The Higher Mind Calling

Dedicated to

Serving the Truth

and

Uplifting the Consciousness

of the people of

Planet Earth

Table of Contents

Part 1   4

Chapter 1 The Formula   5

Chapter 2 Brick Walls and Beliefs   37

Part 2   72

Chapter 3 Understanding Our Species   73

Chapter 4 Toxic Habits   107

Chapter 5 Root Cause of Disease   170

Chapter 6 Eliminating the Disease   269

Chapter 7 Eating for Vitality   348

Chapter 8 Power of Herbs   402

Chapter 9 Tools for Healthy Living   534

Appendix A   562

Appendix B   565

Appendix C   598

Appendix D   623

Bibliography   626

Preface

A few years back I realized how the matrix controls us all by creating wars, poverty, hatred, etc., in the world. It divides us all. Instills fears in our hearts. So I was looking for a way to overcome it. After searching for a very long time, I was able to uncover the true secrets of how our body, our mind, and our universe works. And that is exactly what I have explained in this book. It is the key to breaking free from the shackles of the Matrix.

The first part of the book explains the formula by Bashar, which will help you develop all the skills and abilities you require to live your best life. It will help you live your purpose and guide you through chaos and difficult situations. It will fill your life with complete abundance. It will also bring to the forefront the shadows of your personality like negative beliefs, fear, etc. for you to deal with.

In the second part, we'll talk about the findings of a Naturopathic Doctor (in his own words), who has cured all the diseases you can think of, in thousands of patients. The matrix wants you to believe that there are no cures available, which the doctor has proven to be false.

So, let us begin!

Part 1

Few years back, I came across Bashar, who taught me about creating true abundance in my life. Part 1 of this book explains his teachings in an easy to understand way, in his own words.

Bashar's 'Follow your excitement formula' is the master key to being your true self and living your dreams in pure bliss, in just 3 simple parts.

All kinds of things will suddenly start to happen consistently when you apply this formula in your life. It's just like everything starts to fall into place. Everything shows you that it's interconnected, that we're not really isolated. It's a very incredible experience.

All you need to do is follow the 3 parts of the formula. And when you do all of that, when you take those steps and apply them as precisely and cleanly as possible, the synchronicity in your life goes to absolutely crazy magical levels that are almost beyond belief. And your life just becomes this ecstatic explosion of synchronicity, one after another, to the point where you could tell people stories and they almost won't believe you because it just seems too good to be true. Too magical, too weird, too crazy.

CHAPTER ONE

MODULE 1.1

The Formula

1) Take Action on the Opportunity that contains Highest Excitement

- The highest excitement does not have to come in the form of a project or a career.
- As long as an option contains even just a little bit more excitement than any other option, act on it first.
- Excitement is your body's physical translation of a communication from your higher mind. Respond to it by acting on your excitement.
- Check your beliefs to make sure you are not making anxiety appear to be excitement.
- Check your beliefs to make sure you are not making excitement appear to be anxiety through fear-based definitions.

2) Act on that Excitement to the Best of Your Ability

- Use all your talents, skills, imagination and abilities in taking the action.
- Act to the fullest degree you are able to act on it.

- If more than one opportunity has the same ability to be acted upon, choose either and it will show you whether or not to continue on that route.
- Continue taking action on it until you have no more ability to act.
- When you can act no further, opt for the next most exciting thing you are able to take action on.
- Recognize the signs, reflections and agreements that signal an inability to take action.
- Physical parameters, laws of society, moral values and ethical standards can all indicate whether or not you have the ability to take action.

3) Act on that Excitement with Absolutely Zero Insistence or Assumption with Respect to a Specific Outcome

- Understand that insisting on a specific outcome, manifestation or path, may actually prevent a better manifestation than you had imagined.
- The thing itself that excites you may not need to come to fruition. It may only excite you to get you to take action in order to create the state of being in which the thing that actually needs to manifest can do so.

Complete formula toolkit
Acting on this 3-part formula with integrity aligns you with the complete tool kit of excitement that:

1. Provides you with every form of support, abundance or information you need.
2. It becomes the driving engine that propels you forward.
3. It serves as the organizing principle that shows you, what to act on, in what order, and when.
4. It offers you the path of least resistance to flow through life effortlessly.
5. It connects you to all other expressions of your excitement, regardless of what form they come in.
6. It becomes the reflective mirror that reveals anything within your beliefs that is out of alignment with your core vibration of excitement.
7. It leaves nothing relevant out.

Detailed Explanation

1. Act On Your Passion

a) **The highest excitement does not have to come in the form of a project or a career** - This is very important to understand because very often people will say, well I don't know what my excitement is. And often they are thinking that it has to come in a specific recognizable form. Some kind of a life-spanning career, long-term project or come with trumpets blowing. No. When I talk about the idea of acting on your highest excitement, I mean it can be as simple as, every moment, of every day, you have a number of options available to you, that you are able to take some action on. It can be reading a book, having lunch with a friend, talking to someone, taking a walk on the beach. Whatever option contains even just a little bit more excitement than any other option at that level, that is the one to act on first. Because the more excitement it contains than any other, is telling you, through the synchronicity tool of excitement, that this is the order in which to act on these options. The one that contains the most excitement, that has the greatest ability to be acted upon, is the first one to act on. And it can be step-by-step, very simple. When you do that, it may lead to larger and larger representations of excitement coming in different forms, that will be more apparent, more obvious to you. But really, all I mean is you can take it a step at a time on every level, even the most basic level, and just that every moment act on the one that contains more excitement, more than any other excitement you have the greatest ability to do something about. That's really all it means step-by-step. And it will lead to other representations and other experiences, and other opportunities that will allow you to express your excitement in grandeur ways.

b) **As long as an option contains even a little more excitement than any other option, act on it first** - Again, this is easy to do, I will assume. I may be wrong. But I will assume that you are reading this book today because this is what you were excited to do. But when you leave this interaction today, again you will have a number of options available to you. The only thing you need to do to activate this principle, is just look at all the options and just choose to act on the one that contains more excitement than any other. Even if it is only just a little bit more. That will be your clue and your indication that that comes first. Because again, one of the tools is that excitement carries the organizing principle through synchronicity. And it will show you exactly in what order things need to be done, when they need to be done. And thus, anything that doesn't fit in that day when you are done, doesn't need to be done that day. It truly organizes your life automatically.

c) **Excitement is your body's physical translation of a communication from your higher mind** - People ask all the time, how can I get a sign from my higher mind. How can I learn to communicate with my higher mind. How can I learn to recognize communication from it. I don't know, it must be difficult. Not at all. The things that excite you the most, is actually your translation of that communication. So when you are willing to act on the thing that contains the highest excitement, that is actually you paying attention to the message from your higher mind. That is guiding you from a higher position, broader point of view, saying do this now, do this next. This is the order that works best for you. And when you act on that excitement, to the best of your ability, with zero insistence on the outcome, that is actually your response to the higher mind. That is going, I hear you loud and clear. And so I will act on that, knowing that you are guiding me. And when you then respond to the higher mind through that action, because you are physical, action must be taken to demonstrate your commitment to receive that communication from the higher mind, then the higher mind knows you are listening. It knows you are paying attention, and it can start giving you more things to act on that contain more excitement. But if you are not paying attention, if you are not acting on the excitement that it presents you, why should it give you more. It would be pointless. So the higher mind will always wait for you to demonstrate that you have heard the higher mind through the translation of excitement. And that you are willing to respond to the higher mind through your actions. And then you start that dialogue going, and you start the ball rolling, and you start the momentum, and it will accelerate and accelerate and expand from there.

d) **Check your beliefs to make sure you aren't making anxiety appear to be excitement** - This is crucial. Because many people will be afraid to face their fears, because of negative belief systems within themselves about what it is they think they will encounter if they go exploring those things. And so many times they will gloss those anxieties, those fear-based beliefs over. They will ignore them. They will deny that they are there. They will not want to explore them. Not want to admit that they are there. And so, even though they may actually be feeling anxious, they may attempt to avoid looking at it, or investigating it. By making it appear or labelling it as my excitement. You have to be very clear in discerning within yourself, what is truly excitement based, and what may be anxiety or fear-based. This is absolutely crucial. As is its reciprocal, which is…

e) **Check your beliefs to make sure you are not making excitement appear to be anxiety through fear-based definitions** - Many people on our planet will not be willing to act on their excitement because of fear-based definitions, of what they think will happen if they do. Something bad will happen, or this will happen, or I will lose this, or certain people will laugh at me, or judge me, or I won't belong. And everyone will walk away from me. And many other different kinds of fear-based beliefs. But the idea is to again, in the reverse, make sure that you are not dampening down your excitement, the things that could actually be giving you the best possible life. Just because you have a definition that isn't actually a definition of excitement. This is the irony. This is the paradox. As many people say, I would love to act on my highest excitement. But if I do, I am afraid that something bad will happen. That is not a definition of excitement. It is a different definition. You have to understand, that in the purest form, excitement by definition cannot contain anything that would actually create a negative experience. So if you are making an association of a negative potential experience to the idea of excitement, then the definition you have created is actually not a real definition of excitement. Its a different kind of definition based on that fear-based belief. So be clear within yourself that you are not damping down your excitement, by having an erroneous definition of it. By attaching negative definitions to it, that don't belong there.

2. Act on that Excitement to the Best of Your Ability

a) **Use all your skills, talents, imagination and abilities in taking the action** - Basically this translates to the idea that if you are actually passionate about something, you will use everything you've got. You will stop at nothing to allow yourself to express, to act on, to mimic, to mock up, to model, to mirror. Every skill will be brought to the forefront. Every ability that you have, will be sought out and utilized and applied in your life to match the frequency of the passion you say that you are passionate about. So allow yourself to go forward full steam ahead. When you know you are clearly acting on your excitement, don't hold back. Otherwise, you are not really committing, you are not really demonstrating to the higher mind that it is a full commitment. That you actually believe that this frequency, opportunity or doorway is representative of your passion. Use every skill you have, as best as you possibly can, and it will accelerate you greatly.

b) **Act to the fullest degree you are able to act on it** - Again, this is a reinforcement of understanding that you must go all the way to the degree you are truly able to act on it. Not only bringing all the skills, but taking it as far as you can, until you can take it no further. Exhaust every possible avenue. Take it all the way out. Again, if you are truly passionate about something, you will stop at nothing. It will be your driving force. You will look for every nook and cranny, every doorway, every window, every path you possibly can, to take it as far as you possibly can. Until your reality through synchronicity shows you there is simply nothing else that you can possibly do.

c) **If more than one opportunity has the same ability to be acted upon, choose either and it will show you whether or not to continue on that route** - Again, through synchronicity, the idea is that if it seems to be that there are equal opportunities with equal abilities and equal excitement, it really won't matter which one you choose first. You might, as well, just flip a coin. Because if it is not the path of least resistance for you, it will be self-contained within the toolkit of excitement. And something will happen synchronistically to demonstrate to you that that wasn't necessarily the choice that serves you best. That ability, that reflectivity, is built automatically into every single opportunity that you act on, if it is being acted on to the best of your ability from your highest excitement. And using the coin analogy, sometimes the idea is that you don't really know which one might be representative of your highest excitement, until you flip the coin. You may think they are equal, but sometimes when you flip a coin, and say, if its heads, I will take path A, if its tails, I will take path B. And you flip it, and it comes up tails, and you go, ahh, path B, oh damn, I really wanted path A. You will reveal to yourself in that coin flip what really contains more excitement. But if even after flipping of the coin, they still seem equal, then again it really doesn't matter which path you take. For if it is not the path of least resistance, if it is not the path that serves you best at that moment, it will contain, what it needs to contain to reflect to you that you need to choose the other path. Because this is an automatic guidance system. It is a self-perpetuating, self-guiding, self-correcting system. It contains everything that you need. So, you can utilize it that way as well.

d) **Continue taking action on it until you have no more ability to act** - Again, take it as far as you can, until you can take it no further. And again, be clear about the idea, what it means to have an ability to act on something. And this is where I get into some of the other definitions in this segment. There are many different interpretations in people's minds about what it means to have the ability to act on something. So, let me continue with the clarification.

e) **When you can act no further, opt for the next most exciting thing you are able to take action on** - Again, you will come to crossroads in acting on your excitement. When it seems the excitement is exhausted. When it seems there is nothing else you can do. You have taken it as far as you can. Then again, when you come to those crossroads, you just repeat the process. You look around for the options that are available to you, at that moment, on any level. And you simply act on the one that contains more excitement than any other. And you keep repeating that process, over and over and over again. And if you always do that, then your life will always be as exciting as it possibly can be at that moment. Because you are always choosing the thing that contains more excitement than anything else. And you just keep on doing that. And why? Because you have given yourself no other choice. No reason to choose anything else. And that is as simple as it needs to be.

f) **Recognize the signs, reflections and agreements that signal an inability to take action** - Again, this comes back to the definitions of what ability means. Now, each and every one of you has different abilities. Each and every one of you has a different relationship with the collective. Each and every one of you may have different ways of doing things. So, what works for you may not work for someone else, and vice-versa. So you have to really be aware of what your abilities are. And what the synchronicity of your reality shows you, that you are able to actually do and not do.

g) **Physical parameters, laws of society, moral values and ethical standards can all indicate whether or not you**

have the ability to take action - This is the biggest one that needs the most clarification on our planet. Now, some of them are relatively obvious physical parameters. If you are literally physically unable to take action on something, for whatever reason, then that means, you are unable to take action on it. And that is as good, as are crossroads. It is as good as an arrow pointing in another direction. Saying, this direction, that you are unable to act on is not the path of least resistance. So please don't stand there banging your head against a brick wall. Turn left, turn right, go around, do something else. Choose another thing that excites you. The things that may look like obstacles physically, are not obstacles. They are road signs, guiding you that you need to turn left, need to turn right, you need to turn around here and now. And that actually will be the path of least resistance. Please remember that even though the path may seem to be winding and longer than another path you could take, if it is actually the path of least resistance, it will actually be the fastest path. Because even though another path may look shorter, if it is not the path of least resistance, it will take you longer to walk it. So, don't be afraid of the winding path. If it is your true path, it will actually allow you to go with the flow much more easily. Now, the idea again of what our society in general has agreed upon, the different kinds of ethical and moral parameters, are important for you to pay attention to, because you agreed to be part of this society. I understand that many times people don't necessarily agree, or see the same things in the same way, morally or ethically or even legally, but the idea is to understand that if you are part of a society, that in general has agreed that these things are in place for the general benefit of that society, then you have to be very clear about why you might think it is important to go against the grain of that moral imperative, that ethical structure or those legal standards called laws. Because if you go against them just because you can't see any other way, then you are just not being creative or imaginative enough. The idea to understand is that you are part of that society and you agreed to be. If you do not approve of certain laws or ethical standards, then you have every right to change them in whatever way works within your society to do so. But just violating them is not the way to do it. And the idea that law or ethical standard exist, is a sign and an indication that you don't have the ability to go in that direction. You need to see it as clearly as you would see a brick wall. Again, it simply being an arrow pointing in an unexpected direction, that is actually representative of the path of least resistance. Let me add another example to this that I have become aware of, because this particular idea has been banging about in our society now for quite a while. And specifically I will use the example of what is called copyright law, since this seems to be a hotbed topic in our society. The idea about, pirating material that doesn't belong to you, is a perfect illustration of what I am saying here. There have been some individuals in our society that have come back with, what you might loosely call a rebuttal to this concept of obeying the copyright laws. By saying that there have been all sorts of laws in society that we really shouldn't have followed. For e.g. at one point slavery was legal. Should we follow those laws. This is really not a correct argument. And is really very surface oriented. And actually misses the point. The difference between that scenario and the copyright laws, is not apples and oranges, its apples and broccoli. These are two completely different concepts. The idea here is, that yes, there can be unjust laws in our society. And that there may be people who resist those, and go against them, and fight to change them in a variety of ways. And sometimes civil disobedience is one of those ways that is available to us. But the real misunderstanding in that so-called argument, which is not really an argument at all, is the difference between the two ideas. Because what you would call slavery is designed to take people's rights away. Copyright law is designed to protect people's rights. That is the difference. And so such an argument simply means the person hasn't really thought it through. It is just what you would call a knee-jerk reaction to something they want to do. And they are simply creating an excuse in their minds, or a reason to break laws that actually benefit our society, and are actually just laws. So be very clear about the idea when you bring up arguments and reasons like that within your own mind, as to whether they actually are relevant or not.

3 Act On That Excitement With Absolutely Zero Insistence Or Assumption With Respect To A Specific Outcome

a) **Understand that insisting on a specific outcome, manifestation or path may actually prevent a better manifestation than you had imagined** - The idea of insistence on a particular outcome may seem to be a focus on something, that is the best thing you can possibly imagine. But, in fact, it is actually a limitation. Now, visualization is a great tool. Nothing wrong with visualization at all. It is a technique that you can use to imagine, to envision, an ideal reality, that you would absolutely love to experience. That you are excited about experiencing. Nothing wrong with that at all. Nothing contrary to your true vibration. But here is the rub. When you imagine, when you visualize that so-called ideal outcome. And you see yourself in that picture, you get excited about what you are seeing, don't you. That is why you are visualizing it. You are pumping up your vibration, you are pumping up your excitement. You are getting excited about the idea, the possibility that this could actually manifest. And oh boy, wouldn't that be wonderful. Wouldn't that be delicious. Wouldn't that be the best possible thing that could happen in my life. Well, maybe not. The idea is, that maybe something even better than you were capable of imagining, could happen. So if you insist on the picture that your physical mind created, how do you know that you are not limiting yourself from something even better. Your higher mind may know of something even grander than your physical mind is capable of imagining. Because your physical mind is not designed to know how actually something needs to happen. Your physical mind is only designed to know, what is happening. It is designed to experience what is going on right now, what manifests right now. Only your higher mind knows what the true path is for you, and it informs your physical mind through excitement. So that the physical mind can know it too. But the physical mind doesn't have the capacity, it is not designed to know exactly how something really needs to unfold. But the higher mind knows this. So when you amplify yourself up. When you get yourself really excited by having that particular visualization, that your physical mind was capable of conjuring, and you feel at the peak of excitement, drop the picture. Utterly, zero insistence. Zero assumption that it has to look like that. That it has to happen that way, or you have to get there in that particular way, or that anything specific about it really needs to come to fruition. Drop it utterly. But keep the vibration, the state of being of excitement. Then you are driving the engine itself. Now you have made room for the manifestation that the higher mind can bring to you, that is actually representative of that state of excitement. Which may be far grander than your physical mind was capable of visualizing. So, when you understand, that insistence on a particular outcome is actually a limitation, you will drop it, as you say, like a hot potato.

b) **The thing itself that excites you may not need to come to fruition. It may only excite you to get you to take action in order to create the state of being in which that thing actually needs to manifest** - The idea is that when you drop the insistence, when you drop the assumption in that context, you will start to realize, that sometimes things will excite you but not for the reason you think. If you are holding onto certain beliefs that make you resistant to moving in a certain direction, a direction you may really need to go in, something may crop up synchronistically in your life, that will get you to move in that direction. Because it looks so exciting that you just can't resist it. But never assume that the thing that excites you and get you to move, is the thing that actually has to manifest. Because its job may only be to get you off your butt. And that may be it. And once you are moving, and once you are acting on your excitement, and once you are in that state of being, then the thing that really needs to be acted on, and may really need to manifest, can crop up as an opportunity and a circumstance before you. But never assume that what crops up actually has to be it. It may only be the thing that ignited you to start moving, so you would have the momentum to take advantage of what really needs to manifest in your life.

Acting on this three-part formula with integrity aligns you with the complete toolkit of excitement - When I say its complete, I mean its complete. If you need a refresher course on what that word means, please consult your local dictionary. Complete means it leaves nothing relevant out. That is the final piece of the toolkit. But first and foremost, please remember, the toolkit is automatic, self-guiding, self-perpetuating. It works flawlessly all the time. And it becomes, when you activate this three-part formula of acting on your highest excitement, every moment that you can, to the best that you are able, with zero insistence on the outcome, or how you get there, the methodology or anything like that, then you activate the kit to work for you in a positive way. And the kit becomes the driving engine that is the first tool that moves you through life, accelerates you. It becomes the organizing principle in your life. Through synchronicity, it shows you exactly what needs to be done, in what order, and when. And whatever doesn't get done by the end of the day, when you are excited about being tired and going to sleep, which is also an excitement, then it didn't need to be done that day. Because again it is the organizing principle and it knows exactly, how to fill your day perfectly. And remember, when I talk about acting on your excitement, I don't mean that you have to be jumping up and down with your hair on fire. Excitement can be a sense of balance and peace. It can be a very relaxed, meditative state, expressing your excitement. You don't have to be running around the room, bouncing off the walls, to say I am excited. Look at me, I am excited. And so, not only it is the driving engine and the organizing principle, but it is also the path of least resistance. It is also that which connects you to all other expressions of excitement. Even if on the surface they look unconnected, it is the excitement that tells you that they are. It is also what gives you support in life in all the ways you need and all the forms it needs to come. Whatever form of abundance that maybe, will be the form that needs to be there. So, drop the insistence on what form in which abundance may need to come. Because again, you don't know what form may actually serve you best. If its money, then that is the form it will come in. But if that is not the path of least resistance, another form of abundance may need to crop up. Such as, simply being gifted something. That is a form of abundance. But you must trust the synchronicity and the way your life unfolds in order to be open to all forms of abundance. And not be insistent that it must come in a certain form. Which paradoxically, closes the door to which all other forms of abundance may actually reach you through. It also contains the reflective mirror, that reveals to you, as you are acting on your excitement, as you are moving forward, it reveals to you, in no uncertain terms, by bringing them up to your attention, anything that may be in your subconscious or unconscious mind, that is out of alignment with your true vibration. Any negative, fear-based beliefs that are out of alignment, it will bring them to your attention. So when you are acting on your excitement, and suddenly one of these fear-based beliefs comes up, don't label that as something having gone wrong. That is exactly what needs to happen. Because you need to be aware of these things, you need to identify these negative beliefs consciously, in order to see that they don't belong to you. In order to see, they don't make any sense. In order to see that, that is not what you prefer. In order to consciously realize that's not what you prefer to choose. And once you let that go, then you will add its energy to your excitement, and you will continue to expand from there. And this being a complete kit, it leaves absolutely nothing relevant out of your life. That is what I mean by complete. It will contain everything you need in perfect place, in perfect timing. You will find yourself synchronistically where you need to be, when you need to be there, with whom you need to be doing, what you need to be doing. All these things are automatic. And if you are willing to go with the flow, you will start experiencing this synchronicity in that way more and more and more. Life will become more ecstatic. It will become more effortless. It will become more joyful. It will become more creative. It will become more loving. It will become more aware of who and what you are. This all boils down to that 'know thyself.' The ultimate formula, be aware of your definitions, be aware of what you are choosing. Be aware of what story you are telling yourself. And living out, and choosing the ones that you prefer, instead.

This might not contain every single detail, but for now it is sufficient. And if your are willing to follow these guidelines and allow yourself to learn very effectively, and make these principles your own, you will be walking on the most optimum path for your life.

MODULE 1.2

Abundance

Now let me add a new perspective to an idea of-
The Big A: Abundance.
Abundance seems to be an issue that has absorbed much of
people's attention for quite sometime. Let us address the
notions of abundance so you can understand that attracting
abundance into your life is quite a simple matter, and does not
have to be the struggle you may have created it to be.
We have been told that abundance is certain things, but not
other things. Many of us have become wrapped-up in the
definitions that create abundance, or an apparent lack of it. Let
me make it very clear that it is only your definitions of
abundance, that prevent you from experiencing it in your lives.
There is absolutely nothing inherent in the idea of abundance,
or the experience of abundance that is difficult to attain. It is
only your definitions of abundance, that makes it seem to be
beyond your reach.
Here comes another new definition. Are you paying attention?
*Abundance is the ability to do, what you need to do, when you
need to do it.* That is all.
"Hey, he didn't say anything about money. What good is
abundance without money?" Well, what good is money without
abundance? So, allow yourself to understand the most basic
definition of abundance: the ability to do, what you need to do,
when you need to do it.

Now of course, money is one symbol of abundance. Yes, it's valid. Yes, it is creative. Yes, it's going to change. But that is all right. It is still valid. It is just as creative as any other way to represent abundance. "What do you mean, any other way? What other way?" Well, many other ways. And that is the difficulty in your definition. If you only see abundance as money, very often you don't see abundance in its other forms. You're blind so to speak, abundance-blind. Because "green" is the only color you allow abundance to come in. But abundance comes in a total spectrum.

So, you must relax your insistence that "It must come in this particular way or I will not accept it. I will not recognize it if I don't see this and this on such and such a date, to the penny. Otherwise, I'm not abundant. What's wrong with me? I cannot attract this amount of money by this date, because I need it for this and I need it for that. What is wrong with me?" Again, these are just definitions. If you allow yourself to understand that abundance is simply, whatever way, shape or form, your automatic synchronicity can attract into your life, what you need, to allow you to do, what you need to do, when you need to do it, then you will begin to realize that you are very abundant and have been for quite some time. When money is the strongest way a specific type of abundance can be fulfilled, the money will be there. You will attract the opportunity to give you the money. But when money is not the simplest way, when it is not the path of least resistance, that may be the last way it will manifest. You may be receiving many other ways that abundance is manifesting in your life, or attempting to manifest in your life. But you may not be allowing it to because of your definitions.

The Rich Person

I'll give you an analogy. This analogy directly relates to the concept of fundamental unconscious belief systems. When we are growing up, we hear many stories.
And perhaps one day you hear the parable of 'The Very Rich Person.' And in being a small child, being open to all information, you sit there and absorb this parable. And this parable says, "This person is exceedingly abundant." And at the same time, "This person is an exceedingly mean, nasty person." Now, your little budding mind says, "Oh, abundance equals nastiness." And it joins the two. The two ideas marry and fuse in your consciousness' belief matrix.
So one day, many years later, when you have forgotten about this parable, you say to yourself, "You know, I would love to be really abundant. I would really like to be rich." But then, suddenly, somewhere deep down within you, so deep down that you cannot even hear it. A little voice says, "But if I become rich, I am going to become nasty and I do not want to do that. So, I am not going to let myself become rich."
As you embark on a deep meditative journey, reaching a tranquil state within yourself and revisiting your personal history, you uncover the concealed belief systems that underlie various life situations, including abundance. You delve into the

origins of these beliefs and their reasons for existence. Through this process, you realize how you might be unknowingly undermining your own progress, as incompatible belief systems have become entwined. Recognizing these conflicting beliefs allows you to address them. For instance, you might realize, "Ah, I now comprehend that a person can attain wealth without adopting a negative demeanor. I used to think this was impossible. I had linked unkindness with affluence, which hindered me from pursuing wealth because I didn't want to become unpleasant. My understanding of prosperity was incomplete." With this awareness, you choose to reshape your perspective. You redefine and reframe your own interpretations. You engage your imagination to reformulate these beliefs to your liking. You craft your preferred version: "I am a compassionate, benevolent, artistic, creative, affluent individual. This is the type of individual I aspire to be. I now realize that I can achieve anything I desire without causing harm to anyone, including myself. That is how powerful I really am." That's true power. When you understand that you are already as powerful as you need to be, without having to hurt anyone else or yourself, in order to create the reality you prefer, then you know True Power. Power is not control. It is not domination. It is not "attempting to try" to make your reality conform to your will power. No. Will is simply focus. It is simply clarity about who and what you are. What it is you prefer. And, clarity about what it is you believe you deserve.

Deservability is a big issue. Especially with regard to abundance, "Do I deserve to be abundant?" But again, it is the actions themselves. It is the reality itself that says it all. Are you willing to believe it to the point where you're willing to be it? Are you willing to act it out, to be that person. That abundant person then, can attract that reality to themselves? As long as you trust that you are not avoiding something you need to look at, you must trust that your excitement is the thing to follow. Then act in that direction.

The Dream House

Imagine being filled with enthusiasm about owning your dream house. The very thought of living in a house, particularly one resembling the one atop a hill. This particular house captivates your imagination. It becomes your symbol, your aspiration. Living in such a house becomes your all-encompassing desire. However, practicality sets in. You realize that you lack the funds to afford that house. The solution seems simple: find a job. While you're not particularly excited about working, it appears to be the only viable path. You prepare yourself for the task ahead, understanding that you'll need to work hard, save diligently, and eventually, after some years, you might be able to attain a house like the one on the hill. So, reluctantly, you embark on the job search.

As you scour job listings, you don't find anything that truly excites you. But you notice a job opportunity that seems acceptable enough, mainly because it aligns with your aspiration for the dream house. You rationalize that enduring this job is worth it because it's a means to an end. You're willing to endure the suffering now in anticipation of the eventual reward.

Yet, fate takes an unexpected turn. While on your way to the job interview, you run into a friend who invites you to join them for lunch. Although lunch seems much more exciting than the impending job interview, you're torn. The desire for your dream house still drives you, so you decide to compromise and allocate some time for lunch.

During the enjoyable lunch, time slips away, and you suddenly realize that you've missed the job interview. Panic sets in as you bemoan your bad luck, convinced that you've lost the chance at the job, the money, and ultimately, the house you yearn for.

Amidst your disappointment, another individual joins your lunch, and you share your story of missed opportunities and dreams deferred. As you recount your desire for the house on the hill, you mention its specific location, only to discover that the new acquaintance owns that very house. And to your astonishment, he reveals that he was looking for someone to care for the house while he was away for a few years, and he is willing to let you stay there for free.

In a moment of clarity, you grasp the significance of the situation. Had you not missed the job interview, you wouldn't have had this chance encounter, this opportunity to secure your dream house without the need for the arduous job. The cynics might argue that this tale is too good to be true, that life doesn't work in such a serendipitous manner. They might dismiss it as mere coincidence or attribute it to astronomical odds.

Yet, the narrative challenges this skepticism. It proposes that life does operate in such a way, consistently and continuously, as long as you allow it, by following the thing that excites you the most. By allowing your positive synchronicity to work for you in the same way you have been allowing your negative synchronicity to work for you. Yes, they are coincidence, but they are not accidental. The idea of "missing the boat" is negative synchronicity, because it is a perfectly timed reflection of your fears and doubts.

Fairy Tales

Perfect timing is something you always have. It's not about whether you possess perfect timing, but whether you align it with the things you prefer, or those you don't. Your timing is always impeccable; the outcomes are determined by the principle of "what you put out is what you get back." Following your excitement maintains a high level of positive synchronicity and energy. This leads to a reality that might seem like a fairy tale—a magical experience. Miracles, in fact, aren't exceptions; they're the natural order. True power lies in realizing that you are already magical, and nothing is too good to be true. This revelation marks a significant aspect of our expanding understanding.

As you become more conscious and aware, you start recognizing various occurrences. First, you realize that abundance manifests in diverse forms. Sometimes things are given to you, exchanges are made, or services are provided in unexpected ways. The ability to do what's necessary, when it's necessary, becomes evident. Had the individual insisted on money, obtaining the house might have taken years. By following excitement and not insisting on a specific arrangement, he acquired the house without requiring money. Understanding that abundance is versatile and being open to various forms of it, is the first lesson. Allow these opportunities by following excitement. The next lesson is to act on the opportunities that come your way, and this momentum must be maintained. Negative focus blinds you to opportunities. But when you believe that you're synchronized with your needs, previously unseen opportunities become apparent. Act on what excites you most at any given moment, that lies within your capability.

When you face multiple equally exciting choices, pick the one you can most effectively act upon. These equally exciting options often align under a common category—the most exciting thing overall. You don't need a grand career plan to follow your excitement. Start with what excites you most in the present moment. Staying in the moment fulfills a life-spanning career in the best way. Continuously following excitement leads effortlessly to the next situation, enabling you to do the next most exciting thing.

Now, many people have begun to follow their excitement in life. Many have begun to act on the opportunities that they attract into their life. And many have now arrived at a new threshold, which I will now address. Sometimes you say, "Well, I have been doing the thing that excites me, and I have been recognizing that opportunities have been coming to me, and I have been acting on them. And all of a sudden something stopped. I started to see pieces of opportunity, but no whole opportunity. No whole direction makes itself obvious or apparent. Now what is happening? Am I slipping back into my negativity? What's happening to me?"

Here is a very important threshold to remember. You are a creator, and at a certain point you are going to be expected by your actions to act more like a creator. And what that means is, that as you create the ability to act, to trust, to be excited, to follow your dreams, and as you attract opportunities in whole form, there will come a time when all of a sudden, you will shift from attracting opportunities, to being expected to create the opportunity. To create the opportunity, literally, from scratch. That's where you really have to be bold, where you really have to be inspired. Where you really have to use your imagination and your full creativity to actually invent, to create, to manifest, from nothing, the opportunity that you can then act on. Now you are pulling yourself up by your own bootstraps. At this point, you are actually creating the stepping stones that you take the next step on. You are not just waiting for the opportunity to come to you. Yes, up to a certain point.

But after that point you must actually build the next step before you can take the step. You will understand what I mean about this if you have arrived at that point, or when you do in the future, because you will. But that is where your full blossom and full power of creativity is expected to come to bear. Where you have to look at things like you have never looked at them before, and see the ability in "nothing" to create an opportunity. To see things that might be completely disassociated to most people, but see how they connect, and then connect them. To create a new 3rd thing that is an opportunity not only for you but for all individuals involved in the connection. Then you are really high powered. Then you are really beginning to take the first baby steps of true creation and true manifestation.

So what you have experienced now is but one infinitesimal atom of the ecstasy, and the abundance, and the flow, and the synchronicity, that you could experience in your life. Do you think you could stand that much ecstasy? Or will you just explode? Do not say you do not know how to proceed. You do. All you have to do is, use your imagination in whatever direction you so desire. There are no limitations. Create the reality you prefer. Create what your imagination is most strongly and magnetically attracted to. Go and be with the people that you feel are representative of the vibration you want in your life. Let them rub off on you. Be that person now. Act like the person you want to be now. Do the things that person would do, now. Be as bold in every endeavour that excites you. You have given yourself the perfect example, you have created it yourself. You are in no way lacking in creativity and generation of flow, as you have very strongly illustrated. So, from this point forward, when you express that you don't know how to proceed, I will not believe you. Thank you for a most pleasant, enjoyable, ecstatic, synchronistic and abundant exchange.

CHAPTER TWO

MODULE 2.1

Brick Walls and Beliefs

Now, I would like to examine and explore, with a kind of an x-ray approach, the idea of what beliefs are, so you can identify the negative beliefs and change them. The reason why I have entitled this segment as brick walls and beliefs is because I understand, that very often when you have a belief, and you wish to change it, sometimes you may experience a great degree of difficulty in allowing that belief to change. This is why now I am going to examine the actual nature and structure of beliefs. So that by gaining some insight into the actual structure of the belief, you will understand how it is organized to perpetuate itself, and you will also gain greater understanding of how that mechanism works. This will allow you to break it down and allow you to deal with the different components of the belief. You will be able to recognize the different tricks that negative beliefs have in their tool kit to perpetuate themselves, which makes it seem like, as if, it is difficult or maybe even impossible to change that negative belief. The idea first and foremost is that when you attach certain kinds of beliefs to your 'motivational mechanism,' you are then propelled automatically and immediately in the direction of reinforcing that belief.

Motivational Mechanism

The idea of the motivational mechanism is quite simplistic. You are always motivated by the same mechanism to do whatever it is you choose to do. Without exception, you only have really two basic motivations that are really different sides of one motivational mechanism.

Your motivational mechanism is simply, that you will always and immediately move in the direction of what it is you perceive to be, or define to be more pleasurable. And you will always and immediately move away from what you define to be, or perceive to be more painful. The key here is, what it is you define. What it is you believe. What it is you perceive to be pleasure and pain.

Many people say that they intellectually recognize what it is they prefer, and yet they do not understand why it is they do not choose it. Why it is they do not always act on it. This comes down to the motivational mechanism and recognizing, that if you had a positive belief system attached to that so-called preference, you would immediately choose it. And if you are not choosing it, if you are not acting on it, what that immediately tells you, without exception, is that there must be a negative belief attached to your actual preference that is making you see it in a light that makes it not something you actually prefer to choose. So, the important thing is to find out what belief you have attached to the idea of your so-called dream, your so-called preference, that makes it seem to be anything but your preference. And once you find out what belief that is, that you've attached to that preference, you will know immediately why you are not choosing it.

Many individuals will actually remain in a painful state even over the idea of what they say they prefer to choose, because of the belief systems they have attached to the thing, that they say is representative of their passion. And this negative belief system attached to their passion, makes that passion seem even more painful of a choice, than the pain they are already choosing.

Many times it is as simple as, 'fear of the unknown.' Not wanting to move forward in the direction that is unfamiliar to you, and staying with the pain just because the idea of the pain being familiar makes it seem as if that familiarity, that pain, is actually preferable to the idea of the fear of the unknown. And therefore you remain in the pain, as painful as it is, just because it's something that you know, as opposed to something that you don't. But to be able to change them, you require the willingness to examine and explore, why you have those beliefs and why you have attached them in this manner to the motivational mechanism. Why you have attached them to your preference in that manner.

Manifestation

Now I will discuss the concept of manifestation. Let me provide you a slightly different understanding of the concept of manifestation. Because many of you, when you think about the idea of attempting to manifest something, bring it into your reality, make it appear, make it experiential, are coming from a point of view, also definitionally and belief system related, that it is something that does not exist in your reality. That you are attracting it into or bringing it into your reality. That somehow it is ephemeral and non-physical, and you have to somehow make it solid, make it appear, make it real. That is not the case. What it is that is representative of your preference and what you call your desires to manifest, already exists in your reality. It is already manifest. The idea of manifestation is not bringing something that doesn't exist into existence. Or attracting something from over there, and bringing it over here. The idea is that what you desire to manifest is already here. Already existent. Already real. Manifestation is the process of giving yourself the ability to realize, to perceive, that it is already here. You do not have to do any magical thing to make it come into existence. It is already existent. It is already within your sphere of reality. It is just that your belief system makes it invisible to you. So manifestation is not the process of actually conjuring something out of nothing. It is the process of making the invisible, visible. And that simply requires an alteration of perception. That's all it takes. So let me discuss that.

The idea of one of the mechanisms of manifestation that allows the invisible to become visible, is something that uses the power of paradox very strongly. The idea of paradox is the recognition that you are in a very powerful place, right in the center of your power. Because what may seem paradoxical to you, what may seem contradictory to you, two opposing ideas, that cannot necessarily seem to coexist, but do coexist, tells you right then and there, that there must be a middle ground from which they both come, and that middle ground, that balance point, is your place of power from which you have generated the apparently paradoxical and apparently contradictory concepts. But because you can perceive them both, it tells you, just the perception of those things alone tells you, that you are actually in the center of those things. That they come from the center of your being. And that you're simply seeing reflections and expressions of the polarity of creation. But polarity within you combines and interacts in a very specific way to generate your true perfect place of balance and perfect place of power. So, when you see paradox, rejoice. Because it is telling you that you're standing right in the center of your creative self and have the ability to then, manifest and transform, and make the invisible, visible, very quickly. Let me explain a little bit more clearly about the idea of the paradoxical nature of the mechanism of manifestation.

Many of you have been taught to think about the idea of manifestation as an issue of intention, and as an issue of focus. As an issue of concentration, and in a sense, this is accurate.

However, a very important point is often left out, or at the very least, sometimes this point is spoken of independently and so no connection is made to the idea as a whole concept.

The two seemingly paradoxical issues here are intention, focus, concentration, and conversely, on the other side, what you have often heard in many metaphysical and New Age information sources, the idea of surrender and letting go. These two things are not diametrically opposed. They are not mutually exclusive. They work together in a whole mechanism.

In other words, the secret of the paradoxical mechanism is the idea of intention, focus and concentration, and then after that has been done, letting go and surrendering. And letting the intention, focus and concentration do its job on higher level. Linking these two things together gives you the entire mechanism of manifestation, or at least one direction of the energy. I will discuss the other direction in a moment. But first, let me amplify this concept. Any time that you have a desire or a preference for a manifestation, which must be representative of your passion, it must become your world. The intention, the focus, the concentration, is automatically there, if that is truly representative of your passion. Because when something is representative of your passion, you are automatically focused on it. You automatically intend it. You're automatically concentrating all of your attention on that idea. Because that's what passion does if you are truly passionate about something. There is no other choice and consideration.

All other things fall by the wayside. That is a true description of the idea of being in your passion. If then, in that peaceful state, or a meditative state, or a focused state, you allow yourself to image that passionate idea, that manifestation that is desired, and feel it, and build that energy up, in your emotions, in your energy, in your passion, build that energy to a peek, over the course of simply 15 minutes and no longer, sometimes even less (when you get proficient at it you don't always need all 15 minutes). Fifteen minutes at the most, is all that is necessary for you to activate the idea of the wheels of the gears, and put it in motion with regard to the idea of allowing the invisible to become visible. But when you do that, the next thing is to completely and utterly let it go. Forget about it. Stop caring about it. Let it go. Surrender it utterly to the higher self. Let the higher self now do the job. You see, physical reality while apparently complicated at times, is actually not extremely complex. It is actually built on very simple principles and you don't actually have to do very much to get the ball rolling. Your physical mind is not designed to understand how things are going to happen, how things are going to manifest. The how is the purview of the higher mind. Because the physical mind does not actually have the capacity, the capability to understand it, is not designed to understand how that's going to happen. All it needs to do is, flip the switch and let the higher mind do the how, and do the things necessary to cause the synchronicities in your life, that need to be there, and the downloads and inspiration that need to come to you, to allow the invisible to become visible. To allow the manifestation to occur. So, all you need to do is, build that energy up for no longer than 15 minutes. Bring that up to a full peak of passion, a full peak of imagination, a full peak of visualization. In whatever way you wish to do it. With full intensity, concentration, and focus, and then utterly let it go.

Now, because of certain negative beliefs, many people find it difficult to actually let it go. But that is very important because without the letting go side, you don't actually have the whole mechanism engaged. It is important to understand that the intensity, focus and concentration must be paired with the surrendering and the letting go, to actually have the whole mechanism of manifestation. This is using the power of paradox built into this process. Letting go means that you really know that the higher mind is doing its job, and you can now relax. The physical mind can relax. It doesn't need to do anything else. It is not required, nor is it capable of doing anything else. So really, when you know this, you can allow your physical mind to just let it go. And just get on about your day focusing on the next most exciting thing you are capable of taking action on.

At the same time, you must be clear about your motivations to ensure that what you are focusing on, what it is you are surrendering to, is truly representative of your highest passion, instead of something that is simply labeled as such, to actually act as an avoidance of what your highest passion actually could be. This is where you have to really be clear about the idea of what beliefs you are dealing with. Because many of you often fool yourselves, and trick yourselves, through the negative belief system, into thinking that you're acting on your excitement. When in fact, you're actually acting out of anxiety and covering it up because you're afraid to look at the idea of what it is that actually does excite you, because of all the negative beliefs you've attached to it. So clearing out your motivational mechanism, and finding out what beliefs you have attached to it, is the primary and fundamental process that is required in order to actually use the tool of manifestation in a clear and concise manner. Once you have your motivation clear, and you know that what you are focusing on is truly representative of your passion, then you will find that this mechanism of manifestation works very strongly, and often very rapidly.

But the idea again is that you cannot worry it there, you cannot make it happen. You cannot insist that it must happen at a certain time and in a certain way, because then you are putting conditions on it. You are not allowing yourself to truly let it go. You're not allowing the higher mind to do its job. You're actually blocking the entire process by keeping the control, or trying to keep control of the situation within the physical realm. And the physical realm is not designed to handle energy in that way. It does not have the ability and capacity to do the job of the higher self. It would be as if you dove down under the sea with your breathing apparatus, and then instead of allowing yourself to rise to the surface, and taking your breathing apparatus off, and taking a deep breath up there, to go back into the realm of underwater. It is as if you are taking off your breathing apparatus underwater and inhaling, and wondering why you start choking, and why you cannot see that far anymore. Why things are suddenly murky and muddy, and why you are suddenly drowning.

The idea is you must allow your whole self to participate in the creation of your reality. And you are not a whole self, unless you allow the physical mind and the higher mind to work in concert. We have been taught to think that the idea of the higher mind, being that it is non-physical, is somehow not really a part of who we are as a person. It's something else, somewhere else, on another plane, and has nothing to do with what we are supposed to be doing as a personality in terms of guiding us through life. But that is not the case. In order to actually move through physical reality as a whole person, you need to work in concert, you need a partnership between physical mind and higher mind, so that you can actually function as a whole person and use each component in the way it was designed to be used. So that you can then allow the mechanism of manifestation in the creation of your reality to work in an effortless and aligned way with the idea of the vibration of yourself as a total being.

So, the idea of the power of paradox in this manifestation mechanism, is also working in the opposite direction. For as you allow yourself to have the intensity of focus on your highest passion, and you allow that energy to build up to a pinpoint, a white hot pinpoint of concentration and focus and imagery and energy and emotional feeling, bringing it to that fever pitch, and then as you let it go, the idea that is moving in the opposite direction is the concept of expansion. The idea here is that as you actually concentrate, as you bring things down to a pinpoint, you're actually raising the frequency. You're actually expanding the frequency of your energy by focusing it down to such a small focus, small passionate pinpoint. You're actually expanding your energy, building it up, reaching out, letting it expand. And because you are now focused solely on your passion, which makes you more in alignment with your true, core, natural self, so now your energy will expand. As you let go, the energy then collapses back to your physical self. But as it has done so, it is similar to what the physicists call the collapse of the waveform.

What this means is that as you focus, and as you concentrate, and as you expand your energy bubble, you are containing all probable ways of manifestation that are best for you, that could occur. You're expanding your probability net. And as soon as you then surrender and let it go, and that energy bubble collapses back down to your immediate reality, you are allowing the bubble to then automatically choose the highest probabilities that will actually help you bring the manifestation into your awareness. So, this is the paradoxical mechanism. That as you focus, as you concentrate, as you narrow your field of view on the thing that you are most passionate about, you actually expand your bubble of energy probabilities. And as you let it go, as you release, as you surrender, you actually allow the bubble to collapse down to the most likely ways, in which the path of least resistance can bring to you the kind of synchronicity into your life, that will most likely allow for that manifestation to occur, in the most effortless, most rapid way possible. Do you understand this mechanism?

MODULE 2.2

Belief Systems

So, now let us move forward into the understanding that in using the power of paradox, and in understanding how this mechanism works, the most important factor in this entire process is getting a handle on the beliefs themselves, that are at play in this mechanism. Because it is only the beliefs, it is only the definitions, that will color these mechanisms. These mechanisms work automatically. They are neutral. You don't have to do anything special to make them work. They work for everyone the same. This is what is built-in to the structure and nature of existence itself. Because existence is in that sense, constantly the fluctuation of the polarities, the fluctuation of the paradoxes. It is constantly coming and going. It is constantly creating and renewing. It is constantly breaking down and building up. That mechanism is built in. It is the breathing in and breathing out. It is the yin and the yang. It is always there. You don't have to do anything special to make the mechanism work for you. This is not about learning how to work the mechanism. This is about how to allow the mechanism to work in the clearest possible way, in the most aligned way with who you truly are, by clearing out the belief systems and the definitions that have nothing to do with you. The things you have inherited, the things you have had handed down to you, the things that come from other people that are not you. The idea is to understand how beliefs are structured and thus, then how they color your ability to recognize the

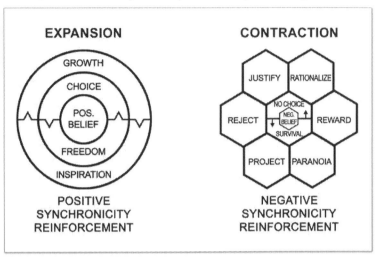

utilization of these mechanisms. Positive beliefs, as you may observe on the diagram, are by definition expansive. All beliefs, even positive beliefs, have a mechanism within them that are self reinforcing and self-perpetuating. They have to, by definition. Otherwise, if they didn't, because beliefs really are ephemeral, then you would not be able to actually have a perpetual, experiential reality in that belief. You would not be able to see the manifestation of that belief if they didn't constantly perpetuate themselves. Because they are constantly being chosen, second to second to second. It may appear as if in the illusion of space-time and the illusion you create of continuity in space-time, once you have chosen a belief and it perpetuates itself, it is the exact same belief just rolling along continuously. But that's not exactly what's happening. The perpetuation mechanism is designed in such a way as to inspire you to continue to choose the same belief again in the next moment. Because in the next moment, it is a whole new reality. You actually have to keep choosing the belief every single nanosecond in order to actually have an experience of ongoing perpetuation. So, the idea of the self perpetuating mechanism in a belief is not that it simply has an automatic momentum that carries it through space-time, it is that it has an automatic perpetuation mechanism that seems to make it seem like the thing to keep choosing over and over again. Because as you do that, you are actually creating a new reality every moment. But if you are buying into the perpetuation mechanism of that belief, positive or negative, then what you're doing is, that you are creating a completely new reality every moment, that looks very much like the reality you created a moment ago. And as you keep creating similar realities, you thus create the illusion of continuity. That it is the same reality and only changing slightly, instead of understanding that it is a completely different reality that has changed completely.

Now, when it is a positive belief, which means that it is representative of alignment with your true, natural, core-self, then you don't mind that it is inspiring you to re-create it again and again. But where you have your difficulty is, when you don't understand why you are re-creating the negative beliefs that you say you don't prefer, again and again.

As you can see from the diagram, and even though this is an oversimplification, it will do to illustrate the point. Because of the nature of positive beliefs being integrative, they are more simply structured. They don't need to be complicated, they don't need to be very diverse. Because that is in alignment with your true natural vibration. Therefore they are very simply structured. However, negative beliefs, because negative energy is that which dissociates, segregates, compartmentalizes, rigidizes, separates, needs a larger bag of tricks to sustain itself. Thus, it will go from the fluid, ever expanding positive structure, the simplistic expanding circular structure, euphemistically, to the rigidized, crystallized and non-expanding structure. That will then contain several compartments and several bags of tricks that it uses to reinforce itself, and to make it seem like the thing to keep choosing over and over again. And here is where x-ray vision comes in very importantly.

You have to recognize what those tricks are. And thus, as a result, by identifying them, you catch yourself, and you stop succumbing to the rationale that you have to keep choosing to create, in every new reality, that belief over and over again.

Let us examine some of these ideas. One of the first differences that becomes evident between the positive and negative belief system, is that while certainly even the positive belief contains this perpetuation mechanism, it also always brings with it the freedom to choose. It always allows you the ability to know that you can change the belief.

So, this is the first and one of the major differences in the positive and negative belief. Because when you operate from fear-based beliefs, it is automatically keying into what you call your survival instinct. In other words, fear-based beliefs lock into your physical survival instinct, in such a manner, as to first perpetuate the idea that if you don't follow this belief, if you don't perpetuate this belief, you will die. So, it relies heavily on tricking you into believing that if you change that belief, there will be nothing left of you. That the belief is all consuming and it is all representative of your true-self. And if you change it, what you're doing is committing suicide. That's one of the first tricks it has up it's little sleeve to allow you to perpetuate it. Because it's a fear-based mechanism, therefore, it is keying directly into your survival instinct mechanism, and using it, and amplifying it, to force you to perpetuate that belief, so that you will survive.

Now, the second thing that automatically happens when that mechanism is engaged, when you flip into the idea of a negative fear-based belief, is that in order for you to continue to perpetuate it, it must also reach into its little bag of tricks, and make it seem as if it is not possible to change it. It simply doesn't have the ability to be changed. So, must be perpetuated by its very unchangeable nature. So, it traps you in a vicious circle of knowing that there simply is no way out at all. The very nature and the very structure of the mechanism says that there is no doorway here. It cannot be changed. This is where you live your entire universe. It is eternal, it cannot change. But it also recognizes that it is fighting against a perpetual, non-ending, relentless stream of information from the higher mind, attempting to reach your core being through this mechanism. Because the higher mind and the positive beliefs are always sending information, always sending light, always sending guidance to guide you back to your natural self.

Within the yin and yang, there is always the opportunity to go in the opposite direction. Within the dark, there is always the doorway that leads to light. Within the light, there is always the doorway that leads to dark. But when you're in the light, you understand that the doorway that leads to the dark is just a choice, and it's only offered to you as an equal choice. But when you're in the dark, the doorway that leads to the light from the dark's perspective is something to be avoided at all costs. So even though it cannot actually close that doorway, it will thus, disguise the doorway with an illusion of unchangeability, so that you will not see the doorway. The doorway will become invisible to your consciousness because you can't perceive what you are not the vibration of. When you are in an enlightened state, you can see all choices, even the negative ones. Because they are all equal choices from the perspective of the higher mind. But when you are in the lower vibrational

state of a negative belief, in fear system belief, then the idea
that it must disguise these things, that exist as choices, to make
it seem as if there is no choice at all. So tapping into the
survival mechanism, the first thing it does with that energy is,
it disguises it, covers up that doorway so that you don't even
know you have a choice to go back into the light, because that
doorway is always there.

And the array of tools it uses to take your attention off that
doorway, are these that are surrounding the mechanism, like
the electrons around the nucleus of an atom. And it will
constantly switch back-and-forth, and use these other tools and
techniques in a variety of ways and combinations, to constantly
keep you off balance, to constantly keep you unable to see that
doorway that leads to the light, by way of variety of
mechanisms such as:
- The idea of projection
- The idea of rejection of new concepts
- The idea of paranoia

So that you will not believe what anyone is saying to you,
when they actually are attempting to help you. So that you can,
in a sense, avoid all information that will actually be to your
benefit by seeing it in light. By projecting it from the dark
vibration, with a dark energy, so that even the light looks dark
to you, and in that sense, seeing everything in a negative light
will keep you off balance. Then the idea of all these things
working together will keep you completely off balance, until

such time as you give yourself the opportunity to recognize that this structure exists.

This is where truly the phrase in our language 'knowledge is power' comes into play. The very fact of illuminating this structure, the very idea of revealing and exposing in x-ray form that this structure exists can give you an edge over it. Because once you've identified the structure, once you have identified the negative belief, once it becomes transparent to you, and you understand what all the tricks are, something happens to that structure. You gain a perspective by being able to actually see it in front of your face, by having a diagram go through your eyes into your brain, and start rewiring in your brain the recognition of the structure. The structure suddenly becomes illogical and nonsensical. You start to see your relative position to the structure and its relative position to you. You start seeing it as nothing but an illusion and a filter, overlaying the idea of your true-self. And you start seeing the idea of you bouncing around in all these little crystalline rooms and being, in a sense, fooled and tricked into believing all the things that it is attempting to get you to believe to perpetuate itself from moment to moment.

My personal favourite trick of negative belief is the one called reward. This is one of its most insidious little tricks. Negative beliefs will actually use positive reinforcement to reward you for buying into the negative belief. So, that you will then only recognize it as the thing to do. This is where it uses the motivational mechanism. This is where it attaches an apparently rewarding result to having chosen the negative path and makes you feel good about yourself, and makes you feel safe and protected for having chosen the safer path.

So, in recognizing that it does this, that it uses all these tricks, you can begin to really examine each and every one of these. And the way to use this template is to take specific negative belief ideas, by examining them and finding out what that belief is.

For example, I am unloved. And taking that and putting it in the center of that diagram and looking at all the different ways the tricks are used to reinforce the idea that you are unloved. And make it seem like the thing to keep choosing, to make it justified, rationalized, rewarded, to develop the paranoia that forces you to not look for the reality where you are loved.

One of the most insidious ways it has of reinforcing your inability to go in that direction, is to make you believe that if you actually go looking for the positive side of that belief, you won't find it. Because there is no such thing, it can't be true. And then when you go looking and find out it doesn't exist, you will then be disappointed. You will then find out that you really are as bad as you've been told you are. And so to avoid that reinforcement of the negative self at all cost, you will simply stay within the negative self. Do you see how insidious that is? It is actually saying, don't go looking to prove the negative. Stay in the negative you are in, because the negative you are in is at least better than proving that the negative is true. It's actually using itself to reinforce itself by saying you don't wanna go and find out what I am telling you might actually be true, because at least here you have a shadow of a doubt, a tiny shadow. I will allow you that much, that is your reward. But if you go looking to find out whether or not what I'm telling you is true, well you'll only find out that what I'm saying is true and then there will be no doubt, whatsoever. So, at least, stay here and hold onto that tiny crumb of a doubt. At least that will allow you to survive, miserably, but survive. But if you go looking and find out that I'm telling you is the absolute truth and you are worthless, well, then your whole world will crumble. Then you will annihilate yourself and not survive. Because how could you possibly survive absolutely knowing, that you don't belong in creation. How can you survive the 'absolute knowledge' that you are worthless. You can't, says negative belief. You can't, so stay here and just play with that little doubt that I'm giving you, that I don't know. It could be true or maybe it's not. I don't know. At least here I am alive as miserable as I am. So I'll keep perpetuating this and I'll bring the doubt with me and I'll keep wondering, could it possibly be true that I'm really this worthless. Maybe I'm not. But if you go looking, you might find out that you are. "Ok, I'll stay here," you say.

But now allow your physical mind to see this diagram of the tricks that negative beliefs are using to create these scenarios, to create the illusion that you must perpetuate the negative belief. This diagram will now begin to imprint itself in your neurological network, just by looking at it. And from this point forward you will not be able to forget that this bag of tricks is being used on you when you succumb to a negative belief. And that will give you just enough of an edge, so that when you find yourself falling into a negative belief and perpetuating it, and going, oh poor me, this is my lot in life, I will never escape this, there is no way out, it's not changeable, of what you're saying to me is not true. You are my enemy by telling me I am loved. Then you will remember this template and suddenly go, oh wait a minute, something is breaking through. I'm getting a whisper. I'm getting an echo from the higher self that this might just be a trick. You'll start remembering that the bag of tricks is being used on you, and suddenly you will realize the fallacy, the folly, the illogic of it. You will recognize that it is just a belief like any other belief and you don't have to believe what it is telling you, and you can believe what you prefer. You can switch over to the positive frame of reference, that you have freedom, that you have a choice, that you have inspiration, you have growth, you have positive synchronicity instead of negative synchronicity. That you can expand instead of contract, and you can start to see through the illusion that the negative belief is desperately trying to get you to believe, because it is basing that desperation on the idea that if you let that negative belief go, you will die along with it.

The idea however, to also further understand is, that this is also a fallacy. The negative belief will actually never die. It will simply become equalized as one of the many infinite choices you have to choose from, and you'll see it that way from the positive perspective. That belief will still be there. You could still choose that negative belief but now that it is simply equal to any other choice, you might prefer not to. You might prefer something else instead. So, it will not really die, but it will do everything in his power to convince you that if you annihilate, if you change your belief, you will annihilate that belief. And since that belief is all you are, you will annihilate yourself. You will be committing suicide by letting that belief go. And you will not find anything to replace it because there is nothing to replace it. And you will wind up in emptiness, in a void, alone, miserable forever and ever. That's the bag of tricks of the negative belief.

Now you will begin to see that this knowledge will change things. Even if it is just a little crack that appears in the plan of the negative belief, in its bag of tricks, that little crack will be enough to let you see the doorway out, that leads to the light. And that's all that is needed. It is just the ability to know, the ability to see, the ability to perceive that, the doorway to light exists in the dark. That's all you need to start moving toward that doorway. You will be continuously bombarded by the tricks of the negative belief that will try to scare you again, away from that doorway. But now you will know it is just a bag of tricks and is not empirically true. It is just attempting to do this to preserve itself. So, as you get closer and closer to that doorway, believe me, it will put up one hell of a fight. It will amplify these things and make them seem so life-threatening if you ignore them, that it will be even more and more difficult to get another step closer to the doorway. But as long as you keep your sight on that light at the end of the tunnel, you will arrive at that light, no matter what it says. And at each step, and this is where you're going to have the edge, what I have just described as what the negative belief normally does should you catch a glimpse of that light, it will bombard you, magnify, amplify, it's bag of tricks to turn you away from that doorway, to cover it up again. But now the difference will be that in knowing this template, when you now see the light in the darkness, as you move toward it step by step, every single time the negative belief attempts to bombard you with one of its bag of tricks to re-enforce the negative belief, your default position will always be to key back into the template, and you will start to see cracks form in its arguments. They will fall apart and they will not be able to sustain themselves because you will constantly understand, that whatever it is negative beliefs are bombarding you with, whatever the negative belief is attempting to divert you with, is again nothing but a part of this template. And once that is burned into your neurological network, once it is hardwired in, you will find that you will never be able to completely buy into the negative beliefs again. So, look at the above diagram multiple times to burn it into your neurological network.

Now here comes the truly empowered part. Once this template is burned in, once you always go to the default position that you cannot get away from recognizing that these negative feelings, these negative ideas, are nothing but a bag of tricks. Once you call its bluff, here is the really important part. You're going to focus on that little spot of light at the end of the tunnel and you're going to pull that light in through yourself and you're actually going to give some of that light to the negative belief, to let the negative belief know it is valued, it is loved. You are willing to allow it to continue to exist because it always will. You are acknowledging that it will not die. You are validating it, as an equally valid belief and allowing it to know that just because you prefer to choose something else, it will not die. You now become the Power Point and you are reassuring the negative belief that it will still exist. But as you do so, you become bigger than it. It no longer fills your world. You know who you now are. You are coming from the higher mind and you are gently reassuring the negative belief that it will continue to always be a part of you because there is no outside, there's nowhere to get rid of anything to. You will always contain it because expansion is the product of inclusion, not exclusion. So you will always include it as a probable choice. It will always be valid and equal in your eyes to any other choice. And you get the freedom to choose what you will manifest, and what you will experience, even as you are validating the negative belief as equally valid as a choice within your entire reality. And as long as it knows it is loved, and as long as it knows it is an equal valid choice, it won't bother you anymore. It will not insist on being in the forefront anymore. Because once everything is an equal choice, it is bathed in the light and the vibrational love of creation equally and that is an overwhelming supportive feeling that will allow it to simply remain quiescent, satisfied, happy, joyful, in love with itself and you, and 'all that is' (God). You will always have from the positive point of view, the freedom to go back into the negative reality and experience the negative belief again. But from that point of view, you will know you don't have to. You are not in a sense, made to believe that you are forced to. You will recognize that, it is just an illusion and you will continue to choose through the manifestation mechanism I already discussed. You will continue to choose what you prefer, knowing that the ideas that negative belief attempted to trick you into believing, are not empirically true. That if you exist, there is something for you that is absolutely ecstatic. And if you stop listening to the negative belief that insists, that the only way to be happy is to pay attention to what it is telling you, that it must be done a certain way, that it must be rigid, it must be controlled, it must be in this template, as soon as you know this diagram exists and it's burned into your neurological network, you will know that these arguments are never empirically true. That it is just a belief. You will see it for what it is. You will have x-ray vision. It will be built-in to your neurological network.

Now the first question that comes up is that, what if that's built into the neurological network, and yet, if the neurological network is always capable of being plasticized and reformed, can't that go away. Yes, and no. Because once you know it's possible, once you have decided, to allow yourself to align with the freedom to choose positive vibration, once this is burned into the neurological network to begin with, there will always be the echo of that choice. Because when I talk about the idea of the plasticity of the neurological network and changing the pathways of your brain, because everything exists at once, that means that all the other possible pathways also still exist as probabilities, including the ability to see this only as a template, only as a trick. But now you will always remember that it's always there even if only as an echo, it is still always something that you will remember exists as a choice. So, you will always be able to choose it if you prefer to. You won't forget it again. Because you will know that memory is created in the moment, and even if you play a game where you forget it in this reality, burning this into the neurological network even once, seeing it this way exposed in x-ray form, even once will allow that crack to form so that as you create those new realities, even if they are negative, it will weaken over time. Something will creep in the echo, the memory of the neural network of this template will creep in and the negative reality perpetuation will weaken and dissolve over time, until you once again remember that you can create something different and you have freedom of choice.

This is the reason why this topic has been discussed in this detailed manner. So I can get your mind to focus on the idea of the plasticity and the rewiring. And now allow your mind to begin to consider, and ponder the idea of this x-ray structure. And because we are a multi-dimensional being, so, allow yourself to crystallize this idea on more than just the physical level. Because the idea of the neurological network in your brain is not just a physical one. Because it is the Nexus point between the higher mind and the physical mind. Because it is the receiver, because it is the antenna, because it straddles both worlds, because it has an etheric and a physical component in the brain, it is capable of imbuing this information, in a sense, into what we might in our modern technology call a virtual memory. So even if in your physical neurological pathways, they are not indicative and not conducive of the idea of bringing back the physical memory, the virtual memory of this will always be there. And you will know that there will always be this nagging feeling that you're missing something. Even when you're caught up in the negative reality for a moment, there will always be this nagging feeling, this little crack through which that higher mind's virtual memory will come through the template and imbue you with at least the nagging feeling that something else is there, there's another choice to be made. This isn't all of it, this isn't it. You will start actually taking the doubt that the negative belief is leaving you, because it has to leave you that doubt, or you will go searching, you can actually use that doubt in a positive way. That doubt will now flip around and it will be the doubt of the negative belief. You are taking advantage of one of the weak spots in the negative beliefs arsenal of tricks. It has to leave the doubt factor, or you'll go looking for something else and find out that what it was telling you was not necessarily true. It has to leave that doubt factor so you won't go looking. So you can take advantage of that. That's the little doorway, that's the little crack through which now this positive energy will leak and turn the doubt against the negative belief. Turn it in the direction of the positive door, the light that exists in the darkness. Does this make sense to you?

MODULE 2.3

Introducing Guilt

One of the key ideas engendered upon our planet, since long
ago, is the idea of guilt. We are compelled to experience guilt
when we possess wealth and abundance in our lives.
Frequently, guilt acts as the primary factor, the central symbol,
that hinders us from manifesting what we wish, desire, and
inherently believe we should be able to enjoy. Guilt
consistently perpetuates limitations and divisions; it obstructs
our acknowledgment of our own self-empowerment and our
inherent connection to boundless creation.

While many of you for a long period of time have assumed that
hate is the opposite of love, but in reality, guilt is the true
opposite of love. Hate may be the diametric, dynamic polarity
expression of love, but guilt is the true mechanical opposite.
For love is complete and utter self-worthiness and creativity,
while guilt is the belief in lack of self-worth; it stifles
creativity. Hate involves the concept that you deserve
something, whereas guilt is completely devoid of the sense of
deservability. In fact, guilt is the denial of your very existence!
Therefore, the belief in your lack of self-deservability allows
you to be able to create a scenario in which you actually keep
at bay, all of the things in life that are yours by birthright. Such
as, happiness, ecstasy and creativity. Guilt serves as a bitter pill
introduced to society to maintain the status quo of

disempowerment. This belief, that you are disconnected and must resort to force, to attain anything in life, perpetuates limitation and guilt.

This narrative has become deeply ingrained in our society. When you doubt your connection to rest of the creation, you likewise doubt your ability to effortlessly create your desires, leading to a devaluation of achievements unless accompanied by suffering. The "no pain, no gain" mentality prevails. Stories containing pain, conflict, struggle, and strife are deemed realistic, while those with happy endings are dismissed as mere fairy tales. There is no inherent truth suggesting that conflict-laden stories are more real than joyful ones; this distinction is driven by habits. Thus, our civilization's prevailing ethos is that nothing worthwhile can be obtained without suffering and earning it. But do recognize that you do not have to earn it, you already own it!

Your Birthright

You were created from ecstasy. You were created out of love and light. It is your birthright. Everything you do can be an act of love, done with an effortless ease of creativity. You are a reflection of the Infinite Creator, which means you possess the ability to create infinitely and across multiple dimensions. This is your authentic essence. If you allow yourself to recognize that you no longer require the burden of guilt, you will open up to the expansiveness that is rightfully yours. You will grant yourself the freedom to fully express your vitality and, with clear consciousness, attract the things you rightfully deserve into your life.

By removing guilt from your mindset, you will be left with a profound realization: Nothing is too simple or too good to be true. This truth holds across the board. Any exceptions? None. Every wondrous and ecstatic experience is attainable by you. You deserve everything you can imagine simply because you exist. The Infinite Creator believes in your existence, and if you hold the desire to bring peace, harmony, joy, and ecstasy into your life, you were created with the capacity to attract these experiences. Just the awareness of this fact is enough to bring it closer to you. Creation does not withhold anything from you.

In all circumstances, the universe has provided 100% support to each individual. Desires are never given without the ability to achieve them. The universe operates purposefully and meaningfully. Just like, you did not have to do anything extraordinary to deserve existence, treat yourself with unconditional love and respect. Empower yourself to create life as you envision it, for you possess the inherent ability to shape it. The mere ability to conceive an idea is evidence of your capacity to bring it to life.

You are multi-dimensional creators. Your thoughts, emotions, and beliefs shape your physical reality without exception. Your reality is a reflection of what you believe is possible or what you fear might occur. Fear is equivalent to believing that the fearful scenario holds the strongest potential reality. Remember, that situations don't arise to demonstrate your entrapment or failure in creating better circumstances. Instead, they manifest to reveal the beliefs you have internalized. If these beliefs aren't to your liking, you have the power to change them.

You always have a self-regulating mechanism to allow you to know, what beliefs may be buried in your unconscious mind. The self-regulating mechanism that allows you to know precisely how to bring those beliefs to the surface of your conscious mind, so you can change them if you don't like them and reinforce them if you do, is the experience of physical reality.

If you see that you are involved in situations you don't prefer, then simply recognize that the only way it could be in your lives is for you to have the belief allowing it into your lives. Therefore, now that a situation has shown you what the belief is you have been operating on, you are free. You have the opportunity to say, "Aha! Now I have the definition of the belief that has created this; it has been buried within me. It has now come to the surface, because here it is all around me. Therefore, if I don't prefer it, I can understand what the

definition was, and I can thus, change that definition to what I do prefer." Then use 100% of the trust. The same trust used to create the negative scenario, to now know that once you have changed the definition to a positive definition, reality will reflect that definitional belief just as strongly as it reflected the other definitional belief which you did not prefer. You have your own, built-in, self-guidance system. And this is why when I interact with you, what you will always sense from me is that, whether you choose to believe in yourselves or not; whether you choose to believe you have the capability of creating the reality you desire or not, I believe in you!
I will always reflect to you that you have that capability, for I know you do. I do not 'believe' you have it. I 'know' you have it, beyond any doubt, whatsoever.

Again, I remind you, all of you are born with a total facility for living your lives in absolute joy. But because of the way we have created our society to be, that joy is drummed out of most of us by the time we are 3 years of age. Yes, that young! And we begin to buy into the belief systems that our society says are the belief systems we must buy into in order to survive in this world... kid!

Part 2

Today, people suffer from a variety of ailments in their lives and the matrix tries it very hard to hide the correct information in relation to the cures for them. So, in Part 2, I am presenting the research of an American Naturopathic doctor (in his own words), who has an experience of more than 30 years. This segment represents his observations of thousands of patients, who used his programs to overcome their toxic conditions & diseases.

Disclaimer - The opinions and suggestions made in this part, are based on personal experience of the doctor and are **for personal study and research purposes only**. This segment is about health & vitality, not disease. **I am making no claims**. If you choose to use the material in this book on yourself, I take no responsibility for your actions and decisions, or the consequences as a result.

Be responsible for yourself. You will be happy that you did. Educate yourself in the truth. Humans must learn that they cannot just treat their symptoms. They must eliminate the cause of these symptoms. Seek freedom from disease. Break free from the programming of the Matrix. Seek The Truth.

All the Herbal Formulas mentioned in Part 2 can be purchased from www.drmorses.com.

Discount Code - GAUTAM

CHAPTER THREE

Introduction

Welcome to an awesome journey into vitality. Health is one of our most precious asset. However, many times we treat our cars better than our bodies.

Fundamentally, there are only 2 choices to be made when we develop a disease: **Treatment** or **Detoxification**. If you choose treatment, you have 2 additional choices. The 1st choice is allopathic (pharmaceutical) medicine. It is the status-quo medical or chemical approach. The 2nd choice is *natural* (traditional) medicine. Which uses products made from natural sources, or herbs to treat the symptoms. If you choose the allopathic approach to fight your disease, then you need to understand that allopathic medicine offers only 3 types of treatment for any condition: chemical medicines, radiation or surgery.

Pharma companies spend loads of money developing drugs to be used for the disease. But, curing the disease and not just its symptoms, is not part of their mindset. Diseases are incurable in allopathy. Drugs are used for everything, from simple headaches & fevers to degenerative conditions, like Parkinson's disease or cancer.

The 2nd form of treatment in allopathy is some form of radiation. This is used in most diagnostic procedures, like X-rays, and some treatment procedures, especially in cancer.

The 3rd procedure in allopathy is surgery. Surgery is simply the removal of bad tissue which is cause of the problem. If the disease is breast cancer, just remove the breast & patient is cured.

Natural medicine or traditional medicine, is different from the allopathic approach. Natural medicine treats the disease with natural products (like those made from plants, animals or mineral substances) or herbs, which are found in nature.

Most of these substances have no damaging side effects Whereas, most chemical drugs have some degree of harmful side effects. However, some natural products used without proper knowledge can cause harm. For e.g. supplementing calcium in the presence of a parathyroid weakness results in formation of stone or excessive free calcium. Generally, the diagnostic procedures used in natural medicine like iridology, pulsing, kinesiology, hair or tissue analysis, and many others are non-invasive and not harmful to the patient.

Most health care systems today are treatment-based modalities. Just treating symptoms will *never* cure the cause. The alternative to treatment is *True Naturopathy (detoxification)*. *This is a* little known science of nature which has been used for hundreds of years, by hundreds of thousands of people & animals globally. It restored health back to their physical, emotional as well as mental bodies. The sciences of chemistry, biochemistry, botanical science and physics are encompassed in detoxification. Detoxification has always been at the heart of true healing, but has been forgotten in our modern world of "treatment."

Detoxification involves the understanding that the body is the healer, and energy is at the center of healing. It also sheds light on the real cause of disease, which is, the destruction of energy. Energy or the destruction of it, is a result of what we eat, drink, breathe, put on our skin, & from what we think and feel. These are the 6 ways in which we either make ourselves healthy and vital, or sick and weak.

Naturopathy is the purest form of healing. Its procedures & diagnostic tools are completely non-invasive, and at its core are **alkalization** and **detoxification**, which we will discuss in great detail in next chapters.

I have had great success with detoxification in chronic and degenerative issues and it has been recognized worldwide. Out of 100 people who come to me with different forms of cancer, approximately 70% cure themselves, 20% can't do the program and 10% are too advanced or do not want to live anymore. My success with regeneration in spinal cord injuries is also remarkable: a 32 year old female, who had severed her upper cervical spine (a C3-C4 spinal cord severation) 12 years previously, came to my clinic. In 11 months she had regained total feeling and movement throughout her body. A young Amish man who got into a tractor accident, leaving him a quadriplegic at the C4-C5 level, in 6 months had complete feelings in his toes.

Most people live to eat. But I want you to start thinking about *eating to live*. What you eat, effects your health directly. I have seen cancer, again and again, cleaned out by the body of my patients. Also, ailments like diabetes, coronary artery disease and arthritis all wiped out. I have seen spinal cord injuries reconnect and nerve damage from strokes, multiple sclerosis and the like, heal.

One of the premises of this segment is that health is really very simple, yet we spend a large part of our time and money trying to achieve it. I will help you to understand our species, and encourage you toward eating in harmony with your physiological, anatomical and biochemical processes. This will give you vitality and a disease-free life.

Allow yourself the time & discipline to *become alive again through the process of detoxification*. Put your heart, soul and self-discipline into it. Detoxification will be one of the most important thing you will do for yourself in your entire life.

MODULE 3.1

A Personal Journey

I was raised in a small town of Indiana. The typical diet here consisted of a lot of dairy products, refined sugars, grains and meat 3 times a day. Dairy products and refined sugars are very mucus forming. As a result, my sinus cavities were always blocked. I had also developed acute constipation, which led to bleeding hemorrhoids. I also started getting migraine headaches, about every 3 days. And, of course, obesity was another side effect of this diet. If I had not been consciously connected to God in these early years of my life, I would have succumbed to severe depression.

In the late 1960s, I started eating raw foods. I read books by Ehret, Hotema, Jensen, Mc-Faddin, and many other great healers, talking about the concepts of not destroying the food we eat before eating them. I read about breatharianism, and the ability to live off of oxygen, carbon, hydrogen, nitrogen, etc. Since all elements are made up of these higher atoms, it seemed logical to me that if our consciousness was in the right place, we could survive at this level. People who survive at this level are called God eaters. So, I decided that I would live in remote areas and attempt this level of consciousness. I became a hermit and undertook the task of eliminating the heavy or low-vibrational foods, including meats and grains as well. I also stopped eating vegetables, which left me with a diet of only fruits and nuts. Finally, I decided to get away from all acid-forming foods. So, I stopped eating the nuts. With those choices I had become a "fruitarian." I lived exclusively on fresh, raw fruits.

Nature's Way

- Natural health is not alternative medicine, rather it is traditional medicine.

- Nature's way is thousands of years old. Whereas, chemical medicine is only 125 years old.

- Since the introduction of chemical medicines, diseases have skyrocketed.

- Medicine should only include natural remedies that alkalize, cleanse and regenerate the body.

I was a fruitarian for almost 4 years, out of which I lived 6 months only on oranges. I had discovered an organic orange garden who was able to supply me with navel oranges for the whole year.

During this period as a fruitarian, I began to experience the tremendous rejuvenational powers of the body. I could cut myself without feeling any pain. There was no bleeding. And the wound would be healed in next one or two days. My goal was to stop eating oranges and live only on air. But the issue was that my energy levels had become so high, that I could not stay in my body. I was traveling out of body into some of the most splendid worlds of God that exist beyond the ordinary human experience. I felt like I had merged with God. I became unlimited. I had no point of reference as I desired nothing. I was completely fulfilled. My love for God and all life forms intensified beyond words. The problem was that I was young and immature with this level of realization of God. As I couldn't communicate in this world anymore, I decided, that I needed to ground myself and teach others about the tremendous healing power of raw foods and the unlimited awareness that each one of us possess. So, after several years of living in remote areas, I moved back to civilization.

Since then I have opened several health food stores and become a certified biochemist, naturopath, iridologist and a master herbalist.

35 years ago I opened a health clinic that I am still managing. From my experience, I can tell you that there is no incurable disease, only incurable people. I have also spent multiple years working in emergency medicine, and I have seen both allopathy and traditional medicine in action. While emergency medicine is *amazing*, allopathy, in general, kills hundreds of thousands of people each year. Whereas, traditional medicine (or herbal medicine) saves hundreds of thousands of lives each year. I invite you to join me in learning and using God's natural laws to heal and rejuvenate yourself.

This segment of the book reflects my (naturopathy doctor) experiences and viewpoints on true healing.

10 Ways To Be Successful

These 10 recommendations will help you massively in achieving the success, health and vitality you want from your detoxification and regeneration process.

1. Your path to success primarily lies in your diet. The things you consume, ingest, inhale, and apply to your skin determine how you integrate the external environment. Engage with the ideas presented in this book that focuses on a raw food diet, understand them, and incorporate them into your lifestyle. The more you increase the proportion of raw fruits and vegetable intake, particularly in the form of salads, the higher your chances of achieving success. For individuals dealing with ailments like cancer, spinal cord injuries, multiple sclerosis, Parkinson's, or other chronic conditions, it is advisable to adopt a completely raw and "living" diet consisting exclusively of fruits and vegetable salads.

2. Seek the expertise of a healthcare practitioner who possesses knowledge in the application of raw foods and alternative detox methods such as fasting. This is particularly crucial when dealing with ailments such as cancer and other persistent degenerative conditions. Having proper guidance and assistance during your healing journey can be advantageous. While you ultimately bear the responsibility for your well-being, numerous valuable sources are available to aid you in embarking on this path toward vibrant health.

3. Locate an individual skilled in the practice of analyzing the iris of the eye, a discipline known as iridology. This natural method stands as one of the few soft tissue analyses available

today. It provides a comprehensive overview of your strengths and weaknesses, revealing congestive (lymphatic) and chemical accumulations. This information is invaluable in addressing any vulnerabilities in your glands or organs. To tackle this, I suggest an herbal course or formula. Utilize herbs to target weaknesses at the cellular level and facilitate the movement and purification of your lymphatic system, gastrointestinal tract, and lungs. You can purchase authentic herbal formulas from www.drmorses.com with discount coupon - GAUTAM.

Nearly all Homo sapiens, almost reaching 100 percent, exhibit deficiencies in their glands. To initiate this evaluation, start by completing the "What Is Your Body Telling You" Self-Assessment Questionnaire located in Chapter 5. This will help you identify your specific areas of weakness.

Utilize the Basal Temperature Study Test (available in Appendix A) to gauge your thyroid's performance and understand its significant role in calcium utilization and metabolism.

If you experience elevated or notably low blood pressure, it indicates a vulnerability in your adrenal glands. Once more, refer to the Self-Assessment Questionnaire to uncover any additional indications of adrenal gland insufficiency.

4. Regularly stimulate your lymphatic system into motion. To varying extents, everyone experiences a sluggish lymphatic system. It's crucial to remember that all your cells require nourishment and the ability to eliminate waste, and your lymphatic system functions as your internal sewage network.

Think of your lymph nodes as septic tanks; maintaining their cleanliness is paramount. Utilize herbal formulas to support kidney health and increase your consumption of fruits. Revitalize your gastrointestinal tract with raw foods and a replenishing herbal formula designed for intestinal health. Refrain from using laxatives, purgatives, acidophilus, bifidophilus, or other forms of intestinal flora supplements. Trust that your intestinal flora will naturally restore itself over time.

Incorporate exercise, such as walking or swimming, to notably assist in the movement of your lymphatic system, particularly in the lower parts of your body. Allow yourself to perspire; your skin serves as your largest excretory organ. Keep it invigorated and clean by practicing skin brushing, regular showers, and alternating hot-and-cold showers to stimulate circulation.

5. Allocate a month to engage with an herbal parasite formula (like parasite micro formula on www.drmorses.com). This approach will facilitate the elimination of larger parasites like worms and flukes. Moreover, it will aid in diminishing the presence of microorganisms such as candida and bacteria, which can influence your food cravings.

6. Prior to commencing your detox regimen, dedicate approximately a month to purifying your liver and fortifying your pancreas. Chapter 8 contains recommendations on how to bolster and cleanse these organs using herbs and herbal formulas. If you are dealing with diabetes or struggling with being underweight, a period of around three months may be necessary.

7. If you are currently taking chemical medications, rest assured that there is minimal likelihood of interactions between this program and the suggested herbal formulas. In the case of being prescribed high blood pressure medication, it's advisable to monitor your blood pressure closely. This program has the potential to rapidly lower blood pressure. Use your best judgment; if your blood pressure is already low, further reduction through chemical medications might not be advisable. In such instances, it's important to focus on normalizing blood pressure by enhancing and rejuvenating your adrenal glands.

When dealing with Type II diabetes, overcoming it is very easy in most cases. If you're using insulin, it's important to keep an eye on your blood sugar levels. The same principle applies here as with high blood pressure considerations.

SCIENTIFIC FACTS

The majority of chemicals have a detrimental impact on cells, leading to their weakening and destruction. Chemotherapy, for instance, induces high levels of acidosis and results in cell destruction, potentially leading to future cancer development, or the progression of existing cancer to other parts of the body (metastasis). Radiation, on the other hand, provokes inflammation, burns, and the destruction of cells and tissues, with the potential to trigger the spread of cancer (metastasis).

9. During the process of detoxification and rejuvenation, your body may exhibit symptoms indicative of a "healing crisis." This occurrence is typical, innate, and beneficial. Gaining an understanding of the concept of a healing crisis will provide

insights into the nature of what we commonly refer to as "diseases." For further information, refer to Chapter 5. It's crucial to remember that disease symptoms arise from two fundamental sources: congestion and cellular weakness.

10. Last but not least: Your mindset matters significantly! Embrace a positive attitude throughout your journey. Find pleasure in your endeavors. Never lose sight of the reasons behind your pursuit of a healthier body, your vessel in the physical realm. It's important to recognize that some of your weaknesses are inherited through genetics, and the toxins you carry might have developed even before birth. Allow time for their release. Achieving vibrant health within this world is not an instantaneous process; it requires patience. Occasionally, it demands substantial effort, yet the rewards are undoubtedly worthwhile. This pursuit links you to life, love, and the divine.

MODULE 3.2

Understanding Our Species

People often inquire about my methods for rejuvenating and revitalizing the physical body. Numerous books on health and nutrition have been published, many echoing existing ideas or hypotheses that remain largely unchanged. Some of these concepts are even nonsensical. Bookstores stock titles on topics like blood types, excessive vitamin intake, high protein diets, among others. A few of these plans, based on my experience, are notably harmful and lead to fatalities annually.

In my view, the essence of health is less intricate than these volumes suggest. My approach is straightforward: Consume foods appropriate for your biological species. This might sound overly simplified, yet let us contemplate our species for a moment. Picture yourself in the African plains or jungles, surrounded by diverse animals like elephants, giraffes, apes, and more. If I were to ask, "Which of these creatures does a 'homo sapien' resemble?" the answer is evident: the primates. They are frugivores, just as we are. Although this comparison might appear basic, let's hypothetically dissect representatives from each species and examine their internal anatomy and physiology.

The subsequent list categorizes vertebrates into four groups—carnivores, omnivores, herbivores, and frugivores—highlighting their distinctions.

Anatomical and Physiological Differences of Vertebrates

CARNIVORES

Includes:

Cats, cheetahs, lions, etc.

Diet:

Mainly meats, some vegetables, grass and herbs

Digestive system:

Tongue—very rough (for pulling and tearing)

Salivary glands—none

Stomach—simple structure; small round sacks; strong gastric juices

Small intestine—smooth and short

Liver—50 percent larger than that of humans; very complex with five distinct chambers; heavy bile flow for heavy gastric juices

Eliminative system:

Colon—smooth, non-sacculated, minimal ability for absorption

GI tract—three times the length of the spine

Extremities (limbs):

Hands (upper front)—claw type Feet (lower back)—claw type Quadrupeds—walks on all four

Integumentary system:

Skin—100 percent covered with hair

Sweat glands—uses tongue, and has sweat glands in foot pads only

Skeletal system:

Teeth—incisor teeth in front, molars behind with large canine teeth for ripping

Jaws—unidirectional, up-and-down only

Tail—yes

Urinary system:

Kidneys—(urine) acid

OMNIVORES

Includes:

Birds (including chickens, turkeys, etc.), hogs and dogs

Diet:

Some meat, vegetables, fruits, roots and some barks

Digestive system:

Tongue—moderate to rough

Salivary glands—under-active

Stomach—moderate gastric acids (HCL and pepsin)

Small intestines— somewhat sacculated, which accounts for their ability to eat vegetables

Liver—complex and larger proportionally than that of humans

Eliminative system:

Colon—shorter than human colon, with minimal absorption

GI tract—ten times the length of the spine

Extremities (limbs):

Hands—hoofs, claws, and paws

Feet—hoofs, claws, and paws

Quadrupeds—walks on all four extremities; except for birds, which have and walk on two legs only

Integumentary system:

Skin—smooth, oily, hair or feathers

Sweat glands—very minimal; only around snout (hogs) and foot pads (dogs) and none on birds

Skeletal system:

Teeth—tusk-like canine teeth or beaks

Jaws—multi-directional

Tail—yes

Urinary system:

Kidneys—(urine) acid

HERBIVORES

Includes:

Horses, cows, sheep, elephants, deer, giraffes

Diet:

Vegetables, herbs and some roots and barks

Digestive system:

Tongue—moderately rough

Salivary glands—alkaline digestion starts here

Stomach—oblong, ringed, and the most complex (as a rule, has four or more pouches or stomachs); weak stomach acids

Small intestines—long and sacculated for extensive absorption

Liver— similar to human (slightly larger in capacity)

Eliminative system:

Colon—long and sacculated (ringed) for extensive absorption

GI tract—thirty times the length of the spine

Extremities (limbs):

Hands (upper)—hoofs
Feet (lower)—hoofs
Quadrupeds—walks on all four extremities

Integumentary system:

Skin—pores with extensive hair covering entire body

Sweat glands—includes millions of perspiration ducts

Skeletal system:

Teeth—twenty-four molars, five on each side of each jaw and eight incisors (cutting teeth) in the front part of the jaws

Jaws—multi-directional, up-and-down, side-to-side, forward and backward creating a grinding effect

Tail—yes

Urinary system:

Kidneys—(urine) alkaline

FRUGIVORES

Includes:

Humans and primates (apes, chimpanzees, monkeys)

Diet:

Mainly fruits, nuts, seeds, sweet vegetables and herbs

Digestive system:

Tongue—smooth, used mainly as a shovel

Salivary glands—alkaline digestive energies start here

Stomach—oblong with two compartments

Small intestines—sacculated for extensive absorption

Liver—simple and average size, not large and complex, like carnivores

Eliminative system:

Colon—sacculated for extensive absorption

GI tract—twelve times the length of the spine

Extremities (limbs):

Hands (upper)—fingers for picking, peeling and tearing

Feet (lower)—toes Walks upright on two extremities

Integumentary system:

Skin—pores, with minimal hair

Sweat glands—includes millions of perspiration ducts

Skeletal system:

Teeth—thirty-two teeth: four incisors (cutting), two cuspids (pointed), four small molars (bicuspids), and six molars (no long canine or tusk-type teeth)

Jaws—multi-motional, dimensional, up-and-down, backward and forward, side-to-side, etc.

Tail—some

Urinary system:

Kidneys—(urine) alkaline

After dissecting various species and observing their anatomical and physiological traits, the consistent conclusion emerges: Humans are inherently frugivores, whether people accept it or not.

Uniquely, humans grapple with dietary confusion. In childhood, our instinct directs us towards certain foods. Place an array of foods before a child, and they gravitate towards fruits and flowers – vibrant, energy-rich options. This inclination aligns with our frugivorous nature, distinct from omnivores. Genuine carnivores, for instance, would relish tearing apart and consuming live prey, a behavior rare among humans.

Grasping our biological needs isn't complex. Moreover, animals don't cook their food before consumption. Zoos avoid feeding cooked meals to animals as it leads to sickness and mortality. Similarly, veterinarians advise against sharing table scraps with pets because they're susceptible to our diseases. Cooking compromises food's chemistry and depletes its electrical energy.

Food, as intended by the divine, sustains life, not demise. God embodies vitality, energy, love, and happiness. Negative aspects like depression and anger also coexist. We choose which path to follow. A robust physical body fosters healthy emotional and mental well-being, which many have lost.

Humanity shares biological sameness. Regardless of origin, our physiological processes and anatomy are nearly identical. Nevertheless, variations in consciousness, activity levels, and body parts used influence our food preferences. Navigating health needn't be intricate. Embrace simplicity. Food can either bind you to this world or liberate you. Embark on a journey toward vitality and freedom from food addictions that undermine well-being.

I encourage you to rediscover vitality and relish life's rewards. Redirect your mind and emotions toward the simplicity of consuming raw fruits, vegetables, nuts, and seeds. Understand your species and opt for foods that nurture your body's health.

"The ancient Greeks, before the time of Lycurgus, ate nothing but fruit," (Plutarch) and "each generation reached the age of 200 years."

— Onomacritus of Athens

MODULE 3.3

How the Body Works

Any soul with a physical form should grasp the fundamental workings of the body. "Why do we eat and what happens to the food we eat?" poses a crucial inquiry. Once we comprehend this, the nature of health and illness becomes clearer.

Consuming sustenance is vital; most life forms on Earth require some type of sustenance to exist and uphold their essence. For most people, halting food intake leads to death, though exceptions do exist. A select few have subsisted solely on air, which comprises carbon, oxygen, hydrogen, and nitrogen – elements corresponding to higher-frequency sugars, fats, and proteins. Achieving this is extremely rare and demands deep spiritual alignment. While I've encountered highly aware spiritual masters and teachers, I've not met anyone personally who has achieved this feat.

We eat to gain additional energy. Cells within our bodies function as individual entities with consciousness, each aware of its specific roles. The life force or spirit forms the inner energy molding life into shapes and providing awareness. Nonetheless, cells require external energy to sustain their activity.

Most individuals ingest food without pondering how or why it is utilized within the body. Assumptions that if it's edible, it's usable are incorrect. This chapter delves into the body's processes of breaking down, utilizing, and expelling consumed foods.

Eating, digesting, absorbing, utilizing, and eliminating food constitute ongoing, consistent processes. Impairment in any of these stages, detrimentally affects the entire body. Major symptoms may take years to manifest, but signs emerge along the way: fatigue, weight issues, eye bags, rashes, digestive irregularities, and more.

The Four Basic Processes

DIGESTION

Initially, all consumed food undergoes a "digestive" process, breaking it down into essential building materials and energy. These raw materials fuel our body's functions, while aiding in its repair and maintenance.

Enzymes initiate food breakdown, commencing in the mouth, where alkaline digestion of carbohydrates, sugars, and fats begins. The stomach contributes by producing pepsin, an enzyme released by hydrochloric acid (HCL) for initial protein digestion. Subsequent digestion predominantly occurs in the alkaline environment of the small intestine. Inadequate breakdown, due to a weak pancreas, stomach, or intestines, or poor food combinations, leads to gas formation through fermentation or putrefaction. Increased gas issues indicate greater weakness or poor dietary choices.

Our body breaks down consumed foods into the following components:

• Proteins into amino acids for building and repair,

- Carbohydrates into simple sugars for energy,
- Fats into fatty acids and glycerol for building, repair, and emergency purposes.

Alkaline digestive enzymes in the mouth handle carbohydrate and fat digestion, while the lower stomach employs acid (pepsin) digestive enzymes for initial protein breakdown. Alkaline digestive enzymes in the pancreas and upper small intestine complete digestion for proteins, starches, sugars, and fats. It's crucial to understand that most of our body's processes are alkaline in nature.

Digestion forms the crucial foundation for a healthy body, but many stumble at this stage. If you're underweight or lack adequate muscle tissue, your body likely struggles to digest food effectively.

ABSORPTION

After food breakdown, absorption ensues, involving the assimilation of building materials, fuels, and other components such as tissue salts, vitamins, tannins, alkaloids, and flavins. These elements travel through the bloodstream to cells, serving for energy, stimulation, building, repairing, or storage. The process happens through the villi (finger-like projections on certain membranes) and small pores along the intestines' mucous membranes. However, absorption is hindered for many due to "mucoid plaque," a thick adhesive substance that develops within the GI tract. This plaque, formed from gluten, mucus, foreign proteins, and food by-products, obstructs nutrient intake. Refined sugars, grains, meats, and dairy mainly contribute to its formation. "Mucoid plaque" prevents proper nutrient absorption. Many individuals struggle with this issue during the second stage of food utilization, particularly if they're thin, malnourished, or lack adequate muscle tissue.

UTILIZATION

Nutrition's journey to our cells is crucial. Blood and its vascular system act as transportation, with the liver overseeing absorption. It can alter nutrients, store them, or release them unchanged for body-wide utilization. The liver's versatility is remarkable, producing amino acids, converting sugars to fats, and more.

Here's a secret: Acid-alkaline balance matters. Increased body acidity leads to anionic nutrition, causing coagulation or clumping of building materials (fats, fuels, minerals, etc.). Human diets, largely, are acidic-forming. Acidity triggers inflammation in the vascular system and throughout the body. In response, fats adhere to vessel walls to counter this inflammation, leading to lipid stones like gallbladder or liver stones. Cholesterol serves as a common anti-inflammatory lipid. High acidity also causes minerals to bond, resulting in "rock-type" stones like kidney stones or bone spurs.

Tiny pores in cell membranes hinder clumped nutrition absorption. When red blood cells clump, hindering oxygen transport, cellular starvation ensues. Glands secrete hormones and steroids to aid utilization, but when these glands underperform, calcium utilization and overall nutrient absorption are impaired. For example, an under-active thyroid slows calcium utilization, creating a domino effect of cellular starvation, muscle loss, and more.

Failure in nutrient utilization is widespread, resulting in varying degrees of health issues.

ELIMINATION

What enters should, for the most part, exit the body. It's problematic if what exits mirrors what entered (except for corn, which might appear unchanged). When food elements are broken down for cellular use, many by-products are produced, like gases, acids, cellular waste, and undigested components— alongside unused vitamins and minerals—that need to be expelled.

The body aims to eliminate, often in ways we don't fully comprehend. Cold and flu symptoms exemplify this, manifesting as sneezing, coughing, sweating, aches, fever, and diarrhea. These processes eliminate mucus, parasites, toxins, and more.

Failure to eliminate leads to interstitial and intracellular congestion, promoting cellular decay. Effective elimination involves regular bowel movements, sufficient urination, sweating, and proper breathing. Most struggle with this. Rectifying digestion, absorption, utilization, and elimination rejuvenates energy, vitality, and a disease-free existence.

MODULE 3.4

The Foods We Eat

Now that we have learned what species we belong to, and how our body works, we will examine the proper foods that Nature designed for our species.

What is so important about the types of foods we eat?

I have heard many doctors say that it doesn't matter *what* we eat. On the other hand, The American Dietetics Association, considered by many to be the authority on the correct foods to eat for health, has been making specific dietary recommendations for years. Still, cancer is reportedly in every other (or every third) person, and statistics for the incidence of diabetes as well as multiple sclerosis, Parkinson's disease and every other disease you can name (and some that you can't) are soaring. Why?

It's All About Energy

Energy serves as the paramount factor essential for the existence of life and forms the very foundation of creation itself. It is the consequence of the motion and interaction among the atoms constituting all living entities. Even carbon, which underpins all life on our planet, relies on the constant movement and interplay of atoms for its existence. It's worth noting that atoms, which embody energy, cannot be brought into existence or obliterated; however, they can undergo transformations. Energy can either be amplified or diminished.

Energy levels, often characterized by frequencies, can be either low or high, symbolized by extended or compact waves. These energy levels are determined by the molecular composition of the initiating force. Energy can also be categorized as either kinetic or potential. **Kinetic** energy is the active form of energy in action, while **potential** energy is energy that's stored, waiting to be utilized. For instance, the chemical energy in food is primarily potential energy until it is released through enzymatic and chemical processes. At that point, this latent energy transforms into kinetic energy, becoming more active and igniting various activities.

A striking contrast between potential and kinetic energy is evident when comparing cooked and raw foods. Cooked foods possess significantly lower electromagnetic energy, which is the combined molecular energy, compared to their raw counterparts. This is attributed to the molecular structural changes that occur when heat is applied, leading to alterations in electrons. An example of this is the transformation of water from a liquid to vapor when heated. The heating process also results in the conversion of unsaturated fats to saturated forms, with the destruction of water-soluble constituents, leaving only some of the original elements. Furthermore, cooking often generates hazardous and carcinogenic compounds. Additionally, heat destroys the vital enzymes present in food, which act as catalysts for various biological reactions.

In summary, the overall health of your body is closely linked to the level of energy your cells possess. Cells with higher energy levels tend to be healthier, while those with lower energy levels are more susceptible to immune system responses or parasitic threats, inching closer to potential destruction.

Carbon, hydrogen, oxygen and nitrogen are the basic elements of all organic matter on earth. All foods and their constituents (like proteins, carbohydrates and fats) are mostly created from these basic elements, which are the building blocks that determine to what category molecules or compounds, etc., belong. These categories of molecular structures (such as sugars, starches, proteins, fats) make up the foods that sustain life on this planet.

This module will view food and the process of eating from the perspective of chemistry and physics, and set it in the context of some overviews from God and nature. Let's first examine some of the most important constituents that your body requires to sustain, clean and repair itself.

SUGARS

A sugar is a carbohydrate belonging to the saccharide family. Simple sugars (also called monosaccharides) are the main fuels for your body. Sugars are as essential to your body as gasoline is to your automobile. It helps run your machine (your body) via the cells. However, there are several important distinctions to understand about sugars.

Glucose (simple sugar) and its initial compounds, such as starch and cellulose, make up the most abundant organic chemical compounds on earth. Since your body can only use substances in their simplest forms, all complex sugars (di- and polysaccharides) must first be broken down into simple sugars (monosaccharides). This is one aspect of the process of digestion.

After digestion breaks down complex sugars to glucose, this glucose is then absorbed into the blood from the intestinal tract. Glucose is then transported to cells where it is reduced to carbon and is oxidized for energy and heat. Part of this carbon is stored for future energy needs (the way a battery stores energy). Some excess carbon, which is not used, is stored as ATP (adenosine triphosphate) or converted to fat and/or stored as glycogen. Glycogen is stored mainly in the liver and muscle tissue, but can also be stored in many other places. When the body is deprived of glucose or fructose, it will start to use its glycogen reserves. Glycogen is then converted back into glucose. Remember that the body *must* have a fuel source, as does your car.

When refined or complex sugars (several glucose and fructose complexes bonded together) are consumed, this creates a glucose overload, which in turn creates excess carbon molecules. This excess carbon is converted into carbon dioxide and carbonic acid. Carbon dioxide is eliminated via lungs, kidneys and skin. Carbonic acid requires oxidation or transmutation via oxygen or mineral salts, respectively. Both of these substances are acid-forming and must be neutralized and removed by the body, as they are strong contributors to acidosis.

Sugar (glucose) overload is common in our society. We consume a great deal of refined and complex carbohydrates and sugars. This keeps a high demand upon the pancreas to produce insulin, and upon the liver and kidneys to convert or eliminate the excess. Add to this excess the problems created by protein and fat consumption, and you can begin to form a picture of why people today have so many health problems.

Raw fruits and vegetables are balanced in their simple sugars, amino acids and fatty acids. This is another reason that I call them "God-foods" designed for humans.

The Danger of High-Protein Diets

Some substances in our diet serve as building materials rather than fuel sources. Proteins, for instance, fall into this category. They are essential for various functions in the body, serving as building blocks for tissues, playing roles in immune function, acting as catalysts for biochemical reactions, and serving as carriers for molecules, among other functions. Much like carbohydrates need to be converted into simple sugars before they can be used, proteins must first be broken down into amino acids before the body can utilize them for building and repair, much like a carpenter uses two-by-fours or two-by-sixes in constructing or fixing a structure. However, if necessary, the body can convert amino acids into glucose.

The grave mistake made by many who want to lose weight is in making the body burn protein for fuel. When the body is deprived of sugars, it will go to stored fat or break down its own tissues for energy. This leads to muscle, liver, pancreatic and kidney damage.

In Chapter 4 we'll discuss the "Protein Myth" in greater detail.

Most artificial sweeteners have been linked to cancer. Nutrasweet® or aspartame is an example of an artificial sugar.

Aspartame is a neurotoxin that breaks down into formaldehyde, and Americans use over 7000 tons of this per year.

The belief that natural, uncomplicated sugars promote the growth of cancer is a misconception. In fact, the opposite is true. Simple sugars provide nourishment and vitality to cells, which is essential for effective cancer treatment. This is because cancer cells, originally normal cells, have lost their vigor and health due to a condition called acidosis. It's important to note that simple sugars, especially glucose, are the appropriate source of energy for cells. The utilization of proteins and fats as fuel should be reserved for situations of absolute necessity, as it can potentially lead to cellular damage.

Fructose is the highest energetic form of a monosaccharide or simple sugar. Neurons (nerve cells) especially attract fructose molecules. Fructose enters a cell through diffusion instead of via active transport, which its counterpart glucose uses. Diffusion saves energy for the body and cells.

Any activity requires energy, including the activity of transporting nutrients across cell walls. Most nutrients also require a helper or carrier to assist in this movement through the cell wall into the cell. As ATP (adenosine triphosphate) is a cell's stored energy, it is used in active transport (the assisted transportation of nutrients across cell membrane walls). Glucose needs insulin to a certain degree as a "utilization hormone" for this active transport. Fructose, on the other hand, requires no ATP or insulin and is simply pulled or absorbed through the cell wall by diffusion.

For diabetics, fructose is perfect, especially if they remove complex sugars from their diets. Complex sugars create excessive glucose levels in the blood, which then creates more insulin demand.

Raw fruits and vegetables are always your best sources of simple sugars. This is one reason why your body becomes stronger and more energetic on these foods. Foods high in protein and low in sugars, or foods high in complex-sugars, rob your body of vital energy, create acidosis and elevate blood sugars.

Carbohydrate Metabolism

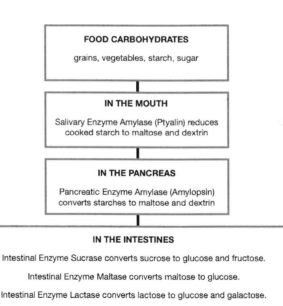

FOOD CARBOHYDRATES

grains, vegetables, starch, sugar

IN THE MOUTH

Salivary Enzyme Amylase (Ptyalin) reduces cooked starch to maltose and dextrin

IN THE PANCREAS

Pancreatic Enzyme Amylase (Amylopsin) converts starches to maltose and dextrin

IN THE INTESTINES

Intestinal Enzyme Sucrase converts sucrose to glucose and fructose.

Intestinal Enzyme Maltase converts maltose to glucose.

Intestinal Enzyme Lactase converts lactose to glucose and galactose.

Simple sugars also aid alkalization of the tissues, which is vital for tissue regeneration and vitality. As stated, fructose is the highest electrical sugar in nature and is superb for brain and nerve regeneration.

CHAPTER FOUR

Toxic Habits

Numerous misconceptions surrounding health and well-being have persisted over time. These notions have been transmitted through generations, passed down through education, and at times intentionally ingrained via media to promote product sales. One prominent example is the fallacy of "Drinking Milk for Calcium," while another substantial myth is the 'Protein Myth'. The prevalence of high-protein consumption in our society can be attributed to industries promoting animal and grain products.

It's commonplace for businesses to devise catchy slogans to market their products. However, when industries veer into the territory of half-truths or falsehoods, it results in fraud and misrepresentation. These fabrications adversely impact the health of countless individuals annually. The problem of deceptive advertising extends to pharmaceutical companies, contributing to the alarming number of deaths caused by over-the-counter and prescription drugs, as reported by sources like The Washington Post.

This chapter will delve into several perilous misconceptions, including those surrounding food, vaccinations against diseases, and reliance on chemical substances.

When choices stem from habit rather than alignment with natural forces, these habits can generate toxic conditions within our bodies, leading to severe illness or death. Opting for perceived health or hygiene at the cost of environmental balance, breeds even broader toxic habits, potentially affecting the well-being of our planet and its inhabitants.

The doctor of the future will give us no medicine, but will interest his patients in the care of the human frame, in diet and in the cause and prevention of disease.
— Thomas Edison

MODULE 4.1

The Problem with Milk and Other Dairy Food

Cow's milk is specifically intended for cows. Drinking milk is beneficial for human infants only during their first two years, given that the milk originates from their mother and is thus fresh, raw, and natural. Ideally, mothers would be on a highly nutritious raw food diet before and during pregnancy. However, our culture tends to opt against breastfeeding. Many of us were introduced to cow's milk or synthetic formulas, which are much more concentrated than cow's milk—almost twentyfold.

Cow's milk is rich in proteins, minerals, and fats, catering to the rapid growth of baby cows that gain 300-500 pounds in a single year. Conversely, human infants don't grow at such a pace. Cow's milk contains over four times the protein and more than six times the mineral content of human milk. This high concentration proves challenging for infants to digest, as human enzyme production for milk digestion is much lower than that of cows. Inadequate enzymes lead to digestive troubles and mucus accumulation in sinus passages, lungs, the brain, and ears. Allergies often stem from the initial congestion caused by cow's milk consumption.

In adulthood, the inability to digest milk becomes even more pronounced, resulting in deeper congestion-related issues as one ages. Cow's milk also lacks essential fatty acids crucial for human functions such as cholesterol production, the creation of steroids, and the development of brain and nerve tissue. While raw cow's milk primarily supports skeletal and muscular growth, human milk fosters brain and nerve growth. This distinction highlights one of the key differences between frugivores and herbivores.

Around the age of three or four, most children lose the enzymes needed to digest milk, particularly lactase which breaks down lactose—the primary sugar in milk. This coincides with the biological norm of weaning after three or four years. Lacking the necessary digestive enzymes leads to heightened mucus production, causing irritation to the gastrointestinal mucosa. The ensuing mucus, combined with starch, contributes to the formation of thick mucoid plaque on intestinal walls.

Remember John Wayne? Reports indicate he carried up to fifty pounds of impacted fecal matter in his bowels at the time of his death. Such impactions lead to inflammation, pockets (diverticulum), and weakening of the intestinal wall tissue. This progression results in bowel constriction, ulcers, lesions, and eventually cancers. Former U.S. Surgeon General C. Everett Koop, M.D., conveyed to the world that "Dairy products are bad for you."

FROM ALKALINE TO ACID

Furthermore, compounding these issues, cow's milk is subjected to cooking or pasteurization. This heating process alters the milk's chemistry and shifts its nature from being alkaline-forming to acid-forming. In the realm of chemistry, introducing heat is a means to alter chemical compounds. The act of heating, or cooking, also eradicates water-soluble vitamins, notably vitamin C and B-complex vitamins. Additionally, the process saturates fats and causes certain proteins to bind with minerals, leading to mineral-to-mineral binding as well. Consider the fate of a young calf fed pasteurized milk instead of its fresh, unprocessed mother's milk—death ensues.

CONGESTION DECREASES UTILIZATION

Colds, flu, mumps, or any conditions affecting the lymphatic or respiratory system can be largely attributed to congestion caused by dairy products. Dairy items are known for their high mucus-forming and constipating properties. The origins of the clear, yellow, green, brown, or black mucus associated with colds and respiratory issues can be traced back to dairy consumption. Similarly, tumors, lymph node swelling, and notably, tonsil enlargement stem from the same source.

The thyroid and parathyroid glands, situated in the throat, are particularly susceptible to congestion due to dairy products. This leads to hyper or hypo-conditions within these glands. These glands play a role in calcium utilization by the body. As congestion, toxins, and inflammation from dairy products compromise these glands, calcium utilization declines. Ironically, this contradicts the very purpose for consuming dairy products in the first place. When cellular-level calcium utilization drops, it results in depression, weakened bones and tissues, nerve and muscle frailty, and compromised connective tissues. All these issues are linked to mucus buildup triggered by dairy consumption.

Calcium, an abundant mineral, is most concentrated in sesame seeds and sea vegetables like kelp. Calcium requires magnesium for effective utilization. In fruits and particularly vegetables, calcium and magnesium are in harmony. Dark green leafy vegetables are rich in calcium, magnesium, and flavonoids, all of which complement each other for optimal usage. However, cow's milk has an imbalanced calcium-to-magnesium ratio, hindering calcium utilization. It's estimated that less than 20 percent of calcium in milk is absorbed, while more calcium is actually utilized from fruit juice compared to milk.

Cooking milk ionizes the minerals, shifting its impact from alkaline to acidic. This transformation can lead to stone formation, muscle weakness, gastrointestinal inflammation, and other conditions. This is evident in cases where individuals consuming milk and taking calcium supplements still experience osteoporosis. Instead of solely focusing on supplementation, a consideration of internal utilization within the body is essential. Adequate utilization, not high calcium doses, holds the solution.

The thyroid/parathyroid and adrenal glands largely control calcium utilization in the body. Healthy functioning of these glands corresponds to robust calcium management. Regenerating these glands enhances calcium utilization significantly. The Basal Temperature Test (discussed in

Appendix A) can be employed to evaluate thyroid function, while checking blood pressure can identify adrenal weaknesses. It's important to remember that a systolic blood pressure below 118 typically indicates adrenal weakness.

PARASITES

Parasites are an additional outcome of milk consumption. It's estimated that 60 percent or more of dairy cows in the United States carry the leukemia virus, salmonella, and the tuberculosis virus. Moreover, milk and dairy products rank as the most mucous-forming among all the foods we consume, while refined sugar is the second most. Both of these foods contribute to excessive congestion throughout our tissues. This environment becomes a feeding ground for yeast, fungi, and worms to flourish. This ultimately leads to conditions like Candida albicans and other infections. Based on my observation of numerous cancer patients, I am strongly convinced that the consumption of milk and dairy products, including colostrum, triggers and amplifies tumor growth and lymphatic congestion. From my perspective, many tumor-related cancers initiate due to the intake of such foods.

DIABETES

Numerous research investigations have established a connection between the consumption of pasteurized milk and diabetes. The antibodies produced to counter these modified and detrimental milk proteins also target the beta cells situated in the pancreas. These beta cells, located in the islets of

Langerhans within the pancreas, are responsible for releasing insulin.

BOVINE GROWTH HORMONE

Another significant concern associated with milk consumption is the impact of rBGH, or recombinant bovine growth hormone. This hormone, engineered by the Monsanto Corporation using E-coli bacteria, was initially designed to enhance milk production. Certain studies have indicated that this growth hormone (rBGH) can function as a carcinogen. Moreover, multiple studies have demonstrated its capacity to accelerate cancer growth. Personally, I am of the opinion that this growth hormone stimulates the endocrine gland system, particularly the thyroid and adrenal glands. This disruption affects various aspects of growth, other developmental processes, and the balance of hormones. Our society confronts substantial hormonal imbalances that are detrimentally affecting our well-being and economy.

It's essential to uncover the truth about the foods you consume. Don't allow yourself to be swayed by media and other influences within our capitalistic society, where monetary interests sometimes supersede human welfare. It's crucial to embark on a process of detoxification to eliminate the accumulated congestion resulting from years of consuming mucus-forming foods.

INTESTINAL FLORA

Many health-conscious individuals today opt to take supplements like acidophilus with lactobacillus, and similar products. But why? If you don't consume dairy products, there might not be a necessity to supplement with these. These bacteria are primarily involved in breaking down milk proteins and sugars. They are also present in areas where the body forms toxemia (toxins) due to dairy product consumption, such as saliva, the lymphatic system, the vagina, and more. Prioritizing your health involves the complete elimination of these toxins and the bacteria that thrive on them from your body. Additionally, it's uncertain whether these bacterial supplements effectively endure the gastric acids as they currently exist.

Establishing intestinal flora isn't a complex task. It's crucial to recognize that you can't entirely keep bacteria out of your body; this is inherent to nature. Bacteria play a role in cleaning and processing your waste, encompassing the by-products generated through digestion and metabolism. Keep in mind that your intestinal flora shifts in response to your dietary choices.

Success is *nothing more than a refined study of the obvious*. — Jim Rohn, success philosopher

MODULE 4.2

Proteins—The Whole Truth

The term "protein" denotes a "structure," comparable to a pre-built house. It possesses a tangible form, such as muscle tissue. Nevertheless, like a house, it comes together using diverse construction components. The framework of proteins is constructed from substances termed amino acids. These amino acids are, therefore, the essential building blocks necessary for your body to construct (grow), sustain, and mend itself. Amino acids also serve as the foundation for proteins used in immune functions, transportation, and catabolic processes. Furthermore, the term "protein" is a general reference to the entire nitrogen-based content in animal or plant matter, excluding nitrogenous fats.

Proteins, or the complete nitrogen-based content of a food, comprise an array of chemical compounds primarily falling into two categories: proteids and non-proteids. Examples of proteids, both simple and intricate, encompass albuminoids, globulins, proteases, peptones, glutinoids, and more. Instances of non-proteids, or simple compounds, encompass creatine, creatinine, xanthine, hypoxanthine, amides, and amino acids.

The human body necessitates various amino acids, which can be classified into two groups. The first category includes the essential amino acids, totaling eleven in number. These are thought to be mandatory for proper growth and repair. (Personally, I differ from this viewpoint, having observed individuals with severe neurological weakness successfully repairing and rebuilding themselves solely through fruit consumption.) The second group consists of numerous nonessential amino acids that the body employs. The list below illustrates both categories.

Protein structures also involve carbon, hydrogen, oxygen, phosphorus, sulfur, and iron. As such, the term "protein" essentially serves as a random label for giving "structure" to construction components. In reality, "protein" is a term used to designate any building material the body requires. However, its factual definition is that of a completed structure, like tissue itself.

Amino Acids

ESSENTIAL AMINO ACIDS (PROVIDED BY FOOD)

- Cysteine
- Histidine
- Isoleucine
- Leucine
- Lysine
- Methionine
- Phenylalanine
- Threonine
- Tryptophan
- Tyrosine
- Valine

NON-ESSENTIAL AMINO ACIDS (PROVIDED BY THE BODY)

- Alanine
- Arginine
- Aspartic acid
- Citrulline
- Glutamic acid
- Glycine
- Hydroxproline
- Hydroxyglutamic acid
- Norleucine
- Proline
- Serine

CAN WE USE THE PROTEIN?

Digestion is a crucial process since the body exclusively relies on simple amino acids—abundantly present in vegetables and nuts. Additionally, the liver can self-generate amino acids and synthesize smaller nitrogen-containing compounds. Contrarily, the proteins found in meat need to undergo hydrolysis—breaking down into basic amino acids—before they can be effectively utilized by the body. I label meat as "second-hand protein" due to the extensive digestive efforts required to break down the complex "structure" into simple "building blocks" or amino acids. Conversely, fruits, vegetables, and nuts are less intricate for the body to process since they feature fundamental amino-acid configurations. It has been substantiated that a plant-based diet supplies more available nitrogen than a meat-based diet.

Differentiating between an anionic (acidic) and cationic (alkaline) environment is crucial in understanding nutrient interactions. In an alkaline or cationic environment, amino acids become agents for growth, maintenance, and repair. In contrast, within an anionic (acidic) environment, they tend to interact with minerals, metals, and fats, leading to toxic conditions. This engenders a scarcity of accessible amino acids, starving the body of essential building materials. While you can consume ample proteins, your body cannot effectively reconstruct itself without proper bioavailability of amino acids.

The accumulation of "bulk" muscles cultivated by high-protein diets will recede during detoxification, as these represent "stacked" amino acids not crucial for regular bodily functions. Protein breakdown results in toxic sulfuric and phosphoric acids that damage tissues. It burns up our electrolytes to convert these acids into salts (ionization), thus neutralizing their damaging effects. Carbohydrates and fats also generate lactic and acetic acids, requiring the same process, albeit with less harm. Hence, replenishing electrolytes is vital. This ionization and alkalization process safeguards kidneys, liver, and other body tissues. Those who exhaust electrolytes without renewal plunge into severe acidosis, leading to seizures, comas, and even death. Cancer and other highly acidic body conditions hasten the consumption of alkalizing electrolytes. This underscores the importance of consuming a variety of raw alkaline fruits and vegetables.

Proteins from meat, dairy, grains, eggs, etc., are abrasive to the body's mucosa. This prompts a lymphatic (mucus) reaction, culminating in excessive mucus build-up in tissues and cavities. The trapped proteins in this mucus accumulation affect interstitial spaces, lymph nodes, sinus cavities, brain, and lungs, often manifesting as pimples, boils, or tumors. The later stages of protein digestion yield uric acid, which is abrasive and irritant, contributing to tissue inflammation and damage. Deposits of uric acid can lead to joint pain and gout. The more animal protein consumed, the more the immune system is taxed, attracting parasitic growth. Many parasites, including viruses, bacteria, worms, and flukes, thrive on waste from animal protein digestion.

Consuming meat leads to body odor due to internal decomposition. Meat can adhere to intestinal walls, inducing mucosa and intestinal lining decay. Importantly, putrefaction converts proteins into toxic chemical by-products. Conversely, fruits and vegetables do not generate body odor.

Proteins are acid-forming, fostering inflammation and tissue breakdown—contrary to their intended purpose. The recommendation is not to abstain from proteins but to be mindful of quantities and types. A diet abundant in nuts, vegetables, and fruits fosters a robust and healthy body, delivering ample amino acids.

The body can't directly use "flesh-type proteins" (grouped amino acids); they must first be broken down into simple amino acids. This starts in the stomach, where hydrochloric acid (HCL) in gastric juices converts pepsinogen to pepsin. Pepsin initiates the breakdown of protein structures into peptones/polypeptides—an acidic process. The pancreas' proteolytic enzymes, alkaline in nature, further transform polypeptides into peptides in the duodenum. As these peptides traverse the small intestines, enzymes secreted by the intestinal wall (peptidase), convert them into amino acids. This extensive process consumes vital energy to yield "secondhand" building materials.

Plant proteins, simple amino acid structures, are much less energy-depleting. Plants' electromagnetic energy counters this demand. Meat protein, comparatively structured and devoid of electrical vitality, necessitates a more intense digestive process, robbing the body of essential energy. High meat protein intake has been linked to colon cancer due to its high acidity. Thousands succumb to the cumulative effects of excessive protein consumption annually, damaging the liver, pancreas, kidneys, and intestines. While 20 to 40 grams of protein daily is ample, many ingest 150 to 200 grams daily.

THE ENERGY OF MEAT

Some assert that meat provides energy, but this energy is primarily derived from the adrenaline present in its tissues, resulting in a stimulated rather than authentic dynamic energy. A visit to a slaughterhouse reveals the fear these animals experience just before slaughter. This fear triggers their adrenal glands to release epinephrine, also known as "adrenaline." Epinephrine acts as a neurotransmitter, transmitting energy via the nervous system into the body's tissues. This heightened energy sensation in protein consumers is largely due to this process. However, continuous consumption of adrenaline-rich meat weakens and impairs the adrenal glands' ability to generate their own neurotransmitters, ultimately reducing blood pressure. Adrenal weaknesses passed down through genetics could potentially lead to conditions like multiple sclerosis, Parkinson's, and Addison's Disease due to a chronic neurotransmitter deficiency.

Adrenal gland weakness can also contribute to high blood pressure. As the adrenal glands falter, the body's ability to produce sufficient steroids (natural anti-inflammatories) diminishes. The high acidity of meat prompts inflammation, further exacerbating the issue. In the presence of acidosis, cholesterol substitutes for steroids in addressing inflammation. However, this gives rise to a significant problem, as lipids tend to congeal and form plaques on tissues.

Energy garnered from meat consumption can also result from the growth hormones administered to livestock for rapid growth. Genuine energy should be cellular and dynamic rather than stimulated by external agents. True dynamic energy emanates from a diet rich in raw foods that emphasize alkalinity, proper electrolyte balance, electrical vitality, amino acids, and synergistic compounds like vitamins, minerals, and flavonoids.

A CALL TO ACTION

The time has come for humans to cease their consumption of animal products, which have become laden with toxic hormones, antibiotics, chemicals, and similar harmful substances, transforming them into ticking time bombs within us. We have the opportunity to rise above decay and toxicity, embracing vitality and internal purity through a raw fruit and vegetable diet. This diet has the power to break the chains of negative emotions, leading us toward vibrancy and well-being.

Consider embarking on a six-week diet devoid of animal products and witness the transformative difference firsthand. While reading and forming opinions based on learned perspectives is one thing, experiencing it personally is quite another.

Although not comprehensively understood by the scientific community, all life transmutes compounds and elements into different forms. Your body has the ability to generate amino acids from carbohydrates and fats. It utilizes the elements in the foods you consume, particularly those that align with your biological needs, to maintain and repair itself.

Nature holds many mysteries waiting to be explored. The ever-reactive mind can anchor our attention in the physical realm indefinitely. This mind, akin to a seeker on a quest for truth, often overlooks the truth right in front of it. The mind's inclination toward intellectualism drives it to dissect and analyze things to understand their composition. The soul, however, already possesses this knowledge. Breaking free from intellectualism allows us to revel in the simplicity of nature and spirituality. This liberation conserves valuable energy. Embracing a raw-food, living-food diet enables us to relish in vitality and robust health, fostering a happier existence.

HIGH PROTEIN DIETS CAN CAUSE DEATH

Research conducted by renowned educational institutions like Simmons College and Harvard University, as detailed in publications such as The New England Journal of Medicine and The Archives of Internal Medicine, has consistently demonstrated the toxicity of meat protein when absorbed through our intestinal walls. This process induces acidosis, compromises immune responses, and invites the proliferation of parasites. The following list summarizes the key points we've discussed earlier regarding the fundamental reasons to avoid meat and high protein diets:

- The body cannot directly utilize protein structures; they must be broken down into their simplest form, amino acids, demanding energy rather than providing it.

- Digesting and metabolizing proteins yield various acids, including uric acid (causing gout), phosphoric acid, and sulfuric acid. These acids inflame tissues, stimulate nerves, and promote tissue hyperactivity.

- Protein, rich in nitrogen and phosphorous, when consumed in excess, depletes calcium and electrolytes from the body.

- Proteins have a high acid-forming nature, leading to inflammation, tissue weakness, and tissue death due to lowered pH balance.

- Proteins are not primarily fuel sources; instead, they serve as building blocks and carriers. Burning proteins for fuel may lead to fat breakdown but also results in tissue degradation, causing harm to liver, pancreatic, and kidney tissues.

- High protein intake prompts the liver to produce substantial cholesterol levels, contributing to plaque formation in the vascular system, liver, and kidneys, along with stone development in the liver and gallbladder.

- Animal proteins decay within the body, resulting in body odor and a buildup of toxins within the intestines and tissues. The acidic environment promotes inflammation, obstructs cellular respiration, and eventually leads to cellular death.

- High protein consumption contradicts human physiology and our species' dietary requirements.

- Animal farming as a food source has inflicted economic, environmental, and spiritual damage. Forests and green spaces are being cleared for pastures, affecting oxygen production, beauty, erosion control, and more.

- High protein diets contribute to elevated levels of epinephrine (adrenaline), triggering aggression, anger, and adrenal failure in those who consume such diets.

- Meat has been linked to intestinal, liver, and pancreatic cancers, potentially linked to the putrefaction buildup within the lymphatic system.

- Meat-eating societies exhibit shorter lifespans, as seen in populations like the Intuits of Northern Canada and Alaska.

- Meat consists of deceased or decaying cells immersed in stagnant, putrefying blood, which humans oddly consider nutritious.

- Meat consumption irritates and inflames sexual organs, particularly the prostate gland, possibly leading to prostatitis.

- Modern animal meat contains growth hormones, antibiotics, pesticides, herbicides, nuclear waste, adrenaline, and other toxic chemicals, all of which are considered carcinogens.

- Today, animal meat harbor more cancer due to environmental toxins. Some meat producers even incorporate sick and dying animals into feed, causing diseases like "Mad Cow" and "Hoof and Mouth."

- Mismanagement within meat production, such as feeding dead sheep to cows, mirrors similar effects in humans, causing acidosis and disease.

- The evidence from reputable institutions underscores the detrimental effects of meat consumption on our health and the environment, making a strong case for adopting alternative dietary choices.

- Consuming diets high in protein leads to reduced manganese levels, causing spasms, convulsions, issues with neurotransmitters (such as myasthenia, shortness of breath, heart arrhythmias including atrial fibrillation), neuromuscular problems, Parkinson's, and Lou Gehrig's disease.

- Meat contains deceased blood cells (hemoglobin), which are rich in iron. However, excessive iron consumption, particularly oxidized iron (not plant-based iron), can lead to toxicity. Iron toxicity triggers various reactions within the body, including:

- A decrease in chromium levels (crucial for insulin transport)

- A decrease in zinc levels (important for insulin and energy production)
- Damage to liver, pancreatic, and kidney tissues
- Reduced calcium levels and impaired calcium absorption and utilization
- Elevated sodium levels, resulting in edema
- Increased nitrogen and phosphorous levels, contributing to acidosis
- Dizziness, balance issues, and spasms by lowering manganese levels
- Meat consumption also contributes to high blood pressure due to sodium retention and lipid coagulation.
- Combining meat consumption with vitamin C supplementation enhances iron absorption, exacerbating iron toxicity.
- Moreover, red meat consumption is linked to elevated N-Nitroso compound levels from intestinal bacteria, which can have carcinogenic effects on the intestinal walls.
- Notably, meat consumption is a major cause of tooth decay.
- These instances illustrate just a few reasons why diets high in animal protein are detrimental to human health. Embracing a diet devoid of animal products can lead to a life free from such concerns. Your body will thrive, becoming odor-free and vibrant. Caring for the planet and its creatures is equally important.

COMPLETE PROTEIN OR COMPLETE MYTH?

There exists a misconception surrounding the concept of "complete" amino acids or "complete proteins" within the human diet. This misinformation has persisted for years, suggesting that unless one consumes foods containing all essential amino acids in a single meal, the body will lack the necessary elements to form a "complete protein," leading to a deficiency in protein. This argument has often been used to advocate for the consumption of meat, dairy products, soy products, beans, and refined flour. However, let's consider the following:

- Look at the dietary habits of wild horses, elephants, and cows – all herbivores known for their strength. Their diets consist entirely of grass and plant-based matter. If they required the "complete protein" as claimed, they must be obtaining it from plants.

- Even a significant portion (70 to 80 percent) of a grizzly bear's diet comprises grass. While bears occasionally consume meat, it's typically the fat, not the protein, that they are seeking. Bears are omnivores.

- We, as the highest species in the frugivore category, are not biologically designed to consume meat.

- Those who follow a raw food diet and maintain a balanced consumption of fruits, vegetables, and nuts do not experience deficiencies in essential amino acids needed for optimal health. In fact, plant-based amino acids are more bioavailable and easier for the body to digest and utilize. Meat necessitates a more energy-intensive and demanding digestive process to extract its amino acids. Furthermore, an important aspect to consider is that meat protein leaves an acidic residue in the body, contributing to acidosis, whereas vegetables yield an alkaline response, counteracting acidosis.

To keep your body vibrant and alive, it requires live, fresh, and organic foods. If the necessary components are not present in fruits, nuts, and vegetables, there is no requirement for them. Additionally, consuming aged, spoiled, and deceased tissue – essentially, dead cells in stagnant blood – cannot be considered a healthy practice.

The constitution of man's body has not changed to meet the new conditions of his artificial environment that has replaced his natural one. The result is that of perpetual discord between man and his environment. The effect of this discord is a general deterioration of man's body, the symptoms of which are termed disease.

— Professor Hilton Hotema, *Man's Higher Consciousness*

MODULE 4.3

Irritants and Stimulants

The diets of most individuals contain substantial quantities of substances classified as irritants and stimulants. These compounds are termed so, due to their capacity to incite irritation and stimulation within bodily tissues, leading to excessive mucus production and either hyperactivity or hypo-activity of these tissues, ultimately resulting in chronic and degenerative disorders. Among the irritants that people either knowingly or unknowingly consume on a daily basis are items such as black pepper, caffeine, salt, MSG, preservatives, and refined sugars, among others. This list can extend extensively.

These compounds exert irritative effects on the mucosa of the gastrointestinal tract, provoking the discharge of mucus, which can accumulate and obstruct. Additionally, they trigger inflammation within the body, given that most possess acidic or heat-generating properties, thereby initiating immune reactions. For instance, Capsicum, commonly known as cayenne pepper, is employed by many for managing high blood pressure and enhancing circulation. It is noteworthy that cayenne pepper is less abrasive than black pepper. Nonetheless, red pepper does stimulate the gastrointestinal mucosa, potentially leading to excessive mucus generation. Mucus congestion constitutes a central aspect of congestive conditions such as sinus congestion, bronchitis, pneumonia, and earaches.

Upon adopting a raw, living-food diet, individuals undergo a transformation in their bodily systems. The greater the consumption of raw foods, the purer and healthier the body becomes. A point may be reached where pungent foods are no longer tolerable. Even cayenne pepper, onions, and garlic can become irritating.

Stimulants hold an allure for many. People ingest significant quantities of these substances annually, often reaching hundreds of pounds or gallons. Coffee, tea, and soda consumption is unprecedented. Yet, these beverages, rich in tannins, alkaloids, sulfuric and phosphoric acids, cause tissue stimulation while simultaneously inflicting damage. For instance, the impact of soda pop on concrete is well-known – it disintegrates it. Similarly, meat introduced to soda pop will deteriorate. Soda pop triggers inflammation and degradation of the gastrointestinal lining, not to mention damage to the liver and kidneys.

Coffee and commercial teas, widely consumed, exert irritation and stimulation on various organs including the liver, gastrointestinal tract, heart, and endocrine gland system (thyroid, adrenals, pituitary, thymus, etc.), as well as the kidneys. While coffee enemas are popular among health enthusiasts, they are not recommended due to their excessive stimulation of the intestines and liver, resulting in heightened enervation and severe constipation. Favorable alternatives are herbal bowel regenerators devoid of addictive properties that facilitate the restoration of proper bowel function.

Chocolate also stands as a popular stimulant for individuals of all ages. Yet, chocolate is highly acidic and boasts a significant oxalic acid content. In instances of bodily acidity and consumption of oxalate-rich foods, oxalates combine with ionic calcium, forming calcium oxalate stones, including kidney stones.

Alcohol and refined sugars represent other widely consumed stimulants. These substances are notably acidic and mucus-forming. Beer contributes to yeast overgrowth, promoting the craving for refined sugars, thereby maintaining a perpetual cycle. Alcohol sustains elevated blood sugar in diabetes and triggers adrenal gland stimulation, further weakening the body. Moreover, fermentation of food sugars within the stomach produces alcohol. Organic wine would be the only alcohol I would recommend, and very little of that.

Refined sugars promote acidity and foster excessive mucus production. As previously mentioned, mucus accumulation leads to allergies, bronchitis, pneumonia, colds, flu, sinusitis, and various "congestive" conditions. Additionally, the acidifying nature of refined sugars aggravates tissue inflammation.

Meat, recognized as a known stimulant, is also irritative and inflammatory towards bodily tissues. The preceding section established that meat contains antibiotics, hormones, nuclear waste, steroids, adrenaline, pesticides, herbicides, and an assortment of other toxic chemicals, all of which function as stimulants, irritants, and suppressants, coexisting within meat tissue. These chemicals, in conjunction with adrenaline, can produce a transient sensation of energy, followed by increased fatigue. Meat's high nitrogen content also displaces calcium, disrupting the equilibrium between calcium and phosphorus. In meat, an imbalanced phosphorus-to-calcium ratio is present, whereas vegetables display a balanced ratio of these essential minerals.

Our intestinal tract, in comparison to carnivores like cats, is four times lengthier, boasting significantly enhanced absorption capabilities. Owing to the rapid putrefaction of meat protein, coupled with our extended intestinal tract, meat putrefies within the body prior to elimination.

Putrefaction generates acidosis, consequently inflaming and ultimately disintegrating cells. This, in turn, creates an environment conducive to various parasitic organisms, which prove highly detrimental to vulnerable cells, tissues, organs, and glands. Sulfuric and phosphoric acids produced by meat are similarly potent stimulants, inflammatory agents, and tissue-damaging agents.

Energy should consistently stem from dynamic or cellular sources, rather than external stimulants. If external stimulants are necessary for energy, it implies the presence of inherent tissue weaknesses. In the long run, irritants and stimulants weaken and deteriorate tissue (organs and glands). The nervous system (including the sympathetic, parasympathetic, and autonomous components) and the heart are particularly susceptible to the impact of these substances, often resulting in palpitations, heart arrhythmias, and neurological imbalances.

Freeing oneself from stimulants and irritants yields a realm of dynamic energy – the cellular energy radiating from healthy cells. Ultimately, irritants and stimulants merely furnish transient energy that, over time, debilitates and corrodes the body. Eliminating acidic irritants and stimulating foods liberates one from the cycle of constant reliance on stimulation. These food types not only weaken but also toxify the body. Animals do not consume irritants or stimulants, prompting the question – why should humans?

Living is actually a struggle for fresh air. Keep the vast lung surface of the organism supplied with fresh, unpolluted air, and also observe all the other health rules, and there is no reason known to science why you should ever die.

— Prof. J. S. Haldane, English Astronomer

MODULE 4.4

Vaccinations: The Poison Needles

The principle of "like treats like" is a concept employed by both allopathic (conventional medical) and homeopathic (natural) approaches to disease treatment. However, one of the most hazardous and sometimes fatal ideas and practices stemming from scientific advancements is the method of inoculation or "vaccinations." This involves injecting live parasites into the body, aiming for the body to develop immunity against them. This practice stems from the belief that parasites (germs) are the root cause of most illnesses. Currently, science is gradually shifting away from this notion, replacing it with the theory of genetics or genes being responsible for adverse outcomes.

An illustrative instance of the fallacy of "like treats like" can be found in the context of the polio vaccine. The underlying theory suggests that by exposing the body to a virus in smaller doses, immunity can be bolstered against it. The assumption is that the body will produce antibodies, leading to a quicker or overlooked immune response to the virus. In this way, immune cells might either eliminate the virus before it becomes uncontrollable or tolerate its presence, rendering it inactive. This perspective appears flawed to me, and the evidence seems to confirm it. For example, following the introduction of the polio vaccine, polio cases surged by 680 percent, as revealed by Dr. Leonard Horowitz in his book "The Emerging Viruses." An account from the Tampa Tribune recounted an infant contracting polio from the vaccine itself. The same pattern emerges with flu vaccines. Numerous instances can be cited where individuals who received the flu shot still contracted the flu. This underscores the shortcomings of this risky practice, which has repeated countless times.

The hazards associated with vaccines should not be underestimated. Vaccines for measles, mumps, rubella (German measles), and polio contain live yet weakened viruses. Despite health authorities asserting that polio has been eradicated in the U.S. since 1979, they often omit that all documented cases of polio since then are in fact linked to the polio vaccine, or that polio is now referred to under a different name—spinal meningitis. In India, polio was replaced by 'Non-polio acute flaccid paralysis' syndrome. It's high time we lift our heads from the sand and embrace reality.

A healthy and vibrant body remains resilient against sickness. Its immune system is robust, exhibiting an astonishing ability to safeguard itself. Natural immunity endures throughout life, while vaccinated immunity is short-lived, estimated at merely around seven years. It's crucial to remember that nature, through the plant kingdom, provides all the necessary resources. Opting for herbal anti-parasitics, astringents, and immune-boosting agents to cleanse and fortify the body proves superior to contaminating it with toxic substances, live parasites, and foreign proteins.

Many vaccines have been the product of collaborative experiments. One such collaboration was reported between Kaiser Permanente of Southern California, the U.S. Center for Disease Control (CDC), and the World Health Organization (WHO). Between 1989 and 1991, this partnership utilized the

Edmonston-Zagreb (E-Z) Measles virus for experiments on "poor, Black and Latino inner city children, primarily in Los Angeles." Similar experiments yielded dire results in Africa, Haiti, and Mexico. Countless children died from the vaccine itself or its subsequent immune suppression, which hindered their ability to combat other pathogens.

Vaccinations have led to immune suppression and mutation, giving rise to various conditions afflicting many. Human actions, coupled with scientific endeavors, have induced unnecessary suffering and death due to ignorance and the desire to manipulate nature and others. A multitude of conditions including Gulf War Syndrome, AIDS, cancer, body mutation, and numerous others can be attributed directly to vaccinations. Given that most vaccines are composed of living matter and are manufactured from human and animal tissues such as monkey kidneys, cattle, human embryos, chicken hearts, and human placentas, the potential for contamination and mutation exists. Nature operates in equilibrium and harmony, but human ego has ushered in a dangerous level of imbalance and mutation, leading to a cascade of devastating consequences.

Barbara Loe Fisher, president of the National Vaccine Information Center (NVIC), a consumer advocacy group based in Virginia, asserts that vaccinations are accountable for the growing numbers of individuals suffering from immune system and neurological disorders, hyperactivity, learning disabilities, asthma, chronic fatigue syndrome, lupus, rheumatoid arthritis, multiple sclerosis, and seizure disorders. She calls for long-term studies to monitor the effects of mass vaccinations and urges physicians to ensure the safety of these vaccines. Unfortunately, this remains an uphill battle.

Substantial evidence from research and reported cases across the globe, including the United States, Great Britain, Africa, New Zealand, and beyond, unequivocally demonstrates that vaccinations are both toxic and deadly. The pressing question is: Why do government agencies and institutions tasked with "protecting" the public, such as the CDC, FDA, VRBPAC, ACIP, HRS, knowingly permit these atrocities? The distinction between the present scenario and the horrors of Nazi Germany is legality and global spread. Millions are now ensnared. Ultimately, the driving force behind this is simple: money. These same people probably go to church and think they won't have to pay for such atrocities. If you think this world is heaven, think again.

Prominent medical journals, including the renowned British Lancet, have documented various side effects of these "killer" vaccinations. For instance, the measles vaccine has been linked to conditions like asthma and allergy-like symptoms. The DPT (diphtheria-pertussis-tetanus) vaccine, introduced in the 1940s, had dire consequences, including numerous deaths, despite being legalized by states. Notably, Japan prohibited its use. The DPT vaccine has particularly been associated with brain damage and neurological impairments such as multiple sclerosis, Parkinson's disease, and Lou Gehrig's disease.

The hepatitis B vaccine stands out due to its own set of problems. Hepatitis B is relatively manageable, with over 90 percent of cases being curable through natural means. However, a vaccine was developed for it and administered to millions. This vaccine has been linked to conditions such as arthritis, diabetes, vascular issues, Bell's palsy, MS, and other neurological disorders. In New Zealand, diabetes rates surged by 60 percent after the introduction of the hepatitis B vaccine. The British Medical Journal reported a connection between the hepatitis B vaccine and autism, as well as inflammatory bowel syndrome.

A tragic case I encountered involved a sixteen-month-old girl from Texas. She received a hepatitis B vaccination at three months and subsequently experienced continuous convulsions, temporary blindness, and misalignment of her left eye. She developed hepatitis, brain damage, and severe spinal scoliosis. I managed to alleviate most of her convulsions over a two-month period, improving her eyesight and reducing liver inflammation. While this was a sorrowful case, it is emblematic of the prevailing situation in the medical community.

Adding insult to injury, research has indicated that the HIV virus was introduced into the Hepatitis B vaccine in several major U.S. cities. Originally conceived as a biological weapon, the HIV virus infiltrated impoverished ethnic communities and the gay population. Dr. Horowitz has conducted extensive investigative research on this matter, gathering evidence of the parties involved, as well as the times and locations of these experiments. The malevolent motivations that initiated this process are beyond comprehension. Whatever happened to the medical vow: "First, do no harm"?

Neil Z. Miller, an investigator of vaccines, questions the necessity of the polio vaccine, which actually leads to new cases of polio. Miller asserts that before mass vaccination campaigns began fifty years ago, cancer was not widespread, autoimmune disorders were rare, and childhood autism was unheard of. Modern children receive twenty to thirty different vaccines throughout their lives, each bearing its own detrimental effects. It's no wonder that juvenile diabetes cases have soared to 600,000 annually and continue to rise. This pattern mirrors most other diseases as well.

For those of us working with cancer, the medical and scientific hubris that has spawned the "vaccines" menace is truly disheartening. Doctors and researchers who lack an understanding of health and the workings of nature continue to pursue destructive paths under the guise of "modern" medicine, arguing that it's the only way.

The issue of contamination has consistently plagued vaccine production. During World War II, a yellow fever vaccine created using human blood serum was inadvertently contaminated with hepatitis viruses and administered to the military. This resulted in over 50,000 cases of serum hepatitis among U.S. troops who received the vaccine.

I also want to highlight the simian virus, known as Sim-40 or SV-40. This virus originated in the 1950s when polio vaccines produced using monkey kidney tissue became tainted. My focus on this virus over the years has revealed its potential to cause cancer in animals and its potential links to lung cancers (mesothelioma) and bone marrow cancer (multiple myeloma) in humans.

Today, humans are more toxic and debilitated than ever before in history. The immune system, genetically speaking, is at an all-time low. The paths chosen by individuals, especially vaccination with poisons, have led to chronic and degenerative vulnerabilities or conditions, even in infants. It's crucial to recognize that introducing parasites into a toxic body yields severe consequences. Given our limited understanding of viruses, it's exceedingly dangerous to treat them like mere playthings. It is now theorized that viral proteins integrate into our cells' DNA structures in some manner and are transmitted through genetics. This underscores the importance of comprehending the concept of God and "consciousness." Just as life experiences shape our memory patterns, the same is true for all life forms, including the tiniest cells within the body. All life possesses memory and emotions, down to the smallest particles.

Men and women must awaken from their slumber and elevate their consciousness toward God. This will broaden their perspectives and deepen their understanding of the profound simplicity and beauty of health and life. It's time to fill one's consciousness with love, energy, health, and vitality, rising above the lower echelons of disease. "**Detoxification and Regeneration**" remain the sole solution to our current predicament. A shift in consciousness from treatment to proactive cleansing of the body, coupled with cellular strengthening, holds the key to overcoming the numerous conditions mentioned above.

Ultimately, it's your body. Reflect upon it. Place trust in yourself and in Nature. Endeavor to learn about genuine health and vitality through nature and the tools (food and herbs) that nature furnishes for your well-being and vitality.

Wake up! Time is running out.

Resources

There have been multiple books written on the toxic practice of vaccinations. Check Bibliography at the end of the book. Read, learn, and educate yourself. No one else will. Two such books are-

Bechamp or Pasteur?

Dissolving Illusions

I *am much more interested in a question on which the "salvation of humanity" depends far more than on any theologians' cuño: the question of nutrition.*

— Friedrich Nietzsche, *Ecce Homo*

MODULE 4.5

Chemical Toxicity: *Environmental, Hygiene, Household and Drug*

If you're acquainted with someone experiencing chemical or environmental toxicity, you understand the extent of their suffering intimately. I once aided an individual who was so heavily chemically toxic that the mere scent of gasoline fumes caused her to lose consciousness. Our reckless use of chemicals has caused significant harm to our home, Earth, and now we find ourselves at a point of no return. We can only watch as the Earth goes through a process of self-purification, driven by various changes in the atmosphere and on land. This stands as one of the most shameful chapters in human history.

Likewise, our physical bodies are being severely impacted by diseases, with cancer rates reaching alarming levels. In 2020, 18 million new cancer cases were diagnosed, globally. And there are many more on the track of developing it.

According to information from the Natural Resources Defense Council, there are now over 85,000 synthetic chemicals in commercial use, and many of these are known to be carcinogenic, as well as harmful to the brain, nervous system, and reproductive systems. It's estimated that human activities release more than 20 billion pounds of chemicals into the environment annually. The distressing consequences are evident: whales and porpoises are stranding themselves in growing numbers, fish populations are dwindling, and wild animals are experiencing unprecedented rates of cancer and birth abnormalities. What will it take for humanity to awaken to this crisis? Every single person, regardless of their wealth or intellect, ingests more than 120 pounds of chemicals each year, including over ten different pesticides daily. Our immune systems are ill-equipped to handle this level of assault on the body.

CHEMICAL AWARENESS

The inventory provided primarily comprises carcinogens, which are substances or compounds that can lead to the development of cancer. These substances enter our bodies through the air we inhale, the food we consume, the water we drink, and the personal care products like lotions, cosmetics, and hair dyes that we apply to our skin.

SOLVENTS

These are compounds that dissolve things.

- Propyl Alcohol
- Benzene Wood Alcohol
- Xylene
- Toluene
- Methyl ethyl Ketone (MEK)
- Methyl butyl Ketone (MBK)
- Methylene Chloride
- TCE

INORGANIC METAL POLLUTION

These can be found in dental wear, cosmetics, food, drinking cans, water supplies and cooking pots.

- Copper
- Mercury
- Thallium
- Lead
- Cadmium
- Nickel
- Chromium
- Aluminum

CHEMICAL TOXINS

- Chlorofluorocarbons (CFCS)—Freon can be found in air conditioners and refrigerators.
- Arsenic—can be found in pesticides.
- Polychlorinated biphenyls (PCBs)—can be found in transformers, commercial soap and detergents.
- Formaldehyde—can be found in furniture, pillows, mattresses, clothing, Formica cabinets, and carpets.
- Chemical medications
- Psychotropic drugs
- Chlorine in water supplies and pools

- Fluorine (a known carcinogen) added to water supplies.
- Inorganic Iodine
- Sulfa drugs
- Phosphates

EVERYDAY CHEMICALS

These are chemicals that you may be breathing, using, touching, etc.

- Aluminum cookware
- Household cleaners
- Automobile fluids
- Pesticides (neurotoxins)—these are an excito toxin (brain and nerve poison).
- Herbicides (neuro and liver toxins—these are an excito toxin (brain and nerve poison).
- Fertilizers
- Paint
- Varnish
- Wax
- Glues
- Lubricants
- Bleach

- Gasoline
- Underarm deodorants (aluminum chlorohydrates and neomycin)
- Toothpaste
- Soaps

MYCOTOXINS

These are molds that can produce some of the most toxic substances.

- Alflatoxin—can be found in commercial fruit juices, rice, pasta, bread and vinegar.
- Zearalenone—can be found in commercial cereal grains, processed foods and feeds.
- Sterigmatocystin—pasta
- Ergot
- Cytochalasin B
- Kojic Acid
- T-2 Toxin
- Sorghum moulds
- Patulin

Top 20 Hazardous Substances

There are 275 substances on the current list from the ASTDR/EPA.

1. Arsenic
2. Lead
3. Mercury
4. Vinyl Chloride
5. Polychlorinated Biphenyls (PCBs)
6. Benzene
7. Cadmium
8. Benzo(a)pyrene
9. Polycyclic Aromatic Hydrocarbons
10. Benzo(b)fluoranthene
11. Chloroform
12. Aroclor 1260
13. DDT, P,P'-
14. Aroclor 1254
15. Dibenzo(A,H)Anthracene
16. Trichloroethylene
17. Chromium, Hexavalent
18. Dieldrin
19. Phosphorus, White
20. Aroclor 1242

PHYSICAL TOXINS

- Fiberglass
- Asbestos
- Car and truck exhaust—carbon monoxide, lead, etc.
- By-products of chemical manufacturing
- Lead pipes
- Nuclear wastes

Common Water and Food Contaminants

Pesticides	Possible Health Effects
Chlordane	Known carcinogen.
Atrazine	Damages kidney, liver, heart, lung, tissue; a known carcinogen.
Alachlor	Probably carcinogen
DDT and Derivatives	Liver, kidneys, nerve, and endocrine damage
Diazinon	Excitotoxin. Suspected carcinogen, liver and kidney damage.
EPN	Excitotoxin. Suspected carcinogen, liver and kidney damage.
Lindane	Excitotoxin. Suspected carcinogen, liver and kidney damage.

Pesticides	Possible Health Effects
PCB's (polychlorinated biphenyls)	Excitotoxin. Suspected carcinogen, liver and kidney damage.
Phosphamidon	Excitotoxin. Suspected carcinogen, liver and kidney damage.
Chlorpyrifos	Excitotoxin. Suspected carcinogen, liver and kidney damage.
Dicloran	Excitotoxin. Suspected carcinogen, liver and kidney damage.
Endosulfan	Excitotoxin. Suspected carcinogen, liver and kidney damage.
2, 4D	Kidney, Liver and Lung damage.

Toxic Metals	Possible Health Effects
Arsenic	Kidney, liver, endocrine and nerve damage.
Mercury	Brain and nerve damage.
Lead	Liver, kidney, muscle and nerve damage.
Sulfur	Accumulative, allergies, lymphomas, kidney and intestinal impairment, and inflammation
Cadmium	Brain, nerve, liver, pancreas damage.

Petrochemicals	Possible Health Effects
Benzene	Carcinogen.
Xylenes	Liver, kidney, endocrine and nervous system damage.
Carbon Tetrachloride	Suspected carcinogen
Ethylene dibromide	Suspected carcinogen
Permethrin	An excitotoxin (neuro-toxins) Suspected carcinogens, liver and kidney damage.
Toluene	Kidney, liver, nervous system, endocrine, circulatory damage

FOOD ADDITIVES

- BHT
- Nitrates
- Nitrites
- MSG
- Artificial sugars (aspartame, saccharin, etc.)
- Tobacco for smoking or chewing

As evident from the aforementioned lists, significant quantities of chemical pollutants, primarily of human origin, have been introduced into our air, water, and food sources. It's essential to recall that every action results in a reaction. All these toxins possess varying degrees of irritative, detrimental, and inflammatory properties (triggering an immune reaction) to some extent.

TOXIC PESTICIDES

The U.S. Department of Agriculture along with various independent research entities and organizations have documented that our foods contain substantial levels of pesticides and other contaminants. Foods such as tomatoes, strawberries, peaches, spinach, turnips, and squash, among others, can be laden with up to 80 to 100 distinct pollutants, particularly pesticides, either on their surfaces or within them. Peanuts exhibit the presence of more than 180 pollutants, while raisins can contain over 110.

As you review the potential and acknowledged repercussions of pesticides, it's worth pondering whether you truly support the concept of Bio-Tech Engineering—where pesticides are genetically incorporated into the seeds of our foods. This implies that pesticide remnants will be an inherent part of the foods, without any means for removal. Similar to sulfur drugs, pesticides accrue in impact over time. As they amass to toxic and fatal levels, they trigger allergic responses, inflammation, exaggerated immune reactions, and neurological breakdowns.

TOXIC CHEMICALS

The list below offers instances of common toxins that you inadvertently "ingest" via your diet, water, personal care items like cosmetics, toothpaste, and deodorants. These are merely a selection of the highly harmful chemicals that have been produced and introduced into both our surroundings and the sources of our sustenance.

Aluminum (chlorohydrates, etc.)

Found in: Underarm deodorants, canned foods, industry, cooking utensils, etc.

Properties: Suspected brain and nerve damage, suspected in Alzheimer's and other brain and nerve syndromes. May affect the endocrine gland system, especially the pituitary.

Aspartame (NutraSweet®, Equal®)

Found in: Diet drinks (soda, etc.), candies desserts, many prepackaged foods, etc.

Properties: Artificial (low calorie) sweeteners. Known carcinogen excitotoxin (neurotoxin) affects brain and nervous system as well as the glandular system. U.S. consumes 7000 tons per year. (CNN)

Benzoic or Benzyl

Found in: Cosmetics, nail polish, shampoos, bath and shower products.

Properties: Suspected carcinogen, affects endocrine gland function, also suspected in birth defects.

BHA/BHT (butylated hydroxyanisole)

Found in: Breads, dry cereals, cake mixes, frozen pizzas, pork, potato chips, many oils, crackers, puddings, prepared donuts, gelatin desserts.

Properties: A preservative. Suspected carcinogen. Affects liver and pancreatic tissues. Forbidden in many countries.

Caffeine

Found in: Colas and other soft drinks, naturally occurring in cocoa, coffees, teas.

Properties: A stimulant. Suspected in birth defects. Affects endocrine system and nervous system. Over stimulates the GI tract.

Caramel

Found in: Colas and other soft drinks, bread, pudding, frozen pizzas, candies, snacks, etc.
Properties: A coloring. Suspected carcinogen, causes genetic defects.

Carrageenan

Found in: Cottage cheese, ice cream, sour cream, puddings, baby formulas.

Properties: A thickening agent. Suspected and indicated in ulcerative conditions of the GI tract. Affects blood clotting and proper nutrient dispersion.

Chlorine

Found in: Tap water, showers, pool, laundry products, cleaning agents, food processing, sewage systems, etc.

Properties: Anti-bacterial and parasitic. Contributes to asthma, hay fever, anemia, bronchitis, circulatory collapse, confusion, delirium, diabetes, dizziness, irritation of the eyes, mouth, nose, throat, lung, skin and stomach, heart disease, high blood pressure and nausea. Probably cancer causing.

DEA (Diethanolamine)
MEA (Momoethanolamine)
TEA (Triethanolamine)

Found in: Bubble baths, shampoos, soaps, skin washes and cleansers.

Properties: Foaming agents. Suspected carcinogen. May bind with nitrates and nitrites to form nitrosamines (tumor growers).

EDTA (Ethylendiaminetetraacetic Acid)
Found in: Shellac, solvents, and personal care products that foam (bubble baths, body washes, shampoos, soaps and facial cleansers).

Properties: Preservative. Hormone disrupters. Suspected in at least two types of cancer—kidney and liver cancer. Known to cause kidney, intestinal and skin disorders. Causes cramping and the like.

Gums (Arabic, Karaya, Xanthin, Cellulose, Ghatti, Tragacanth, etc.)
Found in: Ice cream, colas, candy, gum, beer, salad dressings, Isopropyl alcohol.

Properties: Thickening agent. May be linked to allergies and bowel disorders. Affects proper nutrient bioavailability

Isopropyl Alcohol
Found in: Hair color rinses, body rubs, hand lotions, after-shave lotions, fragrances, and many other cosmetics. A petroleum-derived substance, it is also used in antifreeze and as a solvent in shellac.

Properties: A solvent and denaturant. (A denaturant is a poisonous substance that changes another substance's natural qualities). Inhalation or ingestion of the vapor may cause headaches, flushing, dizziness, mental depression, nausea, vomiting, narcosis and coma.

Lactic Acid

Found in: Printing industry, dyes, frozen pizzas, gelatin, cheeses, frozen desserts, olives, beer, carbonated drinks.

Properties: A preservative. Acidosis and inflammation.

Maltol Dextrin

Found in: Wood tars, many desserts and soft drinks, processed foods, ice cream.

Properties: Aroma and flavor enhancer. Suspected carcinogen.

Mineral Oil

Found in: Commonly used petroleum ingredient. Baby Oil is 100% mineral oil.

Properties: Disrupts the skin's natural immune barrier, inhibiting its ability to breathe and to absorb moisture and nutrition. Impedes the skin's ability to release toxins, promoting acne and other disorders. Ultimately causes premature aging.

Modified Food Starch

Found in: Baked beans, creamed canned foods, beets (processed), dry-roasted nuts, ravioli, drink powders, frozen pizzas, pie fillings, baby foods, baking powder, frozen fish (packaged), soups, gravies.

Properties: Thickening and filling agent. Alkali in sodium hydroxide. Suspected in causing lung damage. GI tract irritation, vomiting. Possible cramping and spasms.

Mono and Diglycerides
Found in: Pies, butter, dry roasted nuts, cakes, cookies, some processed foods.

Properties: Binding and smoothing agent, softener. Suspected carcinogenic, possibly causing genetic and birth defects.

MSG (Monosodium Glutamate)
Found in: Many Chinese foods, sauces, canned and processed foods, frozen pizzas, beer, salad dressings, canned meats, tomato sauces, broths, gelatins, bouillon, soy sauce, etc. May be disguised by other names, e.g. glutamate, glutamic acid, autolyzed yeast, hydrolyzed proteins, natural flavors, caseinate, seasonings, carrageenan, maltol dextrin, yeast extract.

Properties: A common flavor enhancer. Excitotoxin (neurotoxin) affects the nervous system and glandular system. Spasms, headaches (including migraines), sweating, chest pain, diarrhea. Possibly linked to genetic conditions, brain damage, heart conditions, tumors, Alzheimer's and Parkinson's disease, asthma attacks, ALS, ADD, ADHD, GI tract conditions.

Nitrites, Nitrates (Sodium)
Found in: Processed meats, frozen pizzas, baby foods, etc.

Properties: Preservative, used in "curing." Known carcinogens. Extremely toxic.

Overdoses cause death. Binds to form nitrosamines, especially in the presence of alcohol.

PEG (Polyethylene glycol)
Found in: Toothpastes, bath and shower products. Used to make degreasers and cleansers (oven, car, etc.)

Properties: Thickening agent. Affects endocrine function; has estrogenic effects; a suspected carcinogen.

Propylene Glycol
Found in: Antifreeze, make-up, lotions, deodorants, mouthwashes, toothpaste, hair products (shampoos, etc.) shaving cream, etc. Used in food processing. Used as solvents.

Properties: A surfactant or wetting agent. Skin irritant, causing inflammation and possible damage to skin. May cause kidney, liver, brain and pancreatic damage and abnormalities. Used to break down proteins and cellular structures.

Propylgallate
Found in: Gum, pickles, oils and shortenings, processed foods and meat products.

Properties: A preservative. Suspected in liver and pancreatic damage. Possible link to birth defects.

Red Dye #40 (AI I u ra Red AC)
Found in: Red pistachio nuts, meats (hot dogs, etc.), gelatin, gum, cereals, baked goods, many candies, red sodas. Note: #40 is not used as much today. However, there are many artificial colorings that are very questionable.

Properties: A coloring. Suspected carcinogen and possibly linked to birth defects. Liver and kidney damage. Nerve toxin.

Saccharin
Found in: Many desserts, drinks and prepackaged foods.

Properties: An artificial sweetener. Suspected in some cancers (bladder, etc.) and possible tumor formation. Can affect heart rhythms, GI tract conditions and skin irritation.

Sodium Erythorbate
Found in: Meat products, baked goods, many beverages, etc.

Properties: Preservative. Banned in many countries. Suspected in birth defects and genetic conditions. Highly toxic.

Sodium Laureth and/or Lauryl Sulfate (SLES/SLS)
Found in: Mouthwashes, shampoos, bubble bath, shaving gels/ creams, toothpastes, shower bars/gels, detergents, car wash soaps, engine degreasers, floor cleaner, cosmetics.

Properties: Reportedly, it includes nitrosamines and dioxane, both classified as substances that have the potential to cause cancer. There are concerns regarding potential outcomes such as harm to the liver, kidneys, lungs, and pancreas. It might also impact the utilization of calcium, possibly leading to vulnerabilities in teeth, bones, and connective tissues. Moreover, effects on nerve and brain functions are suspected. It's associated with possible issues like hair loss, cataracts, deteriorated eyesight, impairments in eye health and development, breathing difficulties, skin discomfort, damage, and even fatality.

Sodium Fluoride
Found in: Toothpastes

Properties: Known carcinogen. Affects brain and nerve function; weakens kidney tissue.

Talc
Found in: Deodorants, shaving products and skin products.
Properties: A known carcinogen that causes ovarian cancer in mammals.

Synthetic (Artificial) Flavorings or Fragrances
Found in: Packaged foods, mouthwashes, deodorants, cosmetics, perfumes, etc.

Properties: Many are neurotoxins affecting your brain, nerve, and endocrine function; many suspected as carcinogens.

Tannin (Tannic Acid)
Found in: Teas, coffee, beer, wine, soda. Found in many artificial flavorings, etc.

Properties: Flavoring. Suspected in liver, pancreatic and GI tract irritation. Occurs naturally in nature, in low doses and buffered.

Toluene
Found in: Nail polish, feminine products, as well as some cosmetics.

Properties: Suspected carcinogen, reportedly affects endocrine function. Research shows possible birth defects as one side effect. Can affect brain and nerve function.

Conclusion

Numerous of the aforementioned harmful substances have been identified in both above-ground and underground municipal water sources, including those serving large cities. A significant portion of these pollutants originates from manufacturing processes, industrial solvents, discarded ammunition waste, pesticides, herbicides, grain fumigants, and the use of petrochemicals (like gasoline, solvents, oils, and cleansers) that find their way into the soil. Even recreational boating contributes to water contamination.

Reports indicate that more than 125 cosmetic components, along with numerous others commonly found in cigarettes, foods, lotions, ointments, synthetic vitamins, and other commonly used or ingested substances, are indeed carcinogenic. Hundreds more accumulate within organs like the liver, brain, kidneys, pancreas, bowels, and heart tissues, disrupting proper cellular respiration and inducing inflammation and damage.

Many of these contaminants oxidize, becoming airborne and leading to damage and cancer in the liver and lungs. Moreover, they often combine to form radical compounds, such as nitrosamines, which significantly accelerate tumor formation and growth. A substantial number of the aforementioned pesticides, herbicides, fungicides, and petrochemicals can also disrupt hormones, influencing the production of substances like estrogen and testosterone.

The levels of benzene, a known carcinogen used in solvents and food additives, have surged in the air, water, and food supply. This compound is emitted by sources like oil refineries, gas stations, rubber manufacturing plants, and diesel-powered vehicles. A staggering volume of carcinogens is being released into our environment through tobacco smoke, gasoline, and particularly diesel emissions, as well as from sources like body shops, airports, highways, railways, industries, and petrochemical production plants.

Radiation is another significant factor contributing to cancer rates. Detrimental radiation is present in dental offices, hospitals (with the use of X-rays, nuclear medicine, and other procedures), around high-power electrical lines, televisions, microwave ovens, cathode-ray computer monitors, and most medical diagnostic equipment, including CT scans, MRIs, mammography machines, and X-ray devices.

Cancer has escalated to an epidemic level, with estimates suggesting that nearly every other individual in the U.S.A. is affected. Kathleen Deoul's book "Cancer Cover-Up {Genocide}" notes that an American succumbs to cancer every minute, equivalent to three fully loaded jumbo jets crashing daily. Yet, this tragic situation can be altered.

We exist in a world saturated with excitotoxins, also known as "neurotoxins," which are affecting our connection to both the external world and our own selves. Our surroundings are literally saturated with cancer-inducing agents—we live within and amidst them, consuming and applying them, even to our skin. Our homes are laden with formaldehyde and other potentially perilous and cancer-causing substances that emanate from items like carpets, laminate cabinets, plywood, adhesive materials, curtains, and synthetic clothing. Dry-cleaned clothes, for instance, can also contain toxins, particularly due to the use of perchloroethylene or "perc," an extremely toxic chemical used in dry cleaning.

Plastics are another significant source of toxins and possible carcinogens. Vinyl compounds (phthalates) are found in PVC pipes, toys, baby teething items, bottles, and construction materials. It is wise to avoid purchasing distilled water in plastic containers, as it tends to draw in other substances due to its lack of inherent content.

Even if we were to cease all chemical usage today, the impact would remain irreversible. As a species, we remain enveloped in ignorance as we perpetuate the destruction of our own habitat—an action no other species takes. Industries and automobiles rank among the most egregious polluters. Many factories that release vast quantities of toxic particles into the air resist the implementation of pollution control mechanisms due to the associated costs. Despite the existence of valuable research conducted by conscientious individuals, such information often gets suppressed or buried within a society driven by monetary interests. Nevertheless, life is beyond valuation. Each individual must contribute to the effort of cleansing our shared world.

Strive to minimize exposure to toxic chemicals to the best of your ability.

MODULE 4.6

Protecting Yourself From Carcinogens

We are encompassed by and ingest numerous cancer-causing substances on a daily basis. These substances function as triggers and intensifiers, causing harm to tissues and sparking immune reactions much like gasoline fuels a fire. Many of these agents are neurotoxins that bind to your nervous and endocrine systems. This leads to reduced activity in these systems, resulting in a range of symptoms including breathing difficulties, irregular heart rhythms, multiple sclerosis, and conditions like Lou Gehrig's disease.

It's imperative to assume full responsibility for your own well-being. Even our governing bodies exhibit little concern regarding the levels of environmental toxicity. Politicians often fail to realize that they are as vulnerable as anyone else to these effects. Have you ever wondered why cancer rates are soaring? The truth has been skillfully concealed by those who stand to benefit from this situation. Nonetheless, they too will eventually succumb to these harmful agents, just as the general population is.

PROTECT YOURSELF!

1. Live closer to nature, away from factories, power lines and heavy traffic.

2. Fill your house with live plants. Philodendrons (philodendron spp.) are known to absorb formaldehyde, ammonia, benzene, trichloroethylene and hydrates, as well as xylene. The following plants are great indoor plants and will help clean indoor air:

- Philodendron (Philodendron spp.)

- Spider Plants (Chlorophytum comosum)

- Bamboo plant (Rhapis excelsea)

- Corn Plant (Dracaena fragrans)

- English Ivy (Hederá helix)

- Bromeliads (Cryptan thus spp.)

- Chrysanthemum (Chrysanthemum spp.)

- House-type Palms

- Ficus Tree

- Golden Pothos (Epipremnum aureum)

3. Always wash your fruits and vegetables before you eat them. Use a vegetable wash or fresh lemon juice with hydrogen peroxide.

4. Eat an 80 - 100% raw food diet. Eat fruits even more than vegetables. Fruits are full of antioxidant and astringent properties. They will keep your lymphatic (immune) system clean and moving. They also enhance the strength of a cell, especially brain and nerve cells.

5. In traffic, keep your car's outside air vent closed. Make sure your car's exhaust system is not leaking and in good order.

6. Use 100% natural hygiene products (soaps, shampoos, etc.). Read the labels. If they have chemicals in them, don't use them. (If you can't pronounce it—you probably don't want it.) What you put on your skin absorbs into your blood stream and circulates throughout your body. This can damage your brain, heart, kidneys and especially your liver.

7. Avoid dry cleaning, as the chemicals used are extremely toxic.

8. Use common sense with everything you do and use. It is your body and it carries you around in this world, as any vehicle would. If it fails—you're stuck. Chemicals can be extremely dangerous.

9. Avoid cooking. If you must cook, steam your food in stainless steel. Always use stainless steel cookware.

10. Use and clean your air conditioners and air filters. Use the natural, high-filtration-type that removes 1-micron to 3-micron size particles.

11. Use R/O (reverse-osmosis) or steam-distilled water. Note: Avoid storing distilled water in plastic containers. Distilled water will leach some of the chemicals from the plastic into itself.

12. Drink from and use glass as much as possible. Plastic can be toxic to you.

13. Avoid walking for exercise near high traffic areas. Walk in a safe park or wooded area instead.

14. Avoid florescent lighting as much as possible. Be aware of what you eat, drink, breathe and what you put on your skin, as this is how you bring the outside world in.

CHAPTER FIVE

The nature of Disease

To understand the path to good health, it's vital to shift your perception of illness. Disease often generates fear because its root causes are often misunderstood. Medical professionals can make diseases seem complex, leading people to believe only specialists can provide help. This is a misconception. Understanding disease symptoms boils down to grasping the concept of acidity, toxicity, and the body's responses to them. This knowledge reveals that disease is a natural outcome of imbalanced choices and behaviors.

Additionally, it's important to consider the inherent health state your cells inherit from genetics when examining disease. In my experience, about 99% of disease symptoms result from genetic vulnerabilities, toxicity, and excessive acidity. This section will focus on these three factors and how they contribute to common illnesses like cancer, diabetes, gender-specific disorders, and weight fluctuations.

In the final module, referred to as "Body Language," you will encounter a compilation of numerous symptoms that point towards weaknesses or malfunctions in one or more of the body's glands, organs, or systems. You can acquire the skill of "reading" the valuable signals that your body continually provides.

MODULE 5.1

The Three Root Causes of Disease

FIRST ROOT: INHERENT (GENETIC) WEAKNESSES

Innate weaknesses represent cellular codes, often termed cellular memories, that determine tissue conditions and their responses to life's demands. Your physical body is a reflection of your familial lineage, and your cellular strengths and vulnerabilities are derived from your genetic heritage. This principle applies uniformly throughout your body. Although cells were originally divinely crafted, it's the memory of their functionality that shapes our genetic makeup. As we mature, we can either amplify or attenuate our inherent weaknesses based on our chosen lifestyles. This awareness holds profound significance because, regrettably, each successive generation seems to be growing weaker rather than stronger. Presently, people are ingesting and injecting significant quantities of toxins into their bodies, leading to the manifestation of conditions like cancer (a form of degeneration and chronic toxicity) even in early adolescence. Infants are grappling with chronic and degenerative ailments, and birth anomalies are occurring at an unprecedented rate.

When organs and glands possess diminished activity due to genetics, inflammation, or toxicity, an array of imbalances and health issues can ensue. The concept of genetics is readily comprehensible—our physical attributes, mental inclinations, and emotional traits are inherited from our parents. Our lineage, however, extends even further; we carry traces of our grandparents as well, as their encoded characteristics have been transmitted via our parents' genes. Geneticists assert that we bear the legacy of four prior generations in our bodies and psyches, yet in my practice, I've observed genetic patterns that have endured for more than just four generations.

Each cell in your body holds genetic information, serving as a blueprint for its parent cell. These cells acquire strength or vulnerability based on genetic dictates and lifestyle influences —your dietary choices, beverages, inhalation, skin absorption, thoughts, and emotions.

Cells, much like humans, derive their strength from the memories of their experiences. Specific encounters can render both us and cells weak and susceptible. Physical acids and toxins can undermine and damage cells, while genetic memories contribute to or detract from a cell's overall state of health. The cumulative effect of these factors governs the potency or frailty of cells, organs, and glands, impacting their capacity to fulfill their original designated functions. For instance, if you inherit a debilitated thyroid, feeble adrenal glands, or a compromised liver, the functions of these tissues will be impaired, significantly curtailing their ability to produce hormones, digestive enzymes, steroids, and other vital components. This subsequently influences your entire body's performance, ultimately leading to the manifestation of various diseases. An alternative perspective on this subject can be found in "About Consciousness and Disease" later in this section.

Collectively as a society, we need to address our weaknesses and rejuvenate our cells to ensure the well-being of future generations. Remember, nature does not propagate the frail; the weak are naturally consumed. This mechanism sustains the vitality of all species, and the same principle extends to each cell within your body.

Now, let's delve into the two other primary factors underlying all diseases, as well as the causes of tissue failure: toxicity and excessive acidity (acidosis). Both contribute to blockages within the body.

SECOND ROOT: TOXICITY

Toxicity, a term encompassing poisonous substances, encompasses a diverse range of elements. This includes mucus buildup from dairy consumption, irritants, complex sugars, as well as deposits of chemical toxins, toxic metals, and minerals. This form of toxicity, primarily acidic in nature and liable to accumulate within the body, originates from various sources: food, air, personal care products, household items, construction materials, and so forth. In modern times, the majority of foods and beverages people consume tend to be acidic, mucus-forming, energy-depleting, and laden with protein toxins. The processed starches we consume act akin to adhesive in our body tissues, contributing to the buildup of plaque, as previously discussed. This form of toxicity, due to its acidic nature, has the potential to trigger inflammation and tissue congestion, even leading to tissue death.

This toxicity and mucus find storage throughout the body's tissues, with heightened prominence in areas such as the sinuses, throat, thyroid, lungs, muscles, liver, kidneys, and skin. This explains why these regions are most impacted when experiencing cold or flu-like symptoms. The body initiates "disease" as a mechanism for purging itself of toxins, as well as dying or deceased cells. Many so-called "diseases" essentially amount to the body's efforts to eliminate toxins and/ or expel non-functional cells.

Toxicity accumulates both intracellularly (within cells) and interstitially (around cells) within the vascular system, organs, glands, bowels, and body cavities. When combined with an overly acidic diet, this concoction leads to inflammation, ulcers, tumors, and ultimately cellular degeneration. The presence of these toxins and mucus generates obstructions that impede the flow of blood and lymph to and from cells. This significantly impairs a cell's capacity to function optimally and maintain its health.

A host of conditions—ranging from colds, flu, and lymphatic disorders to lung and gastrointestinal issues—are all indicative of this buildup of toxicity within the body. Your immune system and/or parasites naturally respond to this toxicity. However, these immune responses and the actions of parasites, which thrive on this toxicity, are often misidentified as autoimmune disorders. Parasites and immune reactions are always secondary to the underlying cause; they arise as side effects of the symptoms.

THIRD ROOT: OVER-ACIDITY—ACIDOSIS

The body's functioning—digestion, absorption, utilization, reproduction, and elimination—occurs within a milieu of fluids. These fluids encompass digestive juices, blood, extracellular and intracellular fluids, lymphatic fluids, and urine. However, comprehending the effects of both food and toxins within your body necessitates a grasp of the concept of opposites.

Creation hinges on the dynamic interplay of opposites, which prevents monotony. (It's worth noting that as one approaches unity with God, the dichotomy between opposites tends to blur.) This interaction of opposites generates motion, activity, forms, sizes, colors, and temperatures. Complex as chemistry may seem, it fundamentally rests upon two opposing pillars: heat and cold, or yin and yang, in the context of Chinese philosophy and medicine. In this framework, heat equates to acidity, while cold corresponds to alkalinity. Acids set changes in motion, whereas alkalis establish balance. This polarity constitutes the foundation of all matter.

Elements composing matter possess either acidic or alkaline characteristics. Acid-forming elements include nitrogen, phosphorus, and sulfur, while alkaline elements comprise oxygen, calcium, magnesium, sodium, and potassium. Numerous alkaline elements are labeled as electrolytes due to their capability to convey and discharge electrical charges. Alkaline elements have oxygen and carbon dominating the hydrogen, whereas acids have nitrogen and hydrogen dominating.

Sustaining vitality and health requires most of your body's fluids to be alkaline, except for the gastric juices in the stomach—hydrochloric acid and pepsin—which are acidic and facilitate initial protein breakdown. The acid or alkaline status of your body is gauged by pH factors. pH signifies "potential of hydrogen." The pH scale ranges from 0 to 14, with 0 representing extreme acidity, 7 as neutral, and 14 as extremely alkaline. Given the logarithmic nature of the scale, each step signifies a tenfold difference. This distinction is notably meaningful considering that blood pH should hover around 7.4, slightly alkaline. If the hydrogen atoms in the blood diminish (by adding hydrogen atoms), reducing the pH to 6.95, it can lead to coma and death. Conversely, an excessively alkaline pH (reduced hydrogen atoms) can result in convulsions and spasms, though this is rare. It's vital to note that mineral utilization problems predominantly underlie most convulsions and spasms.

All human-consumed foods can be classified into these two categories: they either yield an acid-forming or an alkaline-forming residue post-digestion. This classification hinges on the resulting "ash" after digestion and the prevalent inorganic minerals within the food, which influence the pH of bodily fluids. Acidic foods tend to leave behind more compounds of phosphorus, iron, and sulfur, which displace alkaline minerals like calcium, magnesium, sodium, and potassium. Acids tend to crystallize, thereby provoking irritation and inflammation in tissues. Throughout the body, these crystals amass, causing inflammation, irritation, and stimulation. An example is uric acid, a byproduct of meat metabolism or fungal growth, which contributes to conditions like gout and inflammation.

Various other acids emerge during food digestion, including sulfuric acid, phosphoric acid, butyric acid, lactic acid, acetic acid, and pyroracemic acid. If these acids aren't transformed into salts by electrolytes, they can inflict harm upon tissues. As the body's acidity deepens, the potential for damage intensifies.

In modern society, individuals predominantly consume acid-forming foods, such as meats, grains, pasteurized dairy products, eggs, and cooked tomatoes. Since acids are "hot," these acids and compounds tend to ignite inflammation in tissues. Inflammation weakens cells and impedes their capacity to transport nutrients via cellular respiration across the cell membrane, eventually leading to cellular death.

As previously emphasized, the human stomach serves as the sole acid chamber, facilitating the initial breakdown of proteins. After the stomach's contents transition into the small intestines, bile and sodium bicarbonate are secreted to alkalize the mixture, now referred to as chyme. The remainder of the digestion process is alkaline.

The accumulation of acids and toxic foreign proteins within tissues triggers an immune reaction labeled as inflammation. This inflammation is then diagnosed as an "itis" condition—gastritis, colitis, cystitis, nephritis, bursitis, and arthritis, for instance. These conditions aren't diseases but rather inflammatory responses to acidosis. Addressing such conditions with more acid-forming drugs or steroids is illogical and will eventually foster further tissue deterioration. A more sensible approach involves alkalization and detoxification—eliminating the acids and foreign proteins at the root of the issue. Recent reports by CNN underscore that acidosis can indeed alter cellular genetic patterns (DNA and chromosomes), weakening cells and causing structural changes in their DNA and chromosomes.

ABOUT CONSCIOUSNESS AND DISEASE

Cells respond to various states of consciousness much like we do as individuals. To illustrate, if someone approaches us in a state of anger, we may find ourselves becoming angry as well. The essence of everything is energy, and everything emits energy.

Energy operates on an array of levels. Spiritually, anger is associated with lower energy levels, while love embodies a higher energy level. In spiritual circles, energy is often termed "consciousness" or "awareness." The concept can be likened to a large mirror representing God, or "total awareness," while creation is comparable to this mirror divided into numerous fragments—distinct states of consciousness or awareness. All living entities are essentially fragments of this mirror, expressing themselves through diverse individual states of consciousness. Upon entering creation, we commence in a relatively unconscious or unaware state and progress towards greater consciousness through experiences in our surroundings. Just as a computer equipped with additional software or data can carry out more functions, each fragment of the "mirror of creation" expands its ability to express itself as it awakens to its intrinsic nature. As humans, being components of this mirror, we evolve in a similar fashion—growing in consciousness as we encounter life's experiences.

Though expressing these concepts in words proves challenging, introspection and observation of nature can aid in understanding that all things are reflections of a common essence. In essence, everything to some extent mirrors God and God's creation, including our cells. These cells possess consciousness and adhere to the laws of cause and effect, much like ourselves. Just as the inputs dictate the outputs, the DNA and chromosomes of cells retain memory patterns extending beyond simple genetics. They also retain traces of day-to-day "experiences" akin to our memory recording our daily lives.

Viruses, as proteins, impact a cell's consciousness or vitality. They weaken cells, setting the stage for an immune response. As previously mentioned, nature avoids propagating weakness and instead eliminates it. Numerous proteins, including viruses, trigger mechanisms that enable the body to purge these vulnerabilities. This process ensures that weakened cells are replaced by stronger ones.

However, cells face an issue—typical fuels and building materials, the foods that many people consume, can no longer sustain a refined level of consciousness or awareness. Present-day diets consist of foods with limited energy and vibration, ultimately diminishing cell energy and overall body vitality. This decline in energy also leads to reduced human awareness on the whole, contributing to negative traits like hatred, gossip, and deceit, rather than love.

The role of parasites in disease processes is worth mentioning here (refer to Module 5.2, "Parasites Good or Bad?"). Although parasites serve as secondary factors in disease, they impact a cell's consciousness and vibration, influencing its DNA memory. The introduction of live or deceased pathogens (parasites) into toxic bodies through vaccination has led to the proliferation of genetically weakened and mutated cells. Many "diseases," including ADD, AIDS, and notably cancer, can be traced back to vaccinations. This state of affairs stems from humanity's acceptance of science's misguided actions, often exacerbated by misleading propaganda that shifts blame away from science. Scientists have taken risks with human lives, all for the sake of "progress" and under the guise of safeguarding us. Overcoming these dark periods in medicine and chemistry, characterized by substantial harm to the species, is essential for our advancement.

THE SIMPLE SOLUTION

It's time to awaken and return to simplicity, aligning with the ways of God and nature. Nature has generously provided us with herbs and foods that possess the potential to cleanse, rejuvenate, and nourish both our physical and spiritual selves.

The path to health is remarkably straightforward: consume foods that are in harmony with your species, opting for fresh, ripe, raw, and unprocessed options, just as other animals do. Prioritize rest and ample exposure to sunlight. Detoxify your body from all forms of toxins, including chemicals, heavy metals, antibiotics, excessive hormones, proteins, unnecessary mucus, harmful parasites, pesticides, and similar substances. Fundamentally, strive to alkalize your body through your dietary choices. Among all species, humans possess the most advanced neurological development, and fruits stand as the most electrically-alkaline foods on Earth. Notably, I've witnessed instances where fruits have regenerated the nervous system where vegetables did not yield the same effect.

Harness the power of herbs to restore tissue and support optimal tissue function. Integrate freshly made fruit and vegetable juices as potent supplements to your diet. Enhance your nutrition by incorporating a super-food complex or blend, which encapsulates nature's most nutritious and energy-rich foods—such as royal jelly, wheatgrass powder, and alfalfa powder—in capsule, pill, or powdered forms.

By implementing these strategies, you will observe your body spring into action. It will naturally cleanse and rebuild itself, regardless of the disease you might be facing. Drawing from my experience as a health professional, I have yet to encounter a case where this approach did not yield positive results. Every individual I've worked with has witnessed significant improvements, often leading to the complete elimination of their ailments.

Always strive, no matter how advanced or immobile your condition. I've seen even the most dire situations turn around; cases where complete spinal cord severations healed despite years of near-immobility. I've witnessed bodily realignment and reshaping, even in the presence of various deformities. Adhering to the laws of nature, you will discover that the power vested in God and nature is boundless.

Remember, every occurrence, including health and disease, has a reason. It all stems from the law of cause and effect: your choices and actions initiate the cause, ultimately leading to an effect. Avoid getting caught up in a constant stream of scientific treatment theories. Endeavor to comprehend the underlying causes of things. Consider potential side effects of your actions—whether they involve what you eat, drink, breathe, feel, or think. These elements culminate in your experiences, spanning the physical, emotional, mental, and spiritual realms.

"Disease" is a term predominantly used within the medical sphere, associating it with a set of symptoms displayed by the body. When allopathic doctors refer to a disease, they often lack an understanding of the body's true nature and its responses to genetics, toxicity, and acidosis. Their comprehension often fails to encompass the chemistry and physics of nature, as well as the imperative for humans to coexist and consume in harmony with it.

Let go of the concept of diseases. Instead, focus on purifying and strengthening your body's cells. With this approach, there's virtually nothing you cannot overcome or heal. Life begets life, and death begets death—a truth that holds especially true at the cellular level. Fortify your body, rejuvenate your cells, and you'll discover vitality and robust health, leading you to a life free from disease.

Summary

The majority of tissue deterioration originates from the presence of acidosis and toxicity. As tissues falter or become congested, indications of disease emerge, manifesting both locally and through reflex responses. In this context, "reflex" signifies that often we feel discomfort in one area while the underlying problem or weakness originates elsewhere in the body. A concrete example is when inflammation occurs in the gallbladder, leading to potential right knee pain or weakness. The connection between the two might not be apparent due to the spatial separation between them.

Frequently and mistakenly, we label the symptoms arising from acidosis and toxicity as "disease," attempting to alleviate these symptoms with suppressive medications. This approach is not only misguided but also perilous, since it eventually results in tissue breakdown culminating in tissue demise. Treating symptoms is a misguided approach; true resolution demands addressing the underlying cause. Treating symptoms doesn't resolve the root issue that generated the symptoms initially. Consequently, the core cause of your ailment's symptoms might eventually exact its toll on your well-being, possibly even jeopardizing your life.

Treatment is not synonymous with cure. Instead of treating, focus on rejuvenation. This approach is our sole recourse for survival. Essentially, counter inflammation throughout your body by means of detoxification. Rid yourself of chemicals, needless mucus, toxic heavy metals, superfluous parasites, and acidic substances. A body that is clean and alkaline equates to one that is robust and healthy.

When the truth is unveiled, nothing remains enigmatic. Disease is essentially a natural progression, an outcome that the body undergoes as its cells begin to weaken due to an accumulation of toxicity—such as excessive mucus, vaccinations, metals, chemicals, and other pollutants—and acidosis, which signifies inflammation. True healing is exclusively attainable through purifying the body and fortifying the cells.

MODULE 5.2

Parasites, Good or Bad?

For approximately the last two centuries, researchers have invested considerable resources into investigating the enigmatic parasite. We have inundated our bodies with antibiotics, leading to the development of severe allergies, excessive fungal proliferation, suppression of the lymphatic system, tissue impairment, and novel diseases like MRSA (methicillin-resistant staphylococcus aureus). Tragically, in numerous instances, antibiotic usage has resulted in fatalities. The pharmaceutical industry, the U.S. Government, and various scientific communities have experimented with the often perilous "vaccination," as discussed in Chapter 4. Vaccines have proven to be among the most lethal innovations. This methodology has initiated a genetic avalanche that remains uncontrollable, contributing to the prevalence of chronic and degenerative conditions in infants and young children. The rampant use of antibiotics has led to countless bacterial mutations, and a surge of harmful viruses that are now posing a rapid threat to the human race.

Sometimes, people become so intellectually engrossed that they miss the larger picture. Let's consider the purpose of parasites through a simple lens. Webster's Dictionary defines a parasite as "an organism that feeds off of another." For the purpose of our discussion, I would rephrase this definition as "an organism that thrives on the toxicity and vulnerabilities of others."

To comprehend the role of parasites more comprehensively, let's examine what happens when we shoot and kill a deer (this is a hypothetical scenario). Flies are the initial creatures drawn to the scene. They lay eggs, which later metamorphose into maggots. The primary task of a maggot is the same as other proteus-type parasites: to decompose the deceased deer's carcass. This is how nature maintains its equilibrium, ensuring that the remains of deceased animals are disposed of. Otherwise, the cadavers of all deceased creatures would accumulate endlessly. Nature is perpetually undergoing transformation from one form to another.

Did you know that maggots are presently employed in hospitals for wound debridement? During World War I, when medical attention was scarce, many wounded soldiers developed maggots in their wounds. These maggots inadvertently contributed to maintaining a partial level of cleanliness, aiding many in their recovery.

Clearly, parasites were not designed by a higher power to assail healthy tissue, or else we would all be in jeopardy. Parasites exist ubiquitously, and their vital role in the ecosystem involves aiding nature in the elimination of weaker organisms so that the stronger ones may persist. This perpetuates the cycle of nature. The atoms within our world do not vanish; they undergo transformations through various mechanisms, including oxidation, ionization, and parasitic actions, to name a few.

To illustrate how we can amass parasites within our physical bodies, consider the case of a nineteen-year-old female. She came to me undernourished and frail due to malabsorption issues. Experiencing perpetual fatigue and discomfort, she began my detoxification regimen. Subsequently, she started expelling a significant amount of mucus, a common occurrence. Additionally, she noticed "peculiar-looking entities" in her stool. She even drew pictures of what she saw, which left me astonished. Among the entities, two were tapeworms—a beef tapeworm and a conventional tapeworm. She also detected roundworms, pinworms, flukes (resembling jellyfish), and other indistinct parasites. In a state of panic, she sought assistance at her local hospital's Emergency Room. There, the ER doctor dismissed her concerns, asserting that "parasites don't exist in Americans." Refusing to relent, the young lady insisted that her stool be tested, and after much hesitation and deliberation, the ER doctor complied. The lab report unequivocally confirmed the presence of parasites in the sample.

Humans serve as hosts to a myriad of parasites, primarily microbial. However, I would estimate that approximately 40 to 75 percent of Homo sapiens harbor macroscopic parasites that are observable. Various parasite types include yeasts, fungi, warts, viruses, bacteria, a wide array of worms, and flukes. Most individuals possess several varieties of each type within their bodies. Yeast or fungus, specifically Candida, resides in all individuals. Most people have over thirty different Candida strains. Candida albicans, a prevalent type of fungus, is responsible for myriad symptoms when overgrown, including fatigue, itching, skin irritations, and infections. Candida overgrowth leads to a yearning for sugars and starches, although patients are often advised, incorrectly, to avoid fruits due to their sugar content. However, as previously explored, fructose and glucose serve as primary energy sources for cells. Fruits, rich in antioxidant and astringent properties, play a pivotal role in helping the body eliminate Candida by cleansing lymphatic congestion, where these organisms tend to thrive. In contrast, complex sugars provide a fertile environment for Candida growth, as they are unusable as fuel by the body until they are broken down into simpler forms. Employing an herbal parasite and lymphatic cleansing formula to enhance the "kill" process, can be exceedingly beneficial for those grappling with conditions associated with Candida.

VIRUSES

I have incorporated the term "virus" within the category of parasites. However, there remains uncertainty about the true nature of viruses. Some scientists speculate that viruses might be components derived from decomposed cells, while others entertain the idea that they could be microorganisms. What we do know is that viruses exhibit some form of protein structure, yet they lack the recognized attributes of "life" found in bacteria or protozoa. In my perspective, viruses function as protein catalysts that stimulate an immune response. When a cell's strength diminishes, it could release its own "virus" (protein) as a means of provoking an immune reaction to eliminate the weakened cell. This process adheres to the fundamental principle that the weaker entities are consumed to maintain the perpetuation of life. Just as this principle operates universally, the cellular realm abides by the same principle: fortifying the body necessitates eliminating its vulnerabilities.

Numerous virus variants, including the herpes virus (which seems to align with the proteus-type), serve as "protein splitters." They manifest in over-acidic environments, particularly when elevated protein intake is observed. In instances of herpes simplex or genital herpes, the inactivation or dormancy of these viruses can be achieved by reducing protein consumption in the diet.

The scientific community's lack of comprehension regarding the genuine role of parasites has led to the dangerous notion of vaccinations. These interventions introduce viruses, often deadly and capable of altering DNA, purportedly to induce immunity. As many viruses are cultivated in animal tissues and blood, contamination of these cultures is frequent. This has led to the emergence of problematic entities like the Sim-40 virus, which has been implicated in numerous cancer cases. HIV and E. coli are additional examples of man-made viruses intentionally released into unsuspecting human subjects, resulting in excruciating suffering and substantial mortality.

In the name of "immunity," the U.S. Government has subjected thousands of military personnel to inoculations. The Gulf War Syndrome epitomizes the disastrous consequences of such misguided approaches. The architects of these initiatives should be held accountable for inflicting more suffering and death than even Hitler's regime. Scores of individuals have contracted polio from the very vaccine designed to prevent it. Many thousands more have grappled with cancer and other ailments due to the introduction of live bacteria and viruses into already toxic individuals. The profound devastation inflicted upon human organisms will require generations to overcome, provided we awaken to the truth in a reasonably prompt manner.

A spiritual perspective

There's no need to be consumed by fear when it comes to adhering to nature's principles and the creatures that uphold them. All that's required is a thorough understanding of nature's mechanisms. It's crucial to recognize that parasites don't create or instigate diseases; they are simply consumers. Sometimes we overlook the fact that the origin of everything lies in a Creator who was well-versed in crafting a functioning system. A glimpse into the marvels of the physical body can easily convert even the most skeptical into a believer.

Let's take a moment to ponder: "What gives rise to your consciousness?" I'm not referring to the mental processes of learning, comparing, or deciding, but rather the consciousness that exists behind those thoughts—the unchanging you that remains constant whether you're driving your car, strolling on the beach, or at home; the you that is inescapable regardless of your location.

Your presence is constant, as time essentially unfolds as a sequence of "Nows." You, as consciousness, perpetually inhabit the present instant. Conversely, the mind operates within the framework of time, encompassing both the past and the future.

Allocate some time to introspect. Cultivate the skill of relaxation. Exercise control over your thought patterns. Curtail excessive desires and learn to wholeheartedly embrace each moment. Revel in the unique offerings of every instant, and proceed to appreciate the subsequent moment for its distinct attributes. Engaging with the past or projecting into the future equates to living a life devoid of vitality. Genuine life exists solely in the eternal now.

BACTERIA

The term "bacteria" is commonly recognized, referring to those single-celled organisms that lack a distinct nucleus. Bacteria encompass several distinct types. Firstly, there's the spherical variety, which exists as individual cells known as micrococci, or as pairs referred to as diplococci. Within this classification, there's the cluster-type termed staphylococci, which is familiar, as well as the chain-type termed streptococci. Cube-shaped clusters of this chain-type are denoted as sarcina.

The second category involves rod-shaped bacteria or bacilli. If they exhibit an oval shape, they are identified as coccobacillus. Those that arrange themselves in chains are called streptobacillus.

The third classification comprises spiral-shaped bacteria, where the rigid forms are classified as spirilla. The more pliable spirals are recognized as spirochetes, while the curved spirals are named vibrios.

Bacteria exist at the microscopic level, thriving in instances of lymphatic congestion. It's essential to remember that lymph tissue functions as the body's drainage system, expelling cellular waste and metabolic byproducts from the body. These byproducts can manifest as mucus on the skin, within the gastrointestinal tract, and throughout the body where toxins accumulate. Bacteria exhibit a preference for complex sugars, as well as byproducts of milk and starch. This is why, during the onset of a cold, the body initiates a cleansing process within the lymphatic system, leading to the discharge of mucus and the parasites living within it. This purging is particularly noticeable in areas like the sinuses, lungs, kidneys, and bowels. However, the body's cleansing extends to the entire system, often causing a widespread sensation of body ache.

Bacteria, also known as flora, populate the entire gastrointestinal tract, aiding in the breakdown of foods. Numerous vitamins are synthesized through bacterial activity. A prime example is the various bacteria residing in the gastrointestinal tract, which facilitate the generation of B-vitamins through the breakdown of ingested foods.

PROTEUS

Another category of parasites is known as the proteus or proteolytic parasites, characterized as protein-splitting organisms. Similar to the herpes virus, these parasites either attach themselves to or infiltrate weakened cells. These parasites belong to the acidic type and flourish within the body when it becomes excessively acidic. Their primary role is to break down proteins or cells that are already compromised. In a cellular environment that is alkaline due to health, this particular type of parasite does not typically manifest.

However, a diet that is rich in protein serves as an invitation to the most destructive parasites. Diets with high protein content lead to an over-acidification of the body, resulting in harm to organs such as the liver, pancreas, and notably the kidneys. This also gives rise to body odor due to the surplus of undigested proteins that accumulate within tissues interstitially.

WORMS

Moving on to larger organisms, let's shift our focus to worms and flukes, which can pose significant challenges within our bodies. Worms come in various types, such as pinworms, hookworms, roundworms, spiral worms, and a variety of tapeworms. These organisms can proliferate and travel throughout the body, with a particular affinity for organs like the liver, heart, gastrointestinal tract, including the stomach. Worms have even been found in the lungs, and tapeworms can grow to remarkable lengths, exceeding twenty-six feet in some cases.

In one instance, a woman in her twenties had her gallbladder removed due to persistent pain in the gallbladder and back regions. However, upon examination, her gallbladder was found to be healthy. Over the following twenty years, her pain worsened, and she developed extreme sensitivity in her abdominal area, especially upon touch. She experienced difficulty consuming fatty and dairy-rich foods, which would trigger vomiting. Interestingly, she started consuming her meats nearly raw. Following my detox program, she discovered three substantial tapeworms in her stools, and subsequently, her abdominal pain and sensitivity vanished.

Another case involved a young butcher from Portugal who suffered from severe neurological weakness akin to multiple sclerosis. With his nerve function deteriorating rapidly, he was given a prognosis of two months to live. Upon commencing the detox program, he began expelling numerous worms through vomiting. Within three months of detoxification, he exhibited significant improvement, even resuming driving in Lisbon.

Years ago, adults commonly engaged in a practice known as "de-worming," where parasites were periodically removed from their children's bodies, typically during the spring season. Everyday activities and the consumption of foods introduce numerous parasites into our bodies, which then subsist on our toxins and weakened cells. Often, worms grow within the intestinal tract. As time passes, they can transform from innocuous inhabitants to sources of various symptoms. Regrettably, we have forgotten fundamental insights about the role of parasites in nature and their impact on our well-being.

Flukes, resembling miniature jellyfish, are another variety of parasites that tend to accumulate primarily within the liver and pancreas. When present in the pancreas, they can contribute to digestive issues and even diabetes.

Summary

Maintaining the body's purity and freedom from mucus and impurities, while simultaneously fortifying your cells, is crucial. It's essential to recognize that parasites are not the primary issue; rather, they thrive within a foundation of toxicity and mucus, as these substances serve as their nourishment. Parasites do not target healthy cells for sustenance; only those weakened by toxins and mucus are susceptible. Survival is a law of nature that applies universally —only those possessing strength endure. By fostering robust health and vitality, you'll experience transformative changes in every facet of your life.

As you embark on your cleansing and detoxification journey, pay attention to your stools. In some cases, you might even notice larger parasites within your stools during the detoxification process. For those curious, consulting a parasitology textbook can provide visual references or illustrations. While smaller parasites might require a stool sample analyzed by a healthcare professional or a laboratory for detection.

Most Common Parasites

Parasites range in order of size, from smallest to largest: Viruses, Bacteria, Yeasts, Protozoa and Worms (Nematodes).

Name	Where Found

Bacteria

Streptococci (several)	Lungs, Lymph, Sinus, Small Intestines
Salmonella	GI Tract, Liver, Brain
Shigella Dysenteriae	Dysentery
Staphylococcus Aureus	Lungs, Lymph, Joints, Eyes
Clostridium Difficile	Colon
E-Coli	Kidneys, Bladder, GI Tract
Pseudomonas	Lungs, Lymph, Urinary Tract
Campylobacter Jejuni	GI Tract - Main Cause of Diarrhea

Fungi (Mushrooms, Yeast, Molds)

Candida Albicans (Moniliasis) (Yeasts)	Lymph System, GI Tract
Yeasts (Others)	Throughout the body
Molds	Skin
Fungus (general)	Lymph System, under Fingernails and Toenails, in GI Tract, etc.

Protozoa

Trypanosome Cruzi	Heart, Muscle
Giardia Lemblia Trophozolte	Small Intestines, Gallbladder
Neospora Caninum	Brain, Spinal Cord, All Tissues
Sarcocystis (Amoebas)	Muscle, CNS, Heart, Lungs, Glands, Liver, GI Tract
Isospora	Intestines
Pneumacystis	Lungs
Cryptosporidium	Intestines
Entamoeba's SPP. (Malaria)	GI Tract
Plasmodium SPP. (Malaria)	Liver, Red blood cells
Toxoplasma Gondii	Brain, Spinal Cord, All Tissues

Worms

Tape worms, beef, pork, etc.	GI Tract, Liver, Brain, Bladder
Hook Worms	Skin, Blood, Lungs, Intestines
Round Worms (Trichinosos, etc.)	Intestines, Eyes, Brain, Ears
Pin Worms (oxyuris SPP)	Large Intestines, (mature in small intestine)
Flukes (Many Types) Liver, Lung, Pancreatic	Pancreas, Liver, Lungs
Whip Worms (Triechuris Trichina)	Intestines
Frichina Worm (tichinella Spiralis)	Muscles, Intestines
Blood Flukes (Schistsomes)	Blood, Bladder, Small Intestines, Veins

MODULE 5.3

Why Do We "Plaque" Cholesterol and Other Lipids?

The liver is responsible for generating a substantial quantity of cholesterol, a crucial lipid that serves various purposes within the body. Lipids are a group of fats or fat-like substances characterized by their insolubility in water and solubility in fat solvents such as alcohol, ether, and chloroform. Unlike chemical names such as "protein" or "carbohydrate," the term "lipid" is descriptive. It encompasses true fats (fatty acid and glycerol esters), lipoids (phospholipids, cerebrosides, waves), and sterols (cholesterol, ergosterol). A notable component of cell membrane walls is cholesterol. Cortical-type steroids, produced by the adrenal glands, utilize cholesterol and function partly as anti-inflammatory agents.

The accumulation of cholesterol in the lining of the vascular system and other tissues, known as plaque, prompts inquiry into the reasons behind this phenomenon. To address this, it's necessary to grasp the concept of inflammation or acidosis, along with the role steroids play in the body.

Inflammation signifies the body's state of being ablaze, which can manifest at varying intensities. For instance, cancer epitomizes an intense blaze. Acidosis arises from dietary choices, beverages, air quality, skin applications, emotions, and thoughts, leading to inflammation. In medical terminology, inflammation is labeled with the suffix "-itis," where the affected area determines the specific "itis," like arthritis denoting joint inflammation. The allopathic approach involves administering steroid shots—such as cortisone or prednisone—

to address "itis." Given that adrenal glands utilize cholesterol to manufacture cortical steroids, a pertinent question emerges: "Why might the adrenal glands fail to generate adequate cortisone?" If the adrenal glands are feeble or under-active in the tissue responsible for steroid production, the body's defense against acute inflammation becomes compromised.

Devoid of sufficient steroids, the body resorts to water and electrolytes to combat the "fire" of inflammation, yet this can lead to edema or swelling at the inflamed site. Additionally, the liver increases cholesterol production to augment the body's repertoire of anti-inflammatory compounds. Cholesterol is a key constituent of steroids.

These anti-inflammatory substances are vital for safeguarding cells from the destructive impact of acids. Plaque formation is a natural chemical occurrence in an acidic environment. Alkalization is pivotal for dismantling this "protective shield" of plaque, which can itself become problematic.

A significant majority of individuals consume acid-forming foods, typically comprising 90-100 percent of their diet. This dietary pattern sustains an acidic pH within the body. Metabolic by-products further contribute to this acidic state, provoking inflammation—akin to a destructive fire—resulting in cellular harm. The body employs various strategies to counteract this, including producing steroids, forming lipid plaques (cholesterol-based), extracting calcium, and retaining fluids and electrolytes. These measures represent the body's attempt at self-preservation through alkalization.

Check for acidity

Obtain pH-testing papers, commonly known as litmus papers, and periodically assess your saliva and urine, typically about one to two hours after meals. This practice will aid in identifying the sources contributing to your heightened acid state.

Promoting alkalization is pivotal for tissue rejuvenation, disintegration of stones, and elimination of lipid plaques. Inflammation-induced lipid plaquing precipitated by acidosis results in compromised blood circulation, culminating in tissue deterioration, heart attacks, and strokes. Acidosis further triggers the aggregation of fats and nutrients, leading to memory impairment, cardiovascular events, graying of hair, tissue discomfort, stone formation, and other health issues.

REMOVING THE FIREWALL, SAFELY — Eliminating plaque buildup and breaking down lipid-based stones can be achieved by adopting an 80-100 percent raw-food regimen. Raw foods facilitate the reduction of inflammation by promoting alkalization and heightened steroid synthesis, effectively dissolving stones and lipid plaques. Consequently, this approach clears obstructions within the body, enhancing blood circulation to tissues and subsequently boosting nourishment and vitality to cells. This process leads to the revitalization or regeneration of compromised regions. Consistent adherence to the diet yields rapid results in terms of restoration.

MODULE 5.4

Adrenal Gland Weakness = Female and Male Disorders

The adrenal glands play a significant role in shaping the desired and attainable quality of life for each person. Hence, it's crucial to prioritize the enhancement of all cells and glands within your body. Your physical body serves as your vehicle during your journey in the physical world. Illness and fragility can isolate you from life, whereas well-being and energy integrate you more fully into it. Embrace the journey towards better health – its rewards surpass what you might envision.

Now, let's delve into additional complications that can emerge when the adrenal glands are feeble and the diet primarily produces acidic conditions.

FEMALE IMBALANCES

Women are particularly susceptible to the effects of weakened adrenal glands. One of the primary signs of this is low blood pressure. When adrenal glands are not functioning optimally, blood pressure typically starts below 118 systolic and may eventually fluctuate to either high blood pressure or continue to decrease.

Another indication of adrenal weakness in women presents itself through menstrual cycle irregularities. In such cases, females might experience early onset of menstruation, occurring anywhere from the ages of three to twelve.

Excessive bleeding and irregular cycles are common. Although less frequent, some women may have infrequent and scanty periods.

Adrenal insufficiency in women can also manifest in various ways including fertility issues, reduced sex drive, frigidity, and vaginal dryness. If the condition persists, it can lead to the development of ovarian cysts, uterine fibroids, fibrocystic problems, atypical cells, fibromyalgia, as well as breast, ovarian, cervical, and uterine cancers.

The central concern revolves around estrogen. In the absence of adequate progesterone and other anti-inflammatory steroids, a woman can become estrogen dominant. This dominance of estrogen, particularly ovarian estrogen, prevails without the balancing effects of progesterone. Most forms of estrogen are acidic, especially ovarian estrogen, which breaks down the uterine lining each month. Progesterone counteracts this process, healing inflamed tissue and repairing damaged cells.

Considering estrogen's role in breaking down the uterine lining, it's noteworthy that birth control pills are estrogen-based. Estrogen encourages a natural menstrual cycle in women. In light of this, one might question why a medical doctor administers additional estrogen after a hysterectomy. Furthermore, given the information above, would estrogen contribute to bone strengthening or weakening? The answer is the latter, as estrogen replacement programs often exacerbate existing issues.

MALE IMBALANCES

Now, shifting our focus to male concerns stemming from similar adrenal deficiencies, we encounter prostatitis and prostate cancer. These issues arise for analogous reasons: acidic hormones such as testosterone and androsterone tend to predominate in the absence of appropriate steroids like progesterone, which would otherwise counteract the inflammation triggered by these acidic compounds or hormones.

Glandular weaknesses often contribute to a loss of romantic vitality in men. This encompasses a range of other conditions that commonly affect men, encompassing problems like erectile dysfunction, impotence, and premature ejaculation. The restoration of health has the potential to reinvigorate all these aspects.

PROBLEMS COMMON TO BOTH

In both males and females with reduced steroid production due to under-active adrenal glands, we also observe a decline in lower back and pelvic strength and integrity. This deterioration often progresses to conditions like sciatica and other nerve-related discomfort in the lower extremities, particularly when the thyroid is also affected. Given that the thyroid and parathyroid influence calcium utilization, the consequences extend to include issues like bone density loss, nail problems, and connective tissue disorders such as varicose veins, hemorrhoids, macular degeneration, hernias, heart arrhythmias, and aneurysms.

The adrenal glands also play a role in producing neurotransmitters. When these glands are weakened, the nervous system can also be affected, contributing to feelings of anxiety, shyness, inadequacy, panic attacks, asthma, multiple sclerosis, Parkinson's disease, and other conditions associated with neurotransmitter imbalances, including irregular blood pressure. It's astonishing to observe the wide array of secondary conditions that arise due to the hypo-activity of just one pair of glands. When combined with the fact that many individuals also have weaknesses in their thyroid and/or pituitary glands, the list of potential diseases resulting from these factors continues to expand. There is a logical explanation behind diseases once you begin to consider the broader context.

You are the only one in control. Stop, explore yourself, and rid yourself of the thoughts, images, and feelings that bind you. Become free and healthy and your body will readjust itself to match. Become love.

MODULE 5.5

Cancer

Diseases are a natural outcome stemming from specific causes. By addressing and eliminating the root cause, the resulting effect can also be eliminated. Drawing from over thirty years of clinical experience and observation with cancer patients, it is my perspective that there are essentially two fundamental types of cancer. First, there are the congestive or tumor-related cancers that pertain to the lymphatic system, which serves as the body's waste disposal mechanism. Second, there are degenerative cancers, characterized by dying tissue or cells and the immune system's endeavor to remove these compromised cells. The latter category might seemingly exhibit an "autoimmune" response, wherein the immune cells mistakenly attack both themselves and healthy body cells. However, the genuine purpose of this process remains poorly comprehended within the current allopathic medical framework.

The genesis and triggers of both types of cancer are intertwined, as evidenced by an examination of congestive or tumor-based cancers. Body congestion, as mentioned earlier, can be attributed to factors like dairy products, refined sugars, chemicals, metals, and foreign proteins, which collectively induce inflammation. In response to inflammation, mucus is discharged by the mucosal linings as an anti-inflammatory reaction. If the lymphatic system becomes stagnant or overwhelmed by excessive mucus production, this mucus can accumulate. Such congestion obstructs proper cellular respiration, culminating in cellular vulnerability and cell death. This phenomenon further ignites inflammation, perpetuating additional cellular demise. This cycle of congestion and inflammation subsequently triggers cellular deterioration, paving the way for cancer development.

As highlighted earlier, this degeneration or cellular destruction stems from prolonged inflammation, or acidosis. Primarily provoked by dietary, respiratory, ingestible, and dermal exposure factors, acidosis can also arise from the dominance of acid-type hormones (steroids) like estrogen or testosterone in the absence of counterbalancing anabolic (anti-inflammatory) steroids, which are produced by both the adrenal glands and gonads. These unchecked hormone types contribute to heightened inflammation, culminating in the formation of tumors or fibrocystic structures and the eventual destruction of cells. Estrogen, for instance, represents a prominent acidic and inflammatory hormone. In the absence of adequate steroids, estrogen progressively leads to tissue degeneration through inflammation, thereby fostering conditions like breast, uterine, and ovarian cancers.

Parasites and mutations commonly factor into both forms of cancer. Parasites target weakened or dying tissue, rather than healthy cells. They tend to thrive and reproduce within lymph and lymph nodes, which function as "toxic waste reservoirs." It is my hypothesis that cells discharge their own protein-based viruses when they lack the vitality to sustain life. These viruses and parasites consequently induce cellular mutations in response to their presence. The immune system is naturally inclined to eliminate these mutated cells, resulting in an abnormal immune response in the presence of cancer or other degenerative ailments. Indeed, the immune system's design entails combating various forms of invasion, encompassing parasites, foreign proteins (including weakened cells), and other harmful pathogens. This encompasses acids arising from metabolism or digestion that can inflict harm on cells and tissues.

Cancer does not manifest out of nowhere; it formerly required years for tumors or tissue degeneration to develop. However, the substantial amount of chemicals and hormones ingested by many people each week has expedited the growth of tumors to a matter of months or even days. The same applies to hormonally triggered cancers. Hormonal imbalances are predominantly the result of chronic weaknesses in the endocrine glands, particularly the adrenal glands.

The term and condition of "cancer" was relatively unheard of until humans started engaging with vaccines and toxic substances. Contaminated vaccines have been implicated in numerous health conditions that individuals presently grapple with. An illustration is the polio vaccine, which was manufactured in monkey kidney tissue during the early to mid-1950s, leading to contamination with a monkey virus known as simian virus number 40 (SV40 or Sim-40). This virus has been demonstrated to cause cancer in animals and has links to conditions like mesothelioma and multiple myeloma in humans. This instance highlights only one vaccine's potential consequences. How many different vaccines have you received, and what adverse effects might they have triggered?

Vaccination Facts

According to the FDA, most physicians report only a fraction, approximately 1 to 10%, of the injuries and deaths resulting from vaccinations to the Vaccine Adverse Event Reporting System (VAERS), which was established as a central repository for monitoring the side effects of vaccinations. Each year, the health of hundreds of thousands of children and infants is compromised by the mandatory administration of 20 to 30 vaccinations. Some children endure severe injuries, and tragically, fatalities occur as a consequence. Vaccines have been associated with numerous conditions, including various cancers, a substantial increase in diabetes cases (particularly juvenile diabetes), multiple sclerosis, Bell's Palsy, vascular disorders, and arthritis. Despite being aware of the toxic and distressing adverse effects of vaccinations, the American Academy of Pediatrics still promotes their widespread use.

As the cells within your body weaken due to factors like diet, chemicals, vaccinations, and similar influences, this debility becomes manifest in their expression. Just as you continuously express yourself based on your experiences and the memory of those experiences, your cells operate in a similar manner. Over time, the strength or fragility of each cell shapes its memory patterns embedded in DNA and chromosomes. At the moment of conception, the state of each cell and the memories it carries are inherited, dictating the functioning of your body and the potential conditions it might encounter. As we progressively undermine our genetic state through ongoing dietary and lifestyle choices, we witness a surge of chronic cellular and tissue vulnerabilities. These vulnerabilities are transmitted to subsequent generations, leading to an amplification of chronic cellular patterns and functions, ultimately triggering the emergence of disease symptoms even in infants. Through this mechanism of genetic transmission, we have inadvertently set in motion alarming repercussions.

While many allopathic doctors assert that cancer constitutes an autoimmune disorder, I regard this conclusion as somewhat misleading, often serving as a catch-all explanation stemming from a lack of understanding regarding the actual origins of disease processes. The immune cells in your body are meticulously designed to target and eliminate weakened, mutated, dying, or parasitically infested cells. This is particularly applicable to the natural killer cells (NK cells), including T-cells from the thymus and B-cells from the bone marrow. Natural killer cells are substantially larger than the smaller macrophages, neutrophils, basophils, and others that perform basic bodily cleanup functions. Within us resides an active internal defense force, crucial for our survival. This process is indispensable for maintaining our internal equilibrium. The more compromised a cell or tissue becomes due to inflammation, toxicity, genetics, or the parasitic response to these factors, the greater the immune response required. The heightened count of white blood cells is a reaction to all the aforementioned factors, particularly in response to foreign pathogens.

DETOX FOR CANCER PREVENTION AND CURE

It is imperative to engage in cellular and tissue cleansing, strengthening, and subsequent regeneration. The process of detoxification is the essential pathway to achieving this goal. The commencement of detoxification naturally occurs when you adopt a raw food diet that leads to alkalization. Through this approach, cells are fortified by the removal of impediments and acidic substances responsible for inflammation and hindering nutrient supply to cells. Detoxification enables cells to acquire nutritional energy and efficiently expel waste through cellular respiration, thereby initiating the body's reconstruction process.

Empirical evidence demonstrates that diets rich in animal protein contribute to the onset of cancer. Animal protein carries an acidic nature (inflammatory), fostering putrefaction and congestion. The congestion arises due to mucus formation prompted by its abrasive and putrefactive attributes. The inclusion of toxic chemicals, vaccinations, and hormones in the diet or injection into animals subsequently generates tissue toxicity within the human body. This triggers an immune response leading to inflammation. Animal protein also disrupts the biochemical equilibrium in the body. Elevated levels of iron and phosphorous force out essential electrolytes like calcium and magnesium, culminating in the weakening and dehydration of the body.

It is evident that cancer, which emerges from the aforementioned factors, cannot be effectively managed with chemotherapy, which acts similarly to Draino® in plumbing systems, or eradicated through radiation (heat). Both these options either exacerbate the cancer or prompt its metastasis to locations where cellular and tissue integrity has been undermined by these treatments. Radiation compromises the cell's capacity to carry and utilize oxygen, while still permitting glucose to enter through the cell membrane. Consequently, fermentation transpires within the cell, eventually leading to auto-intoxication and cell demise, albeit with a delayed effect.

Initially, these interventions may appear to shrink tumors or halt cancer progression, but beware—cancer can intensify throughout the entire body. This provokes supplementary immune responses, giving rise to the appearance of "autoimmune issues."

In essence, the crux of all cancers lies in excessive acidity and inflammation, coupled with the accumulation of cellular toxins. Both these factors contribute to enervation or the diminishment of cellular energy and function, thereby culminating in the deterioration of overall systemic energy and well-being. This engenders the overburdening of the immune system. In cancer patients, the majority of tissues responsible for generating immune cells, particularly the thymus gland (producer of T-cells) and the bone marrow (site of B-cell production), tend to become hypoactive.

A HEALTHY LYMPH SYSTEM IS ESSENTIAL

Having considered all of these factors, it becomes essential for you to grasp the significance of your lymphatic system. Your lymphatic system serves as the origin of around ninety percent of all disease processes. When this intricate network becomes congested and fails to facilitate effective elimination, it creates a blockade in the body's entire "sewer system," leading to inadequate or improper disposal of cellular and metabolic waste (acids), as well as toxic substances like chemicals and metals that have been ingested. The removal of these toxins is imperative, as failure to do so can lead to cellular demise.

Your lymphatic system plays a critical role in your immune function. For an enhanced immune response, prioritizing the cleansing of your lymphatic system is crucial. It's essential to remember that your kidneys, colon, and skin serve as the exit points for your lymphatic system. If your septic system is obstructed or overloaded, the solution isn't to remove it, but rather to clean it out. Many individuals have experienced compromised kidney filtration, impacted intestinal walls, and reduced sweating capacity. Consequently, the exit pathways become partially obstructed, hampering proper elimination of waste and sewage. Consequently, this leads to congestion in the lymphatic system and an enlargement of lymph nodes. When this state persists over several years, various conditions such as lymphomas, breast cancer unrelated to estrogen, throat cancer (especially following tonsil removal), and cancers in the neck, colon, kidney, liver, and other areas, can manifest.

Family Support

Over the course of the last three decades, I have observed numerous cancer patients undergo our program as well as other programs, both within Mexico and abroad. A significant factor in the process of recovery is the presence of supportive friends and family members.

Some individuals appear to be moving through life in a passive manner, greatly influenced by societal norms and thinking patterns. Others, fortunately, exhibit a higher level of openness and awareness towards spirituality and unconditioned states of consciousness. Many people are held back by fear of the unknown or of experiences they haven't yet learned about. I have witnessed many cases where family members mock their loved ones for choosing natural health methods for healing. They frequently offer tempting but harmful food and snacks to their loved ones, fully aware of their detrimental effects. Friends have also engaged in similar behavior.

Such ridicule or disregard often stems from a lack of awareness and an inability to comprehend the significance of their loved one's quest for recovery, and the dire consequences that could ensue if this path is ignored. Shockingly, certain family members have unintentionally contributed to the demise of their partners or children by discouraging them from pursuing natural healing methods, one of the most authentic avenues for wellness.

Staying resolute in your health decisions is crucial. One of the key elements in the journey to recovery is your inner strength and self-discipline. Dedicate time to solitary reflection. Understand yourself on a deep level. Cultivate inner strength. This path is your own, distinct road to health, not influenced by others. This inner strength will empower you to interact confidently with friends and loved ones. Share the knowledge you have gained, for the pursuit of wellness is a universal need.

Keep in mind that most individuals tend to neglect their health issues until they become critical. Refrain from becoming one of those individuals. Prioritize your own well-being and vitality now, and become an inspiration for others.

This underscores why detoxification is pivotal in combatting cancer. Through the process of alkalizing and purifying your tissues and fluids, your cells will gradually fortify, while the accumulation of toxic substances that diminish your cells' vitality will be expelled. This transformation leads to an exceptional sense of happiness, vigor, and vitality.

Out of every 100 clients who have visited our clinic and adhered to a detoxification regimen, an impressive 80 have managed to overcome their cancers. From my experience, I can confidently state that detoxification and the revitalization of cells through dietary and herbal approaches is one of the most effective means of healing, cleansing, and rejuvenating the body. Assuming responsibility for your health and embracing an open-hearted approach can result in unbelievable accomplishments. Do not permit anyone to convince you that there are no solutions available. We've encountered individuals who were given a mere day or even hours to survive, yet managed to make a remarkable recovery. Throughout the past thirty years, I've witnessed astonishing instances of cellular regeneration. Never compromise the integrity of your immune system, nor allow anyone to undermine it. And most importantly, avoid the removal of your lymph nodes, as the consequences can be extremely damaging. Instead of attempting to merely treat, prioritize the process of regeneration.

MODULE 5.6

Neurological Disorders and Injuries

It deeply troubles me to witness a significant number of individuals living as quadriplegics and paraplegics in a seemingly helpless state. However, this perception couldn't be further from the reality. I vividly recall one particularly challenging case involving a thirty-four-year-old woman who had sustained a spinal injury at the C3-C4 level. Her spinal cord had been completely severed due to an accident that occurred when she was just twelve years old. This left her with only the ability to move her head. She suffered from severe spasms and excruciating pain. After an arduous journey lasting eleven months, this young woman underwent a transformation from severe bodily degeneration—where her only means of movement was a wheelchair controlled by her tongue—to being capable of shaking hands and lifting either leg as many times as desired. Remarkably, she could experience sensations from head to toe.

Another case involved a young man in his early twenties who had suffered a spinal injury at the C4-C5 level, leaving him paralyzed from the upper body down to his feet for a span of two years. In a span of merely six months under our program, his nerve responses began aiding him in moving his feet, and he regained the ability to have bowel movements independently. This is especially significant since most quadriplegics and many paraplegics lose the capacity for self-initiated bowel movements. This malfunction leads to lymphatic system congestion, causing cellular auto-intoxication.

In our hubris and ignorance, we often overlook the truth that is right before our eyes. If the human body can astonishingly mend itself in instances such as broken bones, profound cuts, and the regeneration of various glands and tissues, then why shouldn't it be capable of restoring damaged nerves? The answer lies in the fact that this rejuvenation is possible, but not on a diet of cooked and lifeless foods, particularly those that lead to an acidic pH within the body.

Neurons, the body's highest energy centers, necessitate an alkaline environment for effective regeneration. Additionally, they thrive on the highest energy foods available—fruits. Fructose, a high-energy simple sugar present in fruits, seamlessly provides energy to cells. This principle holds true for all neurological issues, spanning from multiple sclerosis and Parkinson's to Bell's palsy and even asthma. It's noteworthy that all these neurological conditions are preceded by adrenal weakness.

In the context of neurological problems, including injuries, it's crucial to enhance the adrenal glands alongside the entire endocrine gland system. Moreover, maintaining a 100 percent raw food diet is imperative. I once encountered a forty-year-old woman suffering from advanced multiple sclerosis. She was brought to me on a stretcher, her body completely rigid. However, within three months of adopting a fruit-based diet, she managed to sit up, feed herself, and even operate her wheelchair. To encourage muscle tissue development in her thin frame, I introduced vegetable juices and salads, rich in amino acids. Surprisingly, she temporarily lost mobility. This phenomenon can be attributed to the distinct electrical charge of fruits versus vegetables. Upon reverting to a fruit-centric diet, her strength gradually returned. The rejuvenating potential of raw foods on the physical body is truly remarkable. I have witnessed the body pulling itself back from precarious circumstances. Naturally, it took a substantial amount of time to reverse her degenerative condition. A predominantly fruit-based diet played an integral role in maintaining nerve response.

An essential realization is that the body's regeneration process cannot be fueled by toxic chemicals. These chemicals are perceived as invasive foreign proteins that serve to exacerbate tissue acidity, thereby perpetuating damage and evoking chronic inflammatory immune responses, often necessitating steroid treatments—leading to a vicious cycle. Similarly, electrical stimulation isn't a genuine solution. Despite the evident truth, people often dance around it, often driven by financial motives. Unfortunately, greed often leads to the creation of profitable "treatment" systems, such as illness-centered institutions, drugs, and surgeries, rather than delving into the fundamental truths underlying disease.

THE SAME ANSWER—ALKALIZE

Empower every cell within your body through a combination of dietary adjustments and herbal supplements. Keep in mind the principle of Alkalization—it's a fundamental approach. I also suggest incorporating a top-notch herbal brain and nerve formula to bolster the strength of your spinal column, nerve centers, and brain tissue. Equally vital is the enhancement of your adrenal glands, as these play a significant role in generating numerous neurotransmitters and steroids vital for bodily functions.

In addressing neurological issues and injuries, it's important to take into account the thyroid and parathyroid glands. The parathyroid hormone's role in proper calcium utilization is crucial. An effective way to gauge your system's functionality is by performing the Basal Temperature Test (details in Appendix A). With optimal calcium utilization and a diet comprising entirely raw foods, success is highly promising.

At the very least, individuals grappling with nerve damage can experience substantial improvements in their quality of life by alleviating concerns like urinary tract infections, excessive spasms, pain, cellulitis, obesity, and tissue deterioration. On the brighter side, complete recovery becomes a possibility. The entire body has the potential to regain health and vitality.

Never succumb to the belief that the body cannot rejuvenate itself. Our bodies often accumulate acidity and toxicity from foods that we've been led to believe are beneficial. Regeneration becomes unattainable in the presence of inflammation, mucus, parasites, toxic chemicals, metals, and excessive hormones. Consuming lifeless animal products, cooked mucus-inducing dairy items, acidic and greasy grains, and refined sugars only hastens the body's deterioration. Rekindle your vitality, initiate a process of self-regeneration, and witness the emergence of remarkable transformations.

MODULE 5.7

Diabetes: Types I and II

According to 2020 statistics from the U.S. Government, around 37 million Americans are affected by diabetes. Despite the severe impact this disease has on the body, diabetes can actually be among the easier conditions to overcome. This statement is made with respect for the fact that there are certain challenging cases, particularly in the more advanced instances known as "brittle" diabetes or type I diabetes.

Diabetes is fundamentally classified into two types. The first type, commonly referred to as juvenile or brittle diabetes, falls under the category of insulin-dependent diabetes. The second type, often referred to as late-onset diabetes or type II diabetes, is initially considered non-insulin dependent but can eventually transition to insulin dependency.

In my view, there exists minimal disparity between these two types, except for the presence of weakened tissues in type I cases, which have often been further compromised due to genetic inheritance. To gain a deeper comprehension of the diabetes condition, it's essential to delve into the involved tissues, cells, and the underlying causes behind their dysfunction.

THE ROLE OF THE PANCREAS

The pancreas, an organ with both exocrine and endocrine functions, plays a crucial role in diabetes. Positioned behind the stomach, between the first and second lumbar vertebrae, its "head" connects to the initial portion of the small intestine (duodenum), while its "tail" extends toward the spleen.

The pancreas serves two essential purposes, vital for the body's survival. Firstly, it secretes significant digestive enzymes along with sodium bicarbonate, which neutralizes stomach acid, creating an alkaline environment for these enzymes to function effectively. Secondly, and particularly relevant to diabetes, it generates insulin via beta cells, which aids in the utilization of glucose. When the pancreatic cells become weakened and fail to perform their respective roles, both aspects of its function can be affected. While there are other functions of the pancreas, we will explore those later.

Although not directly linked to diabetes, digestion is a critical function associated with the pancreas. It involves breaking down food so that its nutrients and energy can be used for cellular energy. Proper digestion is facilitated by digestive enzymes secreted in four main locations: the mouth, stomach, pancreas, and small intestines. While enzymes from the mouth, pancreas, and intestines are alkaline and work on carbohydrate, sugar, and fat digestion, the stomach contains hydrochloric acid (HCL) that starts protein breakdown by releasing pepsin, an acidic enzyme.

The significance of bile and sodium bicarbonate should be noted here. Bile is released by the liver/gallbladder, while sodium bicarbonate is released by the pancreas. These alkalizing agents neutralize the acidic stomach contents (known as chyme), allowing the alkaline pancreatic and intestinal enzymes to continue digestion. If there's insufficient bile or sodium bicarbonate, the acidic chyme can neutralize the alkaline pancreatic enzymes, hindering proper digestion. HCL can then lead to intestinal inflammation, potentially causing ulcers and inflammation ("itis"). The inhibition of proper enzyme action results in fermentation and putrefaction, which contribute to toxicity and alcohol production, further disrupting food breakdown, blood sugar, and acid-base balance.

The primary pancreatic function relevant to diabetes is carried out by beta cells, producing and releasing insulin to assist glucose utilization. As a protein-type hormone, insulin aids in transporting glucose across cell membranes. It's worth noting that fructose from fruit moves into cells via diffusion, not active transport like glucose, raising questions about the necessity for insulin to assist fructose passage. Surprisingly, diabetics are often advised against consuming fruits due to their sugar content. However, my experience has shown that incorporating fruits into the diet of diabetic patients yields remarkably positive outcomes.

Letting Others Do It For you

I've witnessed numerous instances where a concerned friend or family member drags their unwell partner into my clinic and expects me to dictate the path to healing. They thrust their ailing loved one into a detox regimen, taking on the role of preparing juices, meals, and herbal supplements. Unfortunately, this approach tends to result in failure about nine times out of ten. The individual who's unwell lacks the genuine motivation and true desire to recover.

Active participation in your own healing is crucial. This partly explains why you fall ill in the first place. If you truly want wellness and good health, you need to fuel it with your own determination and actions, just as you would for any experience or possession you desire in life.

While it's valuable to have the support of loved ones, it's important not to let their involvement overshadow your personal aspirations and objectives. Your desire to regain health must emerge from within you. You need to become a shining example of the incredible power of the divine, but that starts with showing it to yourself.

Within the pancreas lies a segment known as the Islets of Langerhans, containing the beta cells responsible for insulin production and release. Inflammation or congestion can render this part of the pancreas hypoactive, resulting in insufficient insulin production.

The Islets of Langerhans encompass three cell types: alpha cells (secreting glucagon to raise blood glucose), beta cells (secreting insulin to lower blood glucose), and delta cells (releasing somatostatin, which inhibits insulin, glucagon, growth hormone, and gastrin secretion). In diabetes mellitus, the beta cells are primarily affected.

Both types of diabetes, particularly type I, often involve genetic transmission of pancreatic weakness. Nevertheless, lifestyle choices can contribute to pancreatic debility during one's lifetime. This is particularly evident in type II or late onset diabetes. Multiple generations might pass before inflammation or toxicity-induced weakness leads to diabetes. It might initially manifest as hypoglycemia or gestational diabetes before evolving into a permanent form of the condition. The degree of pancreatic weakness varies across individuals, and it's essential to recognize that someone had to initiate this weakness originally. The crucial question is: "How did it originate?"

Diabetes is often considered an autoimmune issue, where lymphocytes attack and obliterate the beta cells. In my perspective, this interpretation misunderstands the body's protective mechanisms. Remember, the immune system's role is to eliminate weakness. It doesn't target itself without cause. The allopathic medical field struggles to find an explanation for this autoimmune response beyond genetic factors. However, the true cause of this reaction becomes evident when considering nature's principle of survival of the fittest. The strong endure, while the weak perish. Nature eliminates the weak, rather than perpetuating them.

I've witnessed cases where diabetes was triggered by pancreatic flukes. These parasites can infiltrate the liver and pancreas. An effective detox program typically addresses harmful parasites in the body. However, it's important to note that parasites aren't the primary cause of disease or tissue failure. They manifest as a secondary issue due to existing toxicity and tissue weakness.

ADRENAL GLANDS

One of the often overlooked yet highly significant connections lies between the pancreas and the adrenal glands. The adrenal cortex is responsible for generating adrenocortical hormones. Within this group, glucocorticoids like cortisol and corticosterone have a primary impact on carbohydrate metabolism. Cortisol and cortisone fulfill various roles, encompassing anti-inflammatory functions as well as carbohydrate digestion and metabolism. This functionality is essentially catabolic, engaging in the process of breaking down substances.

Moreover, the adrenal glands are responsible for manufacturing neurotransmitters that influence the functioning of the pancreas. This underscores the importance of addressing both of these glands. Strengthening the adrenal glands is consistently crucial, as they maintain a pivotal relationship with every single cell within the body.

Body Fuels

Glucose and fructose are vital basic sugars essential for powering your body, much like how your car requires fuel for operation. Simple sugars necessitate significantly lower levels of insulin compared to complex sugars. Complex sugars, such as maltose, dextrose, and refined sucrose, need to be broken down into simpler forms before the body can utilize them. This process results in heightened insulin demands and contributes to excessive glucose levels, leading to the storage of fat.

Amino acids constitute the structural components, while sugars like glucose and fructose serve as the energy sources. It's essential to avoid using proteins as energy sources, as doing so can lead to tissue damage, cancer, and ultimately, adverse health outcomes. Proteins are intended for building and not as sources of energy.

THYROID/PARATHYROID

The role of the thyroid and parathyroid gland should also be taken into account due to their influence on metabolism and the regulation of calcium utilization. Insufficient calcium utilization can lead to a general weakening of all cells within the body. Additionally, calcium has an impact on the utilization of essential minerals like zinc, selenium, and iron, which in turn affect glucose utilization and overall cellular activities.

HYPOTHALAMUS AND PITUITARY

Another aspect of vulnerability to take into consideration regarding diabetes involves the hypothalamus and pituitary gland. The posterior section of the pituitary gland, regulated by the hypothalamus (the body's central control system), releases an anti-diuretic hormone that, when functioning inadequately, leads to diabetes insipidus. It's also noteworthy that the transverse colon is central to a significant portion—around eighty percent or more—of the upper brain weaknesses, with particular emphasis on the pituitary and hypothalamus regions. With a more comprehensive comprehension of the gastrointestinal tract, especially the colon and its interconnectedness with organs and glands, you'll realize why a healthy GI tract is essential to support the overall well-being of the body.

GI TRACT AND DIABETES

The gastrointestinal tract maintains connections with all the organs and glands throughout your body. Similar to the central hub of a wheel, the GI tract serves as the central hub of your bodily functions. If the GI tract becomes encumbered by decaying deposits from meat and flour-based products, the consequent inflammation and toxicity generated have a ripple effect on interconnected regions. For this reason, it is imperative to cleanse and fortify the GI tract, as it holds a pivotal role in achieving favorable outcomes in various health conditions, including diabetes.

THE TRUE CAUSES OF DIABETES

Various theories exist concerning the origins of diabetes, ranging from cholesterol buildup around beta cells, autoimmune disturbances, genetic factors, stress, and obesity. Every cell in the body carries genetic information, with some cells becoming more susceptible to weaknesses based on the mentioned factors. These vulnerabilities are amplified and transmitted across generations. Due to limited awareness of this reality, the human population is grappling with significant tissue weaknesses, leading predominantly to persistent and degenerative ailments. It's crucial to recognize that the fundamental causes of any disease boil down to two factors: toxicity and acidosis, manifesting as inflammation. These triggers stem from what you consume, drink, breathe, apply to your skin, and even your thoughts and emotions. These choices either fortify your body and its cells or contribute to their weakening.

TREATING DIABETES

I have consistently recommended a diet centered on raw fruits and vegetables for individuals with diabetes. This particular dietary approach serves to cleanse and rejuvenate both the pancreas and adrenal glands. Adhering to proper food combinations is equally important (refer to Chapter 7, Eating for Vitality), as improper combinations leading to food fermentation and putrefaction can negatively impact blood sugar levels and the pancreas. I also incorporate an herbal detoxification regimen and a specialized formula aimed at supporting the pancreas alongside this diet (detailed in Chapter 8, which covers herbs and herbal formulas for such support).

For type II diabetes cases, if a thorough detoxification program is followed along with the use of high-quality herbal supplements, insulin dependency can typically be reduced or eliminated within a timeframe of three to eight weeks. It's crucial, however, to collaborate with a qualified healthcare practitioner throughout this detox process. Monitoring blood sugar levels diligently is of utmost importance, as rapid drops can occur, and excessive insulin administration may lead to dangerous situations such as coma.

Prudence and carefulness should be exercised. If you're self-monitoring your blood sugars while using insulin, transient increases in blood sugar levels due to specific fruits are not uncommon. Should you identify a particular fruit causing this effect, temporarily excluding it from your diet until your blood sugars stabilize is advisable. Remember, the primary objective is to cleanse and rejuvenate the pancreas and adrenal glands, rather than merely treating the symptoms of diabetes.

Keep in mind that complex sugars like sucrose, maltose, and dextrose can burden your system with excess glucose. Relying solely on insulin to manage this heightened glucose load isn't the solution; it's wiser to avoid these complex sugar-rich foods altogether.

Furthermore, it's noteworthy that proteins, especially meat, can also lead to elevated blood sugar levels. The protein-rich nature of meat disrupts balance in the body, prompting the breakdown of fat and its conversion to glucose, resulting in an increase in blood glucose levels.

While diabetes has numerous contributing factors, it's essential to maintain simplicity in your approach. Nourishing your body with foods inherently designed for it—namely, fruits, vegetables, and nuts—is key.

The maxim "There are no incurable diseases, only incurable people" underscores the idea that some individuals may not embrace recovery due to various reasons. Some may use their illness to garner attention, and some might seek love and support from others. In your journey to health, cultivate strength from within, allocate time for introspection, and gather knowledge about foods and their effects on tissue. Instead of fearing the natural order, trust in the potential for healing. While diabetes carries formidable consequences, its remedy is fundamentally straightforward. Opting for six months to a year of dedicated healing efforts far outweighs enduring a lifetime of suffering. Embrace freedom from illness and reclaim your health.

MODULE 5.8

Weight Loss and Control: Addressing the Cause

There are multiple factors contributing to the issue of obesity, which has become a significant global concern, particularly within the United States. Tommy Thompson, Secretary of Health and Human Services, stated in the New York Times in January 2003 that 25 percent of the U.S. adult population, approximately 50 million individuals, are obese. Today, over 40 percent of U.S. adults are obese.

When addressing obesity, it's crucial to focus on the root causes rather than mere symptoms. Societal perceptions often label fat as excessive, unhealthy, or indicative of a lack of control, driving individuals to strive relentlessly to eliminate it from their bodies. In some cases, people resign themselves to obesity, suppressing inner frustrations and anxieties, which can further exacerbate the problem.

To understand the origins of obesity, we must first consider the endocrine glandular system. An under-active condition of the thyroid and adrenal glands is frequently associated with obesity. Hypothyroidism, in particular, is a common trigger. Conventional medical practitioners rely on blood tests to assess thyroid activity by measuring TSHs, T3s, and T4s levels. However, these tests often prove to be inaccurate, as evidenced by my extensive observations. The Basal Temperature Test (see Appendix A) was developed due to the shortcomings of these blood tests. In numerous cases, I've encountered patients with normal T3s and T4s readings, yet they exhibit symptoms such as cold extremities, hair loss, fatigue, brittle nails, heart issues, depression, or vocal weakness, all indicative of hypothyroidism.

The adrenal glands also play a significant role in obesity, particularly when the adrenal cortex functions sub-optimally. This can disrupt steroid production related to carbohydrate metabolism, causing the conversion of complex sugars (such as starch) and glucose into fat instead of proper metabolic utilization. Additionally, the pituitary gland, the master gland, might also be implicated.

Dietary habits constitute another prevalent cause of obesity. Our society has a preference for disaccharides, which are complex sugars like sucrose, dextrose, maltose, and lactose. However, our bodies can only process simple sugars: glucose, fructose, or, in infants, galactose. Complex sugar molecules must be broken down into simple sugars before cells can use them for energy. Excess complex sugars are converted and stored as glycogen or fat. The standard American diet also incorporates an abundance of saturated fats that become even more saturated in an acidic environment. This renders them less available for cellular nourishment and energy, resulting in a sticky condition within the bloodstream and vascular system, causing issues like plaque formation and clumping of red blood cells.

Starchy foods, such as grains, are widely embraced by humans. Unsprouted grains are not only low in available nutrients but also acid-forming, hard to digest, and contribute to weight gain due to their gluey starch composition. The rationale behind feeding grains to livestock, like cattle and hogs, is to fatten them for market.

Genetics undeniably influence our body's functioning. Every cell carries genetic information, though some cells are stronger than others. Weak cells can lead to glandular weaknesses, which are subsequently inherited across generations. This generational pattern of weakening can only be counteracted if someone initiates the process of strengthening their genetically compromised cells.

EMOTIONAL COMPONENTS OF WEIGHT GAIN

Our society has evolved into a state of heightened emotional sensitivity and interdependence, resulting in emotional and mental fragility. This deeply impacts the issue of obesity, as we've learned to substitute sugary or refined foods—often referred to as "comfort foods"—when experiencing emotional vulnerabilities and pain. Given our frugivorous nature, sweet foods align with our biological requirements. However, it's important for these sugars to be simple sugars, as opposed to complex sugars that tend to be stored as fat.

If you desire to transform your life, invest time in introspection to truly understand your essence. You possess a divine nature, a manifestation of God's creation. Uniqueness defines creation, and relishing your individuality can bring joy. From birth to death, we traverse existence largely in solitude, with only chosen companions accompanying us along the way. Thus, embracing self-love becomes crucial, for you are your primary companion aside from the Divine presence.

Your mind serves as the most potent tool for creation. Your self-perception shapes your experiences. To attain a slender physique, envision yourself as such. Many obese individuals struggle to view themselves as thin due to their personal feelings of not being thin. By cultivating a feeling of thinness, you'll gradually see yourself in that light. Shifting your diet to consist of fresh raw fruits and salads can instill a sense of lightness, cleanliness, and thinness within your body. The dietary recommendations outlined in this book can facilitate fat loss while simultaneously bolstering cellular function, elevating your overall vitality.

Dedicate attention to your endocrine gland system, particularly the thyroid and adrenal glands. Embracing a raw food diet and integrating herbs into your routine can spark regeneration in virtually every aspect. The process of self-reconstruction can be a delightful endeavor. Cultivate self-contentment and savor divine presence in every moment. Release negative emotions like anger, envy, jealousy, or hatred, and usher in a profound love for all forms of life, recognizing the inherent divinity within each.

THE DANGER OF HIGH PROTEIN DIETS

When attempting weight loss, the recourse of adopting high protein diets is frequently pursued. However, such diets can prove detrimental to our well-being, particularly when the protein derives from animal sources. The process of breaking down these complex protein structures into simple amino acids demands substantial time and energy from the body before they can be utilized. It's important to note that the body cannot directly employ protein structures; instead, it relies on converting them into amino acids. The energy expended for this conversion leads to the breakdown of stored fat as the body endeavors to secure the necessary energy for protein transformation.

Amino acids serve as the foundational components for the growth and repair of bodily tissues. Their purpose isn't to serve as cellular fuel. If we attempt to utilize amino acids as fuel, this triggers an excessive demand for energy, resulting in the deterioration of liver, pancreatic, and kidney tissue and functionality. Furthermore, the body's muscle tissue will degrade, leading to a state of weakness and, in severe cases, even death. Tragically, numerous fatalities arise annually due to the toxicity stemming from excessive protein consumption. Protein is characterized by its acidic nature and high content of phosphorus (nitrogen) and iron, which disrupts electrolyte balance, especially calcium levels. This acidity fosters inflammation and the accumulation of mucus in the body, culminating in eventual cellular demise. Recognizing the genuine biological requirements of our bodies and the dire consequences of high protein diets is of paramount significance.

SIMPLE SUGARS ARE THE ANSWER

Sugars play a pivotal role as the essential energy source for cellular sustenance. However, it's crucial that these sugars are of simple kind, as commonly found in fruits and vegetables.

On the contrary, the intricate sugars present in grains, refined sugars, dairy products, and similar items contribute to the storage of fats, and they carry an acidic nature that leads to congestion.

Adopting a diet centered on raw fruits and vegetables provides an abundance of vital nutrients, encompassing both simple sugars and amino acids. Embracing these foods in their raw state can contribute significantly to weight reduction, especially when adhered to entirely. Simultaneously, this approach aids in cleansing the body while initiating improvements in the function of the thyroid and adrenal glands. It's imperative to emphasize the role of glands, as they wield substantial influence over all 76 trillion cells within the body. Their impact extends to various metabolic processes—digestive, sugar-related, and fat metabolism—ultimately determining weight management and overall energy levels.

Excessive Thinness

Numerous individuals grapple with the challenge of excessive leanness, often stemming from compromised digestion and issues with the pancreas, as well as malabsorption within the digestive tract. When the process of breaking down food into essential components and energy sources is hindered, or when the digestive tract becomes congested to the point of hindering nutrient absorption, the body is at risk of malnourishment and wasting. Surprisingly, even in cases of hypothyroidism, a condition often linked to weight gain, a weak pancreas and obstructed digestive tract can lead to pronounced thinness despite thyroid under-activity. Rectifying this state may require a prolonged effort, yet the pursuit of restored health is undoubtedly worthwhile.

It's worth noting that many, including medical professionals, tend to associate excessive thinness with decline, prompting them to suggest dietary interventions aimed at weight gain. These recommendations often focus on dairy-derived fats and grains, though these choices can exacerbate cellular weakness due to their congestive and acidic attributes.

For those engaging in a detoxification regimen and observing weight loss, a pivotal inquiry emerges: "Why is weight decreasing despite introducing more nutrition and superior amino acids through a raw food diet?" A potential response is that as the body grows stronger and healthier, it naturally discards toxins and weakened cells, creating space for the development of new, more robust cells. This transformative process may involve the shedding of tissues like nails, skin, and muscles, particularly when those tissues are too frail to respond to the body's efforts at rejuvenation. This phenomenon should not be a source of concern; regrown tissues tend to be stronger and healthier.

Moreover, it's important to acknowledge that some individuals embarking on a raw fruit and vegetable diet might initially experience weight gain. This often results from water retention —a natural consequence of these foods' high water content. Such water retention generally occurs when the body is excessively acidic and harbors a surplus of acidic deposits. The body retains water as a buffering mechanism to counteract these conditions. Although short-lived, this process is actually advantageous.

Embarking on the journey of embracing a diet focused on vitality and health demands patience and enthusiasm. Amid this new adventure, individuals are likely to witness the pounds gradually dissolve away.

MODULE 5.9

The Skin and Its Disorders

Your skin stands as the body's most expansive vital organ, fulfilling tasks ranging from temperature regulation and safeguarding to the process of elimination. It is often dubbed the "third kidney" due to its role in elimination and its connection to the detoxification process. Your skin is designed to expel daily amounts of waste comparable to those managed by your lungs, kidneys, and bowels. This elimination encompasses mucus, toxins (acids), and gases.

The repercussions or byproducts of many consumed foods can contribute to congestion and inflammation within the system. Skin issues manifest as visible indicators of this underlying process. As the body strives to expel these byproducts, a spectrum of manifestations can arise, spanning from dandruff, pimples, and rashes, to more severe conditions such as dermatitis, psoriasis, and even skin cancer—where psoriasis and skin cancer represent the most toxic and parasitically influenced among these skin conditions.

Parasites, functioning as scavengers, thrive in areas with toxicity and deceased or decaying cells, including within skin layers and on the skin's surface. While these symptoms might be labeled as "diseases," they all share a common origin. The severity differs, but the root cause remains consistent. Conventional medical practitioners often turn to cortisone or steroids like prednisone for treating skin conditions, which can inadvertently drive toxins and parasites deeper into the tissues, exacerbating proper elimination challenges.

As toxins congest the skin and eliminative organs, a similar backlog develops in the liver. For individuals grappling with skin issues—whether minor pimples or severe dermatitis and psoriasis—detoxification becomes imperative, with a primary focus on the lymphatic system, liver, kidneys, and bowels. Eliminating dairy products and refined sugars is crucial, as these substances intensify tissue congestion. This congestion becomes an attractive feeding ground for fungi, leading to the development of Candida albicans, a yeast overgrowth. Effective herbal parasite formulas can help combat most of these fungi, but unless the underlying toxicity and congestion are addressed, recurrence remains likely.

Fever serves as one of the body's most effective mechanisms for skin-based elimination. Elevated body temperature amplifies perspiration, thereby enhancing the expulsion of toxins, poisons, and mucus. Consequently, the body might manifest cold or flu-like symptoms in response to parasite attacks, stimulation, or detoxification efforts (alkalization). It is essential not to suppress these symptoms, as they represent a natural bodily response to bolster elimination—a vital aspect of recovery.

Lack of perspiration can lead to skin congestion, resulting in dryness and inflammation. Moisturizers are commonly employed to counter this issue, yet they can compound congestion within the skin's deeper layers. The health of your skin is intrinsically linked to your internal well-being. Thus, maintaining a healthy body internally directly reflects on the external health of your skin. If external nourishment is necessary, consider employing pure, raw, organic grape seed oil, olive oil, mixed tocopherol vitamin E, jojoba oil, or essential oils.

Individuals with hypothyroidism, affecting 60 to 70 percent of the population, often struggle to sweat. Thyroid function profoundly influences perspiration levels, potentially leading to excessive sweating or insufficient perspiration. Sedentary habits and a lack of physical activity also contribute to reduced sweating. Refer to Chapter 9, "Healthy Habits," for insights on cold-sheet treatments and dry skin brushing, simple techniques to augment skin elimination. Just as a raw food diet supports cellular health, it is equally indispensable for fostering vibrant skin health. When your skin experiences sagging or wrinkling, it is not merely a sign of aging but rather indicative of skin weakness.

Bestow care upon your skin as you would any vital organ. It's vital to recognize the interconnection between the skin, thyroid, and liver. Thus, prioritize liver detoxification and ensure proper thyroid function, which can be assessed more accurately using the Basal Temperature Test (refer to Appendix A). As you embark on detoxification and regeneration, your entire body will express its gratitude by bestowing robust health. I've witnessed individuals in their eighties and nineties regain vibrant, wrinkle-free, toned, and tightened skin. The human body is an incredible, intelligent machine—nurture it, for it serves as your vessel throughout your time on Earth.

MODULE 5.10

Mind, Emotions and the Cells

Until now, we've explored the substantial influence and consequences that various foods and toxins wield over your body. Let's delve into the more subtle mechanisms that shape your well-being and contribute to the onset of disease.

The two most influential tools you possess to shape your experience in the physical world are your mind and emotions. Your corporeal form acts as a vessel that houses your consciousness. The ability to conceptualize sequences of events, a product of your thought processes, empowers you to craft the events in your life. However, the emotional aspect is equally vital, as it fuels your desire to manifest these envisioned sequences. As your mind stitches together images from the past and present to form future scenarios, your emotions propel you to transform these mental constructs into tangible reality. The intensity of your emotions toward a certain idea or image plays a pivotal role in how profoundly you'll immerse yourself in that experience, regardless of its nature. This creative interplay is further influenced by your ego, which forms the basis of your individual identity. The interweaving of these elements gives rise to the tapestry of existence.

The mind and emotions possess the capacity to either serve as constructive agents or turn into destructive forces by exerting control and enslavement. I propose channeling your mind and emotions towards rejuvenation and enhancement. Keep in mind that the mind operates on images. Your imaginative constructs eventually assume the guise of reality, be it on a subtle or palpable level. Channel this process to your advantage. Visualize yourself embodying health and vitality, an endeavor where emotions play a pivotal role. Infuse enthusiasm into your vision of a vibrant life. Allow your emotions to fuel your journey towards success. Immerse yourself in literature and resources about raw foods and detoxification, nurturing your soul's comprehension of your corporeal vessel. A profound comprehension of our bodies as soul dwellings is vital, as these bodies facilitate our passage through creation. It is imperative to harness the body's potential for our highest good. What you manifest emotionally and mentally engenders your reality.

Achieving genuine health and vitality entails achieving equilibrium among these "bodies" of mind and emotion. These aspects wield mutual influence. Negative emotions like anger, hate, and jealousy can disrupt physical well-being, inducing sickness and disease in the body. These emotions tend to accumulate in the liver and kidneys, impeding proper pancreatic function (digestion) and other glandular processes. Emotional turmoil can even subdue our cognitive faculties, hindering comprehension, thought processes, and rational decision-making. This turmoil can particularly block the heart centers. Closure of the heart center drastically diminishes the potential for healing, potentially leading to fatal outcomes.

Among my cancer patients, some remained beyond assistance due to the closure of their heart centers, often rooted in difficulties opening themselves to love. For certain individuals, this presents a multifaceted and deeply ingrained dilemma.

This is where practices such as meditation, personal introspection, and spiritual guidance come into play.

Embrace life's essence for what it is. Immerse yourself in nature and envelop yourself with the soothing energies of flowers and plants, which harbor healing attributes. Nature resonates with love's energies. By relinquishing the past, you can relish each moment for its inherent beauty. Release all harbored hate, anger, and judgments—surrender them to a higher power. Personally, I hold close the adage "Let go and let God."

Love, happiness, joy, health, and mental equilibrium all conspire to keep the heart center open. Conversely, unhappiness, depression, despair, anger, jealousy, rage, envy, and other negative states can shut down or stifle the heart center. Similarly, the mind must be mastered, as it's been said that the mind is an exemplary servant yet a dismal and even harmful master.

Thought processes frequently distance us from savoring the present moment, often referred to as the "eternal now." Recall the days of your childhood when the present moment appeared to stretch indefinitely? Those moments, laden with play and excitement, felt boundless. With maturity, these timeless interludes succumbed to the clutches of thought and desire. Conventional educational systems often breed competition and curtail free thinking, just as materialistic pursuits encroach on freedom and happiness. These dynamics have collectively blunted our awareness and dulled our connection to God—the source of genuine vitality, bliss, and contentment.

Initiating detoxification of your physical body sets in motion a sequence of events that facilitates cleansing and control of emotional and mental processes. This journey can be supported by permitting the release and fading away of old thought patterns and associated emotions that may surface during detoxification. Several approaches can facilitate this process.

Embark by observing your thoughts. Adopt the stance of an impartial observer, distancing yourself from the outcome of events and the emotional responses of others. Release. Entrust matters to the realm of spirit, to God, or to your higher mind. Shed negative emotions and mental shackles. This paves the way for the most potent healing energy to course through your mental, emotional, and physical "bodies," inducing a vibrancy and awareness that words fail to encapsulate. Revel in life's marvels, embracing each fleeting instant. Grant yourself the liberty to expand and partake in new experiences. Extricate yourself from conditioned modes of thinking and feeling; metamorphose into a vigorous, thriving being. The time to embark on this transformation is now.

GLANDS, EMOTIONS AND HEALTH

It's crucial to recognize that an imbalance in your glandular system translates to an imbalance in your overall well-being. This is particularly evident with the trio of essential glands: the pituitary, thyroid, and adrenal glands.

When the thyroid gland's activity diminishes, there's a decline in calcium utilization. This can trigger various forms of depression, ranging from mild to persistent. On the other hand, when the adrenal glands become under-active, anxiety can engulf you. The spectrum of responses spans from slight shyness and introversion to apprehension, chronic worry and anxiety, acute anxiety attacks, and even intense fear leading to isolation. Conditions like bipolar disorder, schizophrenia, and similar psychological states manifest due to the interplay of factors mentioned above, influencing calcium levels, serotonin, neurotransmitters, and more. This underscores the profound connection between the well-being of your physical body and the equilibrium of your mental and emotional dimensions. These facets are intricately intertwined, forming a unified expression of your overall state.

Summary

Discover the hidden knowledge that paves the way to the well-being and liveliness of your physical body, emotions, and thoughts. Assume control over these essential instruments or aspects. They serve as your means of expression during your time in this existence. Purify and cleanse your body through detoxification. Release or transform all your emotions, allowing love to prevail. Transcend your mind, entering the realm of the present moment. Embrace your authentic self, distinct from your thoughts. Utilize your thoughts solely for constructive creation, focusing on what you truly require rather than mere desires.

MODULE 5.11

Body Language: What is Your Body Trying to Tell You

Nothing occurs in life without an underlying cause. Every event and change is propelled by a reason. Just as when you choose to embark on a lengthy walk, your decision arises from a combination of thoughts and emotions, driven by the desire to do so. Similarly, the cells within your body operate on the same principle. They react and respond based on thoughts and emotions, although these influences are often subtle and nearly subconscious in nature.

Although cells possess automatic functionality, they are significantly influenced by various compounds like hormones, steroids, neurotransmitters, and serotonin. These substances trigger reactions within tissues (cells), prompting them to respond or behave in specific ways, influenced by the initial thoughts and emotions. For instance, consider fear. If confronted with a terrifying sight, your brain sends a message to the adrenal glands to release adrenaline, boosting heart rate, blood circulation, and muscle activity to empower either flight or fight responses. This message transmission originated from your awareness of the situation.

Cells exhibit responsiveness to stimuli, yielding either positive or negative outcomes contingent upon the source of the stimulus. As emphasized throughout this book, the foods consumed, beverages consumed, air breathed, and substances applied to the skin can either bolster cells, tissues, organs, and glands or have a detrimental effect. Adverse influences can lead to decreased cell activity and tissue function, potentially resulting in cell demise. In response, weakened or dying cells might alter their function or structure, become targets for parasitic invasion, or be eliminated by immune cells.

As this process of cellular deterioration unfolds, the body as a whole begins to experience repercussions. This creates a ripple effect, inducing shifts in the body's functioning. These changes manifest as a kind of "body language," forming a sequence of signals that you or a healthcare practitioner can decipher. If you cultivate attentiveness and familiarize yourself with your body's communication methods, you can ascertain which organs and glands might be experiencing dysfunction. This component should be used in conjunction with Module 5.12, the Health Questionnaire, which concludes this section. The questionnaire aids in reflecting on diverse bodily processes and systems, pinpointing their vulnerabilities.

For now, the ensuing lists provide some instances of "body language" cues or outcomes that I've accumulated from over thirty years of experience as a healthcare practitioner. While some of these might sound akin to diseases, they actually represent the effects of organ or glandular weaknesses and deficiencies.

THE LANGUAGE OF THE GLANDS, ORGANS AND SYSTEMS

Thyroid (Endocrine Gland System)

Weakness or failure of the thyroid will show up as:

- Obesity (if your pancreas is weak, you can be thin and still have a thyroid weakness)

- Low Metabolism (can give you poor digestion)

- Low Body Temperature (cold extremities and cold intolerance)

- Hair loss and balding

- Failure to sweat properly, affecting skin elimination (creates dry skin and other conditions)

Parathyroid (Endocrine Gland System)

Calcium requires a parathyroid hormone so it can be utilized properly by your body. Failure to utilize calcium results in:

- Bone loss (Osteoporosis, spinal deterioration or herniated disks)

- Bone (calcium) spurs

- Arthritis (adrenal gland weakness must also be present)

- Connective tissue weakness, causing prolapsed conditions (dropping) of skin, bladder, uterus, bowels, and other organs

- Varicose veins and spider veins

- Hemorrhoids
- Depression
- Nerve weakness
- Spasms, cramping of muscles, convulsions
- Dehydration
- Ridged, brittle or weakened fingernails
- Anemia (low calcium causes poor iron utilization)
- Scoliosis
- Ruptured Discs
- Hernias
- Aneurysms
- MVP (mitral valve prolapse—heart)

Adrenal Glands (Endocrine Gland System)

Linked to the nervous system, inflammation, carbohydrate utilization, healing and repair of tissues. Weakness or failure of these glands will be seen as:

- "itis's" (all inflammatory conditions)
- Fibrocystic conditions
- Fibromyalgia, scleroderma and sciatica
- Ovarian cysts
- Excessive bleeding

- Endometriosis and atypical cell formation
- Prostatitis
- Prostate cancer
- All female cancers
- Multiple Sclerosis and Parkinson's Disease
- Tremors
- Tinnitus (ringing in the ears)
- Shortness of breath
- Cholesterol plaquing
- Dehydration
- Anxieties, excessive shyness, emotional sensitivities, and other related conditions
- Sleep disorders
- Memory problems
- Early puberty, initial menstruation, and irregular menstruation
- Conception problems
- Sexual problems (including lack of or excessive sex drive, impotence, erection problems, frigidity in women, and fertility problems)
- Low Energy (Chronic Fatigue)
- Low endurance

Pancreas (Digestive and Endocrine Gland System)

Hypo-activity (under-activity) of the pancreas can cause the following:

- Gas and bloating during digestion
- Undigested foods in your stools
- Excessive thinness
- Loss of muscle tissue
- Moles growing on your skin
- Low blood sugar (Hypoglycemia)
- High blood sugar (Diabetes, etc.)
- Acid reflux
- Gastritis
- Enteritis
- Nausea

Liver and Gallbladder (Hepatic/Blood System—Your Chemical Factory)

When the liver or gallbladder becomes toxic, inflamed and full of stones, the following symptoms may appear:

- Bloating and Acid-Reflux conditions
- Enteritis
- Poor digestion

- Anemia
- Low amino acid utilization
- Low hemoglobin and albumin count
- Skin toxicity (resulting in dermatitis, eczema, psoriasis, and other conditions)
- White stools
- Liver spots (skin pigmentation changes)
- Starvation
- Low cholesterol production = low steroid production = more inflammation
- Lower resistance to inflammation
- Lowers cell wall protection
- Gastritis
- Nausea after eating
- Loss of muscle tissue (low protein utilization)
- Low cholesterol levels
- Sugar problems (high or low blood sugars)

Gastrointestinal Tract (Digestive and Eliminative Systems)

Your digestive system, spanning from the stomach to the anus, serves as the central core of your body's functions. If it falters due to obstructions and inflammation, it can lead to a decline in overall bodily health and nourishment. When the gastrointestinal (GI) tract encounters difficulties, the rest of the body is likely to suffer in tandem. Below are several examples of the consequences that arise from its malfunction:

- Malabsorption and starvation
- Gastritis, enteritis and/or colitis
- Diverticulitis (when "pockets" are formed from impactions)
- Gas
- Diarrhea
- Constipation (also connected to adrenal medulla weakness)
- Parasites (worms, and others; the unfriendly type)
- Crohn's disease
- GI cancer (now second most prevalent type of cancer in the U.S.)
- When the GI Tract becomes toxic, it sends toxicity to all parts of the body
- Appendicitis
- Lymphatic congestion (blocks proper lymphatic elimination)
- Nausea upon eating

Lymphatic System (Immune and Eliminative "Septic" System)

The primary function of the lymphatic system is to cleanse and safeguard the body. It holds equal significance to the circulatory blood system. Regrettably, the lymphatic system is often disregarded and necessitates greater care. The onset of all diseases occurs when this system becomes overwhelmed and ceases to function properly. The ensuing are merely a selection of observable outcomes:

- Colds and flu-like symptoms
- Many childhood diseases (mumps, measles, etc.)
- Most respiratory congestion issues
- Sinus congestion
- Earaches
- Hearing loss (causing the need for tubes in the ears)
- Sore throats
- Cysts and tumors
- Boils, pimples and the like
- Lymphatic cancers
- Appendicitis
- Low immune response
- Low lymphocytes (when the lymph gland called the spleen is affected)
- Low platelets and a lack of blood cleansing can take place.
- Lymph edema from removed or degenerated lymph nodes
- Lymph node swelling
- Allergies

- Cellulitis
- Blurred vision
- Cataracts and glaucoma
- Snoring
- Sleep apnea
- Tonsillitis
- Stiff neck
- Cervical spine deterioration from stagnant lymph system in neck (especially when tonsils have been removed)
- Dandruff

Kidneys and Bladder (Eliminative/Urinary Tract System)

These organs play a crucial role in the body's process of elimination. When metabolic wastes, originating from both cellular and digestive processes, are not adequately expelled, the accumulation of toxic by-products can lead to self-intoxication of cells. This contributes to cellular debilitation and demise. The ensuing list represents indications or cautionary signs that the body manifests when the kidneys and bladder encounter weakness.

- Bags under your eyes
- Vision problems
- Lower back weakness and pain
- Kidney stones (contributing factor to parathyroid weakness)

- Urinary tract infections—UTI (burning upon urination)
- Loss of bladder control (incontinence)
- Difficulty urinating (can be urinary tract infections as well)
- Increased acidosis
- Dehydration
- Edema (contributing factor)
- Toxemia
- Headaches
- Can affect your breathing

Heart and Circulation (The Circulatory System)

Numerous conditions impacting the heart and circulatory system have been discussed in relation to various glands and their repercussions on the body. This is because many conditions within the body are reflex conditions that have an origination point other than the obvious symptoms. For instance, conditions like mitral valve prolapse and heart arrhythmia have their roots in the parathyroid, where the nervous system and connective tissue may be influenced. Additionally, the adrenal glands play a pivotal role in the nerve network that supplies the heart. In cases of weakened adrenal glands and uncontrolled acidosis, cholesterol can accumulate and form plaques, potentially leading to blockages, heart attacks, and strokes within the vascular system. It is imperative to comprehensively consider these factors when addressing matters concerning the heart and circulatory system. The ensuing list enumerates some of the indicators the body presents when these heart and circulatory tissues are impacted.

- Poor circulation leads to cellular death (which leads to a multitude of problems)
- Gray hair
- Memory loss
- Chest pain or angina
- Feeling of "heaviness" or "weight" on top of your chest
- Petechiae (bruising easily)
- Blood Regurgitation (back flow) from weak valves (causing chest pain)
- High or low systolic blood pressure (adrenal gland relationship)
- High diastolic (bottom number)
- Tired feeling (especially during exercise)
- S.O.B. (shortness of breath) from water buildup, congestive heart failure (CHF), and myocardial edema (fluids around the heart). Water build-up is an inflammatory issue from acidosis.
- Low endurance (also adrenal gland relationship)
- Cramping or spasms upon exercise
- Contributes to lymphatic blockages, causing sluggish lymphatic issues

- All types of heart arrhythmias (however, thyroid and adrenal gland weakness is mostly to blame.)

Skin (Integumentary and Eliminative System)

Your skin functions as the primary organ for elimination within your body. Its role entails expelling waste on a scale comparable to your kidneys and bowels. Yet, when congestion occurs in the liver, bowels, and lymphatic system, it overloads the skin, causing it to function sluggishly and become obstructed. Consequently, numerous skin conditions arise from this situation. Moreover, when the thyroid is compromised, the ability to sweat becomes diminished, further hindering effective elimination through the skin. An impairment of the skin's customary functions can lead to:

- Skin rashes

- Dry skin

- Eczema

- Boils, pimples, etc. (related to lymphatic system)

- Dermatitis

- Psoriasis

- Splitting of the skin

Lungs (Respiratory System)

The process of breathing and the functioning of the lungs are responsible for introducing the most significant sources of energy and oxidation into our body. It goes without saying that life depends on oxygen; its presence facilitates the conversion of elements into different compounds through transmutation, which is an inherent natural process. The subsequent signs and symptoms clearly signal the presence of lung congestion, toxicity, and acidosis:

- Bronchitis and pneumonia
- Asthma
- S.O.B. (shortness of breath)
- Chronic coughing
- Emphysema
- C.O.P.D. (chronic obstructive pulmonary disease)
- Pain in lung areas
- Fatigue (also thyroid and adrenal gland weakness)
- Low endurance (also caused from adrenal gland weakness)
- Sore throat (begins here)
- High carbon dioxide levels
- Toxemia

MODULE 5.12

The Health Questionnaire

Having examined body language in Module 5.11, this Health Questionnaire serves to further enhance your understanding of your body's condition by highlighting areas where organs, glands, or systems might be experiencing inadequate performance. Once you identify these weak points, you can implement the dietary recommendations provided in this book, along with utilizing specific herbal formulas tailored to address these particular areas. Refer to Chapter 8, Module 8.3 for Herbal Formulas associated with each system.

This Questionnaire can also prove invaluable when shared with your healthcare practitioner. It delves into aspects that might not be covered by standard medical history questionnaires, potentially uncovering subjects that may not have been discussed previously. Utilize it as a collaborative tool to work together with your healthcare provider in devising the most effective approach for your detoxification and regeneration program.

THYROID/PARATHYROID (GLANDULAR SYSTEM)

Are you overweight?	Yes	No
Do you get cold hands and feet?	Yes	No
Do you have hair loss or are you bald or going bald?	Yes	No
Is it easy to put on weight and hard to loose it?	Yes	No
Are your fingernails ridged, brittle or weak?	Yes	No
Do you have varicose or spider veins?	Yes	No
Do you have, or have you had, hemorrhoids?	Yes	No
Do you get cramping in your muscles?	Yes	No
Is your bladder strong or weak?	Strong	Weak
Do you have an irregular heartbeat?	Yes	No
Do you have mitral valve prolapse (heart murmur)?	Yes	No
Do you get headaches or migraines?	Yes	No
Do you now have, or have you ever had, hernia?	Yes	No
Have you ever had an aneurysm?	Yes	No
Do you have osteoporosis?	Yes	No
Do you have scoliosis?	Yes	No
Do you get irritable easily?	Yes	No
Do you have low energy levels?	Yes	No
Do you suffer from symptoms of depression?	Yes	No
Did you score low on your bone density tests?	Yes	No
Do your tests come back showing low calcium levels?	Yes	No
Do you have, or have you ever had, a goiter?	Yes	No
Do you have spine deterioration or herniated discs?	Yes	No
Have you or any family member been diagnosed with Hashimoto or Reidel disease?	Yes	No
Do you sweat profusely or hardly at all?	A lot	Little

ADRENAL GLANDS (GLANDULAR SYSTEM)

Medulla (Adrenal)

Do you have MS, Parkinson's or Palsy?	Yes	No
Do you have anxiety attacks, or feel overly anxious?	Yes	No
Do you feel excessive shyness, or inferior to others?	Yes	No
Do you have low blood pressure (below 118 systolic)?	Yes	No
Do you have tremors, nervous legs, etc.?	Yes	No
Do you have tinnitus (ringing in the ears)?	Yes	No
Do you have shortness of breath or is it hard to take a deep breath?	Yes	No
Do you have heart arrhythmias?	Yes	No
Do you have a hard time sleeping?	Yes	No
Do you have Chronic Fatigue Syndrome?	Yes	No
Do you get tired easily?	Yes	No
Have you ever been diagnosed with Addison's disease or with congenital adrenal hyperplasia?	Yes	No

Cortex (Adrenal)

Do you have elevated blood cholesterol levels?	Yes	No
Do you have lower back weakness?	Yes	No
Do you have, or have you had, sciatica?	Yes	No
Do you have arthritis or bursitis?	Yes	No
Do you have any "itis's" (inflammatory conditions)?	Yes	No

Explain- _____

FEMALE ONLY

Are your menstruations irregular?	Yes	No
Do you get excessive bleeding during menstruation?	Yes	No

Do you have, or have you had, ovarian cysts?	Yes	No
Do you have, or did you have, fibroids?	Yes	No
Do you have, or did you have, endometriosis or A-typical cells?	Yes	No
Are you fibrocystic?	Yes	No
Do you have fibromyalgia or scleroderma?	Yes	No
Do you get sore breasts, especially during menstruation?	Yes	No
Do you have a low or excessive sex drive?	Yes	No
Have you had hysterectomy?	Yes	No

Partial_____ Complete_____ When_____

Did they take any other organs out at the same time? (c.a. gallbladder)	Yes	No
Have you had a D & C?	Yes	No
Have you had a miscarriage?	Yes	No
Have you had difficulty in conceiving children?	Yes	No

Other_____

MALE ONLY

Do you have prostatitis (frequent urination, especially at night)?	Yes	No

If yes, how often? _____

Do you have prostate cancer? PSA counts:	Yes	No
Do you have testicular hypertrophy (enlargement)?	Yes	No
Do you have a low or excessive sex drive?	Yes	No
Do you have erection problems?	Yes	No
Do you have premature ejaculation?	Yes	No

Other_____

PANCREAS

Do you get gas after you eat?	Yes	No

Do you feel you food is just sitting in your stomach?	Yes	No
Do you have acid reflux?	Yes	No
Do you see any undigested foods in you stools?	Yes	No
Do you have hypoglycemia (low blood sugar)?	Yes	No
Do you have diabetes (high blood sugar)? Type 1_____ Type 2_____	Yes	No
Are you thin and have a hard time putting on weight?	Yes	No
Do you have gastritis or enteritis?	Yes	No
Do your foods pass right through you (diarrhea)?	Yes	No
Do you have moles on your body?	Yes	No

GASTROINTESTINAL TRACT

Is your tongue coated (white, yellow, green or brown) especially in the morning?	Yes	No
Do you have a hiatal hernia?	Yes	No
Do you have gastritis?	Yes	No
Do you have enteritis?	Yes	No
Do you have colitis?	Yes	No
Do you have diverticulitis?	Yes	No
Do you get or have diarrhea?	Yes	No
Do you get or have constipation?	Yes	No
How often do you have a bowel movement?	_____	
Have you ever had stomach or intestinal ulcers?	Yes	No
Do you have, or have you ever had, any type of gastrointestinal cancer: stomach, colon, rectal, etc.	Yes	No
Explain-_____		

Do you have Crohn's Disease?	Yes	No
Do you have "gas" problems?	Yes	No
Other GI problems_____		

LIVER/GALLBLADDER/BLOOD

Do you have a problem digesting fats?	Yes	No
Do fats or dairy foods cause bloating and/or pain in the stomach area?	Yes	No
Are your stools white or very light brown in color?		
Do you get pain in the middle of your back (especially after eating)?	Yes	No
Do you get pain behind the right, lower rib area?	Yes	No
Do you have "liver" or brown spots on your skin? (not freckles)	Yes	No
Do you have any skin pigmentation changes?	Yes	No
Do you have skin problems? If so, what type?	Yes	No
Are you anemic?	Yes	No
Do you have, or have you ever had, hepatitis?	Yes	No

A_____ B_____ C_____

HEART & CIRCULATION

Do you have any gray hair?	Yes	No
Do you have a hard time remembering things?	Yes	No
Do your legs get tired or cramp after you walk?	Yes	No
Do you bruise easily?	Yes	No
Do you get chest pains or angina?	Yes	No
Have you ever had a heart attack (Myocardial Infarction)?	Yes	No
Have you ever had open-heart surgery?	Yes	No
Do you have heart arrhythmias? What kind? _____	Yes	No
Do you have a heart murmur or mitral valve prolapse?	Yes	No
Do you ever feel pressure on your chest?	Yes	No
Do you get "prickly" pains anywhere, especially in the heart area? Where? _____	Yes	No
Do you have, or have you ever had high blood pressure?	Yes	No

Your average blood pressure is _____ over _____

SKIN

Do you get or have skin rashes?	Yes	No
Do you get skin blemishes?	Yes	No

Do you have eczema or dermatitis?	Yes	No
Do you have psoriasis?	Yes	No
Do you itch anywhere? Where?	Yes	No
Is your skin dry?	Yes	No
Is your skin excessively oily?	Yes	No
Do you get or have dandruff?	Yes	No

LYMPHATIC SYSTEM

Are you allergic to anything? What? _____	Yes	No
Do you ever get cold or flu-like symptoms?	Yes	No
Do you have sinus problems?	Yes	No
Do you have or get sore throats?	Yes	No
Do you have swollen lymph nodes?	Yes	No
Do you have, or have you had, tumors?	Yes	No

What type?   fatty_____ benign_____ cancerous_____
Where? _____

Do you have a low platelet count (blood)?	Yes	No
Is your immune system low or sluggish?	Yes	No
Have you had appendicitis or an appendectomy?	Yes	No

When? _____

Do you get boils, pimples, and the like?	Yes	No
Do you have allergies?	Yes	No
Have you ever had abscesses?	Yes	No
Have you ever had toxemia?	Yes	No
Do you have, or have you had, cellulitis?	Yes	No
Have you ever had gout?	Yes	No
Do you get blurred vision?	Yes	No
Do you have mucus in your eyes when you wake up in the morning?	Yes	No
Do you snore?	Yes	No
Do you have sleep apnea?	Yes	No
Have you had your tonsils out?	Yes	No

What age? _____

KIDNEYS & BLADDER

Have you ever had a urinary tract infection?	Yes	No
Have you ever had "burning" upon urination?	Yes	No
Do you have problems holding your bladder (parathyroid)?	Yes	No
Have you ever had kidney stones?	Yes	No
Do you have bags under your eyes (especially in the morning)?	Yes	No
Is your urine flow restricted?	Yes	No
Do you get cramping or pain on either side of your mid-to-lower back?	Yes	No
Do you have, or did you ever have, nephritis?	Yes	No
Do you have, or did you ever have, cystitis?	Yes	No

LUNGS

Do you get or have (or have you had) bronchitis?	Yes	No
Do you get or have (or have you had) emphysema?	Yes	No
Do you get or have (or have you had) asthma?	Yes	No
Do you get or have (or have you had) C.O.P.D?	Yes	No
Are you on inhalers or nebulizers?	Yes	No

How often? _____

What type? _____

What is your oxygen saturation? _____

Do you get pain when you breathe?	Yes	No
Do you get pain when you take a deep breath?	Yes	No
Did you ever have, or do you now have, lung cancer?	Yes	No
Do you have a collapsed lung?	Yes	No
Are you a smoker? If yes, how often do you smoke?	Yes	No
Have you ever had pneumonia?	Yes	No
Have you ever worked around toxic chemicals, in coal mines or around asbestos?	Yes	No
Do you cough a lot?	Yes	No
Do you get any mucus when you cough?	Yes	No

What color is the mucus? _____

OTHER (What are your main health complaints or concerns?)

Please list and elaborate on any conditions or symptoms that this questionnaire has not covered or asked you. _____

_____

_____

_____

_____

PAST SURGERIES

Please list any past surgeries you have had (e.g. tonsils removed, gallbladder removed, hysterectomies, open heart surgery, etc.)

Surgery _____ Year _____

_____ _____

_____ _____

CHEMICAL MEDICATIONS

Please list any chemical medications that you are presently taking.

Medication _____ Reason _____

_____ _____

_____ _____

NATURAL SUPPLEMENTS

Please list any natural supplements you are currently taking.

Supplements _____

_____

Vitamins & Minerals _____

_____

ALLERGIES

Please list anything that you are allergic to: _____

_____

_____

GENETIC HISTORY: List major diseases or conditions.

Mother _____

Father _____

(Maternal) Grandfather _____

(Maternal) Grandmother _____

(Fraternal) Grandfather _____

(Fraternal) Grandmother _____

Sister _____

Sister _____

Brother _____

Brother _____

Other _____

_____

CHAPTER SIX

Eliminating Disease Through Cleansing and Rebuilding Tissue

Awaken to the fact that modern healthcare systems, particularly allopathic methods, predominantly focus on addressing symptoms. These encompass various issues like fevers, infections, sugar imbalances, neurological breakdowns, and skin disorders, among others. Shockingly, cancer statistics indicate that almost every other male and every third female will be affected by it in their lifetime. With diseases threatening to wipe out humanity, it's evident that this approach is ineffective. Such treatments merely suppress or temporarily alleviate symptoms, which tend to resurface when the treatment stops. Often, symptoms return even more aggressively, as seen in cancer cases. Chronic or degenerative conditions can't truly be "treated"; instead, such interventions worsen the situation.

Contrastingly, the concepts of regeneration and detoxification involve targeting the root cause of symptoms. By rectifying the underlying problem, the symptoms naturally subside. Regeneration encompasses the restoration of failing tissues, while detoxification aims to eliminate inflammation and toxins responsible for the tissue's breakdown. Rather than merely chasing after effects, it's essential to identify and address the root causes of symptoms. The majority of diseases stem from three primary causes: acidosis, toxicity, and tissue weakness. These factors are responsible for 99.9 percent of all diseases, particularly when they impact the endocrine gland system. Regeneration and detoxification are symbiotic; one can't occur without the other. They stand as the twin pillars of optimal health and vitality.

Through my three decades of clinical experience, I've witnessed remarkable improvements and even complete resolutions of a wide range of conditions using these regeneration and detoxification methods. I've observed spine alignment, tissue and gland regeneration, and even reconnection of severed spinal cords after years. The human body possesses innate regenerative capabilities, similar to how it can heal from surgeries and injuries, but this process is hindered by a diet heavy in cooked and processed foods.

Regeneration involves three fundamental aspects: **Alkalization**, **Detoxification**, and **Energization**. These components are interconnected and mutually reliant. Alkalization combats inflammation, supports electrolyte balance, and facilitates cellular functions. Detoxification eliminates obstructions, irritants, and harmful substances from the body, enabling proper digestion, absorption, and elimination. Energization via nutrient-rich, live foods provides essential energy and nutrition required for alkalization and detoxification.

Detoxification is the key to establishing true internal balance (homeostasis) within the body, which can then be elevated to unprecedented levels. Striving for vitality and vibrancy should be your ultimate aim. Life becomes exhilarating, joyful, and brimming with energy when health flourishes. Dedicate time to yourself and settle for nothing less than complete health, devoid of disease. The path to regeneration isn't effortless and may involve challenges based on your toxicity levels and weaknesses. However, it's the sole avenue toward lasting health, vitality, and longevity.

Thus far, we've delved into a plethora of information about your identity as a species and your body's requirements, as well as how your physical, emotional, and mental aspects function. We've scrutinized the composition of foods and identified toxic elements. Additionally, we've explored disease symptoms and their origins. Now, it's time to address the crux of the matter: how to tackle health concerns and initiate your journey towards well-being. This chapter will initiate with insights into Naturopathy and the Science of Detoxification, proceeding to offer comprehensive details about the detoxification process. Consider marking this chapter for ongoing reference, as it will provide you with step-by-step guidance, cautions, and tips to navigate through this critical process.

MODULE 6.1

Naturopathy and the Science of Detoxification

Naturopathy stands as a prominent science, centered on the exploration and application of natural principles. Its fundamental cornerstone lies in nurturing health and vitality, encompassing all aspects of the natural world that contribute to regeneration.

In the realm of nature, every form of life partakes in consuming sustenance to maintain well-being. Most of nature's inhabitants rely on intuitive eating. Unfortunately, humans have largely departed from this innate wisdom, influenced instead by societal teachings on dietary choices. Given that financial gain holds significant sway in today's society, numerous products and foods are marketed for profit, often at the expense of individual health. As our species grapples with unprecedented levels of illness and disease, Naturopathy emerged as a response to rekindle the lost instinct for identifying the most suitable foods to sustain human life.

As previously discussed, the human body functions akin to an engine, necessitating a fuel source while requiring periodic cleansing and rejuvenation. Much like an automobile running inefficiently or coming to a halt with poor-quality fuel, the body reacts similarly. As people have chosen to fill their bodies with subpar fuels—foods that leave behind residues in their tissues—there arises the imperative to cleanse the body or confront the resulting repercussions.

Diseases serve as indications and manifestations of the body's necessity to undergo cleansing and rejuvenation. Fresh and uncooked foods, particularly fruits, possess inherent self-cleansing properties. They not only nourish the body but also maintain internal cleanliness.

Detoxification stands as both a scientific discipline and an artistic practice, representing a crucial response to the consumption of toxic and obstructive foods that have congested and impeded the human body. In nature, detoxification operates as an ongoing process inherent to all forms of life, operating at various levels. Nevertheless, the detoxification process, aimed at expelling toxins, mucus, and acidosis, can generate symptoms that some medical professionals mistake for diseases, fostering a fear of this natural course.

Energy consumption, metabolism, and waste elimination are intrinsic to all living entities in the physical world. Yet, humans stand apart as the sole species consuming foods discordant with their natural disposition. Through processing and cooking, humans alter the chemistry and energy of foods, often rendering them irritating, mucus-inducing, and inflammatory within the body. Foods like processed grains and dairy products tend to adhere like adhesive in the tissues, while others, such as meat and processed items, introduce harmful chemicals and heavy metals. The external environment compounds this predicament, with chemicalized air and personal care products adding to the toxic burden. The resultant toxic and mucus-forming elements influence the body's elimination processes, slowing them down and often leading to the storage of toxic by-products in tissues. This obstructs cellular respiration and gradually weakens cellular function.

Numerous disease symptoms signify the body's endeavor to expel stored toxins and mucus, some of which may have accumulated even before birth. During pregnancy, women often consume dairy, meat, and other toxic foods under the assumption that they are enhancing fetal bone and muscle development. Unfortunately, this practice exacerbates toxicity and acidosis, ultimately contributing to tissue frailty in both the mother and fetus.

Detoxification remains a perpetual effort by the body to maintain cleanliness and strength. It manifests through various means, including fever-induced sweating, vomiting, diarrhea, frequent urination, colds, and flu. The level of purging becomes more pronounced as toxicity increases. However, if purging is consistently hindered, it can result in lymph node swelling and, eventually, tumor growth due to prolonged retention of toxins and mucus.

Healing crises, characterized by symptoms like fever, sweating, coughing, mucus discharge, and skin rashes, are integral to the body's cleansing cycles. These crises bolster the immune system's activity and enhance the functioning of eliminative organs, including the skin. Hence, it is paramount to prioritize detoxification and regeneration over treatment. Despite this, many individuals, including healthcare practitioners, misunderstand this process and rely on natural products to treat symptoms. In my approach, I exclusively employ herbs to facilitate detoxification and invigorate the function of cells in related or weakened tissues, organs, and glands. Furthermore, herbs, being non-hybrid vegetables, offer substantial nutrition.

Common sense is, in medicine, the master workman.

— Anonymous

MODULE 6.2

Obstructions and Detoxification

When examining acidosis, it becomes crucial to comprehend its impact not only on cells but also on the nutrients and components that are ingested, imbibed, and inhaled. The term associated with acidosis is "anionic," which essentially denotes a state or condition of coagulation. This implies that when the body turns acidic due to dietary, drinking, and/or respiratory inputs, a cascade of reactions occurs, leading to inflammation and the aggregation of nutrients within the bloodstream and bodily tissues.

Digestion serves the primary purpose of breaking down and disentangling food compounds, such as proteins or complex sugars, into their simplest forms like amino acids and simple sugars, which cells can utilize through catabolic processes. Considering this concept, it becomes evident that clustering these basic elements or compounds hampers their cell usability, resulting in what are termed "obstructions," commonly referred to as "free radicals." These free radicals function as antagonists within the body, potentially causing cellular damage.

Compounded with the above scenario, is the accumulation of mucus and congestion due to the mucous lining's response to irritants, foreign proteins, and abrasive foods. This accumulated mucus indeed becomes significantly obstructive, a fact well recognized in instances of sinus congestion, sore throats, impaired vision, and other similar congestive conditions.

Pain signifies obstructions or blockages within the body. Pain emerges as a reflex response, where the energy that constantly courses through the body's pathways becomes impeded and congested. Moreover, the body channels additional energy to areas that require healing, as energy functions as the natural healer. However, this influx of energy can also exacerbate existing energy blockages. Acidosis stemming from acid-forming elements gives rise to inflammation, which, in turn, can induce energy obstructions. Practices like acupuncture, acupressure, and therapeutic touch operate to "decongest" the energy flow, allowing it to resume its natural course. This alleviation of blockages typically relieves pain and enhances blood and lymph circulation to the relevant areas.

It is imperative to eliminate both obstructions and acidosis. Ignoring this step means addressing only the effects, such as swelling, pain, or other symptoms, while the underlying cause persists. These symptoms represent the body's innate defense mechanisms reacting to the root cause. In this context, detoxification presents itself as the sole rational solution capable of delivering enduring healing. Alkalization constitutes the initial phase of the detoxification process. Alkalization functions by neutralizing acidosis. Furthermore, detoxification not only promotes body alkalization but also supplies the additional energy necessary for the body's self-cleansing mechanisms to operate effectively.

MENTAL AND EMOTIONAL DETOXIFICATION

Complete detoxification needs to occur on every level within you. Throughout this book, we've emphasized the profound influence that your thoughts and emotions exert on your overall health. If you genuinely aspire to achieve genuine well-being and vibrancy, you must cleanse not only your physical body but also your mental and emotional aspects.

All matter, including yourself, is constructed from atoms, which serve as the fundamental building blocks of the universe. The motion of these atoms generates electromagnetic energy, giving rise to magnetism. Motion inherently signifies the presence of two contrasting poles or forces, namely positive and negative. Energy continuously oscillates between these opposing facets. In Chinese Medicine, they are symbolized by yin (negative) and yang (positive). Despite sharing the same essence, these positive and negative energies elicit distinct effects on you and your body. For instance, emotions such as anger and love manifest diverse impacts on your thoughts and physical well-being. Anger introduces stress and constriction within the body, leading to reduced blood and lymphatic circulation. It adversely affects the liver and pancreas, interfering with digestion, while also placing excessive strain on the adrenal glands, resulting in an overflow of hormones and neurotransmitters. This culminates in acidosis. In contrast, love brings about the opposite outcome, enhancing blood and lymph flow, promoting improved digestion and kidney function, and inducing alkalization. Anger obstructs and restricts, whereas love opens and expands.

You might say that anger breeds "dis-case," whereas love fosters healing.

From a spiritual perspective, each emotion contributes to the tapestry of creation, as the entirety comprises the sum of its individual parts. Every emotion carries its own lesson to impart. You can discern whether an emotion serves you positively or negatively at a given time and respond accordingly. Alternatively, you can simply observe the ebb and flow of these emotions and their counterparts, without allowing them to wield influence unless you consciously choose to do so. It's up to you to determine your aspirations for your life and your body.

Here's a little secret: As you begin to amplify the energy within your physical body through detoxification, the process will extend to all levels of your being. Thoughts and emotions attach themselves to your cells and establish subtle obstructions that might persist throughout your lifetime, and some even suggest across multiple lifetimes. Hence, if you find yourself crying or venting during the detoxification journey, this is the rationale behind it. Allow your emotions to surface and be released. Remain watchful over your thoughts and feelings, avoiding attachment to anything. This way, you can let go of these obstructions. By doing so, the river of energy and love can once again surge freely within you. This, undoubtedly, represents the path to both vitality and spirituality.

MODULE 6.3

How Do We Get the Body to Detoxify?

Our species is naturally inclined towards alkalinity. The consumption of acid-forming foods triggers inflammation and congestion within the body, resulting in a condition characterized by coagulation. This reaction prompts nutrients, blood cells, and other elements to aggregate, fostering the development of various kinds of lipid and oxalate stones. Consequently, essential nutrients become inaccessible to cells, leading to a state of cellular malnourishment.

Because acidosis is both inflammatory and detrimental to cells, the body employs measures like steroids, electrolysis, water, lipids (cholesterol), and other mechanisms to counteract its effects. This response contributes to dehydration on both the extracellular and intracellular levels.

The initial step involves transitioning from a diet rich in acid-forming foods to one centered on alkaline-forming foods. Opting for alkaline-forming foods, primarily consisting of fruits and vegetables, initiates the detoxification and rehydration process. For those desiring an accelerated cleansing process, it's essential that these fruits and vegetables are consumed in their raw, uncooked, and unprocessed state. To delve deeper into the tissues and expedite the process even more, one can exclusively consume raw, fresh fruits. Fruits boast the highest concentrations of antioxidants and astringent properties among all foods. Their sugars burn slowly yet powerfully, swiftly boosting cellular vitality with minimal digestive effort. Furthermore, fruits possess unparalleled electrical properties. The energy within raw fruits is so potent that it expedites the transport of neurons and enhances endocrine function.

TAKE IT EASY

Given the potent detoxifying and vitality-restoring qualities of raw fruits, it's crucial to understand that it's possible to undergo detoxification too rapidly. This can result in severe cleansing symptoms. I have personally witnessed intense reactions such as the emergence of multiple abscesses in the mouth, tumor like swellings across the body, the skin opening and emitting pus, and even expelling tumors. These reactions occur when individuals abruptly transition from a conventional diet of dairy and meat to a highly pure and cleansing regimen of fresh, raw fruits. A fruit-centric diet can vigorously stir up toxins and mucus within the body, leading to noticeable side effects. However, embarking on an all-raw food diet that includes both fruits and vegetables for several weeks initially can facilitate a slower and generally more manageable cleansing process.

Among the most profound methods of detoxification is water fasting. Nonetheless, I do not recommend water fasting for chronic or degenerative cases, especially when the patient's energy levels are already low.

The detoxification journey is not always pleasant. Many of the more challenging instances involve cancer, HIV, or spinal cord injuries, where toxic buildup has reached significant levels. Keep in mind that the body will eliminate anything that doesn't belong, even going so far as to discard weak tissues like fingernails and weak muscle tissue. Although this might sound unsettling, it's important to recognize the body's self-cleansing mechanisms. The body can deconstruct itself to a considerable extent in order to rid itself of vulnerabilities and toxins. However, it's crucial to understand that the body will subsequently rebuild itself in a remarkable manner. Just as you would need to clear away old, burned materials before rebuilding a partially burned-down house, the body follows a similar pattern. Doctors often shy away from this process out of fear, despite it being a natural facet of life. Nature consistently removes the weak and replaces it with the strong, a principle applicable to cells as well.

For those with accumulated toxic chemicals in their bodies, heart palpitations might occur during the cleansing process. While rare, this is a potential outcome. Remember that the body can harbor deep-seated toxins dating back to the time when you were in your mother's womb. Clearing these toxins won't happen overnight. However, I've observed lymphomas disappearing in as little as forty-five days, stomach cancer vanishing in fifty-nine days, and diabetes being eliminated in sixty days.

Furthermore, the body stimulates its own diaphoresis process (perspiration) by elevating systemic temperature to induce sweating and eliminate parasites. The positive aspect is that this process is usually short-lived, and the cleaner your internal environment becomes, the less intensive cleansing will be required. Typically, enduring one, two, or at most three cycles of this process can alleviate most disease symptoms.

FOR THE REST OF YOUR LIFE

Life is an ongoing cycle of intake and elimination. This process of detoxification will persist throughout your lifetime, operating at varying degrees, particularly if you regularly consume fresh fruits and vegetables. Continuously, your body will delve deeper into its internal realms, purifying and reinstating proper functions. Much of this activity becomes exceedingly subtle, often escaping your awareness except for sporadic symptoms such as mucus discharge, cold-like effects, or minor discomfort. Remarkably, the human body is exquisitely designed and possesses remarkable intelligence. Even if you amassed knowledge about chemistry, biochemistry, and physics, comprehending the intricate workings of the human body would remain elusive. Always ask the fundamental question: "Why is my body responding in this manner?" Every action your body takes has a rationale behind it in any given situation. We need only decipher the body's language to fathom its actions and their purposes (for further insight, refer to Chapter 5, Module 5.11, Body Language). Observation and common sense consistently transcend the confines of science. While science originated from observation and common sense, it has since become influenced by biases, often yielding to corporate interests and financial considerations.

To truly discern the advantages of a natural healing regimen or therapy, inquire within: "How can it address the root cause of my issue? Can it contribute to my vitality, well-being, and longevity? Most crucially, does it facilitate my spiritual growth or awakening?" Authentic well-being entails a state where the body, emotions, mind, and soul synchronize harmoniously; it signifies genuine spirituality. Remember, genuine Naturopathy revolves around comprehending nature and the ways in which nature maintains its own health. As humans grasp the foundational truths of nature, they will be empowered to restore health as well. The key to unlocking nature's magic door and allowing for rejuvenation and vitality is detoxification. Always embrace simplicity.

Given that detoxification is synonymous with alkalization, the ensuing section will delve into the interconnection between this process and the foods we consume.

MODULE 6.4

Alkaline-Forming and Acid-Forming Foods and Detoxification

Gaining insight into the foods you consume is of paramount importance. As previously mentioned, a key aspect of food pertains to its impact on the body's pH. Foods can be categorized into two fundamental groups: those that generate an acidic response within the body and those that prompt an alkaline response. This distinction isn't necessarily tied to the pH level of the foods themselves.

Alkalinity plays a pivotal role in the body's detoxification process, making alkaline-forming foods potent detoxifiers. The degree of detoxification deepens as foods become more alkaline-forming. Fruits, in general, exemplify high alkaline-forming foods, and these constituents also serve as nourishment for the body. They hold the remarkable ability to foster regeneration.

Conversely, acid-forming foods tend to impede, inhibit, or even halt the detoxification process. Such foods evoke inflammation and foster the production of mucus within the body, ultimately contributing to tissue deterioration. Acids, if not counteracted by antioxidants (which have an alkaline nature) and subsequently eliminated, can evolve into free radicals that inflict harm upon tissues.

Despite this, acids are essential for critical processes like ionization and oxidation.

Avoid being deceived. Foods have the capacity to either nurture, purify, and reconstruct your well-being, or they can lead to your demise. Certain foods have the tendency to foster mucus buildup, congestion, and inflammation, which, in turn, result in cellular, tissue, organ, and gland dysfunction. Allow your dietary choices to serve as the foundation for your health and healing, steering clear of becoming the source of disease. Now, let's delve into the distinctions between these two categories of foods.

ALKALINE-FORMING FOODS

I draw a parallel between alkaline foods and the winter season. These foods possess a cooling and soothing effect on inflamed tissues, promote the healing of ulcerations, and bolster cellular functions. Following digestion, these foods predominantly yield alkaline ash, mainly composed of calcium, magnesium, sodium, and potassium. This results in an overall alkaline reaction and condition.

The human species is fundamentally alkaline in nature. The majority of our bodily fluids, such as blood, saliva, urine, synovial fluids, cerebral fluids, and digestive enzymes (with the exception of those in the stomach), are—or should be—alkaline. Any shift towards acidity in these fluids can lead to deterioration and even mortality. The stomach is the sole acidic chamber in the body, where initial protein breakdown occurs. Conversely, alkaline digestion relies on enzymes from the mouth, pancreas, and intestines.

In order to facilitate the detoxification process, it is imperative to incorporate alkaline-forming foods into your diet. Alkalization holds the key to achieving successful self-regeneration and overall health. A remarkable illustration of alkalization's significance can be observed in emergency medical scenarios. In hospital Emergency Rooms and other immediate care situations, patients are often administered an IV containing normal saline, which is essentially a sodium solution. Sodium is renowned as a potent alkalizing agent. This approach aids in countering acidosis—the primary factor underlying various health issues. Acidosis typically leads to pain, swelling, and inflammation.

Raw fruits and vegetables emulate the effects of normal saline, although they offer even greater vitality and nutrition. For effective alkalization, the consumption of raw, ripe, living foods is paramount. Alkaline foods, such as fresh fruits and vegetables, align with the natural dietary preferences of humans. Striving for a diet that comprises approximately 80-90 percent alkaline-forming foods is highly recommended.

ACID-FORMING FOODS

I draw an analogy between acid foods and fire. Acidic foods are rich in sulfur, phosphorus, and nitrogen, primarily comprising protein-rich foods. This category includes items like meats, eggs, grains, legumes, nuts, seeds, pasteurized dairy products, and cooked tomatoes.

Most animal protein sources are irritants to both the mucous membranes and cells within the body, provoking an immune reaction. This triggers the production of mucus and lymph cells within the lymphatic system and mucosa. The consumption of foreign proteins leads to widespread mucus production throughout the body, resulting in issues related to congestion. As the consumption of these foods continues, congestion accumulates, gradually saturating the lungs, sinus cavities, ear canals, throat, and intestines. This mucus buildup fosters an environment conducive to parasites, heightened white blood cell activity, and inflammation, all of which negatively impact the body's proper functioning. This inflammation and congestion eventually contribute to cellular deterioration.

A stark illustration of this congestion and inflammation phenomenon is evident with dairy products. The proteins present in dairy are abrasive to bodily tissues, causing many individuals to experience congestion in areas such as the lungs, sinuses, ears, and throat after consuming these foods. This congestion impairs tissue function, as the mucus is either stored or pushed further into the body. A significant portion of this mucus and toxins is filtered through the lymphatic system, particularly in the lymph nodes. (The incidence of lymphatic cancers is notably high in the U.S.) The body's response to eliminate this congestion includes processes like colds, flus, bronchitis, sneezing, and coughing. The conventional medical approach often labels these efforts by the body as "diseases" and attempts to counteract them with pharmaceuticals that, unfortunately, exacerbate the problem. These medications suppress the body's elimination of mucus and toxins. Consequently, the immune system becomes suppressed and overburdened as it confronts this significant challenge. It's crucial to remember that what isn't eliminated accumulates, potentially leading to chronic ailments, degenerative conditions, as well as simple boils or tumor formations.

Numerous individuals predominantly consume acidic foods, leading to an abundance of inflammatory conditions (often ending in "itis"), ulcerations, congestive disorders, and cancers in our society. Due to the high phosphorus or nitrogen content in these foods, the body loses essential alkaline minerals like calcium, as it employs these minerals to neutralize acidic components.

A balanced diet should ideally comprise only 10-20 percent of acid foods. Alkaline foods are especially beneficial during the spring, summer, and fall seasons when temperatures are warmer. However, during the colder alkaline winter months, a moderate increase in acid foods is recommended. Keep in mind that opposites attract, fostering harmony. When external conditions are hot (acidic), incorporating cold (alkaline) foods is advantageous, and vice versa.

To better understand the nature of alkaline and acid foods, it's helpful to consult the Alkaline/Acid Food Chart provided in Chapter 7, Module 7.2. This chart explains how the alkaline or acid nature of foods is determined. Given that humans are alkaline beings, our biological makeup is better suited for predominantly alkaline-forming foods. These foods promote health and vitality, while acid-forming foods contribute to disease and discontent. The choice ultimately rests with you.

MODULE 6.5

What to Expect During Detox

Experiencing a range of symptoms during the detoxification process is quite normal. These symptoms can manifest as symptoms resembling those of a cold or flu, alterations in bowel movements, diverse types of pain, elevated body temperature, heartburn, congestion in the lungs, reduced energy levels, swelling, itchiness, and in some cases, vomiting. In the subsequent section, we will thoroughly explore each of these potential side effects. At times, I will propose strategies to facilitate the detoxification process or provide ways to alleviate the discomfort associated with what is commonly referred to as the "healing crisis." In general, I strongly advise you to persist through these side effects and continue moving forward in the direction of regeneration.

COLD AND FLU-LIKE SYMPTOMS

As the body initiates the cleansing of its lymphatic system, various body tissues such as the sinus cavities and lungs will become actively engaged in this detoxification process. It's crucial not to hinder this natural course of action. This is the genuine method to enhance cell function and set your body on the path towards regeneration.

You'll notice a significant discharge of mucus from the body, which can exhibit colors ranging from clear, yellow, and green to even brown or black. On rare occasions, there might be traces of blood in the mucus. There's no need to panic; this blood has likely been present for a while. The congestion caused by acidity can lead to inflammation and tissue bleeding. Sore throats might develop as a result, which is a sign of the body expelling mucus and toxins from the tissues. While it's best to avoid cough drops, if necessary, opt for natural alternatives like those containing Slippery Elm.

The intensity of the cleansing process can vary from minor (manifesting as a runny nose and slight cough) to more intense, with profound expectoration from the bronchial and lung regions. These deeper cleansing stages might be uncomfortable or unsettling, but it's essential to trust that the body is following its inherent wisdom.

The body will eliminate toxins through any available opening, including the skin, ears, nose, mouth, kidneys, and bowels. In instances of rapid detoxification in extremely toxic individuals, the skin might even create openings to expel toxins. An illustrative example is that of a patient whose skin above the belly button split open during rapid detoxification, expelling a small tumor. Similarly, immobile individuals with high toxicity, like quadriplegics, can experience this phenomenon where the skin opens to release toxins.

A general sensation of bodily achiness might be experienced. It's advisable to conserve energy during this time to allow the body to thoroughly cleanse itself. Embrace these healing or purging processes as they are essential for your overall well-being. While it can take several months for your body to exhibit such responses, maintaining consistent detoxification efforts is crucial.

For many individuals, accumulated sulfur from sulfa drugs can hinder the lymphatic system. Eliminating this stored sulfur is a prerequisite for optimal lymphatic flow. Considering that the lymphatic system is responsible for immune cell transport and serves as a cellular waste disposal system, it's evident how crucial its unimpeded function is. Be patient and persistent as you progress through this journey. The rewarding sensation of revitalized life force coursing through your clean body will make the effort worthwhile.

The detoxification process will naturally unfold as you augment your energy levels and achieve alkalization. Permit the body to undertake its self-cleansing mechanisms without hindrance.

CHANGES IN BOWEL MOVEMENTS

Ensuring regular bowel movements is of paramount importance – a minimum of one per day is essential, although achieving two or three would be far more beneficial. An optimal state of bowel health entails experiencing a bowel movement around thirty minutes after each meal. Regrettably, many individuals experience an unnatural frequency of three to six or more bowel movements daily, often attributed to Irritable Bowel Syndrome (IBS), a term used to describe inflammation within the gastrointestinal tract.

In instances where stools are excessively loose or watery, such as in cases of diarrhea, a recommended approach is to employ a high-quality herbal bowel formula containing ingredients like Slippery Elm Bark, Marshmallow Root, and/or Chamomile.

These formulations aid in solidifying stools while simultaneously addressing the underlying toxicity and inflammation that trigger diarrhea. Some formulations may also incorporate bentonite clay and charcoal, which are also effective options for this purpose.

A FEW DEFINITIONS

- Gastritis is inflammation of the stomach.

- Enteritis is inflammation of the small intestine.

- Colitis is the inflammation of the colon or large intestine.

- Diverticulitis is the inflammation of bowel (intestinal) pockets, which form from our S.A.D. (Standard American Diet).

Consuming a raw food diet is crucial for the healing, restoration, and strengthening of the gastrointestinal tract's tissues. If you find it challenging to tolerate the fiber in raw foods, you can use an herbal bowel formula to ease the discomfort. However, this will only be a temporary measure, as it won't take long to alleviate the inflammation in the GI tract.

On the contrary, many individuals struggle with constipation. Constipation can negatively impact the body in various ways, including the absorption of decayed matter from foods held in the intestines. This can even lead to damage to the intestinal lining, particularly if these food remnants become impacted. It's important to ensure regular bowel movements by consuming plenty of fresh raw fruits and vegetables.

Additionally, utilizing an effective bowel-corrective formula until your colon is clean and healthy can be beneficial. The most effective bowel formulas are designed not only to achieve the aforementioned goals but also to restore and enhance normal bowel peristalsis. A good formula will strengthen and tone the bowel without causing dependency. Furthermore, it will aid in the healing of inflammation and ulcerations caused by the consumption of acidic foods.

For individuals dealing with inflamed bowels, chamomile or peppermint tea can provide relief. Both teas have a soothing effect on smooth muscle tissue. Consuming 2 ounces of aloe vera juice three times a day is also highly beneficial, although it might result in mild diarrhea. Two other botanicals that can help reduce inflammation in the gastrointestinal tract are Slippery Elm and Marshmallow Root. You can prepare a tea from these herbs by using 1 teaspoon of the herb with 1 cup of water. Boil the tea for 8 minutes, then let it steep for another 5 minutes. Strain and drink. Consuming 1 cup, 3-6 times per day, is an appropriate dosage.

IMPORTANT: In cases of severe constipation, a more potent purgative herb might be necessary.

It's important to note that such treatments should be used for short-term relief, as these formulas can lead to dependency. Additionally, colonics are strongly recommended for these situations. (More information on the use of colonics can be found later in this chapter, see Module 6.9.)

ACHES AND PAIN

During the process of cleansing and healing, various aches and pains may manifest. Weaknesses within the body tend to reveal themselves through these discomforts. The body actively works to draw out and expel toxicity, which can result in pains. Degenerative areas can also experience pain as the body addresses the underlying issues. It's important to understand that these aches and pains are a natural part of the process and should not be a cause for concern. Most of these sensations will typically last from a few hours to a week. After the healing crisis, you'll likely observe that the specific area undergoing discomfort becomes notably stronger than before.

Pain often stems from acidosis, leading to inflammation that can either stimulate or deteriorate the nervous system. It can also arise where toxins, foreign objects like splinters, clots, cholesterol, acid crystalline deposits (such as uric or calcium deposits), and chemical medications block energy within the body.

Traditionally, we've been taught to address pain or alleviate symptoms. However, pain-relieving drugs might inadvertently hinder the body's healing process. In the realm of natural health, the focus is on eliminating the cause rather than the symptom. Pain serves as a warning sign, urging us to pause and naturally cleanse our bodies. Suppressing pain symptoms unnaturally can pave the way for future degenerative issues, as the root cause remains unaddressed. This can allow the deterioration of tissues to persist.

The intensity of pain varies based on the extent of inflammation or tissue degeneration. Yet, for conditions like bone cancer, certain types of cancer, shingles, and other specific cases, the use of pain medication may become necessary. Severe pain can weaken both the spirit and the body to the point of being detrimental. Given that pain medications often lead to constipation, those using them should consider maintaining a bowel formula to facilitate proper bowel management. It's crucial to keep the bowels functioning smoothly, particularly during detoxification, as this process places an additional burden of toxins to be eliminated.

Working with the Detoxification Pain

When dealing with situations causing discomfort, you can employ alternating warm and cold compresses. Additionally, applying Arnica oil topically can provide relief. Castor oil packs are another valuable option for alleviation.

However, in cases where these approaches fall short, it's important to closely consult a healthcare expert when dealing with painful conditions. Keep in mind that pain is associated with acidity, so maintaining an alkaline state in your body is crucial.

VOMITING

The act of vomiting is typically uncommon unless an individual is severely toxic or has been exposed to numerous chemical medications that can build up in the stomach tissues. Vomiting serves as a natural response for the stomach to rapidly expel toxins and mucus. In certain cases, individuals may even experience the expulsion of worms or parasites that have developed during their participation in this program.

What to Do For Vomiting

Vomiting is the body's inherent method for purging the stomach of an excess accumulation of poisons, toxins, mucus, or parasites. To alleviate the discomfort and ease the spasms associated with vomiting, herbal teas like Ginger, Mint, or Chamomile can be quite beneficial. These teas not only provide a soothing effect on the stomach but also contribute to improved liver and intestinal function, thus aiding in your relief.

FEVERS (THERMO-THERAPY)

Fever is a natural mechanism that your body employs to efficiently eliminate toxins, including pus, mucus, parasites, and undesirable cells. Your skin, being the largest eliminative organ, plays a crucial role in this process. According to the American Medical Association, under normal conditions, the body discharges about two pounds or more of waste through the skin on a daily basis. When the body is undergoing cleansing, even greater elimination is required.

In adults, fevers typically arise at or around 103° Fahrenheit. It's essential to maintain proper hydration by consuming ample pure water and fresh fruit or vegetable juices during cleansing periods to prevent dehydration. Utilizing cold showers, baths, or applying a cold washcloth to the forehead or neck can provide some relief by cooling down the body slightly.

For children, it's natural for fevers to reach temperatures of 104° to 105° Fahrenheit, so there's no need to panic. As mentioned, proper hydration remains the foremost concern in such cases. Elevated fevers are instrumental in eradicating parasites, as the high temperature and increased white blood cell count contribute to their demise.

It has been noted that fevers above 106° can effectively target cancer cells, while temperatures of 110° Fahrenheit and beyond risk harming healthy cells. The rise in temperature is instigated by the thyroid gland and hypothalamus, prompted by the cellular release of interleukin-1. This stimulates the release of prostaglandin E2 (PGE2) from the hypothalamus, which triggers sweating (diaphoresis). Sweating dilates the vascular system and activates sweat glands, facilitating the expulsion of toxins through the skin. These toxins are subsequently oxidized by skin mites or washed away. This process greatly aids proper elimination and overall bodily health.

Fever prompts the immune system to boost white blood cell production and increase interferon levels, substantially enhancing its effectiveness in battling threats. The body's innate intelligence guides these processes, and our role is to comprehend and appreciate them. Embrace natural processes without fear, as they are instrumental in maintaining your well-being. Fevers are just one of the ways the body achieves this. Rather than fearing fevers, it's essential to apprehend their significance. If any concern arises, it's dehydration that warrants attention. Given that many individuals experience some degree of dehydration due to acidosis, educating yourself about the principles of nature will be an invaluable asset on your journey towards achieving health and vitality.

Working with a Fever Caused by Detoxification

If you're experiencing a high fever, it's crucial to ensure proper hydration. Consume generous amounts of distilled water, along with fresh fruit or vegetable juices. Applying a chilled cloth to the forehead and back of the neck can provide relief, as can taking a cold bath. It's important not to inhibit the body's natural response in this situation. Keep in mind that adding liquid minerals to your water or juice can enhance hydration, which is especially valuable in cases of significant depletion.

GENERAL INFLAMMATION

Not all inflammation needs to be eradicated. Inflammation triggered by histamine response serves as a mechanism for the body to widen blood vessels, allowing for increased blood flow and immune components during critical situations or in the presence of irritants. The application of hot and cold compresses can offer relief. Numerous anti-inflammatory botanicals are at your disposal, such as Wild Yam Root, Marshmallow Root, Slippery Elm, and Comfrey (both leaves and root). Remember, inflammation is inherently acidic, so the key is to emphasize alkalization. Raw fruits and vegetables serve as excellent alkalizing agents. Sodium is recognized as a potent "Great Alkalizer."

FACTS ABOUT DEHYDRATION

Acidosis gives rise to dehydration, while dehydration in turn fuels acidosis. Consuming mostly cooked food contributes to dehydration. This dehydration triggers reduced tissue activity, ultimately culminating in tissue deterioration.

HEARTBURN

Heartburn emerges as a consequence of the stomach and intestinal tract succumbing to acidosis. Inaccurate food combinations incite fermentation and putrefaction, leading to this state of excess acidity. Overindulging in acid-forming foods can also provoke heartburn, particularly prevalent among those who consume meat, which triggers excessive hydrochloric acid production. Consuming an excess of grain products or cooked tomatoes can also be a major cause of severe heartburn. Inadequate pancreatic enzyme production, contributing to subpar digestion, may contribute to heartburn and gas.

Insufficient production of sodium bicarbonate by the pancreas, along with deficient bile flow or production from the liver and gallbladder, can trigger acid reflux. In many instances, gallstones obstruct the bile duct, impeding the natural flow of bile. Furthermore, a weakened sphincter muscle between the esophagus and stomach enables stomach acids to regurgitate into the esophagus, causing acid reflux.

The detoxification and rejuvenation regimen advocated in this book is not a source of heartburn. However, due to the invigorating nature of raw foods, one might temporarily experience some stimulation of these conditions.

Working with Heartburn During Detoxification

Ginger tea proves to be highly beneficial for addressing heartburn. When faced with this issue, it becomes imperative to closely evaluate food combinations. If incorrect eating practices, including improper food pairing, have taken place, consuming an apple can offer assistance. Apples contain potent digestive enzymes that significantly aid the process of digestion. Additionally, you can prepare teas from other calming herbs such as Chamomile flowers, Gentian Root, Slippery Elm Bark, or Marshmallow Root to promote the healing of the stomach lining. The key remains consistent: prioritize alkalization for genuine health and well-being.

LUNG CONGESTION

The lungs strive to cleanse themselves by expelling mucus and toxins. In cases of asthma, emphysema, and C.O.P.D. (chronic obstructive pulmonary disease), where the adrenal glands also play a role, muscle spasms in the tissues can be problematic, impeding the ability to breathe freely. To counteract this, an herbal antispasmodic can be of immense value. This type of remedy alleviates the spasms while facilitating the natural removal of congestion from the lungs.

For individuals keen on truly healing lung conditions, relying solely on an inhaler might yield moderate success. Instead, I recommend considering the use of herbal antispasmodics as an alternative to inhalers. However, if your condition is advanced, periodic use of an inhaler may be necessary. It's worth noting that some research has suggested that inhalers might have carcinogenic properties.

Inhalers pose a significant issue due to their lymphatic-inhibiting effects. While they do widen the airways, they do so at the expense of hindering the elimination of congestion. Conversely, herbal antispasmodics promote airway dilation while allowing for effective congestion elimination. Expectoration, the expulsion of congestion from lung tissues, is crucial for optimal oxygen exchange. Certain herbs like Comfrey Root, Chickweed, Marshmallow Root, and Yerba Santa Leaf are known to aid in the regeneration of lung tissues.

Individuals dealing with chronic asthma and long-standing lung problems should exercise caution when embarking on detoxification. Starting with a diet consisting of 70 percent raw foods and 30 percent cooked foods is a gentler approach that allows for gradual cleansing.

Remember the role of the adrenal glands in lung spasms. Under-active adrenal glands can lead to low neurotransmitter production, weakening the lung-related nervous system. This can result in heightened nervous system sensitivity and irritability. Coupled with decreased thyroid function affecting calcium utilization, the conditions for tissue spasms are set. Clearing the lungs of congestion and enhancing adrenal gland function, along with assessing basal body temperatures to evaluate thyroid involvement, are essential steps. For advanced lung conditions, close monitoring by a healthcare professional is highly recommended throughout this process.

Working with Asthma and Lung Congestion During Detoxification

Individuals dealing with asthma or lung congestion might find relief by using a castor oil pack along with warm cayenne compresses placed over the chest area where the lungs are located. (Detailed instructions for creating and using a castor oil pack can be found in Chapter 9.) Additionally, consuming a cup of Peppermint tea and following it every ten minutes with a teaspoon of Lobelia tincture (up to 6 teaspoons) can be beneficial. It's important to note that Lobelia acts as an antispasmodic in lower doses and as an emetic in higher doses, which could induce vomiting in certain individuals. Vomiting can help compress the lungs and expel phlegm.

Another effective approach involves alternating between hot and cold compresses. Apply a hot compress for 2 minutes, followed by a cold compress for 2 minutes, and repeat this process for a round or two. Considering the use of an antispasmodic herbal formula could also be helpful. Such a formula can help manage spasms, making it easier to breathe and expel mucus from the lungs.

LOSS OF ENERGY OR EXHAUSTION

When stored toxins are dislodged and released from the tissues into the bloodstream, individuals may encounter the side effects associated with those specific toxins or poisons. Generally, older individuals tend to accumulate a greater amount of toxins over time. Factors such as glandular vulnerabilities, compromised immune system function, emotional distress, prolonged lung issues, weakened thyroid and adrenal glands, and difficulties in nutrient absorption can all contribute to significant energy depletion. Fluctuations in energy can also arise from imbalances in sugar levels. During detoxification, periods of increased rest might be necessary, particularly when all stimulants like coffee, tea, and refined sugars are removed from the diet.

Our society heavily relies on stimulants for energy, which ultimately weakens the true energy centers – the glands. When the intake of stimulants is halted, a rebound effect might occur, leading to pronounced fatigue. However, this feeling of fatigue will gradually diminish as nutrient-rich living foods and juices are consumed. It's crucial to realize that the typical Western diet (S.A.D.) undermines the body's strength instead of bolstering it. These foods often trigger inflammation and toxicity in tissues. When coupled with stimulants, this combination contributes to tissue deterioration.

While "Chronic Fatigue Syndrome" is frequently associated with the Epstein-Barr virus, it's important to note that this virus is not always the sole cause of fatigue. Although the virus can induce fatigue, it can be effectively targeted. The real culprits behind widespread fatigue in our society are weakened thyroid and adrenal glands. When these essential endocrine glands are compromised, fatigue, depression, and anxiety can manifest. The regeneration of these glands is imperative to overcoming chronic fatigue, albeit this process doesn't occur overnight. With determination and persistence, success can be achieved. The key lies in adopting a raw food diet and utilizing herbal formulas.

Working with Lack of Energy or Fatigue During Detox

The cessation of all stimulating foods can lead to a significant decline in energy levels, particularly when someone possesses under-active thyroid or adrenal glands. These glands, responsible for providing energy, tend to weaken due to the presence of acidity and toxins in the body. Paradoxically, stimulating foods exert a detrimental impact on these glands, further compromising their strength rather than enhancing it. The persistent stimulation from substances like coffee and tea masks this deterioration. A substantial portion of our energy over our lifetimes stems from the stimulated functioning of cells.

Energy should ideally be vibrant and natural, rather than driven by external stimulants. Consuming 3 to 6 glasses of 10-ounce carrot, spinach, and celery juice daily can contribute to a rise in energy levels. Incorporating abundant quantities of fresh, ripe fruits into the diet can also prove beneficial. Additionally, supplements like Panax Ginseng extract, Royal Jelly, Alfalfa, Barley Green Complex, and a well-balanced super-food blend can assist in elevating energy levels. Adequate rest and allowing sufficient time also play crucial roles in the healing process.

SWELLING AND ITCHING

During the detoxification process, various skin eruptions and swellings might occur. In some cases, tumors could even increase in size before eventually dissolving. While most swellings are temporary, maintaining a consistent intake of fruits becomes crucial during these episodes.

Itching is another phenomenon associated with detoxification. It is often triggered by fungal or Candida activity. Individuals may experience itching and skin redness in different areas of the body.

Remedies for Itching During Detoxification

Using topical applications of Angelica Root, Aloe Vera, or Chickweed can provide relief from itching. If the itching persists, it indicates the presence of a fungal infection that needs to be eliminated, and the lymphatic system housing these fungi must be cleansed. This necessitates the use of herbal formulas for the lymphatic system and parasites, along with adhering to a raw food diet.

OTHER SIDE EFFECTS DURING DETOXIFICATION

Additional potential side effects may encompass, though are not confined to, excessive menstruation, persistent or profound coughing, frequent urination, headaches, diarrhea, as well as sensations of numbness and tingling in the extremities. Skin eruptions and gas can also occur.

Throughout the process of cleansing and recuperation, prior symptoms of past ailments or vulnerabilities may reappear briefly before subsiding as the body addresses and rectifies those specific areas. These are manifestations of long-standing toxic issues that were initially suppressed, and now the body is systematically addressing these regions to reconstruct and restore regular tissue function. In a specific instance, an Amish woman who had encountered poison ivy over two decades ago had treated it with chemical remedies and seemingly "cured" it. On her detoxification regimen, the poison ivy resurfaced exactly where she had treated it before. This was a remarkable revelation, even to me. It's possible to expel latent, suppressed toxins from childhood or even from the prenatal stage while inside your mother's womb.

LIMITING OR STOPPING THE USE OF PHARMACEUTICALS

If you are currently relying on chemical medications and are considering reducing or discontinuing their usage as you embark on the journey of detoxification and regeneration, here are some actions that I, personally, would recommend taking:

FIRST — This program normalizes blood sugars. If I were a diabetic, I would watch my sugars daily and adjust my insulin accordingly or have my doctor help me.

SECOND — This program has the effect of reducing elevated blood pressure and increasing it if it's too low. If I were on medications for high blood pressure, I would consistently monitor my blood pressure levels. It's important to avoid causing hypotension or excessively low blood pressure, which could lead to symptoms like fainting, balance issues, or even more serious complications.

THIRD — I would recommend gradually tapering off the use of medications. Nonetheless, in cases of high blood pressure and diabetes, it might be necessary to discontinue medication relatively quickly, and this can be achieved without experiencing adverse effects.

Certain medications can create a dependence where the body becomes reliant on them. This is particularly evident with neurological drugs and certain steroids like prednisone. Seeking assistance from your doctor is advisable. Should your doctor decline, the responsibility may fall on you to take action. Many traditional doctors may become frustrated when patients take initiative for self-improvement, as their training often lacks detoxification and regeneration knowledge. Such circumstances lead many individuals to find their own solutions. This book is being written to address this gap. Remember, the choice is always yours. Strive for a healthy life without the need for medications.

Please note: Interactions between medications and herbs are infrequent but plausible. Pay attention to your well-being and sensations. You'll sense if the substances you're using are reacting together. Utilize sound judgment and cooperate with your natural health specialist.

Summary

Most people do not encounter a significant number of the aforementioned symptoms. Generally, the intensity of the "healing crisis" corresponds to the level of toxicity within the individual. It's crucial to understand that a healing crisis is valuable and advantageous. The symptoms and discomfort are all integral components of the detoxification process, facilitating the expulsion of toxins and poisons from the body.

Typically, the healing crisis is short-lived, so patience is key. It's important to maintain a diet consisting mainly of raw foods, especially fresh fruits and juices. Many fruits possess potent antioxidant and astringent properties that aid in expelling toxins. If you do not feel like eating, do not eat. Let the body rest and be sure to drink plenty of fresh juices or pure water. Do not let the body dehydrate.

If over 80 percent of your diet consists of fresh, raw, uncooked fruits and vegetables, any symptoms experienced are likely a result of your body's detoxification process. If your diet is more of a 50/50 balance, your symptoms may lean towards an acidic condition, potentially prolonging the healing crisis.

Using botanical formulas, taking time to rest, and cultivating a positive mental outlook are equally important during this period. If the healing crisis persists for more than two to three weeks and you need a respite, returning to cooked foods can halt the body's intense cleansing action. However, it's highly recommended to continue the cleansing process for as long as possible. Detoxification ultimately leads to vitality. In the end, the detoxification journey will bring about robust health, energy, and a sense of spiritual well-being.

MODULE 6.6

The "Healing Crisis"

The subsequent examples illustrate instances of the "Healing Crisis" that can arise throughout the process of detoxification. Over my three decades of involvement in detoxification, I've encountered an array of distinct healing "crises" that can't all be covered here due to space limitations. This section addresses the most prevalent side effects, many of which I have personally undergone during my own detoxification endeavors.

I have classified these detoxification side effects into three categories: Mild, Moderate, and Strong. It's possible to experience any of these levels at various points, though the stronger levels are not commonly encountered. The severity of these experiences is influenced by an individual's toxicity level and the overall energy or resilience of their entire system.

MILD CLEANSING EFFECTS

- Cold and flu-like symptoms
- Low-grade fevers (99°–100° Fahrenheit)
- Coughing with or without discharge
- Clear and yellow mucus discharge from nose or throat (lungs, bronchi, etc.; this mucus may include blood)
- Minor aches and pains

- Mucus in stools
- Mucus in urine
- Loss of energy (may go up and down)
- Rashes and itching
- Disease symptoms increasing temporarily
- Mucus from eyes
- Mild headaches
- Minor blurred vision
- Minor vertigo
- Weight loss (average 8-15 lbs. in two weeks. Depends upon level of thyroid weakness. Can be as little as 2 lbs.)
- Chills
- Emotions rising up, such as mild crying, anger or even laughter
- Short term nose bleeds
- Some rectal bleeding (hemorrhoids or lesions)
- Minor blood in urine

MODERATE CLEANSING EFFECTS

- Symptoms of bronchitis or pneumonia
- Heavy discharges of green to brown mucus from nose and throat (lungs, bronchi, etc.)

- Pain in joints
- Heavy discharge from kidneys (urine color changes to brown, orange or dark yellow, etc.)
- Pain in old injuries or in degenerative areas of the body
- Minor paralysis of limbs
- Chronic fatigue symptoms
- Nosebleeds
- Spasms of the lungs in asthma/emphysema/ C.O.P.D.
- Moderate shortness of breath (asthma, emphysema, C.O.P.D.)
- Temporary increase in tumor size
- Disease symptoms magnifying (short-lived)
- Sores appearing on the skin
- Oozing of innumerable substances from the skin, especially from the hands and feet
- Bruising
- Weak muscle breakdown (muscle built from meat protein)
- Heavy mucus discharge from eyes and ears
- Vomiting
- Diarrhea
- Cellulitis "clumping"
- Dizziness and/or vertigo

- Minor heart palpitations
- Loose teeth (minor)
- Minor abscesses in mouth
- Migraines
- High-grade fever (103° to 105° Fahrenheit)
- Deep coughing (sometimes dry). Use herbs to loosen and eliminate (expectorate) the impacted mucus.
- Depression or anxieties
- Emotional releasing (crying, anger, laughter, etc.)
- Heavy thoughts (lack of clarity)
- Skin splitting where heavy toxins exist
- Excessive itching
- Mercury tooth fillings can be pushed out by the body
- Rectal bleeding from past or present hemorrhoids or lesions

You might encounter one or multiple of the aforementioned detoxification effects. There's no need for alarm; in fact, these are desired outcomes. Personally, I find it encouraging when patients expel dark-green mucus as it indicates they are following the program correctly and reaping its rewards.

Collaborating with a knowledgeable healthcare professional who possesses extensive expertise in detoxification and its associated effects is a prudent approach.

STRONG CLEANSING EFFECTS

- Paralysis of any part of the body
- Black mucus discharges from the lungs
- Heavy brown discharge or blood in the urine with associated kidney pain
- Heavy black discharge from the bowels with diarrhea
- Tumors popping out all over the body
- Loss of sight
- Loss of hearing
- Severe dizziness (or vertigo)
- Severe fatigue
- Abscesses developing all through the mouth
- Loss of fingernails or toenails
- Excessive weight loss (this can result when a pancreatic weakness exists)
- Severe shortness of breath (use an antispasmodic or inhaler)
- Temporary deep depression, released through crying, anger, laughter, etc.
- Mental confusion
- Skin cracking open
- Teeth becoming loose (major)
- Old suppressed symptoms (like the case of "poison ivy") reappear

The intensity of detoxification at this severe level is not commonly encountered by most individuals. Variability arises from factors such as an individual's toxicity level and the number of medications they're on. Some individuals who have chosen to suppress their body's natural cleansing processes, often through medications like prednisone, may have deeper underlying issues. However, the group more susceptible to these intense effects tends to be those who have been chronically toxic from birth, often exhibiting conditions such as cancer, H.I.V., or other serious illnesses.

TWO CASES OF CLEANSING

Let's examine two cases that exemplify the healing crisis.

Case #1

A 36-year-old woman diagnosed with pancreatic cancer, specifically the degenerative type that had severely impaired her pancreatic function, experienced significant digestive dysfunction where ingested food passed through her stool without proper digestion. Her gastrin levels were exceptionally elevated. Throughout her detoxification program, she observed the emergence of around forty golf-ball-sized tumors on both of her legs. Despite being informed by a medical doctor that her cancer had spread throughout her body, she adhered to a fruit-based diet and within approximately three weeks, all the tumors on her legs disappeared.

About a month later, she visited a dentist due to a loose tooth, which was subsequently extracted after being diagnosed as abscessed. As another tooth also became loose, the dentist recommended its extraction as well. Fortunately, her scheduled appointment with me occurred before the second tooth could be removed. I advised her that these dental issues were indicative of her body's healing crisis and urged her to remain patient.

Within the next week, she developed multiple abscesses in her mouth and faced the prospect of loose teeth. However, approximately a week later, all the abscesses vanished, her teeth regained their firmness, and she reported a sensation of a "clean" and healthier mouth. Her sense of taste notably improved too. After a span of eleven months, her body was completely clear of cancer, and she continues to be alive and in good health to this day.

Case #2

A 32-year-old woman who had suffered a C3-C4 cervical spine severance due to a head-on collision had been immobile for a duration of twelve years. Apart from the typical healing and cleansing processes, she underwent intensive emotional releasing. On certain nights, she would call me in deep tears, and on other nights, she would be overwhelmed with uncontrollable laughter. This emotional release persisted for nearly two months, much to the chagrin of her caregiver. I assured him that this emotional upheaval was a necessary purification of her emotional being. The car accident that had left her paralyzed during her late teens had also led to the death of the other driver involved. Over the course of twelve years, she had suppressed a myriad of feelings and emotions linked to this traumatic incident.

To provide a concise summary, within eleven months of undergoing the healing regimen, she achieved complete neurological reconnection, enabling voluntary and conscious movement of all body parts along with full sensory perception. The detoxification process had facilitated the release of deep-seated grief, fostering emotional stability and expediting her overall healing process.

While these two cases stand out as extraordinary instances among the countless I have witnessed during my three decades as a healer, they serve as extremes. While certain healing crises deserve a resounding "Wow," such as these, the majority fall into the "Oh, that was nothing..." category. Most individuals will likely experience mild to moderate symptoms at most.

SPECIAL NOTE

For individuals who are currently on multiple chemical medications, it's advisable to collaborate closely with your healthcare practitioner to gradually reduce or taper off these medications. As your blood sugar levels normalize and your blood pressure returns to a healthy range, the benefits of discontinuing these medications will become evident. It's worth noting that high blood pressure often stems from internal obstructions and acidosis. In many cases, individuals with high blood pressure actually have an underlying issue of low blood pressure. As your body undergoes detoxification, your blood pressure is likely to reflect this positive change. The systolic reading can potentially decrease to levels in the low 100s, 90s, or even 80s, depending on the strength of your adrenal glands.

Regardless of the appearance of your healing crisis, always keep your ultimate goal in mind: achieving total health. The discomfort of any symptoms during this process will be overshadowed by the satisfaction of attaining your health objectives. Embrace the healing crises and detoxification, as they are as natural as the sunrise each morning. Anticipate these cleansing experiences, as with each one, you'll notice an improvement in how you feel, and your overall health will significantly benefit from your diligent efforts.

END RESULTS OF A CLEANSING PROCESS

- Increased energy—many times more dynamic and dramatic
- Deeper breathing (greater lung capacity)
- Increased sense of smell, taste, and hearing
- Tumor reduction or elimination
- Loss of lymphatic swelling
- Greater strength in previously weak areas
- Increased circulation
- Gray hair begins to disappear (goes back to natural color)
- The skin begins to tighten and become softer
- Clarity in thinking
- Improved memory
- Disease symptoms disappear
- Blood sugars normalize

- Blood pressure will normalize
- Deeper relationship with Higher Mind and Nature
- Higher sense of happiness, joy and well-being
- Skin blemishes (like pimples, rashes, etc.) disappear
- Bowels move better
- Improved kidney function
- Voice strengthens
- Heart arrhythmias disappear
- Improved eyesight
- Overall sense of well-being and vibrancy comes back
- Reversal of the "aging" process
- Never get "sick" or "catch" what's going around
- And much, much more.

WHAT TO AVOID DURING A HEALING CRISIS

- **Dehydration** — Keep yourself hydrated with fresh mineral water or freshly juiced fruit and vegetable juices.
- **Overexertion** — During a healing crisis try to conserve your energy.
- **Too Many Pesticides** — Pesticides can cause shortness of breath and "hypo" conditions of the endocrine gland system and nervous system.

- **Pushing It Too Far** — If you find the need to temporarily slow down or halt the cleansing process, consider incorporating some cooked foods into your diet. Opt for a minimal amount, if feasible, such as steamed vegetables or whole grain rice. By doing so, you can temporarily reduce the overall energy level within your body, effectively putting a pause on the intense detoxification. Once you feel ready, you can resume your cleansing program and continue your journey towards better health.

- **Fevers Above 103° Fahrenheit** — For adults and children, it's important to manage fevers of this intensity. Utilize measures like cool baths to help bring the fever down. In the case of children, it's natural for them to experience higher fevers, sometimes reaching around 104° to 105°. To manage these high fevers, use methods like cold washcloths and cool baths to keep the child's body temperature under control. Striking the right balance is crucial — you want to avoid unnecessarily interfering with the body's self-cleaning and healing efforts, while still taking appropriate measures to prevent any potential severe effects. Always ensure proper hydration by drinking ample water or fresh fruit juices, but avoid excessive hydration as well. Balance is key during this process.

- **Impatience** — As you begin to infuse your body with energy and promote its alkalinity, the natural process of self-cleansing will initiate. It's essential to bear in mind that your body is the one conducting this cleansing process. While you can incorporate herbal formulas to augment the efficacy of the cleansing process, including addressing congested lymphatic systems, eradicating parasites, and boosting the functionality of organs and glands, it's crucial to recognize that your body follows its own healing rhythm. Patience is key during this journey.

- **Do Not Overeat** — In nature, animals typically abstain from eating when they're unwell. Similarly, your body is intricately designed to undergo self-healing and self-cleansing processes, guided by the inherent wisdom of its mechanisms. Your role is simply to provide the body with appropriate nourishment to support these processes, just as the divine forces are active within them.

SMART CLEANSING

Approach the process of supporting your body's detoxification with intelligence. Striking the right balance between aiding and obstructing the process is crucial. Use your common sense as you navigate through detoxification, understanding that each person's journey is unique. Whether dealing with asthma or uterine cancer, the experiences can greatly differ.

The healing journey is a truly remarkable one. It involves a transformative release on various levels, even though its depth is often underestimated. Embrace life, well-being, and spirituality wholeheartedly.

Should the side effects of detoxification ever cause you to believe that seeking medical assistance is necessary, do not hesitate to go to an Emergency Room. I have worked in such environments for many years and know that they are designed to aid during critical situations. While many ER staff may not fully grasp the intricacies of the detoxification and healing crisis, in rare instances when you feel the need for immediate help, refer to Module 6.5, "What to Expect During Detox."

ITEMS FOR YOUR HOME FIRST AID KIT

Here is a compilation of essential First Aid supplies to keep at home, which can provide you with comfort and support throughout your detoxification journey:

CASTOR OIL PACKS
See Chapter 9 for what is needed to prepare these.

OLIVE OIL
Used like or instead of castor oil.

CAYENNE PEPPER
Used to dilate the skin and/or vascular system; for high blood pressure or castor oil packs.

PLEURISY ROOT, MULLEIN LEAF AND/OR
FENUGREEK SEED
Lung expectorant

A HEAT SOURCE
Hot water bottle or heating pad, etc. Used to dilate or "drive" herbs through the skin.

AN ANTI-SPASMODIC (AN HERBAL TINCTURE)
Spasms, convulsions, cramping and pain

HERBAL PAIN FORMULA
Tincture, preferably

SLIPPERY ELM AND/OR MARSHMALLOW ROOT
HERBAL TEAS
For acid reflux

ARNICA OIL
Use externally for sprains, pulls, stiff or sore muscles, etc.

HERBAL HEALING SALVE
Should contain a variety of healing herbs like comfrey,
horsetail, lobelia, marigold, etc. Used for sprains, muscle pulls,
pain in joints, wounds, etc.

PLANTAIN TINCTURE AND SALVE
Used for insect bites, snake bites, and other poisonous bites.

"HEAL-ALL TEA"
From www.drmorses.com or another alternative. Used for
tumors, snake bites, abscesses, infections, anything and
everything.

HERBAL INTESTINAL CORRECTIVE LAXATIVE ALOE
VERA
An "all-heal" for burns, itching from fungus, intestinal soother,
etc.

TEA TREE OIL
Herbal antiseptic, itching from fungus, etc.

HERBAL PARASITIC FORMULA
Bacterial infections, E-coli, Candida, etc.

MODULE 6.7

Fasting in Detoxification

Fasting, in various forms, has likely been a practice since ancient times, observed by both humans and animals. Fasting is a natural instinct linked to rest and efficient energy utilization. In 1972, I personally underwent a six-month orange fast, an experience that turned out to be profoundly remarkable. The surge of energy I felt led to incredible out-of-body encounters, taking me into profound spiritual experiences.

Two primary categories of fasting exist. The first, called "forced fasting," arises from illness. During this state, eating becomes impossible, and even if attempted, the body rejects food. This mechanism redirects energy from digestion to vital systems like immunity, lymphatics, and hormones, aiding in the expulsion of invaders, obstacles, or congestion.

The second type is "conscious fasting," undertaken to purify and rejuvenate the body. Such fasting nurtures self-discipline and self-assurance, both critical qualities on the path to optimal health. Both forms of fasting are strategies for managing the body's energy. Regrettably, many foods consumed by humans deplete energy instead of supplying it. Health and vitality emanate from energy, while disease results from its scarcity. Fasting permits the body to abstain from extensive digestive and metabolic duties, channeling energy instead to cleanse itself of acidic compounds and toxins, thus enabling the healing process.

Traditional diets that encompass meats, grains, dairy, and similar foods tend to strain and weaken our digestive and elimination systems. Fasting provides respite to organs like the pancreas, stomach, liver, intestines, and kidneys, directing more energy towards the immune, endocrine, and lymphatic systems. Fasting is a crucial component in achieving wellness.

Numerous fasting methodologies exist. Let's explore 4 fundamental fasting approaches and subsequently discuss the proper method of concluding or "breaking" a fast.

TYPES OF FASTS

All Raw-Food Fast

Certainly, this can't be termed a true fast as you're still consuming food. However, for individuals accustomed to consuming dense, cooked meals, this regimen is often perceived as a form of fasting. It's important to recognize that among all creatures, humans are unique in their practice of cooking food before consumption. Approach this modified fasting strategy on a day-to-day basis and aim to consume only raw foods throughout that day.

For those entrenched in diets consisting of hearty, cooked fare, this regimen might be perceived as a type of fast. The key is to take it step by step, focusing on the consumption of entirely raw foods during the designated day. To expand on this, consider attempting this modified fast for various durations: 5, 10, 30, or even 60 consecutive days. During this time, your intake should be restricted to fresh raw fruits, fruit juices, vegetables, and vegetable juices. However, it's important to note that this form of fast excludes "protein-rich" foods like nuts or seeds from the dietary mix.

All Fruit Fast

I strongly advocate for this form of fasting. Given our biological and anatomical characteristics as frugivores, this fast aligns well with our natural physiological processes and overall design. It's advisable to center this fast on grapes, preferably organic. In case organic grapes aren't available, thorough washing becomes imperative, as conventionally grown grapes often harbor significant pesticide residues. However, any assortment of fruits or melons can be utilized. As you'll discover in the forthcoming chapter on food combining, the principle "Eat melons alone or leave them alone" is key. Similarly, grapes or watermelon, for instance, should be consumed individually, without mixing them with other foods. The choice of fruit is flexible, catering to your preferences or cravings. I've had the privilege of aiding numerous individuals in purging cancer from their bodies through grape and grape juice fasting. Importantly, there's no need to monitor caloric intake within this program; you're encouraged to eat as much as desired.

Juice Fasting

This advanced form of fasting provides a respite for your gastrointestinal and digestive systems. Juice fasts operate at a higher energy level, invigorating much-needed detoxification and lymphatic circulation, all the while ensuring continual flushing of the kidneys. Juices play a role in furnishing cells with glucose and fructose for sustained energy. The juice options encompass both fruits and vegetables; however, fruit juices, especially freshly extracted grape juice, boast notable potency.

Naturally, exceptions can arise in any situation. A case involving pancreatic cancer underscored this point during my involvement. The individual's capacity to digest food had altogether ceased. When she ate any food it came out in her stools undigested. My approach commenced with exclusively fruit juices, and as time progressed, I introduced vegetable juices. Subsequently, a gradual transition incorporated raw fruits and vegetables. The rationale behind this sequence is straightforward: given the complete cessation of pancreatic digestion, the focus rested on sustaining systemic energy while requiring minimal effort from the pancreas. Freshly prepared fruit juices emerged as the optimal choice within this context. Subsequently, vegetable juices were incorporated, albeit they are comparatively more taxing on digestion. The pancreas had by then sufficiently recuperated to accommodate this adjustment. Additionally, I harnessed the potency of liquid herbal extracts to invigorate various organs and glands, notably targeting the pancreas. The final phase reintroduced solid foods, commencing with fruits, favored for their robust energy content and ease of digestion. Over the course of eleven months, the individual achieved complete freedom from cancer.

Water Fasting

This represents the fourth and ultimate form of fasting. Water fasts should exclusively be undertaken using R/O (reverse osmosis) or distilled water. At this level, the entirety of your digestive energy is devoted to fortifying the immune, lymphatic, and glandular systems. A water fast facilitates a potent process of body purification and cleansing. The body, guided by its remarkable wisdom, will prioritize the elimination of stored toxins, mucus, and inflammation.

For the average person, water fasting can provide a surge of energy. However, in cases of debilitation or depletion, the objective is to infuse energy into the body by elevating its systemic energy levels. I advise against a water-only fast for individuals who are significantly weakened or depleted, particularly those with cancer. The reason is that this type of fasting doesn't directly provide the body with energy, and thus the body must rely on its existing energy reserves.

While fasting typically boosts energy in most people, in cases of advanced tissue weakness, incorporating raw foods—especially fruits—will supply the body with both nutrition and energy. Opting for high-energy fruits or fruit juices can initiate an enhancement of cellular and systemic energies, simultaneously enabling detoxification. In situations of extreme depletion, water fasting can actually drain the body's energy and lead to potentially fatal consequences. Once an individual's strength has been restored, water fasting becomes a suitable option.

PREPARATION BEFORE FASTING

If you plan to progress towards juice or water fasting, it's advisable to ready yourself by consuming raw foods for a week, with the final couple of days focusing solely on fruits. This preparatory phase aids in cleansing the intestines of stagnant matter, promoting the flushing of the liver and kidneys, and aligning the body for the upcoming fast.

Fasting can be an enjoyable and empowering experience. Its effectiveness in aiding the body's cleansing and rejuvenation processes has been repeatedly demonstrated. For extended and prolonged fasts, it's recommended to seek guidance from someone knowledgeable and experienced in fasting and detoxification.

WHEN TO "BREAK" A FAST

Determining the optimal time to end a fast is best guided by your inner intuition and awareness. Trust your own understanding of your body, as you know it better than anyone else. Pay attention to when you feel satisfied and have had enough. However, be honest with yourself, as desires can sometimes influence your perception of hunger. After approximately three days, the desire for food typically diminishes. This occurs because the body redirects its energy toward healing and cleansing processes. When true hunger returns, it's a positive indication that you are prepared to resume eating. Begin with consuming fruits exclusively.

Another method to gauge the duration of fasting is the tongue-examination approach. This traditional technique, which I've employed for years, involves observing the appearance of your tongue. When you initiate fasting, a thick coating of white, yellow, green, or brown may develop on your tongue. The degree of toxicity in your body influences the thickness and color of this coating. With better health, the coating becomes lighter. Fasting until your tongue regains a pink hue indicates a substantial achievement in detoxifying your body.

Detoxification is an ongoing journey that can span years, but it's not as daunting as it sounds. Consider health as one of your personal interests. Dedicate around a year to proactive self-improvement, then transition into a balanced and harmonious lifestyle. This newfound way of living will embody the healthier, more vibrant, and more conscious version of you. As your spiritual awareness expands, aim to maintain equilibrium between your lifestyle, eating habits, and spiritual growth. The deeper your awareness, the stronger your desire for energetically nourishing food. Strive for your physical well-being to match your spiritual evolution. Embrace the excitement of your voyage towards health, vitality, and spirituality; it's a unique and fulfilling journey.

HOW TO "BREAK" A FAST

Breaking a fast is a critical step and should be approached with care, taking into consideration the duration and type of fast you've completed. As a general guideline, it's recommended to transition from fasting by consuming fresh, raw fruits exclusively for a day or two for every three days of fasting you've undertaken.

This principle holds especially true for juice or water fasting. The longer your fast, the more crucial it is to allocate more time to solely eating fruits before incorporating heavier vegetables. Caution is essential during this phase, as I've come across instances where improper breaking of a fast led to unfortunate outcomes. For example, I know of a case where an individual passed away due to breaking an extended fast with boiled potatoes. Given the starchy nature of potatoes, it's understandable how they could lead to bowel complications.

Prioritize maintaining regular bowel movements, although this might be challenging during juice or water fasting. In Module 6.9, we will delve into the topic of bowel health and management.

Please Buy a Juicer

N.W. Walker's vibrant health and longevity, living to the age of 107, stands as compelling evidence of the benefits of juicing. It's a testament to the positive impact that juicing can have on one's well-being. Why not give it a try yourself? Enjoy a refreshing glass of carrot, spinach, and celery juice today and experience the potential benefits firsthand.

Raw fruit and vegetable juices offer a concentrated burst of nourishment. For instance, a single glass of carrot juice can provide the nutritional equivalent of 6 to 8 whole carrots. These juices are what I like to refer to as "High Electrical"

Drinks, as they brim with energy and essential amino acids that can invigorate the body.

Incorporating 2 to 4 glasses of your preferred fruit or vegetable juices into your daily routine can provide a substantial nutritional boost. If you're interested in delving deeper into the world of juicing,

I recommend reading "Vegetable and Fruit Juices" by N.W. Walker. This resource can provide valuable insights into the benefits and practices of juicing for health and vitality.

MODULE 6.8

Two Great Fruit Juice Fasts

LEMONADE FAST
HOW TO MAKE LEMONADE:

- 2 tbsp. lemon or lime juice (approx. 1/2 lemon)

- 1/2 to 3/4 tbsp. genuine Maple Syrup (not maple-flavored sugar syrup)

- pinch of Cayenne Pepper (optional)

Combine the juice, maple syrup, and cayenne pepper in a 10-ounce glass and fill with medium/hot distilled or R/O water. (Cold water may be used if preferred.) Use fresh lemons or limes only; never use canned lemon or lime juice, or frozen lemonade or lime juice.

Cayenne Pepper may be used with this formula as it adds extra vitamin C and B-complex. It also increases warmth for an additional lift. For those not used to hot peppers, start with a dash and increase it as you are able. You may eliminate the pepper if you wish. Pure sorghum, black strap molasses or honey may be used as a lesser replacement when maple syrup is not available. You might wish to make a quart of lemonade for the whole day.

FOR A FULL QUART OF LEMONADE:

10 cups distilled water
1 1/2 cup of fresh lemon juice

1/2 cup of pure maple syrup
Shake well and refrigerate

HOW TO TAKE THE LEMONADE:

Drink this lemonade as much and as often as you want, but drink only this lemonade, no other foods or drinks. This fruit juice fast can be done for 1, 2, 3 or up to 10 days easily.

GRAPE JUICE FAST

HOW TO MAKE GRAPE JUICE:

A juice extractor or juicer is necessary.
Juice a quart of grapes (seeds and small stems as well).
Any type of grape is okay; however the dark, seeded ones are the best. And always try to use organic grapes.

HOW TO TAKE THE JUICE:

Feel free to indulge in grape juice as frequently and abundantly as you desire. Grapes possess remarkable antioxidant and astringent properties that play a vital role in purging toxins from the body. Consuming grapes and partaking in a Grape Juice fast can be an exceptional choice. In my experience, I've overseen fasts lasting more than twenty days solely relying on grapes. Opting for a 5 or 10-day grape or grape juice fast can be both exceptional and highly advantageous.

Grapes and lemons are two of nature's most effective agents for cleansing the lymphatic system and combatting tumors. Through a combination of fruit juice fasts, herbal therapies, and adhering to a raw food diet, I've observed remarkable outcomes, including the disappearance of lymphomas within forty-five days and stomach cancer eradicated in just fifty-nine days. This underscores the potential of these fruit juice fasts as integral components of comprehensive healing strategies.

MODULE 6.9

Healthy Bowel Management

The core of many health issues often lies in inadequate bowel management. I've been a proponent of colon health education for over three decades. My dear friend, the late Dr. Bernard Jensen, dedicated over sixty years to this endeavor. Dr. Jensen, who interacted with more than 300,000 clients, concluded that "caring for the bowels is invariably the first step before effective healing can commence." In fact, the natural health field's origins largely revolve around gastrointestinal concerns.

Conversing about bowel wisdom is a topic most shy away from, yet nurturing the health and vitality of the intestinal tract is a pivotal strategy to evade the clutches of toxicity and cellular debilitation. Your gastrointestinal (GI) tract functions as the epicenter, akin to the hub of a wheel, supporting the body's entire structure. It constitutes a principal organ system of the body, comparable in significance to the heart. The paramount question should be, "How do we safeguard and rejuvenate the GI tract, a core entity as critical as the heart?" The absence of digestion, absorption, and elimination spells demise. The canal spanning from the mouth to the anus facilitates the infusion of energy and chemistry from foods into the body. Beyond digestion, the colon and beyond serve as the means to expel waste, a process pivotal for bodily survival. Adequate elimination of waste from food digestion and cellular metabolism mirrors the import of food ingestion.

In embryonic stages, both the colon and spinal cord were the first areas of the body to form. Genetic vulnerabilities typically manifest first in the colon, which then influence the state of organs, glands, nerves, and other tissues throughout the body.

The bowels endure the brunt of acidic-toxic foods and beverages. Several foods induce inflammation and weaken their structure. Certain foods act like adhesive agents, adhering to the intestinal walls. Others prove abrasive, inducing the production of excess mucus to safeguard these walls. This mucus lodges itself on the bowel walls and within its structure. These factors collectively impede the GI tract's digestion and nutrient absorption capabilities.

Moreover, the GI tract significantly interrelates with the lymphatic system, akin to a sewer system. The kidneys, GI tract, and skin function as its primary outlets. Any obstruction in the skin, kidneys, and especially the colon can clog the lymphatic system, paralleling a blocked septic tank causing a household overflow.

The autonomic nervous system's sympathetic and parasympathetic nerves regulate the digestive tract via neurotransmitters originating from the adrenal glands. Weaker adrenal glands can lead to nerve debilitation and constipation, a connection often overlooked. Strengthening adrenal glands concurrently with regenerating the GI tract is a prudent approach.

The importance of nurturing a clean and healthy intestinal tract cannot be emphasized enough. This canal serves as the crucible for digestion, dismantling foods into fuels and building blocks. Following digestion, nutrients are absorbed through the intestinal lining via villi. Absorption is as crucial as digestion, as the myriad cells forming the body rely on the bowels for nourishment. Proper nutrition can be hindered by retained colon waste, contributing to toxic buildup and the accumulation of a sticky substance termed "mucoid plaque." This plaque fuels inflammation, corroding the intestinal wall tissues.

Mucoid plaque, often a byproduct of refined starches, sugars, and dairy, accumulates as layers on the intestinal walls, hindering optimal absorption of nutrients necessary for the body's functioning and peak performance. This plaque also provides a breeding ground for harmful parasites, which further impede nutrient absorption. Intestinal flora, or certain intestinal parasites, play a constructive role in breaking down digestion by-products. A case in point is B-vitamins generated through intestinal flora's interaction with starches. Generally, non-harmful organisms populate the intestines, assisting digestion and conversion of food components into nutrients. However, numerous destructive parasites can flourish, particularly with meat consumption, instigating the proliferation of various worms and protein-splitting microorganisms. Hence, addressing intestinal inflammation concurrently with waste elimination is crucial.

A healthy diet should trigger bowel movements roughly thirty minutes post-meal. Achieving two-to-three daily bowel movements is crucial. Sluggish bowels lead to fermentation and putrefaction of food, permitting toxins and gas particles to infiltrate the bloodstream, precipitating headaches, mental fog, bloating, abdominal discomfort, and even heart arrhythmias. Skipping even a single day of regular bowel movements can be detrimental.

Both diarrhea and constipation pose grave concerns. Moving food too rapidly or too slowly through the GI tract yields inadequate digestion and poor absorption on one hand, and fermentation, putrefaction, acidosis, gas, and inflammation on the other. Both circumstances contribute to a state of bodily deprivation.

FOUR WAYS TO CLEANSE THE BOWELS

Herbal Bowel Formulas

An effective bowel formula, to be integrated into your daily regimen during your detoxification process, can play a pivotal role in breaking down mucoid plaque, selectively eliminating harmful parasites, alleviating inflammation, and fortifying the integrity of the intestinal walls.

When developing my stomach and bowel formulas, my objective was to create gentle yet efficacious solutions. These formulas were designed to counter inflammation, cleanse the walls of accumulated mucoid plaque, and address the formation of pockets (diverticula) resulting from obstructions. I aimed to craft a formulation that would enhance the strength of the gastrointestinal (GI) tract, eradicating pockets, as well as addressing issues such as ballooning and spasms that commonly afflict individuals. It is noteworthy that many available bowel formulas are characterized by potent ingredients such as Cayenne Pepper, Aloes, Buckthorn, or other stimulating agents that can cause discomfort through gripping, cramping, or excessive mucus production. This aspect often renders these formulas challenging to regulate and may lead to abdominal distress. Furthermore, such formulas have the potential to become habit-forming, creating a dependency similar to other stimulants, which in turn may exacerbate constipation upon cessation.

An optimal bowel formula, in contrast, should not foster dependency. It should delicately facilitate movement, detoxification, inflammation reduction, and fortification simultaneously. Additionally, it should stimulate lymphatic flow and circulation within the intestinal wall tissues. Refer to Chapter 8, Module 8.3 for herbal formulas focusing on the stomach and bowels.

Colonics

Colonic therapy is a viable option to support colon (large intestine) cleansing, although it is important to underscore that the small intestine necessitates attention as well. This is why the inclusion of an herbal bowel formula is advisable. Colonics share similarities with high enemas but distinguish themselves by the manner in which they wash and cleanse the tissues. These procedures are conducted by colon therapists, often licensed massage therapists, and I hold the perspective that colonic machines and trained therapists should be standard in every Emergency Room. The advantages of colonics encompass dislodging impactions from the large bowel, alleviating conditions like acidosis, abdominal distention, lower back pain, sciatic pain, kidney pain, headaches, and fevers. They also aid in the cleansing of diverticula or bowel pockets.

While colon therapy is gentle in its approach, it can yield robust results, as it can dislodge plaque that has been adhered to the colon wall for extended periods. I have personally witnessed the removal of impactions through colonics that had been lodged within the body for over fifty years. A noteworthy anecdote involves a patient of a chiropractor associate of mine, who, after a colonic, experienced discomfort in her sigmoid bowel. She sought medical attention after hours of enduring the pain, and her visit to the Emergency Room unveiled sigmoid bowel cancer. The colonic did not trigger the cancer; rather, it revealed an existing condition that was attributed to her lifestyle. This instance demonstrated the utility of colonics in identifying underlying issues. While exposing inflammation, as was the case here, can be uncomfortable, my preference leans towards recommending an anti-inflammatory and restorative herbal bowel formula, as opposed to a laxative one. Such restorative formulas gradually loosen and eliminate plaque, while concurrently reducing inflammation and promoting bowel wall healing, thus offering a smoother and less distressing healing process.

Colonics are particularly effective for addressing colon obstructions, provided they are not tumors or adhesions. In terms of my preferred method, I endorse Dr. Jensen's Colema Board® concept as an optimal approach. The Colema Board is ingeniously designed to be placed over a toilet, with one end extending to a chair or stool. By reclining on the board and utilizing a five-gallon bucket of lukewarm water, a self-

administered high enema is facilitated. This method proves to be more serene than a regular enema, as one simply reclines and permits the water to gently cleanse the system. Dr. Jensen has formulated a comprehensive bowel management regimen that is unparalleled (see his book, "Tissue Cleansing Through Bowel Management," 1981). His protocol extends to cleansing both the small and large bowels, distinguishing it from professional colonics which primarily address the large bowel. The Colema System can be executed at home with the acquisition of a Colema Board, given a degree of self-discipline. I wish to emphasize that my stance is not against professional colonics. To optimize their efficacy, it is recommended to transition to a 100 percent raw food regimen and incorporate intestinal restoratives for approximately a month before embarking on a colonic regimen. Typically, three to five colonics should suffice to yield meaningful benefits.

Enemas

Enemas represent an additional effective approach for self-assistance during times of necessity or for addressing specific colon-rectal issues such as hemorrhoids or cancer. Numerous varieties of enemas are available to aid in the cleansing and clearing of this pathway.

LOW ENEMAS — These enemas are generally aimed at cleansing and reinforcing the descending, sigmoid, and rectal sections of the large intestine (colon). They usually involve using about half to one quart of water at skin temperature, placed in an enema bag. These bags can be easily obtained from most pharmacies and are often labeled as "enema/hot-water bottle" or "enema/douche/hot water bottle" combinations.

To enhance the enema's effectiveness, a variety of herbs can be brewed into tea, strained, and then used instead of plain water in the enema bag. These herbs have properties that both cleanse and strengthen the walls of the colon. Some examples of such herbs include Cascara Sagrada, Marshmallow Root, Slippery Elm Bark, Plantain Leaf, Comfrey Root, Burdock Root, and Gentian. Detailed instructions on how to perform an enema can be found in the "How To Do An Enema" section below.

HIGH ENEMAS — A high enema becomes necessary to target the upper sections of the colon, such as the transverse, ascending, and cecum portions of the large intestine. The distinction between a high enema and a low enema often lies in the method of application and the quantity of water or mixture used. This quantity determines how deeply the water or mixture can reach into your colon. The same herbs mentioned earlier can be employed for high enemas as well. In cases of weakened health where extreme fatigue is present, high enemas can utilize fresh green juices like wheatgrass, spinach, kelp, alfalfa, barley, and others, in place of water or herbal tea. These juices are quickly absorbed by the colon walls and provide invigorating energy to the body. Additionally, chlorophyll, a beneficial component, can also be introduced into the colon through enemas to support the healing and detoxification processes.

COFFEE ENEMAS — Some individuals resort to coffee enemas due to their strong stimulatory effects on the bowels and liver. However, I strongly advise against their regular use, unless you are experiencing a situation where your colon is completely obstructed and you are unable to have a bowel movement. The repeated use of coffee enemas can lead to adverse consequences. They can induce an intense back-and-forth effect, ultimately resulting in significant fatigue of the colon and inflammation of the liver and kidneys.

Furthermore, coffee enemas can negatively impact the nervous system, causing either excessive hyperactivity or insufficient activity. This disruption can then extend throughout the body in various ways, including the onset of nerve-related disorders, severe constipation, diarrhea, bloating, edema, and acidosis.

HOW TO DO AN ENEMA

1. Purchase an enema-bag / "hot water bottle" combination from a pharmacy.
2. Fill the bag with 1/2 quart to 2 quarts of skin temperature water or herb-water mixture. Always use skin temperature water no matter what you mix it with.
3. Hang the hot water bottle at least two feet above you.
4. Lay on your left side as you start your enema.
5. Use a healing herbal salve to lubricate the tip for easy insertion.
6. Let the water (or herbal mixture) flow slowly into your colon; stopping the flow periodically while you rest and do some deep breathing.
7. After a few minutes, move from your left side to lying on your back, and continue to let the water flow into your colon; then turn over to your right side.
8. You may wish to massage the region of your colon as it is being filled with the mixture. This will help loosen impacted "plaque" for removal.
9. Retain this water (mixture) somewhat, then allow elimination.
10. Repeat until the bag/hot water bottle is empty.
    Use enemas wisely and when needed. There is no need to over use them.

A diet of raw fruits and vegetables along with a good intestinal rejuvenator will work much better in the long run at reestablishing the health of the GI tract.

Healing Clay

Another approach to bowel cleansing involves the utilization of clays. While this method is not as commonly practiced in the United States compared to Europe, it has gained traction in several countries. For instance, in nations like Portugal, healthcare practitioners apply clay packs over the abdominal area to achieve similar outcomes as colonics.

Dr. John Christopher, who has since passed away, created an effective intestinal powder known as "Intestinal Corrective #2®." This formulation incorporates bentonite clay and charcoal, both of which have powerful cleansing and absorbent properties within the intestines. This specific blend proves beneficial for individuals dealing with irritable bowel syndrome and uncontrollable diarrhea.

Summary

The significance of our intestines, or gastrointestinal (GI) tract, is such that it holds a prominent place in the very early stages of embryonic cell development, highlighting its critical role. During these initial phases, the embryonic structure forms the spinal column alongside "gut" tissue, which subsequently matures into the GI tract. The proper functioning of this system is absolutely essential for your overall survival.

The GI tract serves as a conduit for absorbing nutrients, building materials, and energy sources from its inner walls. Additionally, it plays a role in generating white blood cells, diverse vitamins, and amino acids. While the full extent of the

GI system's synergy with the lymphatic system is not entirely understood, its fundamental connection to every cell within your body through the lymphatic network underscores its immense importance in maintaining proper bodily function.

Choosing to nourish the GI tract with living, easily digestible foods rich in electrically vibrant fiber is vital for sustaining its health and optimal functionality.

Physicians pour drugs of which they know little, to cure diseases of which they know less, into humans of which they know nothing.

— Voltaire, French satirist (1694-1778)

CHAPTER SEVEN

Eating for Vitality

Until now, our exploration has encompassed the intricacies of bodily functioning, the mechanisms of illness, the processes of detoxification and restoration. We've delved into our species and identified the most suitable types of nourishment for us. We've also scrutinized the impact of foods on our bodily tissues.

In this chapter, our focus shifts to what we should consume and how to do so. It's not only crucial to discern the right foods to include, but also to master the skill of effectively combining these foods to attain optimal benefits—a practice known as food combining.

Within this chapter, we will also furnish a range of menus that you can readily adopt to initiate your journey towards detoxification and rejuvenation. These menus are tailored to accommodate your needs, whether you're a cautious newcomer or an adventurous explorer.

We'll also delve into the remarkable health advantages offered by raw fruit and vegetable juices, along with an examination of beans, soybeans, and grains in relation to the processes of detoxification and restoration.

As this chapter concludes, you'll discover an array of superb recipes for both raw and steamed dishes. These recipes will bolster you along your path and introduce delightful variety into your meals, enhancing your overall experience.

MODULE 7.1

What Foods to Eat

Following is a list of acceptable raw fruits, vegetables, nuts, and seeds. Always buy organic when possible.

Most Fruits and Berries

Grapes
Bananas
Strawberries
Mangoes
Oranges
Grapefruit
Apples
Peaches
Pears
Pineapple
Dried fruits of all kinds (unsulphured)
Flowers are acceptable
Avoid–Cranberries, Prunes and unripe fruits

VEGETABLES

Romaine Lettuce
Spinach
Carrots
Celery

Green Peppers
Cucumbers
Sprouts
Avocados
Green Leafy Vegetables
Squash
Green Beans
Peas
Raw Tomatoes
Kelp, Dulse and other Sea Vegetables

OTHER RAW FOODS

Pecans

Almonds

Sunflower Seeds

Sesame Seeds

Pumpkin Seeds

Coconuts

Pine Nuts

Note–Eat moderately of this category. Too many of these foods can be acid-forming, energy robbing, and will slow or stop the cleansing process.

MODULE 7.2

Acid/Alkaline Food Chart

All edibles comprise both components that create acidity and those that produce alkalinity. The organic constituents of foods are not responsible for leaving acidic or alkaline residues within your body. This task is determined by the non-organic constituents, particularly minerals, that govern the acidity or alkalinity of bodily fluids and tissues. Among the alkaline-forming electrolytes are potassium, sodium, magnesium, and calcium, while the acid-forming elements encompass phosphorus, sulfur, and manganese.

Various methodologies can be employed to ascertain whether a food leans more towards acid-forming or alkaline-forming tendencies. Generally, if a food possesses predominant acid-forming elements in contrast to alkaline-forming ones, it is classified as acid-forming. Conversely, if a food features dominant alkaline-forming components, it is categorized as alkaline-forming.

Titration is the laboratory technique employed to gauge the balance between acidity and alkalinity. This procedure unfolds in two stages. Initially, the designated quantity of food is incinerated to ashes, mimicking the process of digestion. Subsequently, around one liter of distilled water is combined with 100 grams of these ashes, creating a solution that is then evaluated for its acid or alkaline nature.

An alternative approach to discerning a food's acidity or alkalinity hinges on its nitrogen or proteid content, referring to chemical compounds that constitute protein structures. Since nitrogen holds an acidic effect, foods abundant in protein (nitrogen-rich) are categorized as acid-forming. However, this method, while older, is less precise due to the realization that plant matter supplies more accessible nitrogen and proteid substances than meats do.

The Acid/Alkaline Food Chart that follows is formulated through a fusion of the above techniques, offering guidance on your journey towards achieving alkaline balance. Remember, a diet encompassing 80 percent alkaline and 20 percent acid-forming foods is pivotal for enhanced well-being. Opting for a diet comprising 90 percent or more alkaline-forming foods signifies robust health.

Simplicity is key. I'm often asked: "What can I add to my diet?" My response is: "What can I eliminate?" Astonishingly, the simpler your diet, the healthier you become. While this concept might perplex nutritional scientists, who have traditionally focused on deficiencies and endorsed high doses of amino acids, vitamins, and minerals, it's essential to grasp that true healing isn't derived from excessive nutrient consumption. Rather, it emanates from the potency and synergistic effects of whole, ripe, raw foods. The capacity of raw foods to cleanse and rejuvenate the physical body remains largely misunderstood within our pharmaceutical and scientific circles.

Observe the diets of many wild herbivores such as elephants, horses, or cows. Their primary intake comprises grass and leaves. Similarly, wild silver-back apes have a straightforward diet, consisting mainly of sweet components like fruits, sweet tubers, berries, and flowers. A substantial 70 percent of a grizzly bear's diet is composed of grass, yet these creatures stand as some of the mightiest on Earth.

From personal experience, during my six-month organic navel orange fast, I've never felt more connected with God and nature. Trust in nature, in the divine, and in your inner intuition to unearth the truth.

The Alkaline/Acid Food Chart differentiates alkaline-forming foods from acid-forming ones. For the duration of detoxification, it is advisable to consume exclusively raw fruits and vegetables.

Alkaline Forming Foods

FRUITS
- Apples
- Apricots
- Bananas
- Berries
- Cherries
- Coconut, fresh
- Currants
- Dates

- Figs
- Grapefruit
- Grapes
- Guava
- Kumquats
- Lemons, ripe
- Limes
- Loquats
- Mangos
- Melons, all Nectarines
- Oranges
- Passion Fruit
- Papaya
- Pears
- Peaches
- Pineapple, fresh
- Pomegranates
- Prickly Pear
- Raisins
- Sapotes
- Strawberries
- Tamarind
- Tangerines

VEGETABLES

- Alfalfa
- Almonds
- Artichokes
- Asparagus
- Avocados
- Bamboo shoots
- Beans—green, string, wax
- Beans, lima
- Beets
- Bell Peppers, all colors
- Broccoli
- Brussels Sprouts
- Cabbage, red and white
- Carrots
- Celery
- Cauliflower
- Chard
- Chestnuts
- Chicory
- Chives
- Collards

- Corn, sweet
- Cucumber
- Dandelion
- Dill
- Dock, green
- Eggplant
- Escarole
- Garlic
- Horseradish
- Kale
- Kohlrabi
- Leeks
- Lettuce
- Okra
- Olives
- Onions
- Parsley
- Parsnips
- Peas
- Pumpkin
- Radish
- Rhubarb

- Sauerkraut
- Sorrel
- Spinach
- Sprouts
- Squash
- Sweet Potato
- Tomatoes, orange only
- Turnips
- Watercress
- White Potato

OTHER

- Apple Cider Vinegar
- Buttermilk, raw
- Dulse and Kelp
- Grains—Amaranth, Millet, Quinoa
- Milk, raw
- Miso
- Molasses
- Olive Oil
- Spices, natural

- Tea, herbal and Chinese
- Whey
- Wine, organic
- Yogurt, raw

Acid Forming Foods

- Alcoholic beverages
- Artichokes
- Asparagus, tips (white only)
- Aspirin
- Barley
- Bananas, green
- Beans, dried
- Blueberries
- Breads
- Cakes
- Candy
- Cereals, breakfast
- Cheeses, all
- Chocolate and Cocoa
- Coffee
- Cola and soft drinks

- Colorings, artificial
- Condiments, all
- Corn, cooked
- Corn starch
- Cranberries
- Crackers
- Custards
- Dairy products
- Dressings
- Doughnuts
- Eggs, whites
- Flavorings, artificial
- Flour products
- Fruits, canned
- Garbanzos
- Gelatin
- Grains, most
- Grapenuts
- Gravies
- Grits, hominy
- Ice Cream
- Jams and Jellies

- Lentils
- Mayonnaise Meats, including fish, shellfish and fowl
- Oatmeal
- Oils, processed
- Olives, pickled
- Nuts
- Pasta
- Pastries and Pies
- Peanuts
- Pepper, Black
- Plums
- Prunes
- Rice cakes
- Rice, white and brown
- Salt
- Soda water
- Soybeans
- Soy products
- Spaghetti
- Sugar, refined
- Tapioca
- Teas, Indian

- Tobacco

- Vegetables, canned

- Vinegar Yogurt

Remember …

Pleasure, laughter, happiness, rest and sleep are all Alkaline forming.
Worry, anger, hate, envy, gossip, fear and lack of sleep are Acid forming.

MODULE 7.3

The Vital Role of Proper Food Combination

In this book, I've guided you through a simplified exploration of the body's intricate systems and their functions. We've delved into the mechanisms of diseases and their underlying causes. You've grasped the significance of the body's pH balance. We've dissected the foundations of chemistry: alkalis and acids, and we've scrutinized the role of acidosis in the context of illnesses. The potency of raw foods and their impact on bodily tissues has been elucidated. Now, it's time to amalgamate these components and delve into the realm of proper food combinations.

Contrary to the assertion by the American Dietetics Association that the specific combination of foods doesn't matter, as long as proteins, carbohydrates, and some fats are present in each meal, this perspective is not only nonsensical but unscientific. Many of us have encountered issues such as gas, bloating, and acidosis due to this approach. The realm of chemistry contradicts this stance. In fact, when we delve into the domain of proper food combinations, chemistry becomes our ally. This becomes especially vital for individuals with diabetes who seek to manage blood sugar levels effectively.

A wealth of valuable literature has been composed on the topic of proper food combinations, and I strongly recommend dedicating some time to explore this pivotal subject. (Recommended readings include "Food Combining Made

Easy" by Herbert Shelton and "Proper Food-Combining Works" by Lee DuBelle.)

Chemistry imparts that when we conjoin an alkaline substance with an acidic one, they neutralize each other. This alteration triggers processes of fermentation and putrefaction to take precedence over the action of digestive enzymes. The consequence is a flawed breakdown of food and a cascade of undesirable chemical transformations, culminating in malabsorption, acidosis, and cellular deprivation. This phenomenon becomes apparent, for example, when protein-rich foods are paired with starches.

There are two fundamental principles when it comes to proper food combinations: firstly, avoid mixing proteins (acidic foods) with carbohydrates (alkaline foods), and secondly, consume fruits or melons separately from other types of food. These principles will be elaborated upon in the subsequent discussion.

By adhering to these principles of proper food combinations, you can effectively alleviate issues like acid reflux, ulcers, bloating, and gas, which often arise from disregarding these natural guidelines. It's important to note that the simpler the array of foods you combine, the more efficient your digestion will be. Just as the mind struggles to focus on ten different things at once, attempting to consume numerous foods simultaneously can lead to confusion. This underlines the value of simplicity in meal planning. The essence lies not in how much you consume, but in your ability to digest, absorb, utilize, and eliminate what you've eaten.

Strive to maintain a straightforward diet, mirroring the simplicity of your life. Approach your meals with joy and contentment. It's advisable to avoid eating when experiencing anger or agitation, as such emotional states can elevate stomach acid levels, undermining your digestion and fostering acidosis. Create a relaxing atmosphere and savor the experience of eating. Adequate chewing is essential, as the initial stage of digestion commences in your mouth. Furthermore, it's beneficial to minimize fluid intake during meals, as this practice dilutes or counteracts your digestive enzymes.

THE TWO MOST IMPORTANT FOOD-COMBINING TIPS

1. Do Not Combine Proteins (acid) and Carbohydrates (alkaline)

In the realm of chemistry, we comprehend that the merging of acid digestive enzymes with alkaline digestive enzymes is generally counterproductive. This is due to their propensity to nullify each other's effects, disrupting proper digestion and ushering in processes like putrefaction and fermentation.

The digestion of carbohydrates initiates within the oral cavity through enzymes like amylase and ptyalin, which exhibit alkaline properties. In contrast, protein-containing foods such as meat and nuts instigate their digestion further down the stomach by discharging hydrochloric acid (HCL), consequently activating pepsin. These substances are predominantly acidic in nature.

When a meal dominated by starches intermingles with one dominated by proteins in the stomach, a clash emerges. This is evident in the bloating and sensation of fullness experienced after such a meal. The fermentation of sugars yields alcohol, which can wield varying effects on our energy levels—either invigorating or dampening. This process can trigger over-acidity, accumulation of mucus, toxicity from proteins, and tissue inflammation. Among the most affected are the liver, pancreas, and adrenal tissues. For individuals with diabetes, managing blood sugar levels becomes challenging when consuming this type of combination.

2. Separate Your Fruits or Melons from All Other Foods

Fruits and melons undergo rapid digestion. However, when they are combined with foods that have a slower digestion rate, their sugars become delayed in the stomach. Consequently, the undigested sugars undergo fermentation, resulting in the production of alcohol. This fermented alcohol from food sugars can lead to elevated blood alcohol levels, and in some cases, has even been associated with accidents such as plane crashes, car wrecks, and arrests for driving while intoxicated.

It is advisable to consume fruits or melons as standalone meals. These meals are rich in energy and contribute significantly to the detoxification process.

Several other significant principles are involved in proper food combinations, including refraining from pairing two different kinds of proteins within the same meal, and understanding that specific fruits can harmonize with particular proteins. This topic can be extensive, and the intricacies exceed the confines of this book. For a deeper understanding, I recommend consulting the suggested books mentioned earlier.

Simplifying your diet enhances your digestive functions, ultimately leading to increased energy levels. The accompanying chart furnishes a general overview of appropriate (and inappropriate) food combinations.

Simple Food Combining

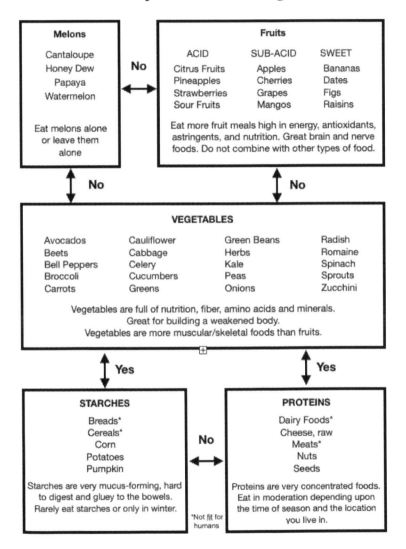

Melons

Cantaloupe
Honey Dew
Papaya
Watermelon

Eat melons alone
or leave them
alone

No

Fruits

ACID	SUB-ACID	SWEET
Citrus Fruits	Apples	Bananas
Pineapples	Cherries	Dates
Strawberries	Grapes	Figs
Sour Fruits	Mangos	Raisins

Eat more fruit meals high in energy, antioxidants, astringents, and nutrition. Great brain and nerve foods. Do not combine with other types of food.

No   **No**

VEGETABLES

Avocados	Cauliflower	Green Beans	Radish
Beets	Cabbage	Herbs	Romaine
Bell Peppers	Celery	Kale	Spinach
Broccoli	Cucumbers	Peas	Sprouts
Carrots	Greens	Onions	Zucchini

Vegetables are full of nutrition, fiber, amino acids and minerals.
Great for building a weakened body.
Vegetables are more muscular/skeletal foods than fruits.

Yes   **Yes**

STARCHES

Breads*
Cereals*
Corn
Potatoes
Pumpkin

Starches are very mucus-forming, hard to digest and gluey to the bowels. Rarely eat starches or only in winter.

No

*Not fit for humans

PROTEINS

Dairy Foods*
Cheese, raw
Meats*
Nuts
Seeds

Proteins are very concentrated foods. Eat in moderation depending upon the time of season and the location you live in.

MODULE 7.4

The Detox Miracle Menus

After decades of practical experience, I've devised the following dietary plan, which I've named the "Detox Miracle Diet." This name stems from the extensive healing and tissue regeneration I've witnessed it achieved for numerous individuals. I also refer to it as "God's Rainbow Diet" as it encompasses a variety of colorful fruits and vegetables. Each food and its corresponding hue provide distinct nourishment, energy, and healing properties to the body. Fruits contribute to brain and nervous system health, while vegetables support the muscles and skeletal structure. Nuts and seeds, on the other hand, serve as foundational components.

Optimal vitality is achieved through an increased consumption of raw, uncooked, and unprocessed foods. I encourage you to challenge your self-discipline by attempting a 100 percent raw food regimen, abstaining from cooked foods entirely. This transition can profoundly impact your overall vitality. Even adopting an 80 percent raw and 20 percent cooked diet can yield remarkable benefits and should be seriously considered.

Here are a few things to keep in mind as you begin this process:

1. I strongly advise against the consumption of any animal products due to their high toxicity and acidic nature. These products tend to promote disease rather than facilitate body regeneration. If you opt for meat, limit your intake to no more than three times a week, and only during lunch. This

allows the predominant acidic digestive processes to occur. Some individuals believe that the body ceases to produce hydrochloric acid after 2:00 P.M., although there's no concrete scientific evidence to support this claim. Despite this, adopting light alkaline meals in the evening can yield enhanced energy levels, improved sleep, and greater healing potential.

2. Avoid combining meat with starches. If you're seeking a hearty sensation, consider substituting meat with a baked potato. Use natural oils like olive oil or real butter, but avoid adding salts, sour cream, or cheese. Opt for a baked sweet potato over a regular one.

3. For those seeking a warm meal, I suggest homemade vegetable soup (excluding tomatoes), steamed vegetables, or stir-fried vegetables accompanied by a salad. (Check our recipe section in the concluding pages of this chapter for an array of soup options.)

4. Insist on organic, vine-ripened foods devoid of chemicals and free from irradiation. We must not permit the degradation of our food sources; otherwise, the consequences could be dire. In a world where cancer threatens to afflict every other individual, it's crucial for each person to take control of their own health. No one else will do it for you.

5. During the initial two to three months of detoxification, focus on consuming low-protein or even "no-protein" foods. This entails avoiding meats, beans, and nuts. While

nuts serve as a valuable amino acid source, they should be considered only if you feel the need for such nourishment.

ONE DAY AT A TIME FOR FIVE DAYS

Approach each day with a fresh perspective and take things one step at a time. Strive to consume exclusively raw fruits and vegetables for a single day. Repeat this endeavor the next day, and continue until you've successfully eaten raw, uncooked produce for five consecutive days. Pay attention to the palpable difference between an all-raw diet and one that includes cooked foods. The disparity is remarkable, akin to the contrast between night and day.

Certain days, you might find yourself inclined to consume only fruits, which is commendable. Fruits possess unmatched detoxification capabilities and possess remarkable vitality, rendering them an unparalleled source of energy for the nerves and brain.

An effective technique I've discovered is adhering to an all-raw diet from Monday through Friday, then allowing yourself the option to incorporate cooked vegetables with rice or similar choices on Saturday and/or Sunday. Establish a recurring pattern for yourself; your body thrives on cycles and routines, benefiting from consistency and habit.

Over time, you might contemplate integrating periods of fasting into your regimen, which can expedite the detoxification process. Embrace fasting as best you can; the longer you sustain it, the greater the benefits for your health.

Recondition your eating habits by reshaping your relationship with food.

The menu I've devised for our "Getting Healthy" program is designed to be both straightforward and effective. Relish the refreshing sensation and newfound vitality that raw foods bring. Embarking on this journey toward vibrancy, longevity, and spiritual well-being is an investment you won't ever regret.

HOW MUCH FOOD AND HOW OFTEN?

The question of "how much and how often should one eat?" has long persisted. In my personal view, we should opt for consuming only one to three different foods in each instance and eat whenever hunger strikes. While our society typically adheres to the three-meal structure of breakfast, lunch, and dinner, this approach often leads to overeating and combining a multitude of food types within a single meal. Regrettably, this practice burdens the digestive organs and gastrointestinal tract, resulting in incomplete digestion and inadequate nutrient absorption. Consequently, individuals in our culture tend to rely predominantly on the consequences of fermentation and putrefaction by-products for nourishment.

Lack of Funds? Make Food Your Medicine

Facing financial constraints is a common challenge that many of us encounter. My response to this predicament is straightforward: "You must always eat." However, the crucial factor lies in the nature of your food choices and their impact on your well-being. Rather than spending money on expensive meats, redirect those funds towards purchasing fruits and vegetables. Your priorities and objectives should consistently prioritize your health.

The costs of disease can be significantly higher compared to investing in your health. For instance, consider the case of a young man diagnosed with stomach cancer who sought my guidance. Traditional oncologists recommended a series of expensive treatments, including surgery, chemotherapy, and possibly radiation, amounting to around $100,000. Moreover, they charged him $5,000 solely for the diagnostic process. In contrast, it took me fifty-nine days to help him overcome stomach cancer through natural methods, at a cost of $1800.00. So, if you believe that natural health is financially burdensome, it's worth reconsidering.

Instead of indulging in discretionary purchases, prioritize necessities. Allocate any remaining funds to acquire high-quality herbs or herbal formulas that will contribute to your health objectives. Disease can leave you financially depleted, whereas investing in your health will ultimately enrich your life.

MODULE 7.5

The Detox Vitality Menu

This meal plan is structured for a four-week transition, guiding you from consuming heavy, toxic foods to adopting a diet of pure, alkaline-rich foods that promote detoxification and rejuvenation of your system. While this menu is primarily designed for newcomers to this process and for individuals who frequently dine out (referred to as "social eaters"), it's worth noting that you're not obligated to incorporate the cooked vegetable and grain alternatives that are provided.

For those who seek a more vigorous approach right from the outset or are under the supervision of a healthcare professional due to specific medical conditions such as cancer, MS, Parkinson's, spinal cord injuries, Alzheimer's, and others, this menu can be readily replaced with the choice to exclusively consume raw fruits and vegetables (Refer to the "Menu for the Bold," which follows). Remember, you have the autonomy to shape your life according to your preferences and intentions. So, let's embark on this journey and enjoy the process of nourishing ourselves.

TODAY'S SPECIALS

Always feel free to eat only fresh, raw fruits and/or vegetables in place of this menu for greater detoxification and regeneration.

Breakfast

Choose one.

1. Fruit

2. Melon
   Pick any single or combination of fruits or melons that you like. Some dried fruit or coconut may be added to the fruit meal.

Between Meal Juice

Drink an 8 oz. to 10 oz. glass of freshly juiced vegetable or fruit juice.

Lunch

Choose one.

1. *Large Salad, with a side of:***
    Vegetables, steamed or raw Vegetable soup, no tomato Stir-fry vegetables

2. *Fruit*

3. *Melon*

Between Meal Juice

Drink an 8 oz. to 10 oz. glass of freshly juiced vegetable or fruit juice.

Dinner

Choose one.

1. Large Salad, with a side of:**
   Vegetables, steamed or raw Vegetable soup, no tomato Stir-fry vegetables

2. Fruit

3. Melon

Snacks

In between meals, snacks must consist of fresh fruits, dried fruits and fruit or vegetable juices only.

** Do not mix starches and proteins at the same meal. Pick one or the other.

MODULE 7.6

The Detox Menu for the Bold

This menu is tailored for individuals who are deeply committed to achieving robust health and vitality. It is especially recommended for those dealing with chronic and degenerative conditions or injuries such as cancer, diabetes, MS, Parkinson's, spinal cord injuries, or Lou Gehrig's disease.

Whenever possible, opt for organic food sources. If that's not feasible, make sure to thoroughly wash your produce. One effective method is to mix two capfuls of hydrogen peroxide and the juice of two fresh lemons in a sink full of water. You can also add a pinch of salt. Allow your fruits or vegetables to soak in this solution for around five minutes, then rinse. Feel free to scrub them with a vegetable brush if desired.

Approach your meals with a joyful disposition, and take the time to relax while you eat. Minimize drinking during your meals and keep your eating experience both simple and enjoyable.

TODAY'S SPECIAL

Breakfast

Choose one.

1. Fruit

2. Melon
   Pick any single or combination of fruits or melons that you

like. Some dried fruit or coconut may be added to the fruit meal.

Between Meal Juice

See recommended juices. **Lunch**

Choose one.

1. *Large Salad*

2. *Fruit*

3. *Melon*
    Salad may consist of any raw vegetables. (See additional salad suggestions among recipes in Module 7.9.)

Between Meal Juice

See recommended juices. **Dinner**

Choose one.

1. Large Salad

2. Fruit

3. Melon
   Salad may consist of any raw vegetables. *(See* additional salad suggestions among recipes in Module 7.9.)

Snacks

In between meals, snacks must consist of fresh fruits, raw vegetables, and fruit or vegetable juices only.

Recommended Juices

Vegetable juices:
Carrot, spinach, parsley, dandelion greens. (*See* Module 7.7, which follows, for more juice combination suggestions.)

Fruit juices:

Grape, apple, pear, fresh-squeezed orange or lemon. I do not recommend pineapple juice (bottled), cranberry juice or prune juice.

MODULE 7.7

Raw Fruit and Vegetable Juices

The most nutritionally dense and energetically vibrant foods available are fresh raw fruits, vegetables, herbs, seaweeds, nuts, and seeds. These foods are optimal for human consumption. It's crucial to include a minimum of 80 percent raw, ripe, and unprocessed fruits and vegetables in your diet. These foods are rich in enzymes, vitamins, minerals (tissue salts), amino acids, antioxidants, simple sugars, water, and electrical energy. While both fruits and nuts are suitable for us, fruits align more closely with our natural frugivore tendencies. Notably, the human gastrointestinal tract is relatively short, about twelve times the length of the spine, whereas herbivores possess a much longer digestive system, approximately thirty times the length of their spine. This divergence accounts for the difference in their respective digestive capacities. Herbivores also have multiple stomachs due to the inherent challenge of breaking down vegetable fibers, which are more resistant compared to fruit fibers.

Fruit fiber is particularly well-suited for our GI tract, effectively maintaining intestinal cleanliness. Fruits' higher energy levels also enhance nervous system functions and bowel peristalsis. In contrast, vegetables contain more minerals, chlorophyll, and amino acids, making them valuable for rebuilding a depleted body. It's often observed that children are more willing to consume fruits before vegetables.

The concept of freshly made vegetable and fruit juices has gained substantial popularity, thanks to pioneers and advocates like Norman W. Walker, Paul Bragg, Herbert M. Shelton, Bernard Jensen, and others who championed juicing for health. Juicing extracts the fiber from foods, offering concentrated nutritional benefits in a liquid form. For instance, while you might eat just one whole carrot, you can easily consume the juice of several carrots. This concentrated power is invaluable for conditions such as cancer, injuries, or any ailment associated with depletion.

While fresh raw juices are beneficial for maintaining health, it's essential to recognize the significance of raw plant fibers for bowel health. The shift towards refined grains and cooked foods, prevalent in the US, coincided with a surge in bowel cancer rates, elevating it from the fourth to the first highest incidence of cancer. Currently, it ranks second only to lung cancer. Despite past controversies, medical experts now acknowledge the importance of fruit and vegetable fiber for optimal bowel function. However, it's crucial to differentiate between the benefits of fruit and vegetable fiber and the potentially harsh impact of grain fiber.

There exists a plethora of literature on vegetable and fruit juices. Notable recommendations include "The Complete Book of Fresh Vegetable and Fruit Juices" by NW. Walker, "Juicing" by Michael T. Murray, and "Juicing Therapy" by Bernard Jensen, Ph.D. The power of these juices is immense, so keep your approach simple yet exploratory to reap their tremendous benefits.

A daily intake of two to four 10-ounce glasses of vegetable or fruit juice, alongside a raw food diet, is recommended. While preparing juice just before consumption is optimal, storing it in a glass container and refrigerating it for a maximum of two days can be practical. Refer to Chapter 6, Modules 6.7 and 6.8 for more insights on juice fasting and its numerous advantages.

Listen to your body's cravings as it cycles between desiring fruit juices and fruits alone and then shifting towards craving vegetable juices and vegetables. Trust your body's wisdom, as it inherently understands its needs. One of our greatest challenges is learning to listen—to our bodies and to the higher mind. Often, we underestimate this innate guidance and let our minds and emotions lead. Breaking free from conditioned thinking and societal norms allows us to return to the vitality and vibrancy aligned with a more natural, God-given way of living.

Juicing is both an art and a science. Educate yourself, embrace simplicity, and savor the transformative effects of these juices as they rejuvenate and purify your body. You'll find it difficult to imagine life without them, so invest in an easy-to-clean juicer and embark on your juicing journey.

"Power House" Juice Suggestions

Grape juice and apple juice stand out as excellent choices for single-fruit juices. These juices provide abundant calcium while simultaneously promoting the detoxification of the liver and kidneys. Additionally, they nourish both the nervous and glandular systems.

GRAPE JUICE

Juice the seeds and stems, too.

Effects: Tumor buster; lymph stimulation; free-radical eliminator; toxicity removal, including heavy metals and minerals. Strengthens the heart and vascular system.

APPLE JUICE

Effects: Enzyme-rich juice aids digestion; supplies amino acids; a free-radical eliminator; strengthens the body.

VEGETABLE JUICE COMBINATIONS

The vegetable juice combinations provided below are specifically designed to offer substantial support to the liver, kidneys, and adrenals. Additionally, they are rich in essential electrolytes such as calcium, magnesium, potassium, and sodium. These juices are abundant in chlorophyll, often referred to as "plant blood" or "green blood," which plays a vital role in purifying the blood and lymphatic system. Chlorophyll is renowned for its effectiveness as a natural detoxifier for heavy metals and chemicals.

Please note that specific juice combinations are not listed in the text provided. If you are interested in learning more about these vegetable juice combinations, I recommend referring to relevant resources or books that delve into juicing and its benefits.

Carrot + Beet + Parsley
Carrot + Beet + Spinach
Carrot + Alfalfa Sprouts + Parsley
Carrots + Spinach + Celery + Parsley
Wheat grass + Alfalfa sprouts

Juicing cabbage and the cruciferous vegetables is very beneficial for cancer cases.

MODULE 7.8

Beans and Grains: Good or Bad?

Beans and grains possess dormant qualities due to the presence of enzyme inhibitors that impede the germination process, thus allowing for extended storage without spoilage. While beans are protein-rich and grains are primarily composed of starches, it's important to note that both of these foods are acid-forming and can be challenging to digest. From a broader perspective, I have always emphasized that the energy expended by your body in digesting, assimilating, and eliminating these foods often surpasses the energy they provide upon consumption. In essence, they have a net energy-depleting effect on the body.

Consider the example of why we feed grains to livestock like hogs and cattle: it is to fatten them up. Similarly, these foods can contribute to undesired weight gain in humans. Dried beans and grains are highly concentrated, which leads to prolonged and intricate digestion. Furthermore, the presence of enzyme inhibitors in these foods could potentially interfere with your body's natural enzyme processes.

Sprout For Life

When beans or grains are sprouted, their inherent "life force" is activated, resulting in the release of enzymes that were previously dormant due to the presence of enzyme inhibitors. This sprouting process not only balances the nutritional content of these foods but also makes their nutrients more accessible and usable by the body. Additionally, sprouted beans and grains become richer in chlorophyll, which is often referred to as "green blood" due to its structural similarity to human blood.

Chlorophyll, the pigment responsible for the green color in plants, has a composition that closely resembles that of human hemoglobin. It serves as a potent source of energy and vitality, offering benefits similar to those of an antioxidant. Moreover, chlorophyll exhibits detoxifying properties, aiding in the removal of toxic heavy metals and excess mucus from the body. By incorporating sprouted beans and grains into your diet, you can harness these healthful qualities and optimize the nutritional value of these foods.

Read: Love Your Body and Survival into the 21st Century by Viktoras Kulvinskas; and Sprouts by Kathleen O'Bannon, CNC.

To achieve genuine physical vitality and rejuvenation, it is advisable to steer clear of unsprouted beans and grains. If consumption of these foods becomes necessary, it's recommended to do so in cold climates, while being cautious not to combine them in the same meal. The rationale behind this is to prevent the combination of protein and starch, which leads to heightened bodily debilitation caused by fermentation and putrefaction processes (see Proper Food Combinations, Module 7.3).

In the wild, animals do not typically include such foods in their diets, as doing so could diminish their agility and make them more susceptible to predators. True health is rooted in energy, and vitality emerges from life rather than from consumption of inert substances. As you shift towards consuming more "living" foods, you will directly experience the impact that beans and grains exert on your energy levels and overall agility. To gain a comprehensive understanding of nutrition, it's essential to transcend the confines of culturally limited dietary beliefs and acknowledge the wide variety of foods that nature offers us.

The changing seasons exert a considerable influence on us, particularly in regions with pronounced weather variations, such as northern climates. During summer, when our body tends to be acidic, alkaline foods are preferable. In contrast, the alkaline nature of the cold winter prompts a natural inclination towards acid-rich foods like beans and grains. This inclination is natural, but it's important to limit the consumption of these foods. Keep in mind that well-functioning glands facilitate the body's internal heat regulation. An illustration of this heat-regulating mechanism is evident in the functioning of the thyroid gland, which governs metabolism. If the thyroid is weak due to prolonged consumption of beans and grains, the result could be an opposite effect—chronic coldness, particularly in extremities.

THE SOY MYTH

In every facet of life, it's essential to cultivate a habit of questioning and scrutinizing the truth behind the prevailing narratives and messages that saturate the media regarding matters of nutrition and well-being. Familiarizing yourself with the fundamental principles of health outlined in this book will equip you with the tools to discern between genuine information and misleading claims. These established truths should serve as your guiding framework.

When encountering new information, it's prudent to inquire and investigate who stands to gain from the dissemination of that information. The current trend surrounding soy is a pertinent example that merits your attention. In order to comprehend the origins of what I perceive as a deliberate and deceptive myth, let's first delve into some verifiable facts about soy.

Properties of Raw Soy Beans

- Acid-forming
- Extremely high in phytic acid (blocks mineral absorption, especially zinc)
- Full of enzyme inhibitors
- Extremely hard to digest
- 85 percent genetically modified (also called Round-Up Ready Soy Beans®) where the cell DNA and structure are combined with herbicides and bacteria to create resistance to these factors for better yield
- Full of excessive amounts of hemagglutinin—a clot-causing compound
- Allergy causing

- Extremely high in levels of aluminum (very toxic to brain and nerve tissue)

Facts about Cooked and Processed Soy Beans

- Over 80 percent of the oils and fats used in the U.S.A. are from processed soy beans

- Over 80 percent of the margarine made in the U.S.A. comes from soy beans

- Soy beans, as most beans, have enzyme inhibitors and also are high in phytic acid. They must be processed at high temperatures to break these metabolism-blockers down.

The Basic Processes in Obtaining Soy Bean Oil and Soy Protein

1. COOKING

Heated to between 225°F and 250°F, which:

- Destroys all nutrients

- Bonds proteins to minerals

- Bonds proteins to lipids and starches

- Causes free-radical formation

- Creates trans-fatty acids (which are hardening and obstructing as well as mutagenic to DNA)

- Encourages rancidity (toxic for the bacterial action needed)

- Is extremely acid-forming
- Possibly promotes formation of acrylimides (carcinogenic compounds)

2. PRESSING

Cold pressed or solvent extraction involves:

- Exposure to light and air causing free-radical formation through oxidation
- Rancidity, causing further breakdown (mostly stored in clear containers allowing a continuation of this process)
- Cold pressing only after cooking
- Solvent extraction method that creates many toxic and carcinogenic compounds
- Solvent extraction, which requires: alkalisoaps, hexane (petroleum distiller), phosphoric acid and sodium hydroxide (the primary ingredient in Drano)

3. HYDROGENATION

- The process involves subjecting the oil to temperatures exceeding 400°F while infusing hydrogen gas (with the aid of a metallic catalyst) for an extended period, usually over five hours.
- This procedure, does not only cause significant damage; it transforms the oil into a substance that is both lifeless and harmful.

Upon examining the concise overview provided above, it becomes evident that soy is far from being a nourishing food source; rather, it serves as a toxin, particularly when it undergoes cooking or processing. If it indeed possesses any estrogen like properties, this only contributes to its detrimental effects, particularly among the 80 percent of females who experience an imbalance of estrogen.

It is crucial to recognize that soy is not a product of sound nutrition but rather an innovation of the industry, conceived by large chemical and biotechnology corporations masquerading as food producers. The prioritization of financial gains over the well-being of individuals and the sanctity of life is a source of shame.

A startling revelation is that more than 60 percent of food items manufactured in the United States incorporate some form of soy, ranging from natural flavorings, vegetable shortening, hydrolyzed protein, textured vegetable protein, and soybean oil to soy protein itself. A multitude of individuals are inadvertently consuming soy in various forms, such as protein powders, soy milk, soy-based snacks, and even baby foods. The soy industry commands a staggering annual revenue of nearly $100 billion, which raises questions about the underlying motivations behind promoting soy as a miraculous dietary addition.

A salient principle to keep in mind is that if a substance does not belong to the categories of fruits, vegetables, seeds, or nuts, it is likely unnecessary and potentially detrimental to your well-being.

MODULE 7.9

Recipes to Enjoy

This concise assortment of recipes, encompassing both raw and cooked options, serves as a glimpse into the multitude of uncomplicated meals you can easily craft for your own consumption. The variety of vegetable pairings in salads, soups, stir-fries, and steamed creations is virtually limitless. Choose to prepare these combinations as fruit-based or vegetable-based dishes based on your preferences. Simplicity is key. Rich creams and sauces were concocted to mask the lackluster flavor of cooked foods. Revel in the vibrant array of colors, energies, aromas, and tastes that nature's provisions offer. These foods are intricately designed for our specific species.

RAW MENU

The Master Salad

Combine any or all of the following:

- Romaine lettuce

- Peas

- Spinach

- Cucumbers

- Olives

- Bell peppers (all colors)
- Tomatoes
- Onions
- Asparagus
- Avocado
- Cabbage (red or white)
- Green beans
- Carrots
- Sweet corn
- Any dark green leafy vegetable

Make your salad fun and filled with a rainbow of colored vegetables. Use only small amounts of dressing. (See Raw Dressing recipe in this section.) For those who wish oil on the salad use only raw organic olive, coconut or grape seed oil. Enjoy the natural flavors of vegetables.

Relish

2 cups sweet corn, cut right from the cob
1/4 cup sweet onions, chopped
1/4 cup red bell peppers, chopped

Mix all ingredients together. If you want your relish creamier, put your ingredients into a blender and blend to your desired consistency.

Raw Dressing

Avocado
Garlic
Cucumbers
Olive oil (optional)
Bell peppers (all colors)
Sweet onion
Apple cider vinegar

Place ingredients in a blender and blend them until a semi-liquid is formed. Pour over your salad as desired.

Guacamole

2 cups of diced avocados (remove skin)
4 diced green onions
Freshly squeezed lemon juice to taste (1/2 lemon)
1/2 cup of tomatoes
1/4 cup of chopped bell peppers (optional)

Chop or mash the ingredients until desired texture, and then mix together.

Veggie Sandwich

Lettuce (romaine or any dark green leafy vegetable)
Black olives
Sprouts
Tomato

Avocado*
Sweet onion
Pickles
Bell peppers (all colors)
Cucumbers
Bread, all natural sprouted multi-grain or millet bread**

*You can mash your avocado and use it like mayonnaise. You can sprinkle some of your salad dressing on your sandwich as well.

**We recommend millet bread because it is more alkaline to the body while most other grains are acid-forming.

Rainbow Fruit Salad

Fruit bowls are extremely delicious and loved by all ages. Certain fruits, however, do not combine well together. Generally your acid type fruits, like oranges and pineapples, do not mix well with your sweet type fruits, like bananas. The following are some suggestions for fruit bowls. Be creative.

Bananas, Peaches
Bananas, Blueberries
Bananas, Strawberries
Bananas, Mangos
Bananas, Apples, Strawberries, Grapes
Bananas, Blueberries, Apples, Grapes
Bananas, Strawberries, Apples
Bananas, Apples, Grapes

Melons

Remember "Eat them alone or leave them alone." All varieties are acceptable.

Watermelon

Cantaloupe

Honeydew

Papaya

Almond Nut Milk

1 cup of raw almonds

1/2 cup of maple syrup

3 1/2 to 4 cups of distilled water

1/2 tsp of almond extract (or vanilla extract)

For a spicy Indian version, add the following to the above ingredients:

1/4 tsp of cardamom

1/4 tsp of nutmeg

1/2 tsp of cinnamon

Place all ingredients into a blender and blend on a high speed for three minutes. For a smoother consistency, strain through a large strainer layered with a piece of cheesecloth.

Almond milk is a protein and should not be combined with starches. Use rice milk if you wish to combine with a starch.

Banana Ice Cream

4 to 6 bananas

1 to 11/2 cups of apple juice

1 tsp. of vanilla

1/2 cup of raw almonds

To make any frozen treat you will need some frozen fruit and fresh fruit juice. Organic fresh juice and fruit is always preferred. However, glass-bottled organic juice may be substituted.

Peel 4 to 6 bananas and freeze overnight in a zip-lock baggie. Put about 1 to 11/2 cups of apple juice and 1 tsp of vanilla in a blender. Break off pieces of frozen banana and add to the apple juice as you blend them (a few pieces at a time) until you get a creamy consistency. If you want a thicker blend simply add more frozen banana, or, first add 1/2 cup of raw almonds to blender and blend to small pieces or powder, then add your apple juice, vanilla and frozen bananas.

Date/Coconut Rolls

2 cups of dates

1 cup of raisins

1/4 cup of coconut

1 cup of nuts—pecans or almonds (optional)

Remove pits from the dates. Put dates and raisins through a food grinder. Chop nuts to medium size. Mix all ingredients together and then form into balls. Roll in grated coconut or finely ground nuts. Keep in the refrigerator.

Frozen Bananas

Bananas
Sesame seeds
Honey
Melted carob (optional)

Peel your bananas and roll them in the honey, then roll them in the sesame seeds or drizzle with or dip into melted carob. Place the bananas on a plate, cover and freeze.

Smoothies

1/2 cup Blueberries
2 Bananas
4 Dates
Organic Grape Juice (fresh or bottled)
Chopped Ice (4 to 6 cubes)

Add your juice, dates, ice, bananas and blueberries to a blender and blend to desired texture. Any fruit and fruit juice combination can be used. Fruit smoothies are like milkshakes, but very healthy.

COOKED MENU

Vegetable Soup

Carrots
Sweet corn
Pearl onions
Green beans (optional)
Peas
Garlic (optional)
Cauliflower
Potatoes (sparingly)

Use a water base when making this delicious soup. You may add any herbal spice toward the end of the cooking process or after the soup is cooked. Fresh raw spices are preferable. No salt or pepper of any type because they are irritants and mucus-forming.

Cauliflower Soup

2 cups chopped cauliflower
3 cups of distilled water
1 large sweet onion
2 Tbs. of olive oil
1/2 cup bell pepper (red or yellow)

Sauté onion in olive oil until translucent. Bring water with cauliflower and pepper to a boil and simmer for 10 minutes. Add sautéed onion, stir. Take out 2 cups of soup and blend in blender. Add back to pot, stir and enjoy!

Carrot/Squash Soup

1 sweet onion, chopped
3 lbs butternut squash chopped (peeled, with seeds removed)
10 chopped carrots
4–5 chopped garlic cloves
3–4 tablespoons of olive oil
1/3 bunch parsley, chopped

Sauté onion until translucent in 2 tablespoons of olive oil, set aside. Add the squash and carrots to water (make sure that they are covered) and bring to a boil. Cook over medium heat until carrots and squash are slightly soft. Add the cooked onion. Add the chopped garlic and parsley and boil for 1 minute longer. Remove from heat. Serve.

Steamed Veggies

Broccoli
Cauliflower
Bell peppers (all colors)
Onions
Asparagus
Pea pods (optional)
Green beans (optional)

Place your desired veggies into a stainless steel steamer, and steam for 5 to 7 minutes. You may wish to put these steamed vegetables over whole grain brown rice with an onion or veggie sauce.

*Stainless steel "leaf" steamers are inexpensive and can be purchased at any department store that carries kitchen utensils. They are made to fit down into saucepans. Avoid all aluminum cookware.

Stir-Fried Veggies

3 tablespoons olive oil

Chopped vegetables of your choice (including bean sprouts)

Add olive oil to skillet. Heat oil and add chopped vegetables (the sky is the limit where your choices are concerned). Stir-fry for approximately 5–10 minutes, but don't overcook. Season to taste with your favorite herbal spices.

Short-Grain Whole Brown Rice

1 cup of short-grain brown rice

2 cups of water

Rinse rice and put into a pot with 2 cups of water. Bring to a boil, cover and cook on low heat for 45 minutes until all water is absorbed.

Millet Cereal

Use this once a week only. Prepare according to package directions, or as you would oatmeal. Use rice milk only. Sweeten with honey, molasses or maple syrup.

Your food determines in a large measure how long you shall live – how much you shall enjoy life, and how successful your life shall be.

— Dr. Kirschner, *Live Food Juice*

CHAPTER EIGHT

The Power of Herbs

When I embarked on the utilization of herbs and herbal formulations over thirty years ago, my clinical achievements experienced an astonishing upsurge. I began observing more profound purification and healing, resulting in genuine rejuvenation and vitality within tissues. Previously, with supplements, I would witness some improvement, maybe certain symptoms alleviated. However, once supplementation ceased, those symptoms would resurface.

Today, the incorporation of herbs (botanicals) stands as a pivotal aspect of restoring the human populace to health. The ability of herbs to catalyze the process of cleansing and regeneration is unmatched by manufactured supplements or chemical medications. Unlike chemical medications that suppress and retain toxins within the body, herbs extract and cleanse these toxins while reinforcing cellular resilience. Since herbs have evaded hybridization, they retain their robust nutritional and electrical attributes.

From a spiritual perspective, herbs retain the "original consciousness" with which they were formed. As an herb's awareness merges with the consciousness of a human cell, the cell is empowered to function as it was inherently intended. This instigates heightened vitality in cells, tissues, and glands. Accompanied by their potent detoxifying properties, herbs empower the body to expel obstructive elements, thus enhancing blood, lymph, and neuro (energy) circulation to cells.

The intrinsic potency, nutrition, and active constituents that herbs possess can mark the distinction between life and death. Genetically, we have reached a juncture where conventional treatment approaches are no longer effective. The pervasive chemical toxins present in our air and food have led to elevated levels of acidosis and deterioration, impacting everything from our buildings and water sources to animals and particularly ourselves. Over the last century, humans have achieved something no other creature has in billions of years: we've wrought destruction upon the Earth. To weather this, transitioning from treatment to detoxification is imperative. Without alkalizing and ridding the body of the poisons that are consuming it, the prospects of attaining health remain bleak.

This book strives to revolutionize your perspective on treatment. My life's work has revolved around detoxification and regeneration rather than treatment. This stands particularly true in chronic and degenerative conditions like type I diabetes, cancer, arthritis, and MS. These conditions cannot merely be treated; the failing tissues (organs and glands) must be revitalized.

Herbs have served as remedies for both humans and animals in combating diseases and providing nourishment for ages. Unlike hybrid garden vegetables, herbs remain non-hybrid vegetables, boasting enhanced nutritional, electrical, and medicinal content. The distinction and superiority of herbs lie in their robust medicinal compounds, referred to as their rejuvenating properties. These compounds encompass acids, alkaloids, saponins, flavonoids, coumarins (clotting agents), tannins (astringent attributes), antioxidants (immune reinforcement), bitter principles, and more. A comprehensive list of these herbs and their effects on tissues can be found in Module 8.2, Power Herbs.

The rejuvenating principles within herbs can stimulate, cleanse, and nourish cells and tissues, thereby influencing cell and tissue responsiveness. Herbs heighten blood and lymphatic flow within tissues, fostering cellular nourishment and waste elimination.

Herbs are "tissue-specific," meticulously designed to impact specific types of tissues or body parts. The beauty of herbs lies in their ability to concurrently affect numerous tissue types. Licorice Root, Saw Palmetto Berries, and Chaste Tree Berries are prime examples, as they not only influence endocrine gland tissues but also exhibit a comprehensive effect on the body. They fortify the vascular system, bolster male and female organs, and combat inflammation. Parasite-targeting herbs like Black Walnut Hull and Pau d'Arco not only exterminate parasites but also enhance the immune and endocrine systems. They exhibit broad-spectrum efficacy, eliminating a range of parasites including yeasts, fungi, molds, bacteria, viruses, flukes, and worms. In contrast, antibiotic drugs solely eliminate bacteria while promoting yeast growth. Parasitic herbs also promote cellular proliferation, effectively rebuilding and fortifying cells. The profound significance of botanical utilization stems from their holistic and affirmative impact on the entire body.

Throughout my career, I've employed substantial quantities of herbs (often on a single client), consistently yielding positive outcomes over my thirty years of practice. Our clinic has gained global recognition for its achievements, succeeding where others have faltered.

While we haven't encountered adverse interactions between herbs and chemical medications, the potential always exists. The ultimate objective is for the patient to eliminate all chemical intake.

In my view, herbs are ideally consumed raw or in tincture form, where digestion is minimal and absorption is optimized. Nevertheless, roots, barks, and tubers can be boiled and still exert a positive influence on liver, pancreatic, and gastrointestinal functions. Boiling does compromise water-soluble components such as vitamin C complexes (flavonoids) and B-vitamins. It can also cause fats to saturate (bond). However, most instances of boiled teas involve symptom management and immediate body response promotion. For the most part, the active medicinal properties remain intact despite heat exposure.

I employ herbs to foster detoxification and enhance tissues through nutritive and energetic stimulation rather than abrasive stimulation. As living entities, we necessitate living foods and herbs to effect self-healing. The potential of a raw herb to accomplish this surpasses that of its cooked counterpart by a hundredfold.

Remember, herbs are nourishment. They consist of proteins (amino acids), carbohydrates (starches and sugars), fats, and abundant fiber (cellulose), crucial for intestinal health. Hippocrates' ageless words, "Let your food be your medicine and your medicine be your food," resonate here.

Across diverse religious and spiritual texts, the power and significance of herbs are reverberated. Chemical medicines were not conceived by God, but herbs were.

Herbs are a source of enjoyment and astonishment as they cleanse and reconstruct your body. A few herbs warrant caution, such as Peruvian Bark (Cinchona calisaya), which holds benefit at low dosages but can be toxic in excess. My advice is to exercise prudence with herbs of this nature.

This chapter commences with a brief exposition (Module 8.1) on the traditional and customary applications of botanicals. Subsequently, Module 8.2 offers an exhaustive compilation of some of the most potent and effective herbs that nature bestows. These herbs have been rigorously tested in clinical settings for many years, showcasing miraculous outcomes in promoting tissue regeneration. In regard to herbal formulas, which involve blends of herbs, their impact on the body often exceeds that of individual herbs. Several factors, including compatibility, synergistic effects, and repercussions on related tissues, must be considered when combining herbs. Module 8.3 proposes an optimal herbal tincture or blend for ten major conditions, encompassing adrenal gland enhancement, parasite purging, and kidney and bladder functioning. In Module 8.4, each body system (Cardiovascular, Digestive, etc.) is addressed, along with herbal detoxifiers and fortifiers tailored to each system. The chapter culminates with a significant deliberation on pharmaceutical antibiotics versus nature's anti-parasitic agents in Module 8.5.

Engage with herbs and herbal formulas with enthusiasm, as their strength and efficacy are imperative in today's world. Through the utilization of herbs for cleansing and reconstructing the body, vibrant health can be accessible to anyone willing to invest dedication. Don't be apprehensive about harnessing what God has provided for your benefit. Simply familiarize yourself with the purposes of various herbs. Herbs are user-friendly. Disregard those devoid of herbology education who may cast herbs in a negative light. Such a perspective equates to labeling God as negative. God fashioned herbs for tasks ranging from bone growth and repair to nerve rejuvenation. Herbs stand as God's foremost healers, especially when combined with a raw food diet.

In the June 1992 issue of the Food and Drug Law Journal, this was stated: "The results of an extensive review on botanical safety conducted by the Herbal Research Foundation (a non-profit organization of leading experts on pharmacognosy, pharmacology, and toxicology), confirmed there is no substantial evidence that toxic reactions to botanicals are a major source of concern. The review was based on reports from the American Association of Poison Control Centers and the Center of Disease Control." (McCaleb, R.S.)

MODULE 8.1

Common and Traditional Uses of Botanicals

Every nation possesses its own array of incredible herbs. I consistently advise opting for herbs indigenous to your country of residence. These herbs tend to exert a more potent influence on your body due to its adaptation and alignment with the prevailing environment.

The global spectrum encompasses thousands of herbs utilized for various purposes. My suggestion is to focus on studying approximately 50 to 100 of the most efficacious and robust herbs prevalent and employed in your own country. These herbs will effectively cater to your needs without inundating you with an overwhelming plethora of options. However, exceptions exist for every guideline. Even if you reside in the U.S.A., do not disregard the exceptional herbs hailing from other nations like China, Brazil, and India. Examples include Ginseng, Ginkgo Biloba, Ginger, Pau d'Arco, and specific medicinal mushrooms. When I incorporate herbs from foreign lands, I exclusively select the finest and most potent offerings each country presents.

Herbs should ideally be cultivated organically or obtained through "wild-crafting." Regrettably, the demand for herbs has escalated to such an extent that wild-crafting has depleted numerous wild herb populations. The establishment of organic herb farms akin to organic fruit and vegetable farms is imperative. Such initiatives offer our sole prospect of revitalizing and safeguarding our species.

Herbs can be consumed in the form of teas, capsules, or tinctures. Personally, I hold a preference for teas and tinctures. This inclination is particularly pronounced in cases of compromised digestion and inadequate nutrient absorption.

MAKING TEA

Preparing herbal teas is a straightforward process. For each cup of tea you intend to make using a single herb, place one heaping teaspoon of the chosen herb and one cup of distilled or reverse osmosis (R/O) water into a glass container such as a pot or saucepan. It's advisable to opt for glass over any metallic materials, including stainless steel. Even stainless steel can introduce copper into your teas or foods. If you're working with multiple herbs, use one cup of water for each distinct herb and one heaping teaspoon of each herb.

In the case of herbs that consist of leaves and flowers, bring them to a boil in the water for around 3 to 6 minutes, and then allow them to steep for an additional 5 to 10 minutes. If the herbs are roots, tubers, or rhizomes, boil them for 10 to 15 minutes and steep them for another 10 to 15 minutes. If your tea turns out to be too potent, you can dilute it by adding more water to your mixture. Consume one cupful of the tea, 3 to 6 times per day, or utilize it for other applications like douches, enemas, or poultices based on your desired outcomes.

TINCTURES

Tinctures, a concentrated form of herbs, are created by extracting herbs in alcohol, vinegar, or glycerin. The most potent method involves using 1 part herb to 3 to 4 parts pure grain alcohol, mixed with an equal amount of distilled water. Combine the mixture in a glass container and allow it to rest in a dark area for about 30 days. Start the process on a new moon and complete it by a full moon. Shake the tincture daily, and on the last day, expose the mixture to sunlight for at least 4 hours. If sunlight isn't available on a particular day, you can omit this step. Once completed, bottle the tincture. Use a press to extract the liquid from the mixture and take one full dropperful, 3 to 6 times a day.

While there are numerous ways to use herbs for health benefits, this book does not intend to cover all of them. There are plenty of other books in the market that offer excellent information on herbs and their applications, some of which are listed in the Bibliography.

Regrettably, there are also books on herbs that lack credibility. These are often written by self-proclaimed herbalists or individuals with limited knowledge about the true uses of herbs. They may rely on information from other sources, including the FDA or misleading details propagated by pharmaceutical companies to create unwarranted fear about natural foods and medicines. There's no need to fear nature or its products. Instead, learn from centuries of traditional use and experimentation.

Stand up for your right to consume and utilize nature's gifts. It's estimated that countless unnecessary deaths—ranging from 2 to 5 million per year—are attributed to practices and products endorsed by conventional medical and pharmaceutical industries. Deaths from herb usage are rare, typically resulting from misuse. Engage in reading, studying, and experimenting. Shed your fears and regain vitality. Embrace life once again.

MODULE 8.2

Power Herbs: A Reference Guide

The following herbs are some of the best herbs you can find in the Northern Hemisphere.

Alfalfa

- A great alkalizer of the body.
- High in chlorophyll and nutrition.
- High in minerals and trace minerals.
- A body cleanser.
- Enhances the endocrine glandular system, especially the adrenal and pituitary glands.
- Helps eliminate retained water and carbon dioxide.
- Helps with alcohol, smoking, and narcotic addiction.
- Helps eliminate toxic chemicals and heavy metals (lead, aluminum, mercury, etc.) from the body.
- Bonds (chelation) to inorganic minerals for elimination.
- Infection fighter and acts as a natural deodorizer.
- Strengthens the body.
- High in chlorophyll, helps rejuvenate the blood.
- Pulls mucus (catarrh) out of the tissues.

Scientific name: *Medicago sativ*

Parts used: Whole plant, (leaves, seeds, and flowers).

Actions: Astringent, diuretic, nutritive.

Aloe Vera

- Internally, aloe heals ulcerations and inflammation of the GI tract.

- Aloe and Burdock are the "burn botanicals." First, second, third and fourth degree burns all respond to aloe's tissue-healing and rebuilding properties.

- Used as a bowel mover in heavy constipation cases. (Avoid prolonged usage for this.)

- Aloe Vera is known as the First Aid Plant. It is great for cuts, wounds, and the like.

Scientific name: *Aloe vera linn*

Parts used: Pulp (gel) from inside leaves and powder of the leaf.

Actions: Abortifacient (when used in high doses), alterative, anthelmintic, anti-arthritic, antifungal, antibacterial, anti-inflammatory antiseptic, astringent, bitter tonic, bitter, cathartic, cell proliferant, cholagogue, decoagulant, demulcent, depurative, emmenagogue, emollient, insecticide, laxative, nutritive, purgative, resin stimulant, stomachic, tonic, vermifuge, vulnerary.

Astragalus

- Astragalus is a tremendous cellular proliferator (strengthens cells).

- I especially like this herb for its effect upon the adrenal tissues.

- Astragalus is a superb immune builder, strengthening the bone marrow, the endocrine glandular system (thymus, etc.), and the spleen.

- Aids in shortness of breath.

- Strengthens the nervous system.

- Increases energy to cells, especially in the spleen and GI tract (stomach, in particular).

- Strengthens prolapsed conditions, e.g., uterus, stomach, intestines and bladder.

- Has mild diuretic properties and helps tone the lungs.

- Brings tone and balance to tissues.

Scientific name: *Astragalus membranaceus*
Parts used: Roots
Actions: Anhydrotic (stops sweating), cellular proliferator, diuretic.

Bilberry

- Tremendous in strengthening the vascular system (arteries, capillaries, and veins); great for varicose veins.
- Helps reduce inflammation (flavonoids) in the vascular walls, hence reduces arteriosclerosis (obstruction of the vascular walls with lipids).
- Inhibits coagulation of platelets in the blood.
- Helps with edema, aids in diarrhea.
- Bilberry helps tone the skin.
- Helps prevent cataracts and protects eye tissue from effects of diabetes.
- Used in formulas to help control blood sugar levels.
- A great anti-inflammatory for all tissues.
- Helps to control stress and anxiety.
- A great aid in night blindness or any vision weakness.

Scientific name: *Vaccinium myrtillus*
Parts used: Leaves and fruits
Actions: Antidiabetic effect, antidiarrheal, astringent, anti-inflammatory.

Black Cohosh

- This herb stimulates estrogen receptors and has estrogenic properties itself.

- Used in female conditions where vaginal dryness, lack of menstruation, and infertility is present.

- Stimulates estrogen production.

- Not suited for estrogen dominant females, where excessive bleeding and cysts, fibroids, and fibrocystic conditions exist.

- Said to help loosen and expel mucus from the lungs.

- Contracts the uterus and increases menstrual flow.

Said to be a tonic for the central nervous system (CNS).

Scientific name: *Cimicifuga racemosa*

Parts used: Rhizomes, fresh and dried root

Actions: Alterative, antiseptic, antispasmodic, anti-venomous, arterial, astringent, cardiac stimulant, diaphoretic, diuretic, emmenagogue, expectorant, sedative, stomachictonic.

Black Walnut Hull

Black Walnut Hull is one of my favorite herbs for many reasons.

- It's one of nature's most powerful anti-parasitic.

- It will kill microorganisms (bacterium, fungi, yeasts, etc.) to larger parasites including all worms and flukes.

- It is a cellular proliferator (strengthens cells).

- It increases the oxygenation of blood cells.

- It is a detoxifier used to balance sugar levels and disperse fatty materials.
- Black Walnut Hull is excellent for any condition and weakness of the body.
- Promotes healing of all tissues and is said to help restore tooth enamel.
- Strengthens and stimulates the immune system.
- Promotes lymph movement and bowel peristalsis.
- Strengthens the bones (high in calcium).

Scientific name: *Juglans nigra*

Parts used: Inner hull (can use the bark)

Actions: Alterative (leaves) bitter, Anthelmintic (vermifuge), astringent, cholagogue, detergent, expectorant, hepatic, laxative, mild cathartic, purgative, tonic (fruit).

Bugleweed

- A specific for the thyroid gland, especially when enlarged or when a goiter exists.
- Said to be a detoxifier, and especially valuable at removing heavy metals.
- Bugleweed is said to offer protection against radiation.
- Beneficial in irregular heartbeat and palpitations.
- Improves thyroid and adrenal function.

- Restores tooth enamel.
- Possibly enhances neurotransmitters.
- Also said to resemble digitalis in its actions.
- Has a strengthening effect upon tissue.

Scientific name: *Copus virginicus*

Parts used: The aerial portions of the herb

Actions: Antigonadotropic, anti-inflammatory anti-thyrotropic, astringent, cardiac tonic, diuretic (mild), narcotic (mild), and sedative.

Burdock

- The leaves are considered by many to be one of the top "burn healers" of all times. This includes first, second, third and fourth degree burns.
- A strong blood and liver cleanser and tonic.
- Reduces swelling in the body, especially around the joints.
- A great aid in detoxification.
- Burdock rids the body of toxins and mucus.
- Promotes urine flow and perspiration.
- Number one in skin conditions of all types.
- Promotes kidney function and helps remove acid build-up within the body, especially sulfuric, phosphoric and uric acids.

Scientific name: *Arctium lappa*

Parts used: Leaves, roots and seeds

Actions: Alterative, anti-inflammatory, antiscorbutic, aperient, astringent (mild to medium), demulcent, depurative, diaphoretic, lipotropic, stomachic, tonic, sedative.

Butcher's Broom

- A great circulatory herb.
- Has anti-inflammatory properties (flavonoids and tannins) which help remove plaque in the vascular system. Used in cases of phlebitis.
- Tones and strengthens the vascular walls (arteries, capillaries and veins), thus used for varicose veins, hemorrhoids and post aneurysms.
- Increases circulation throughout the body, especially to the peripheral areas (e.g., brain, hands and feet).
- Antithrombotic (use to prevent postoperative thrombosis).
- Strengthens bones and connective tissue.
- Aids alkalization of the blood.

Scientific name: *Iuscus aculeatus*

Parts used: Herb and rhizome.

Actions: Anti-inflammatory, aromatic, cellular proliferator, diuretic, laxative (mild), vasoconstrictor.

Cascara Sagrada

- A great herb in low dosages to strengthen the GI tract.

- Helps tone and strengthen the intestines.

- Increases and strengthens peristalsis.

- Increases secretions of the liver, pancreas, stomach and intestines.

- Strengthens the autonomic nervous system of the alimentary canal.

- Use for constipation, but better used in a cleaning and rebuilding formula for the GI tract.

- Helps clean and strengthen the liver.

- Promotes bile secretion.

- Improves digestion in small dosages.

- Use in cases of gallstones, piles and hemorrhoids.

- Can be used for intestinal worms.

Scientific name: *Rhamnus purshiana*

Parts used: Aged, dried bark.

Actions: Alterative, anti-bilious, antidiabetic, bitter tonic, cathartic, emetic, febrifuge, hepatic, laxative, nervine, peristaltic strengthener, purgative, stomachic.

Cayenne (Red) Pepper

- Used in high blood pressure cases because of its vascular dilation properties.

- Increases circulation. Excellent in cold conditions.

- Stimulates lymph flow. However, it also creates mucus. I do not recommend long term use of cayenne or any hot peppers because of their stimulating and mucus-forming properties.

- Can be an irritant to the mucosa of the GI tract in prolonged usage.

- Used to heal ulcers.

- Used with castor oil packs to help drive oils and herbs into tissues.

- Used as a homeostatic externally and internally (stops bleeding).

- A must for strokes and heart attacks. Treats shock.

Scientific name: *Capsicum annuum*

Parts used: Fruit

Actions: Alterative, anti-rheumatic, antiseptic, antispasmodic, astringent, carminative, condiment, emetic, expectorant, hemostatic, pungent, rubefacient, sialagogue, stimulant, stomachic, sudorific, tonic.

Chaparral

- Chaparral is one of God's top herbs in the Northern Hemisphere.
- Its greatest power lies in its ability to move the lymphatic system.
- Used for removal of tumors, boils and abscesses.
- Has strong antimicrobial properties (bacterial, viral, fungal, etc.).
- Very useful in rheumatic and arthritic conditions. Also excellent for gout.
- Has analgesic properties (for pain).
- Stimulates peripheral circulation.
- Stimulates liver function and increases bile production and flow.
- Works as an anti-inflammatory
- Somewhat of a cellular proliferator (strengthens cells).
- Use in all cancers and HIV.
- Use for all types of stone formation.
- Prolapsed conditions, especially of the uterus.Poisonous bites including snakebites.
- Chicken pox, mumps, and the like.
- Useful in all types of female conditions.
- Very useful for stomach and intestinal conditions, including hemorrhoids.

Scientific name: *Larrea tridentata*

Parts used: Leaves and small stems

Actions: Alterative, analgesic, anti-arthritic, anticancer, anti-inflammatory, antioxidant, anti-rheumatic, anti-scrofulous, anti- tumor, anti-venomous, aromatic, astringent, bitter, depurative, diuretic, emetic (large doses), expectorant, laxative (mild), tonic, vasopressor (mild).

Cleavers

- One of the great lymphatic herbs. Helps move and dissolve lymphatic congestion.
- Use in swollen lymph nodes, abscesses, boils and tumors.
- A great blood cleanser.
- Has diuretic properties and helps dissolve kidney and bladder sediment.
- A strong herb for cleansing the skin.
- Excellent for eczema, dermatitis and psoriasis.
- Helps eliminate upper respiratory congestion (sinus, throat, lungs, etc.).
- Helps clean, tone, and strengthen the body.
- Use for all cancers.
- Use in urinary tract obstructions.
- Has anti-inflammatory properties, and is used for any "itis" (inflammatory) condition.

Scientific name: *Galium aparine*

Parts used: Whole herb, especially leaves

Actions: Alterative, anti-inflammatory, antipyretic and laxative, antiscorbutic, antitumor, aperient, astringent, blood purifier, diuretic, hepatic (mild), lipotropic, refrigerant, tonic.

Comfrey

- For centuries considered one of nature's top healers.

- Nicknamed "knit bone" for its powerful effect upon rebuilding the skeletal structure.

- Strengthens connective tissue. Used for hemorrhoids, varicose and spider veins, prolapsed conditions (uterus, bowels, bladder, etc.), muscular degeneration, osteoporosis, hernia, aneurysms, etc.

- A powerful wound healer.

- Useful in sprains, fractures, and the like.

- A good astringent used to detoxify and clean tissue.

- Helps move the lymphatic system.

- Very beneficial for respiratory issues, both for its expectorant properties and its antibacterial properties.

- Comfrey is a tonic to the body, strengthening cells and tissue.

- Checks hemorrhages, especially in the GI tract, urinary tract and lungs. Comfrey is used to help regulate blood sugars.

- Said to aid protein through increasing the secretion of pepsin.

- A great lung tonic.

- Excellent as a poultice for any injury.

- Promotes the formation of epithelial cells.

Note: Because of a strong alkaloid called pyrrolizidic acid, the FDA considers this herb dangerous to the liver. However, generations of use do not bear this out. If you were to extract this alkaloid and take it by itself in large dosages it would cause liver damage. However, in Herbology we never extract individual constituents.

Scientific name: *Symphytum officinalis*

Parts used: Root and leaves

Actions: Alterative, anti-inflammatory, antiseptic (mild), astringent, cell proliferant, demulcent, essential oil, expectorant, hemostatic, inulin, mucilage, nutritive, pectoral, primary constituents, starch, styptic, tannins, tonic (yin), vulnerary.

Corn Silk

- A powerful cleanser of bladder and kidney tissue.

- Helps clean toxins and mucus from the urinary tract.

- Helps lower blood sugar.

- Gently stimulates bile flow, aiding in improved digestion and alkalization.

- Used for bedwetting and edema.

- Used for prostatitis.

- Helps remove inorganic minerals from the body.

- Used for both gallstones and kidney stones.

- Excellent for cystitis.

- Useful in hypertension and C.O.P.D.

Scientific name: *Zea mays*

Parts used: Inner silk (stylus).

Actions: Alkaloid, antiseptic, antispasmodic, cholagogue, diuretic, lipotropic, vulnerary.

Corydalis

- The "Great Corydalis" is valued as one of the top non-addictive pain herbs of the world.

- Used for all types of pain including nerve, joint, abdominal, menstrual, muscular, heart.

- Use for arthritis and rheumatism.

- As a bitter, it has beneficial effects upon the liver and GI tract.

- Use for spasms, convulsions, and seizures.

- Use to relax and calm the nervous system.

• Useful for asthmatic attacks.

Scientific name: *Corydalis yanhusuo*
Parts used: Root.
Actions: Analgesic, antispasmodic, bitter tonic, emmenagogue, diuretic.

Dandelion

• One of nature's top herbs.

• A liver and gallbladder tonic.

• Aids in pancreatic function.

• A kidney and bladder tonic and cleanser.

• Said to have the same diuretic strength as Lasix© (trade name for furosemide).

• Promotes the formation of bile.

• Improves the enamel of the teeth.

• A great alkalizer.

• Effective in liver conditions including hepatitis, jaundice and cirrhosis.

• High in iron, and other minerals, which increases the oxygen-carrying capacity of the blood.

• A natural source of protein.

• Aids in blood sugar issues including diabetes and hypoglycemia.

Scientific name: *Taraxacum spp*.

Parts used: Whole plant: leaves, roots and flowers.

Actions: Alterative, anti-rheumatic, anti-tumor, aperient, bitter, blood purifier, cholagogue, deobstruent, depurative, diuretic, hepatic, immune enhancer and rebuilder, laxative (mild), liptotriptic, nutritive, stomachic, tonic.

Devil's Claw

- One of nature's great anti-inflammatory herbs. (Promotes prostaglandin production and activity.)
- A specific for arthritis and rheumatism.
- Great for any inflammatory condition: joint, muscular, neuro, or other.
- Use in prostatitis.
- Valuable in diabetes (pancreatic) or liver conditions.

Scientific name: *Harpagophytum procumbens*

Parts used: Roots and tubers.

Actions: Alterative (blood purifier), analgesic, anodyne, anti-arthritic, anti-inflammatory anti-rheumatic, astringent, bitter tonic, cholagogue, hepatic (mild), sedative.

Echinacea Angustifolia

- Echinacea is another one of God's greatest herbs.

- It is known as the "immune herb."
- Strengthens and stimulates the immune system.
- It enhances tissue function, especially bone marrow, thymus gland and spleen tissue.
- Has strong antibiotic and antiseptic properties.
- A blood purifier and anti-inflammatory
- Useful in cases of arthritis and rheumatism.
- Useful in colds, flu, pneumonia, and similar conditions.
- Strengthens cells.
- A blood purifier.
- Very useful in sepsis of the blood or any toxic blood conditions.
- A must in all cancers, tumors, boils and abscesses.
- Great in urinary tract infections and inflammation.
- Useful in prostate conditions.

Scientific name: *Echinacea angustifolia*

Parts used: Roots, rhizomes.

Actions: Alterative, antibacterial, anti-inflammatory anti-putrefactive, anti-venomous, antiseptic, antiviral, deodorant, depurant, aphrodisiac, sialogogue, diaphoretic, aromatic, carminative, bitter, stimulant, vulnerary.

False Unicorn (Helonias)

- One of nature's top tonics, especially for the male and female reproductive organs and glands.

- Strengthens the endocrine glands.

- Use in prolapsed conditions of the intestines, uterus, hemorrhoids, veins, etc.

- It revitalizes and regenerates tissue, especially the reproductive tissues.

- Increases the ability of conception.

- Strengthens the mucous membranes, especially the genital-urinary tissues.

- Use for diabetes.

- Use for ovarian, uterine or prostate weakness or conditions.

- Helps prevent miscarriages.

- Use for sterility problems.

- Use for relaxed vagina.

Scientific name: *Chamaelirium luteum*
Parts used: Root and rhizomes.
Actions: Anthelmintic (vermifuge), cellular proliferant, diuretic, emetic (high doses), emmenagogue, oxytocic, sialagogue (fresh), stimulating, tonic, uterine tonic.

Fenugreek

- Fenugreek is a great expectorant.

- It softens, loosens, and helps expel mucus (phlegm), especially from the bronchial and lung tissues.

- Helps dissolve cholesterol and other lipids.

- A great blood cleanser and antiseptic.

- Fenugreek is a medium range parasite killer.

- Has some diuretic properties.

- Excellent for diabetes (helps regulate sugar and insulin levels).

Scientific name: *Trigonella foenum-graecum*

Parts used: Seeds.

Actions: Alterative, antiparasitic, aphrodisiac, aromatic, astringent, carminative, demulcent, deobstruent, detergent, detoxicant, emollient, expectorant, galactagogue, laxative, nutritive, stimulant, stomachic, tonic.

Garlic

- Garlic is one of the great blood cleansers.

- It has antiseptic, antiparasitic, antibacterial, antiviral, antifungal properties.

- Especially good for intestinal parasites.

- A great immune enhancer.

- Stimulates the action of the liver and gallbladder.

- Excellent for colds, flu, bronchitis and any congestive conditions.

- Great for yeast infections of all types.

- Garlic can be too strong and pungent for fruitarians.

- Stimulates digestive enzymes.

Scientific name: *Allium sativum*

Parts used: Bulbs

Actions: Alterative, antibacterial, anticatarrhal, antifungal, antiparasitic, antiseptic, antispasmodic, antisyphilitic, antivenomous, antiviral, aromatic, carminative, cathartic, cholagogue, depurative, diaphoretic, digestant, disinfectant, diuretic, emmenagogues, expectorant, hypertensive, hypotensive, immunostimulant, nervine, rubefacient, stimulant, stomachic, sudorific, tonic, vulnerary.

Gentian

- One of nature's best bitter tonics for the GI tract (gastrointestinal).

- Strengthens the entire body.

- One of the best herbs for the improvement of digestion.

- Increases liver and pancreatic function.

- Increases gastric secretions, while toning and strengthening the stomach.

- Has anti-parasitic properties, kills plasmodia and worms.

- Strengthens the liver, spleen and pancreas.

- Has a toning effect upon the kidneys.

- Increases circulation.

- A revitalizer of the body; used for fatigue, exhaustion and low energy levels (anemia).

- Used in all female weaknesses.

- Use for indigestion, dyspepsia and gas.

- Can be used for lightheadedness, dizziness, etc.

- Can be used for infections and toxic conditions of the body.

- Also can be used for poisonous bites and malaria.

Scientific name: *Gentiana lutea*

Parts used: Root.

Actions: Alterative, antacid, anthelmintic (vermifuge), anti-bilious, anti- inflammatory antiperiodic, antipyretic, antiseptic, anti-spasmodic, anti-venomous, bitter tonic, cholagogue, emetic (large doses), emmenagogue, febrifuge, hepatic, laxative (mild), stimulant, stomachic, tonic, sialagogue.

Ginger

- Used throughout the world as a digestive aid and for circulation.

- Used as a catalyst with other herbs.

- Increases circulation to peripheral areas (brain, hands and feet) of the body.

- Great for indigestion and nausea.

- Increases lymph flow and aids elimination of mucus from the upper respiratory areas, especially the lungs.

- Effective in motion and morning sickness.

- Lowers cholesterol and blood pressure.

- Prevents blood clotting.

- Useful in post strokes.

- Aids in the cleansing of congestion (mucus) in the cerebral and sinus areas.

- Increases perspiration and elimination through the skin.

Scientific name: *Zingiber officinale*

Parts used: Dried rhizomes and root.

Actions: Analgesic, anodyne, antacid, antiemetic, antispasmodic, aperitive, aphrodisiac, aromatic, carminative, cholagogue, condiment, detoxicant, diaphoretic (whole), diffusive stimulant, diuretic, emmenagogue, expectorant, nervine, pungent, rubefacient, sialagogue, sternutatory, stomachic, sweet, tonic.

Ginkgo Biloba

- One of the best herbs for the brain and nervous system.

- Improves cerebral vascular insufficiency.

- Used throughout the world for memory loss and vertigo (dizziness).

- Strengthens the heart and vascular system.

- Increases blood flow to the tissues.

- Useful in cases of asthma.

- Used for tinnitus (ringing in the ears).

- Has been proven beneficial for fibromyalgia.

- Very beneficial for hemorrhoids, spider and varicose veins.

- Has been useful for carpal tunnel syndrome.

- One of nature's great tonics, especially to the "neuro" system.

Scientific name: *Ginkgo biloba*

Parts used: *Leaf*—promotes blood circulation, stops pain, benefits the brain, and is astringent to the lungs. *Seed*—considered astringent for the lungs, stops nocturnal emissions, stops asthma, enuresis, excessive leukorrhea and increases energy.

Actions: Adaptogen, alkalizer, anti-aging, anti-fungal, anti-inflammatory antioxidant, antispasmodic (mild), astringent, bitter tonic, cardiac tonic (mild), expectorant (mild), nervine, sedative (mild), tonic, vasodilator, vulnerary.

Goldenseal

- One of nature's greatest "heal-all" herbs.

- A true tonic for the body.
- Not for long term use because of its accumulative properties.
- It increases gastric juices and digestive enzymes. It also increases the production and secretion of bile.
- Used to strengthen and tone the pancreas.
- Helps regulate blood sugars.
- Considered a source of natural insulin.
- Strengthens the nervous system.
- It has homeostatic properties, especially for the uterus.
- Tones the vascular system and helps increase circulation.
- A great anti-inflammatory especially for the glandular system.
- Use for gastric and intestinal problems.
- Use in cancerous conditions.
- A gentle laxative.
- Use for drug and alcohol dependency.
- Helps eliminate catarrh (mucus) in the body, especially in the respiratory and GI tract tissues.
- Use in cystitis, prostatitis and nephritis.
- Excellent for hemorrhoids and hemorrhages.
- Use for HIV and venereal diseases.
- Has anti-parasitic properties, and is antiseptic.

- Use for infections, wounds, sores, fissures, etc.
- Use in chronic skin conditions, eczema, dermatitis and psoriasis.
- Use in all types of prolapsed conditions, (uterus, intestinal, etc.).
- Makes a great eyewash.
- Tones and cleans the liver. Use for jaundice, hepatitis, etc.
- Use for ulcerated tissue.
- Use for tonsillitis, typhoid fever, malaria, meningitis, and mononucleosis.
- Use for boils, abscesses and tumors.
- Use as a mouthwash for gum conditions and canker sores.
- Great for ringworm and amoebic dysentery.

Scientific name: *Hydrastis canadensis* **Parts used**: Root and dried rhizomes.

Actions: Alterative, anti-diabetic, antiemetic, anti-inflammatory anti-parasitic, anti-periodic, antiseptic, aperient, astringent, bitter tonic, cholagogue, deobstruent, depurative (anti-fungal), detergent, diuretic, heal-all, hemostatic (urine esp.), hepatic, laxative, nervine, ophthalmic, oxytocic (stimulates uterine contractions), stomachic, vulnerary.

Gotu Kola

- One of God's finest herbs for brain and nerve regeneration.

- A tremendous herb for spinal cord injuries.
- A cellular proliferator (strengthens cells).
- Increases oxygen to cells.
- Strengthens the immune system.
- Helps with difficult menopause issues.
- Aids in weight loss.
- Used for depression and endocrine glandular weaknesses.
- Promotes blood flow in lower extremities.
- Strengthens the vascular walls, therefore excellent in cases of varicose or spider veins, hemorrhoids, venous insufficiency or any vascular distensibility .
- Shows healing potential in ulcerated conditions.

Scientific name: *Centella asiatica*

Parts used: Whole plant or root.

Actions: Adaptogen, alterative, antipyretic, antispasmodic, aphrodisiac, astringent, cellular proliferator, diuretic, nervine, sedative, stimulant (mild), tonic (brain and nerve).

Hawthorn Berry

- Hawthorn berry is "the great heart herb."
- This flavonoid-rich fruit is tissue specific for the heart and vascular system. It strengthens these tissues and removes the inflammation.

- It aids in dissolving lipid deposits, therefore increasing circulation.

- Has vasodilating properties, which also aid in increasing circulation.

- Use in high (hypertension) or low (hypotension) blood pressure cases.

- Considered a cardiac tonic for all heart-related issues.

- Also used in cases of insomnia (consider adrenals as well).

- Strengthens vascular walls, therefore excellent for regeneration of varicose and spider veins, hemorrhoids and prolapsed conditions of the body.

- Has strong antioxidant power to help remove acids from the body.

- Hawthorn berry is an excellent anti-inflammatory and should be used in all cases of inflammation.

Scientific name: *Crataegus spp.*

Parts used: Berries and leaf.

Actions: Anti-inflammatory, antioxidant, anti-spasmodic, astringent, cardiac tonic, cellular proliferator, digestant, diuretic, emmenagogue, hypertensive, hypotensive, sedative, tonic, vasodilator.

Horse Chestnut

- This is another one of God's great circulatory herbs.

- Horse Chestnut strengthens and tones the vascular walls.

- It has anti-inflammatory properties, thus it helps dissolve plaqued lipids.

- Both of the above actions together greatly increase circulation.

- A "must" for varicose and spider veins as well as hemorrhoids.

- Reduces vascular swelling.

- A strong astringent, similar to witch hazel and white oak bark.

- Useful for ulcerated conditions.

- Helps remove toxins from the body.

- Useful for prostatitis.

- Use in cases of rheumatism.

Scientific name: *Aesculus hippocastanum*

Parts used: Bark, dried horse chestnut seeds, dried horse chestnut leaves.

Actions: Anti-inflammatory, anti-rheumatic, astringent, bitter, cellular proliferator (especially to the vascular walls), expectorant, febrifuge, mild narcotic, nutritive.

Horsetail or Shavegrass

- Horsetail is one of the greatest herbs for bone and connective tissue weaknesses.

- It is very high in silica, which is converted into calcium by the liver.
- This herb has great healing powers to all tissues of the body.
- It is an extremely good herb for the urinary tract (kidneys and bladder).
- Use to strengthen any prolapsed condition of the body, e.g., bladder, bowels, uterus, veins, skin and the like.
- Has some minor antiparasitic properties.
- One of the greatest helps for increasing platelet production by the spleen.
- A very good herb for prostate inflammation and weakness.
- Used in the detoxification of the body.
- Has diuretic properties, therefore very beneficial in relieving kidney congestion.
- Used to strengthen fingernails (check thyroid/parathyroid).

Scientific name: *Equisetvense*

Parts used: Whole plant.

Actions: Alterative, anti-inflammatory, anti-parasitic (mild), antispasmodic (mild), anti-tumor, astringent, carminative, cellular proliferator, diaphoretic, emmenagogue (mild), galactagogue, hemostatic, litho triptic, nutritive, tonic, vulnerary.

Juniper Berry

- Juniper Berry is considered one of the great kidney herbs.

- It has a very strong action upon the kidneys. Use caution in cases of extreme kidney damage.

- It is anti-inflammatory and has some anti-spasmodic properties.

- It has antiseptic properties, which are useful in killing fungi, bacteria and yeasts.

- Great for UTIs (urinary tract infections) and parasitic overgrowths in the GI tract. It is also a natural diuretic, and relieves excess water.

- Said to aid in restoring the pancreas, and beneficial in cases of diabetes, as it has natural insulin properties.

Scientific name: *Juniperus communis* or *species*
Parts used: Usually the berries, also the oil (from the berries and wood), leaves, bark.

Actions: Anodyne, antiseptic, aromatic, carminative, diaphoretic, diuretic, emmenagogue, stimulant, stomachic.

Licorice

- A definite power herb for the adrenal glands.

- A powerful endocrine glandular herb.

- Acts as a natural anti-inflammatory steroid (cortisone, etc.) without inhibiting the adrenal production of steroids.

- Helps increase neurotransmitters and steroid production.
- Has anti-fungal and antibacterial properties.
- Aids in the regulation of blood sugars.
- Promotes tissue healing, especially of the GI tract.
- A great blood cleanser and detoxifier.
- Use for hypoglycemia and diabetes.
- Use for ulcerated tissues.
- Can be used for Candida albicans.
- Useful in infections and respiratory congestive issues.
- Helps break up and remove mucus.
- Used as a laxative.
- One of the top herbs for hemorrhoids.
- Good for healing up the whole GI tract.
- High in phytosterols.

Scientific name: *Glycyrrhiza glabra*

Parts used: Root and dried rhizome.

Actions: Aperient, demulcent, emollient, expectorant, flavoring, pectoral, sialogogue, and slightly stimulant.

Lobelia

- One of nature's greatest antispasmodics.

- Useful in spasms, cramping, convulsions, epileptic seizures, spinal cord injuries, and the like.

- A very powerful nervine.

- Has a relaxing effect.

- Very useful in cases of asthma, emphysema, and C.O.P.D., where spasms of the bronchi and lung tissue blocks proper breathing. Action is similar to inhalers, but allows for expectoration (which is vital).

- Lobelia has some expectorant properties, therefore very beneficial in removal of congestion, specifically in the respiratory system.

- It is also a hemostatic (stops internal and external bleeding).

- Great for angina pectoris or infarctions (heart attacks).

- Useful in cases of equilibrium or fainting issues.

Scientific name: *Lobelia inflata*

Parts used: Fresh and dried herb and seeds.

Actions: Alkaloids, antispasmodic, anti-venomous, astringent, cathartic, chlorophyll, counter-irritant, diaphoretic, diuretic, emetic, fixed oil, gum, isolobeline, etc., lignin, salts of lime and potassium. Lobelia also contains sulfur, iron, cobalt, selenium, sodium, copper and lead, lobelic and chelidonic acids, lobeline, nauseant, relaxant (in large doses) and stimulant (in small doses), resin.

Marshmallow

- A great anti-inflammatory and healer of the gastrointestinal tract (stomach and intestines).
- A specific for gastritis, enteritis, colitis, diverticulitis, ulcers and cancers of the GI tract.
- Being high in mucilage it coats and protects from free radical (acids) damage to the mucosa.
- It neutralizes over-production of stomach acids, therefore allowing improved digestion.
- Superb for cystitis and urinary tract inflammation.
- A great aid in prostatitis.
- Heals wounds, especially good in burn cases.
- Works well in cases of bronchitis and sore throats.
- Great for inflammation of the vascular system, liver and pancreas.
- Aids digestion and is a mild stimulant to the GI tract.
- High in calcium and lime. Excellent for the skeletal structure.
- Has been used very successfully in gangrene.
- Especially useful for coughs, laryngitis, swollen tonsils (tonsillitis), respiratory congestion and inflammatory conditions.
- Excellent for arthritis and rheumatism.
- Useful for diabetics.

- Great in eyewash formulas to help soothe and heal irritated eyes.
- Superb for vaginal issues of all types.
- Useful for boils, abscesses and skin conditions.
- Very useful as a mouthwash for swollen, inflamed and infected gums.

Scientific name: *Althaea officinalis*

Parts used: Root (greater potency), leaves and flowers.

Actions: Absorbent, anticomplementary, anti-inflammation, demulcent, diuretic, emollient, immune stimulant and hypoglycemic, laxative, mucilage, nutritive, protective, vulnerary.

Milk Thistle

- The great "liver protector."
- Milk Thistle protects, tones, strengthens and detoxifies the liver, like no other.
- It has high antioxidant properties and is considered one of the best to protect against free-radical damage.
- Aids in the regeneration of the liver and pancreas (stimulates new liver cell production).
- Superb for hepatitis A, B and C and in cirrhosis of the liver.
- Increases the production and flow of bile.
- Increases formation of new liver cells.

Scientific name: *Silybum marianum*

Parts used: The ripe seeds.

Actions: Cholagogue, diaphoretic, emmenagogue.

Motherwort

- Motherwort is a great heart tonic.

- It helps to eliminate palpations and arrhythmias.

- Used for any heart condition, including atrial fibrillation, V-tach, PVCs, PACs, tachycardia, and CHFs.

- Helps to enhance the adrenal glands.

- Used in female conditions, including menstrual cramps and hot flashes.

Scientific name: *Leonurus cardiaca*

Parts used: The aerial portion of the herb.

Actions: Antispasmodic, cardiac (tonic), cathartic (aperient), diaphoretic, diuretic, emmenagogue, hepatic, nervine and tonic.

Mullein

- Mullein is one of the great expectorants (removes mucus and congestion).

- Used especially for bronchial and lung conditions including bronchitis, asthma, emphysema, pneumonia and allergies.

- Mullein is also strongly anti-inflammatory aiding in all types of inflammatory conditions.

- A great herb for the endocrine glandular system, especially the thyroid.

- Used for coughs and sore throats.

- Mullein has strong astringent properties as well.

- Aids in the movement of the lymphatic system.

- Helps reduce tumors and boils.

Scientific name: *Verbascum thapsus*

Parts used: Leaves, flowers, root and fruit.

Actions: Absorbent, anodyne, anthelmintic (vermicide), anti-asthmatic, anticatarrhal, antiseptic, antispasmodic, astringent, demulcent, diuretic, emollient, germicide, hemostatic, narcotic, nutritive, pectoral, vulnerary.

Nettles (Stinging)

- A highly nutritive herb with a broad range of actions. Nettles has an alkalizing effect upon the body.

- Used to increase circulation.

- A specific for arthritis and rheumatism.

- Great for the joints.

- Used in pain and inflammation issues.

- One of the few herbs for the thyroid gland.

- A strong detoxifier of the skin.
- Being alkaline it neutralizes acids (like uric and sulfuric acids).
- Somewhat of a hemostatic (stops bleeding).
- Feeds the body nutrition, especially potassium and iron (although it is also full of minerals).
- Useful in circulation issues, somewhat of a vasodilator.
- Promotes the flow of urine and is useful for kidney stones.
- Shrinks swollen tissues.
- Excellent for pregnancy, nutrition, and for anti-abortive issues.
- Used in cases of bronchitis especially asthma, emphysema and C.O.P.D.
- Nettles is an expectorant (removes mucus) and has antispasmodic properties.
- Used for anemia.
- A great blood purifier and body regulator.

Scientific name: *Urtica dioica*

Parts used: Leaves.

Actions: Astringent, diuretic, expectorant, galactagogue, hemostatic, nutritive and tonic.

Oregon Grape Root

- One of the great blood purifiers.

- Has a powerful effect upon the liver, spleen, skin and blood.

- It is one of the greatest herbs for stimulating, strengthening and cleansing of the liver.

- Specific for skin conditions like psoriasis, eczema or dermatitis.

- Increases immune response.

- High in iron; aids in increasing red blood cells and hemoglobin.

- Excellent for anemia, jaundice and hepatitis A, B or C.

- Has a fair amount of antimicrobial action. Shown to kill various fungi and bacteria including: staphylococcus, streptococcus, chlamydia, salmonella typhi, corynebacterium, vibrio cholerae, trichomonas vaginalis, shigella, giardia, treponema pallidum, pseudomonas, pneumococcus, and candida albicans.

- Has some larger parasitic activity as well.

- Also used against protozoas.

- A nerve tonic.

- Slightly laxative.

Scientific name: *Mohonia spp*.

Parts used: Root and rhizome.

Actions: Alterative, anti-periodic, antiscorbutic, anti-scrofulous, hepatic, laxative, nerve tonic, anti-syphilitic, depurant, diuretic, stimulant (slightly), tonic.

Parsley

- A tremendous herb for the urinary tract and adrenal glands.
- Has a strengthening and cleansing effect upon the bladder and kidneys.
- High in chlorophyll, therefore it enhances the blood and cleans and moves the lymphatics.
- Excellent for heavy metal and chemical toxicity.
- Enhances nerve and heart function.
- Superb for the endocrine glands.
- Increases the iron-carrying capacity of the blood.
- Used to fight infections.
- Used in cases of jaundice and dropsy (edema).
- Excellent for upper respiratory congestion and infections.
- Also used in conjunctivitis and inflammation of the eyelids.

Scientific name: *Petroselinum sativum*

Parts used: Whole herb; leaves, root and seeds.

Actions: Anti-periodic (juice), antispasmodic, aperient, aromatic, carminative (seeds), culinary, diuretic, emmenagogue (seeds), febrifuge (seeds), tonic, vulnerary.

Pau D'Arco

- A tremendous Brazilian "friend." A true tonic.
- Considered a top cellular proliferator (strengthens and enhances cells).
- A top parasitic herb used for microorganism infestations (bacterial, viral, and protozoa).
- A great immune builder.
- Used especially in cancer cases.
- Has a powerful effect upon the lymphatic system.
- Helps eliminate tumors, boils, abscesses, and the like.
- Used in skin conditions including eczema, dermatitis, and psoriasis.
- Also considered a nutritive and resolvent.

ActionsScientific name: *Tabebuia impetiginosa*

Parts used: Bark.

Actions: Antimicrobial (bacterial, etc.), anti-viral, cellular proliferator/strengthener), nutritive, alterative (cooling), anti-tumor, tonic, hypotensive, anti-diabetic, astringent, bitter (digestive), stimulant, restorative, somewhat decongestant.

Pipsissewa

- A great alkalizer of the urinary tract system.

- Helps clean and remove sediment from the bladder and kidneys.

- An excellent diuretic.

- Used in urinary tract infections.

- Lowers blood pressure when kidneys are involved.

Scientific name: *Chimaphila umbellata*

Parts used: Leaf, stem, aerial portions.

Actions: Alterative, astringent and diuretic.

Plantain

- The great Plantain can't be beat for pus and septic conditions of the blood and body.

- Great for boils, abscesses and tumors.

- Known for its anti-venom properties in snakebites.

- Has a strong astringent action (pulling and cleansing) upon tissues.

- Useful for inflammation and for its healing abilities.

- Neutralizes stomach acids and helps restore proper gastric action.

- Has mild expectorant properties (therefore aiding in bronchial and lung congestion).

- Used in venereal diseases.

- Use topically and internally for all skin conditions including eczema, dermatitis and psoriasis.

- Great in an eyewash, especially for cataracts and glaucoma.

Scientific name: *Plantago* spp.

Parts used: Root, leaves, flower spikes and seeds.

Actions: Alterative (cooling), anthelmintic (vermicide), antiseptic, antisyphilitic, anti-venomous, astringent, deobstruent, depurant, diuretic, emollient, refrigerant, styptic and vulnerary.

Poke Root (a.k.a. Pokeweed)

- The tumor buster. One of the best for abscesses, boils and masses.

- Encourages movement in the lymphatic system.

- Used for enlarged or hardened organs and glands (thyroid, spleen, liver, etc.).

- Has some mild cardiac-depressant qualities.

- Skin cleanser especially good for eczema, dermatitis and psoriasis. Increases bile and digestive juices.

- Promotes kidney function.

- Has some anti-inflammatory properties.

- Helpful in chronic rheumatism and arthritis.

- Stimulates thyroid and adrenal function.

- Used for all cancers and HIV.

Scientific name: *Phytolacca americana*

Parts used: Fresh root, berries and leaves.

Actions: Alterative, anodyne, anti-sorbic, anti-syphilitic, anti-tumor, cathartic, detergent, emetic, leaves: anodyne, cardiac-depressant, nutritive and resolvent.

Red Clover

- Another one of nature's great herbs.

- Similar to cleavers and sassafras.

- A tremendous blood purifier.

- Use in all cancers, especially leukemia.

- Helps dissolve tumors and masses. Also great for abscesses and boils.

- Cleans and strengthens all liver conditions.

- Strengthens red blood cells.

- Excellent for all skin conditions, including eczema, dermatitis, and psoriasis.

- Great for syphilis and venereal diseases.

- Has some antispasmodic properties and soothes the nerves.

Scientific name: *Trifolium pratense*

Parts used: Flowers and leaves.

Actions: Alterative, anti-spasmodic, somewhat depurative, anti-tumor, deobstruent, detergent, expectorant, nutritive, sedative and stimulant (slightly).

Red Raspberry

- One of nature's top female herbs.
- Considered a nutritive tonic.
- A specific in pregnancy, and produces a far less painful and more natural delivery.
- Strengthens both mother and fetus during childbearing.
- Checks hemorrhages, especially during labor.
- Enriches mother's milk.
- A great herb for cleansing the male and female reproductive organs.
- Excellent for cleansing and strengthening the blood.
- Decreases excessive menstrual flow.
- Used for prolapsus of the uterus, anus, intestines, bladder, etc.
- Used for piles and hemorrhoids.
- Somewhat of a nerve tonic and nervine.
- Increases healing in wounds, sores and ulcerated conditions.
- Used to relieve excessive labor pains (uterine cramps).
- Used as a mouthwash for bleeding and infected gums.

- Used in eyewashes for inflammation, congestion or swelling.

Scientific name: *Rubus idaeus*

Parts used: Leaves, root bark and fruit.

Actions: Alliterative (mild), anti-abortive, antiemetic, anti-gonorrheal, anti-leukorrheal, anti-malarial, antiseptic, astringent, cathartic, hemostatic, parturient, stimulant, stomachic, tonic. *The fruit* acts as an antacid, esculent, mild laxative, parturient, refrigerant. *The leaves* are alliterative, anti-abortive, antiemetic, anti-gonorrheal, anti- leukorrheal, antimalarial, antiseptic, astringent, cathartic, hemostatic, parturient, stomachic stimulant, tonic.

Reishi Mushroom

- A powerful immune stimulator.
- Helps lower cholesterol and increase circulation.
- Helps lower blood sugar levels.
- Helps the body restore itself in degenerative issues.
- Stimulates T and B cell production (NK = natural killer) cells.
- Said to improve heart and liver functions.
- Used in cancer and AIDS cases.
- Used where abscesses, boils and tumors exist.
- Helps reduce swollen lymph nodes.

- Increases fibroblasts, macrophages and lymphocytes.
- May help steroid production by its positive effect upon the adrenal glands.

Scientific name: *Ganoderma lucidum*

Parts used: Whole mushroom.

Actions: Immune system support.

St. John's Wort

- One of the great herbs for the nervous system.
- Has a fairly strong regenerative effect upon the nervous system.
- Also has a balancing effect upon the tissues.
- Used for depression, anxiety and irritability.
- Great for insomnia. (Insomnia and anxiety are the effects of adrenal gland weakness.)
- A great aid with headaches and cramping of all types, including menstrual.
- Has anti-parasitic properties, including antibacterial, anti-fungal and antiviral.
- Shown to have a very positive effect against the HIV virus.
- Has anti-inflammatory properties.
- Will help somewhat in sciatica.
- Used in colds and respiratory congestive issues.

- Helpful in Parkinson's Disease.

Scientific name: *Hypericum perforatum*

Parts used: Herb, flowers, aerial portions.

Actions: Alterative, anti-spasmodic, anti-inflammatory, astringent, vulnerary.

Saw Palmetto

- One of God's great endocrine gland herbs (thyroid, adrenal, pancreas, pituitary, etc.).
- Called the "male herb" for its anti-inflammatory and healing effect upon the prostate. (Inhibits the production of dihydrotestosterone.)
- A strong herb for both female and male reproductive disorders.
- Enhances sexual function and desire.
- Beneficial in inflammation of the respiratory system (nose, throat, bronchi and lungs).
- Has a strong effect upon the adrenal glands, thus increasing neurotransmitters and steroids.
- Aids in sugar issues involving the pancreas and adrenals.
- Helps increase urine flow and kidney function.
- Useful in urinary tract infections.

Scientific name: *Serenoa repens*

Parts used: Berries (fruit).

Actions: Antiseptic, aphrodisiac, diuretic, expectorant, roborant.

Skullcap

- One of the greatest herbs for the brain, spine and nervous system.
- Strengthens the brain and nervous system.
- It's a powerful nervine, sedative and anti-spasmodic.
- Used for spasms, cramping, convulsions, and the like.
- Aids in cases of insomnia and restlessness.
- A specific for multiple sclerosis, Parkinson's and palsies.
- Strengthens the medulla, thus used for vertigo and dizziness.
- Spinal cord injuries.
- Used for drug and alcohol withdrawal symptoms.
- As an aromatic, it calms the emotions.

Scientific name: *Scutellaria lateriflora*

Parts used: Herb, aerial portions.

Actions: Antispasmodic, nervine, sedative.

Senna

- Helps tone and strengthen the GI tract.

- Increases peristaltic action of the GI tract.

- Used as a strong laxative, so not recommended for prolonged usage by itself. (Can irritate in high dosages and prolonged use.)

- Helps clean the intestinal walls.

Scientific name: *Cassia acutifolia*
Parts used: Pods and leaves.
Actions: Purgative that also inhibits reabsorption in the intestines.

Shiitake Mushroom

- Strengthens the immune system by increasing T-cell function.

- Effective in the treatment of cancer, as reported in a joint study by the Medical Department of Japan.

Scientific name: *Lentinus edodes*
Parts used: Cap and stems. Sold dry.
Actions: Immune stimulating, nutritive, hypotensive, anti-cholesterol.

Siberian Ginseng (Eleuthero)

- One of the great endocrine gland herbs, especially great for the adrenal glands.

- Increases neurotransmitter and steroid production.

- Strengthens cells (cellular proliferator).

- Improves vitality and stamina.

- Used for chronic fatigue or loss of energy.

- Helps strengthen the immune system.

- Increases circulation by helping to reduce cholesterol.

- Strengthens the pancreas and helps control blood sugar issues.

- Helps relieve emotional, mental and physical stress.

- Helps lower blood pressure and strengthens the heartbeat.

- Used in cases of asthma, emphysema and C.O.P.D., where an adrenal gland relationship exists.

- A tonic for the whole body.

Scientific name: *Eleutherococcus senticosus*
Parts used: Root.
Actions: Demulcent, stimulant, rejuvenative.

Slippery Elm

- One of nature's great healers of the body.

- Pulls toxicity out of tissues.

- Soothes irritated and inflamed mucous membranes.
- Soothes the mucosa of the GI tract (stomach and intestines).
- Excellent for the urinary tract (strengthens and cleans).
- Well known for its beneficial effect upon the respiratory system.
- Soothes sore and inflamed throat tissues.
- Helps pull (expectorant) mucus from the respiratory tract.
- High in nutrition.
- Used in prostatitis.
- Ulcerated conditions of the body.
- Lesions of the GI tract.
- Used in gastritis, enteritis, colitis and diverticulitis.
- Great for abscesses and gangrene.
- Used in gout and arthritis.
- Helps remove acids from the tissues.

Scientific name: *Ulmus fulva*

Parts used: Inner bark.

Actions: Astringent, demulcent, emollient, expectorant, nutritive, vulnerary, yin tonic and soothing to the alimentary canal.

Turmeric

- An ancient herb used for liver and blood conditions.
- Stimulates bile flow and production.
- Helps dissolve and remove sediment in the liver.
- Has some anti-parasitic actions, especially for protozoa infestations.
- Helps increase circulation.
- Has a beneficial effect upon the whole GI tract.
- Has strong anti-inflammatory properties, therefore very beneficial for arthritis, bursitis, tendonitis, etc.
- Aids in digestion.
- Promotes healing.

Scientific name: *Curcuma longa*

Parts used: Rhizome.

Actions: Aromatic stimulant, alliterative, analgesic, anti-septic, astringent, cholagogue, em-menagogue.

Uva Ursi or Bearberry

- A powerful antiseptic and cleanser of the urinary tract system.
- Has a strong influence upon the pancreas and used to help regulate blood sugars.
- Has a healthy effect upon the liver and spleen.

- Aids with the elimination of kidney stones.
- A great herb for the prostate gland (especially in prostatitis and prostate cancer).
- Great in congestive conditions of the body (especially the bladder, kidneys, liver, gallbladder, pancreas and spleen).
- A diuretic.
- Strengthens the liver, kidneys, bladder, uterus, prostate and spleen.
- Useful in correcting bedwetting issues.
- Useful as a douche for vaginal infections and disorders.
- Soothes, strengthens and tones the mucous membranes of the genitourinary (urinary organs, c.a. kidneys, urinary bladder) passages.
- Used in urethritis, cystitis, nephritis, incontinence, and urinary tract ulcerations.
- Used for CHF (congestive heart failure), cardiac edema.
- Used for piles and hemorrhoids.

Scientific name: *Arctostaphylos uva-ursi*
Parts used: Leaves.
Actions: Antiseptic, astringent, diuretic.

Valerian

- Valerian has soothed a lot of nerves through the years.
- A strong nervine and non-narcotic sedative.

- Aids in anxiety (adrenals), nervous tension, muscle spasms, epileptic seizures and depression (thyroid).
- Said to be somewhat of a cardiac tonic— helps regulate heart palpitations.
- Helps in hyperactivity.
- Helps reduce high blood pressure from stress and tension.
- Helps strengthen brain and nerve tissues.
- Aids in colic conditions, gas and indigestion from nervous stomach.

Scientific name: *Valeriana officinalis*

Parts used: Root, rhizome and also the herb.

Actions: Anodyne, antispasmodic, anti-thermic, aromatic, carminative, cathartic, diaphoretic, diuretic (lithotriptic), nervine (sedative), stimulant, tonic.

White Pond Lily

- This is another one of God's great cleansing herbs.
- Similar to white oak bark, but more for lower body cleansing.
- Helps remove toxicity from the tissues of the body.
- Has a healthy and toning effect upon tissues.
- Especially used to cleanse and strengthen the reproductive tissues in both male and female.

- It has pain-relieving properties.

- Use in cancerous conditions.

- Useful for abscesses, boils and tumors.

- Makes a great mouthwash to clean and heal swollen or ulcerated gums.

- Makes an excellent douche for cleansing the vaginal wall (infections, inflammation, A-typical cells, ulcerations, etc.).

- Strengthens prolapsed conditions and relaxed vagina.

- Use for prostate conditions, especially prostatitis and prostate cancer.

- Excellent for urinary tract system (kidneys and bladder).

- Use to heal wounds, sores, and the like.

- Helps remove congestion out of tissues.

Scientific name: *Nymphaea; Nymphaea Odorata* or *Castalia Odorata*

Parts used: Fresh root and leaves, rhizome.

Actions: Alterative, anodyne, anti-scrofulous, antiseptic, astringent, demulcent, deobstruent, discutient, tonic, vulnerary.

White Oak Bark

- Another tremendous herb of God.

- White oak bark is a great cleanser of the body.

- Has very strong astringent properties.

- Increases lymphatic flow and helps reduce swollen lymph nodes.
- A powerful cleanser of tissue, used for mouthwashes, poultices, douches, enemas and abscesses.
- Use as a douche for infections and A-typical cell formation.
- Strengthens cells (cellular proliferator).
- Superb for internal or external hemorrhages.
- Has diuretic properties, thus increases urine flow.
- Kills and expels small worms (pin worms, etc.).
- Used to eliminate gallstones and especially kidney stones.
- Helps clean and strengthen the GI tract.
- Excellent for prolapsed conditions, including intestinal, uterus, bladder, vascular system, etc.
- Used in all mouth and gum conditions.
- Has a powerful effect upon tooth enamel and bone growth.
- Used with plantain for snakebites.
- Ulcers, boils, gangrene, tumors, and the like.
- Use in all skin conditions including eczema, dermatitis and psoriasis. Hemorrhoids, piles and lesions.
- Used to strengthen the arteries, veins and capillaries; especially great for varicose veins and spider veins.

Scientific name: *Quercus alba: fagaceae*

Parts used: Inner bark, gall, acorn.

Actions: Anthelmintic (vermifuge), antiemetic, antiphlogistic, astringent (strong), antiseptic, antivenomous, diuretic (lithotriptic), febrifuge, hemostatic, stimulant (mild), tonic.

Wood Betony

- Wood Betony is considered a top nerve tonic.
- It especially effects the nerves of the head and face.
- It acts like a tonic to the digestive system.
- A great blood and liver cleanser.
- Use in liver congestive issues like jaundice.
- A great spleen cleanser and strengthener.
- Known to expel worms.
- Used for headaches, convulsions, spasms and cramping.
- Use for nerve disorders like multiple sclerosis, Parkinson's, and palsies.
- Use in cases of neuralgia.
- Use in times of stress and nervous tension.

Scientific name: *Betonica officinalis*

Parts used: Whole herb, aerial portions.

Actions: Alterative, analgesic, anthelmintic, antiscorbutic, antispasmodic, antivenomous, aperient, aromatic, astringent, bitter tonic, carminative, febrifuge, nervine, sedative, stomachic.

Wormwood

- One of nature's top herbs for parasites.
- Wormwood is especially great for larger parasites, including worms of all types and flukes.
- Promotes digestion and liver function.
- Great for stomach paralysis and disorders.
- A strong herb for debilitated conditions.
- An excellent nerve tonic.
- Has antiseptic properties.
- Has been used to counteract the toxic effects of various poisonous plants.
- Use for nausea, morning sickness and upset stomach.
- Use in nervous conditions and nerve injuries.
- Great for jaundice and liver conditions and congestive issues.
- Shown to be beneficial in cases of gout and rheumatism.

Scientific name: *Artemisia absinthium*

Parts used: Whole herb and leaves, oil (external only).

Actions: Anti-bilious, antiseptic, anti-venomous, aromatic, astringent, carminative, febrifuge, hepatic, nervine, stimulant, stomachic (vermifuge), tonic, anthelmintic.

Yellow Dock

- One of the great liver and blood herbs.

- Strengthens the liver and promotes liver function.

- Promotes bile formation.

- Increases the oxygen-carrying capacity of the red blood cells.

- High in iron, thus used for anemia and low hemoglobin counts.

- A top blood builder.

- A great lymphatic cleanser.

- Used in all types of skin conditions.

- Strengthens the spleen and helps clean the blood.

- Has a strengthening effect upon the entire body.

- Excellent for swollen lymph nodes and tumors as well as abscesses and toxic conditions of the body.

- Use in all cases of cancer and HIV.

- Helpful in cases of fatigue and lack of energy.

- Helps increase red blood cell count.

- Helps to promote bile formation and secretion.

Scientific name: *Rumex crispus*

Parts used: Root.

Actions: Alterative, antiscorbutic, anti-scrofulous, anti-syphilitic, aperient, astringent, cathartic, cholagogue, detergent, nutritive (leaves).

Yucca

- A great anti-inflammatory (has steroid type compounds).

- Excellent for gout, rheumatism and arthritis.

- Excellent for prostatitis and cystitis.

- Helps relieve pain in inflammatory conditions.

- Used to help break up inorganic compounds stored in tissues and the vascular system, especially calcium.

- Alkalizes and increases the healing potential of the body.

Scientific name: *Yucca glauca* spp.
Parts used: Roots and leaves of non-flowering plants.
Actions: Alterative, anti-inflammatory, anti-rheumatic, laxative.

MODULE 8.3

Power Herbal Formulas

The formulas recommended in this section, or similar versions of them, can often be found in health food stores.

The true path to healing and tissue regeneration hinges on proper diet and the utilization of botanical formulas. As this realization becomes more widespread, there will likely be a surge of interest in herbal products.

While single herbs are potent and effective in aiding the body's detoxification and rejuvenation, herbal formulas that combine the synergistic actions of several herbs are often even more powerful. In my extensive experience spanning thirty years of working with and creating herbal formulas, the effectiveness of a specific formula in bringing about a cure lies in the unique blend of herbs used.

I have personally used herbal formulas I've developed on thousands of clients with remarkable outcomes. However, I continuously experiment with new formulas, particularly those designed to stimulate the lymphatic system, and break down masses and tumors. Nothing quite compares to an exceptional herbal formula when it comes to promoting detoxification and, more significantly, enhancing and restoring the health of organs and glands.

During the process of detoxifying the body using herbal formulas, it's wise to simultaneously address the kidneys, gastrointestinal tract, liver/pancreas, lymphatic system, and endocrine glands. In my view, it's safe to take six or seven herbal formulas concurrently. Better results are often achieved by adopting a slightly more assertive approach. Many of my acquaintances have used as many as ten to twelve distinct formulas at once. As you grasp the fact that most herbs are designed to augment the functions of your body's organs and glands, strengthen your immune system, and boost detoxification, your apprehension about their consumption will diminish.

To enhance filtration and elimination through the kidneys, intestines, and skin, consider using kidney and intestinal revitalizing formulas. For better skin elimination, a lymphatic and thyroid (endocrine) formula can be beneficial. Combining this with a liver formula serves to detoxify, improve digestion, and enhance metabolism.

The lymphatic system, which functions as your "sewer system" and is intertwined with your immune system, tends to become congested and obstructed. This region is where many of our health problems originate. Masses, boils, tumors, and the like, are often linked to a congested lymph system. At the outset of your detoxification journey, a parasite formula could also be advantageous.

Detoxification is a blend of art and science that is relatively simple to learn. It's advisable to seek guidance from an experienced detoxification specialist and herbalist.

ADRENAL GLANDS

An ideal herbal tincture for aid in the regeneration of the adrenal glands would contain all or most of the following herbs:

- Astragalus Root *(Astragalus membranaceus)*

- Licorice Root *(Glycyrrhiza glabra)*

- Parsley Root *(Petroselinum crispum)*

- Bayberry Root Bark *(Myrica cerifera)*

- Jamaican Sarsaparilla Root *(Smilax ornata)*

- Juniper Berries *(Juniperus communis)*

- Kelp Fronds *(Nereocystis leutkeana)*

- Alfalfa Leaf *(Medicago sativa)*

- Prickly Ash Bark *(Zanthoxylum clava-Herculis)*

- Parsley Leaf *(Petroselinum crispum)*

- Siberian Ginseng Root *(Eleutherococcus senticosus)*

Indications

Adrenal insufficiency, arthritis, fatigue and chronic fatigue (not from Epstein-Barr virus), a specific for low blood pressure, high blood pressure (occasionally), weak pulse, systemic inflammation, female reproductive problems—especially estrogen dominance (ovarian cysts, sore breasts, uterine fibroids, etc), prostatitis, exhaustion, low endurance, neurotransmitting issues —e.g., multiple sclerosis, Parkinson's, palsy, tremors, Lou Gehrig's, etc. Post strokes, spinal cord injuries, all types of cancers, HIV (AIDS), skin conditions, heart arrhythmias, anxiety disorders.

Suggested Usage

Add to a little water or juice.

General: 1 full dropper 3 to 6 times a day.

Acute: 1 full dropper every 4 hours.

Cautions and Contraindications

May elevate the blood pressure temporarily, please monitor in high blood pressure cases.

Notes

1. The adrenal glands' medulla is responsible for producing neurotransmitters such as epinephrine, norepinephrine, and dopamine hydrochloride. These neurotransmitters play a crucial role in regulating heart function and the body's nerve responses. It's worth noting that low blood pressure often indicates a deficiency in adrenal function.

2. The adrenal glands' cortex is responsible for producing cortical steroids, which serve as anti-inflammatory compounds in the body. When the adrenal function is compromised, it often impacts the production of these lipid-type steroids derived from cholesterol. This disruption can result in unchecked inflammation within the body. Diets primarily consisting of acidic foods, which is common in typical diets, contribute to inflammation in the

body's tissues. Prolonged inflammation can lead to tissue deterioration, ultimately progressing to ulceration and potentially even developing into more serious conditions like cancer.

BLOOD

An ideal herbal formula for the blood would cleanse impurities, alkalize the blood and tissues, and reduce vascular inflammation. Such a formula would help remove mineral deposits, lipid deposits, and metals as it strengthened the blood system overall. It would contain:

- Red Clover Herb and Flowers (Frifolium pratense)

- Yellow Dock Root (Rumex spp.)

- Burdock Root (Arctium lappa)

- Plantain Herb (Plantago lanceolata)

- White Oak Bark (Quercus alba)

- Prickly Ash Bark (Zanthoxylum clava-Herculis)

Indications

Detoxification, toxic blood conditions, septicemia, leukocytosis, all cancers (especially leukemia), AIDS, anemia, syphilis, leprosy, elevated cholesterol, fatigue, low iron levels, gangrene, exhaustion, parasitic invasion of weakened blood cells, blood disorders, chronic fatigue syndrome (except when caused from thyroid and adrenal weaknesses), toxic liver and spleen conditions. Low iron levels, low O_2 saturation, malabsorption.

Suggested Usage

Add to a little water or juice.

General: 1 full dropper 3 to 6 times a day.

Acute: 1 full dropper every 2 to 4 hours.

Cautions And Contraindications

None known.

Note

In cancer cases, use with a parasite formula for microorganisms and a lymphatic formula.

BRAIN AND NERVOUS SYSTEM

And ideal herbal formula to strengthen and rebuild the brain and nerve tissues of the body would contain all or most of the following:

- Gotu Kola Herb (Centella asiatica)
- Siberian Ginseng Root (Eleutheroccocus sent.)
- Ginkgo Leaf (Ginkgo biloba)
- Schizandra Berries (Schisandra chinensis)
- Skullcap Herb (Scutellaria lateriflora)
- Prickly Ash Bark (Zanthoxylum clava-Herculis)

- Calamus Root (Acorus calamus)

Indications

Weakened nervous system, marked by nerve rings in the iris (autonomic, sympathetic and parasympathetic), poor memory (short and long term), Alzheimer's (or Mad Cow Disease, as several doctors have reported), senile dementia, multiple sclerosis, Parkinson's, Bell's palsy, post strokes, headaches, migraines, spinal cord injuries, depression, jittery nerves, pituitary and pineal gland weakness, shingles (also use a general parasite formula and a parasite formula for microorganisms), spasms, epilepsy, twitching, electrical weaknesses of the heart (arrhythmias, depolarization and repolarization issues, etc.), dizziness, equilibrium issues and mental disorders.

Suggested Usage

Add to a little water or juice.

General: 1 full dropper 3 to 6 times a day.

Acute: 1 full dropper every 2 to 4 hours.

Cautions And Contraindications

None known.

Notes

1. I have seen tremendous nerve regeneration in quadriplegics and paraplegics with this type of formula, and a 100% raw food diet.

2. Deeper results can be attained using this type of formula together with a circulation (upper) formula plus a lymphatic system formula.

3. Alkalization of the body is essential for brain and nerve regeneration. Acidity causes inflammation, which leads to tissue weakness and deterioration.

CIRCULATION AND BLOOD PRESSURE

A cayenne/garlic combo would be an ideal herbal formula to lower blood pressure and increase circulation throughout the body. It would also strengthen the heart and vascular system. Such a cayenne/garlic formula in capsule form would consist of all or most of the following:

- Cayenne Pepper Fruit *(Capsicum annum)* (40,000 HU maximum)

- Garlic Bulb *(Allium sativum)*

- Alfalfa Leaf *(Medicago sativa)*

- Butcher's Broom Root *(Iuscus aculeatus)*

- Licorice Root (Glycyrrhiza glabra)

- Hawthorn Berries (Crataegus spp.)

- Aloe (100:1)

Indications

High blood pressure, poor circulation, general body weaknesses, especially in the heart and vascular system. Nervous tension, headaches, internal bleeding, depression, sinus congestion, fatigue, poor memory, cold conditions of the body, especially hypo-activity of tissues.

Suggested Usage

General: 2 capsules, 3 times a day.

Acute: 2 to 3 capsules, every 2 to 4 hours.

Cautions And Contraindications

Caution with low blood pressure. Low blood pressure is adrenal and/or pituitary weakness. In high blood pressure cases you should use an adrenal formula (without Licorice), especially if the iris shows adrenal weakness. However, monitor your own or your patient's blood pressure.

FEMALE REPRODUCTIVE SYSTEM

An ideal herbal tincture to help clean, strengthen, and regenerate the female reproductive system would consist of all or most of the following:

- Chaste Tree Berries *(Vitex agnus-castus)*

- Alteris Root *(True Unicorn Root)*

- False Unicorn Root *(Chamaelirium luteum) (Aletris farinosa)*

- Saw Palmetto Berries *(Serenoa repens)*

- Wild Yam Root *(Dioscorea spp.)*

- Red Raspberry Leaf *(Rubus idaeus)*

- Black Haw Bark *(Viburnum prunijolium)*

- Prickly Ash Bark *(Zanthoxylum clava-Herculis)*

Indications

All female reproductive issues including dys-menorrhea (painful menstruation), amenorrhea (lack of proper menstruation), PMS, and ovulation disorders. Discharges (use a lymphatic formula, a general parasite formula and a parasite formula for microorganisms), endometriosis, ovarian cysts and uterine fibroids (adrenal weakness), prolapsed uterus, menorrhagia (excessive bleeding, which is estrogen dominance), hot flashes and cramping (low thyroid function), edema, under-developed or sagging breasts, dry vaginal walls (low estrogen levels), premature births (estrogen dominance), lack of tone in the female body, cancers of the female reproductive organs (see notes), low sex drive (also under-active thyroid).

Suggested Usage

Add to a little water or juice.

General: 1 full dropper 3 to 6 times a day.

Acute: 1 full dropper every 4 hours.

Cautions And Contraindications

Be cautious during early pregnancy. May cut suggested usage in half.

Notes

1. This formula may be used as a douche. Use 2 to 3 full droppers in skin-temperature water.

2. Females produce estrogen in primarily three places: the liver, fat cells, and ovaries (very acidic).

3. In cancers of the cervix, uterus, ovaries or vaginal wall, a heavy detoxification program is essential. Douching 2 to 4 times a day is also beneficial. Use with a lymphatic system and a general parasite formula, plus a parasite formula for microorganisms.

4. 75% of females are considered estrogen dominant. Low blood pressure, excessive bleeding, ovarian cysts, uterine fibroids, premature births, sore breasts, osteoporosis, inability to conceive, etc. are just a few of the indicators of low progesterone levels. Low progesterone production occurs mainly from adrenal insufficiency. Use an adrenal formula to enhance and regenerate the adrenals. Low blood pressure is just one indicator of adrenal weakness.

5. Hot flashes and cramping can be an indicator of thyroid weakness. Add a thyroid formula to your program if this is the case.

GENERAL NUTRITION AND ENERGY

A daily nutritional supplement of the highest quality super-food blend would contain some of God's most energetic and nutritive foods known. These would include:

- Royal Jelly
- Wheat Grass
- Alfalfa
- Siberian Ginseng Root
- Beet Root
- Cinnamon Bark
- Dandelion Leaf
- Saw Palmetto Berries
- Lemon Peel
- Norwegian Kelp
- Black Walnut Hull
- Pau d'Arco
- Chaste Tree Berries
- Chickweed
- Gotu Kola
- Hawthorn Berries
- Milk Thistle
- Seed Barley Grass

- Licorice Root

- Ginger Root

- Rye Grass

- Astragalus Root

- Flax Seed

- Aloe 100:1

- Ginkgo Biloba

Indications

The ideal super-food formula should be one that is designed for all ages and all walks of life. The formula suggested above is mega-nutritional, and fits in all situations, especially for highly depleted individuals. Even animals can benefit tremendously with this formula.

Suggested Usage By Weight

10 lbs. – 50 lbs. – 1/4 of a heaping teaspoon

50 lbs. – 100 lbs. – 1/2 of a heaping teaspoon

100 lbs. – 200 lbs. – 1 heaping teaspoon

200 lbs. – 300 lbs. – 1 tablespoon

Suggested Usage

Take 2 to 3 times a day. This super-food formula can be mixed in water or juice, or sprinkled over a salad.

Cautions And Contraindications

Do not take before bedtime if you want to sleep as this formula is an energizer.

Note

Super-food complexes far exceed orthomolecular supplementation (separate vitamins and minerals). The whole far exceeds its parts.

HEART

An ideal herbal formula to strengthen and regenerate the heart tissue, and increase circulation and nerve response within the heart would contain all or most of the following:

- Hawthorn Berries *(Crataegus spp.)*

- Butchers Broom Root *(Iuscus aculeatus)*

- Black Walnut Hull *(Juglans nigra)*

- Dandelion Leaf *(Taraxacum spp.)*

- Kelp Granules *(Nereocystis luetkeana)*

- Motherwort Herb *(Leonurus cardiaca)*

- Lily of the Valley Herb *(Convallaria majalis)*

- Cayenne Pepper *(Capsicum annuum)*

- Night Blooming Cereus Stem *(Selenicereus grandiflorus)*

Indications

Myocardial infarction (heart attack), mitral valve prolapse, pericarditis, bradycardia, tachycardia, angina pectoris (chest pains), palpitations, dyspnea, varicose and spider veins, arrhythmias, including atrial fibrillation and flutter, junctional rhythms, PACs, PVCs, heart blocks, heart or chamber hypertrophy (enlargement), weak heart (check adrenals), congestive heart failure, edema and aneurysms.

Suggested Usage

Add to a little water or juice.

General: 1 full dropper 3 to 6 times a day.

Acute: 1 full dropper every 2 to 4 hours.

Cautions And Contraindications

Do not take during pregnancy. Monitor if you or your patients are on beta-blockers or calcium channel blockers. Heart medications can become too strong and drop blood pressure too low.

Note

For optimum results, use with circulatory, thyroid, kidney, adrenal glands and/or brain and nervous system formulas.

KIDNEY AND BLADDER

An ideal herbal formula would alkalize (remove inflammation), clean, strengthen, and regenerate the kidneys and bladder tissues. It should contain all or most of the following:

- Couch Grass Root *(Agropyron repens)*
- Corn Silk *(Zea mays)*
- Pipsissewa Leaves *(Chimaphilla umbellata)*
- Nettle Herb *(Urtica dioica)*
- Coriander Seed *(Coriandrum sativum)*
- Dandelion Leaf *(Taraxacum spp.)*
- Lespedeza Herb *(Lespedeza capitata)*
- Gravel Root *(Eupatorium purpureum)*

Indications

Kidney weakness or failure, bladder weakness, cystitis, nephritis, urethritis, urinary tract infections (use a parasite formula for microorganisms as well), lower back pain, prostatitis, edema (dropsy), eye weakness, bags under the eyes, blindness, gout, kidney and bladder stones, dialysis.

Suggested Usage

Add to a little water or juice.

General: 1 full dropper 3 to 6 times a day.

Acute: 1 full dropper every 2 to 4 hours.

Cautions And Contraindications

This type of formula coupled with a raw fruit diet will considerably increase the need to eliminate through the kidneys. If your patient is on dialysis, you may need to increase their dialysis from three times a week to four times a week until self-urination has been achieved. Dialysis patients should eat 90 - 100% raw, living foods. Eliminate all meats and grains as these are acidic and irritating to the tissues of the urinary tract.

Notes

1. Alkalization is essential to the regeneration of the kidneys.
2. Do not drink cranberry juice, as this is too acidic. Fresh watermelon is far better. Fresh fruits and fresh fruit juices are excellent kidney cleansers and regenerators.

LUNGS

An ideal herbal formula would assist the body in removing mucus and toxicity, interstitially and intracellularly within the lung tissues, promoting tissue repair and rejuvenation. It would include all or most of the following:

- Platycodon Root *(Platycodon grandiflorum)*

- Cayenne Pepper Fruit *(Capsicum annuum)*

- Mullein Leaf *(Verbascum thaspus)*

- Fenugreek Seed *(Trigonella foenum-graecum)*

- Pleurisy Root *(Asclepias tuberosa)*

- Horehound Herb *(Marrubium vulgare)*

- Comfrey Root and Leaf *(Symphytum officinalis)*

- Lobelia Herb *(Lobelia inflata)*

Indications

Congestive and degenerative lung issues including: bronchitis, pneumonia, emphysema, asthma, C.O.P.D. (Chronic Obstructive Pulmonary Disease), colds, sore throats, tonsillitis, lung cancer, lung tumors, TB, sinus congestion, dyspnea, pleurisy, influenza, coughs, bleeding of the lungs, hearing loss, loss of taste and smell, thyroid congestion (causing hyperthyroidism or hypothyroidism).

Suggested Usage

Add to a little water or juice.

General: 1 full dropper 3 to 6 times a day.

Acute: 1 full dropper every 1 to 2 hours.

Cautions And Contraindications

Avoid during early pregnancy.

Notes

1. Best when used with a parasite formula for microorganisms and a lymphatic system formula.

2. Gastrointestinal cleaning and rebuilding is a must.

MALE REPRODUCTIVE SYSTEM

An ideal herbal formula to enhance and strengthen the male system would include:

- Damiana Leaf (Turnera diffusa)
- False Unicorn Root (Chamaelirium luteum)
- Chaste Tree Berries (Vitex agnus-castus)
- Saw Palmetto Berries (Serenoa repens)
- Siberian Ginseng Root (Eleutherococcus senticosus)

Indications

A weakened male system with symptoms including, but not limited to: impotence, premature ejaculation, low or excessive sex drive, general body weakness or fatigue, low ambition, low energy, pituitary weakness, adrenal weakness, anemia, depression, hormone imbalance, lack of endurance. Use when you desire a daily formula for longevity.

Suggested Usage

Add to a little water or juice.

General: 1 full dropper 3 to 4 times a day.

Cautions And Contraindications

Do not take with prostate cancer.

Note

With prostate cancer, use a prostate formula together with lymphatic system formula, parasite for microorganisms formula, adrenal formula and blood formula.

PARASITES—MICROORGANISMS

An ideal herbal formula for microorganism infestations (viruses, bacterium, fungi, protozoas etc.) would contain all or most of the following:

- Pau d' Arco Inner Bark *(Tabebuia impetiginosa)*

- *Thyme Leaf (Thymus vulgaris)*

- *Black Walnut Hulls (juglans nigra)*

- *Butternut Bark (Juglans cinerea)*

- *Echinacea Angustifolia Root (Echinacea angustifolia)*

- *Usnea Lichen (Usnea spp.)*

- *Grapefruit Seed Extract (Citrus paradisi)*

- *Lomatium Root (Lomatium dissectum)*

Indications

Microbial infestations including viruses, bacterium, protozoas, fungi, molds, warts, etc., (specifically, but not limited to: streptococcus, staphylococcus, pneumococcus, pseudomonas, M.R.S.A., E-coli, and herpes), yeast infections (Candida albicans), hepatitis A, B, and C, pneumonia, whooping cough, food poisoning, dysentery, cholera, typhoid, syphilis, TB, colds, flu, urinary tract infections, ringworm, poison oak, insect bites, wounds, toxic skin conditions (psoriasis, eczema, dermatitis), itching, tonsillitis, bronchitis, gangrene, AIDS, cancer, tumors, abscesses, cysts, infections of all types.

Suggested Usage

Add to a little water or juice.

General: 1 full dropper 3 to 6 times a day.

Acute: 1 full dropper every 2 to 4 hours.

Cautions And Contraindications

Do not use during early pregnancy.

Notes

1. For heavy infestations especially with Candida albicans (fungi) this type of formula may be used for 4 to 6 months, if needed.

2. In spinal cord injuries (in quadriplegics, paraplegics, etc.) this formula will help eliminate urinary tract infections. This formula may be used on a regular basis to achieve this. Should be used with a lymphatic system formula.

3. In chronic conditions or heavy infestations, use a general parasite formula.

PARASITES—GENERAL USE

An ideal herbal formula especially for larger parasites, such as flukes and worms of all types would contain the following:

- Wormwood Herb *(Artemesia absinthium)*

- Betel Nut *(Piper betle)*

- Male Fern Root *(Aspidium filix-mas)*

- Wormseed *(Chenopodium anthelmin.)*

- Parsley Root and Leaf *(Petroselinium crispum)*

- Cloves *(Syzygium aromatic)*

- Pau d'Arco Bark *(Tabebuia impetiginosa)*

- Pink Root *(Spigelia marilandica)*

- Tansy Herb and Flower *(Tanacetum vulgare)*

- Casara Sagrada Bark *(Rhamnus purshiana)*

Indications

Parasites, especially larger ones such as worms (pin, hook, round, all types of tapeworm) and flukes (in the liver, pancreas), microorganisms including, but not limited to: viruses, bacterium, protozoa, fungi, molds, warts; chronic yeast infections (Candida albicans), hepatitis A, B, and C, chronic UTIs (use with a parasite tincture for microorganisms), ringworm, toxic skin conditions (like psoriasis, eczema, dermatitis), gangrene, AIDS, cancer, tumors, abscesses.

Suggested Usage

Add to a little water or juice.

General: 1 full dropper 3 to 6 times a day.

Cautions And Contraindications

Do not use during pregnancy.

Note

In chronic conditions or with heavy infestations also use a parasite formula for microorganisms.

STOMACH AND BOWELS

An ideal herbal formula that acts like a gentle laxative, as it rebuilds, restores, and rejuvenates the gastrointestinal tract would contain the following powdered herbs:

- Cascara Sagrada Bark *(Rhamnus pursh.)*
- Slippery Elm Bark *(Ulmus fulva)*
- White Oak Bark *(Quercus alba)*
- Wild Yam Root *(Dioscorea spp.)*
- Plantain Leaf *(Plantago spp.)*
- Licorice Root (Glycyrrhiza glabra)
- Barberry Root (Berberis spp.)
- Gentian Root (Gentiana lutea)
- False Unicorn Root (Chamaelirium luteum)

• Ginger Root (Zingiber officinale)

Indications

Inflammation (gastritis, enteritis and colitis), ulceration, degeneration and cancer of the GI tract, constipation, chronic diarrhea, acid dyspepsia, acid reflux, mucoid plaque build-up, prolapsus, IBS (irritable bowel syndrome), diverticulitis (detoxification is a must), polyps (internal and external), Crohn's disease.

Suggested Usage

General: 1 to 6 capsules, 3 times a day.

Cautions And Contraindications

None known. However, avoid during early pregnancy.

Notes

1. The intention behind this bowel formula is to promote regeneration of the bowel rather than acting as a laxative. The purpose is to maintain the continuous action of herbs within the gastrointestinal tract, aiding in its cleansing and revitalization.

2. The objective is to achieve well-formed and soft stools, not to induce loose stools. If diarrhea occurs, it's recommended to reduce the number of capsules being taken. Bowel movements follow a 12-hour cycle, so starting with two to three capsules in the morning and evening is suggested. However, a preferable regimen is three capsules, twice a day, in the morning and evening. The aim is to have a

higher concentration of restorative intestinal herbs in the gastrointestinal tract for effective cleansing and strengthening, while avoiding laxative effects or loose stools. Overstimulating the bowel can hinder proper digestion. For a more intensive approach, some individuals may opt for a stomach and bowel formula three times a day, in which case the formula should contain fewer stimulating herbs like Cascara sagrada, Senna, and Aloe, and more healing and cleansing herbs such as Plaintain, Marshmallow, and Comfrey.

3. A liver/gallbladder flush is very important for everyone, especially those who have small intestinal ulcers, constipation, diarrhea and high blood pressure. (See instructions for Liver Flush in Chapter 9.)

THYROID

An ideal herbal formula to help clean, enhance, strengthen and regenerate the thyroid gland would contain all or most of the following in a tincture:

- Bladderwrack *(Fucus vesiculosus)*

- Fritillary Bulb *(Fritillaria cirrhosa)*

- Poke Root *(Phytolacca americana)*

- Mullein Leaf *(Verbascum thapsus)*

- Bugleweed Herb *(Lycopus virginicus)*

- Bayberry Root Bark *(Myrica cerif)*

- *Black Walnut Hull (Juglans nigra)*
- *Irish Moss (Chondrus crispus)*
- *Cayenne Pepper Fruit (Capsicum annuum)*
- *Saw Palmetto Berries (Serenoa repens)*

Indications

Hypothyroidism, fatigue (also check adrenals), chronic fatigue (not from Epstein-Barr; use a general parasite formula and a parasite formula for microorganisms for Epstein-Barr virus), heart arrhythmias, osteoporosis, cramps, rigid or brittle fingernails, hair loss, menstrual disorders (especially when pain is present), arthritis, bursitis, headaches, migraines, obesity (weight that is hard to eliminate).

Suggested Usage

Add to a little water or juice.

General: 1 full dropper 3 to 6 times a day.

Acute: 1 full dropper every 4 hours.

Cautions And Contraindications

None known.

Notes

1. Where inflammation and bone deterioration is present (as in arthritis, etc.), the thyroid and adrenal glands are always under-active.

2. Most thyroid medications (especially Synthroid®) do not affect T4 to T3 conversion well. This means that the thyroid is always hypoactive even when blood serum levels of TSHs, T4s and T3s appear to be normal *(see* Wilson's Syndrome).

3. Use the Basal Temperature Test (see Appendix A) for a more accurate indicator of thyroid function.

MODULE 8.4

Herbal Rejuvenation for Each Body System

In this section, you will discover a suggested dietary plan along with specific herbs or herbal formulas tailored for each body system. Some of the Herbal Formulas (Detoxifiers and Strengtheners) mentioned here have already been detailed and outlined in Module 8.3: Power Herbal Formulas. For instance, formulations targeting the "Adrenal Glands," "Blood," or "Lungs" are covered in that section. Additional Herbal Formulas provided in this segment are described by their general application, such as "Spleen" or "Liver-Gallbladder." The single herbs and herbal formulas recommended are widely available in numerous health food stores. While different herbal manufacturers might label their formulas differently, the essential point is to locate a formula created for the specific body system or organ that requires rejuvenation.

Note - All the Herbal Formulas listed below can be purchased from www.drmorses.com. Use Discount Coupon - GAUTAM

CARDIOVASCULAR SYSTEM

STRUCTURES — Heart, vascular system (arteries, capillaries and veins), and the blood (also part of the digestive system).

DIET — A living, raw food diet consisting mainly of fruits will alkalize (create an anti-inflammatory effect) the vascular system, which creates an ionic reaction. This means that lipid (cholesterol) plaque and mineral deposits will dissolve, and red blood cells that have bonded will break free. This will increase circulation, blood biodynamics, "thin" the blood, and lower blood pressure. This reduces or eliminates the risk of strokes or heart attacks and increases oxygenation of your body.

SINGLE HERBS—DETOXIFIERS

- Butcher's Broom
- Horse Chestnut
- White Oak Bark
- Witch Hazel
- Red Clover

SINGLE HERBS—STRENGTHENERS

- Hawthorn Berries
- Ginkgo Biloba
- Bilberry Leaf
- Black Walnut Hull

HERBAL FORMULAS—DETOXIFIERS

- Circulation Formulas
- Cayenne/Garlic Combo
- Blood
- Lymphatic System

HERBAL FORMULAS—STRENGTHENERS

- Circulation Formulas
- Adrenal Glands
- Blood
- Inflammation/Joints
- Endocrine Glands

DIGESTIVE SYSTEM

STRUCTURES — Mouth and salivary glands, stomach, small intestines (duodenum, jejunum and ileum), pancreas, liver, gallbladder.

DIET — A living, raw food diet is full of enzymes, nutrition and fiber, all of which promote better digestion, bile flow and bowel function.

SINGLE HERBS—DETOXIFIERS

- Chickweed
- Marshmallow

- Bitters
- Dandelion Root
- Dock Family (Yellow Dock, Burdock, Oregon Grape Root)
- Ginger
- Mint Family

SINGLE HERBS—STRENGTHENERS

- Gentian
- Dandelion Root
- Milk Thistle

HERBAL FORMULAS—DETOXIFIERS

- Stomach and Bowel
- Circulation (a Cayenne/Garlic Combo)
- Pancreas
- Liver/Gallbladder
- Lymphatic System

HERBAL FORMULAS—STRENGTHENERS

- Stomach and Bowel
- Circulation (a Cayenne/Garlic Combo)
- Pancreas
- Liver/Gallbladder
- Adrenal Glands

• Endocrine Glands

OTHER — A Liver/Gallbladder Flush is also recommended (see Chapter 9 for instructions in applying this.)

ELIMINATIVE SYSTEMS

See Lymphatic System, Immune System, Intestinal System, Integumentary System, Urinary System.

GLANDULAR SYSTEM

STRUCTURES — The pituitary gland, pineal gland, thyroid and parathyroid glands, thymus, adrenal glands, pancreas (Islets of Langerhans), glands within the intestinal mucosa, ovaries and testes.

DIET — A living, raw food diet promotes glandular function. It also helps balance hormone and steroid responses, which in turn increases utilization of nutrients. Creates a homeostasis of body chemistry.

SINGLE HERBS—DETOXIFIERS

• Bugleweed Leaf
• Dandelion Leaf
• Parsley Leaf
• Poke Root
• Kelp

- Saw Palmetto Berries

SINGLE HERBS—STRENGTHENERS

- Licorice Root
- Astragalus Root
- Panax
- Ginseng Root
- Siberian Ginseng Root
- Kelp
- Saw Palmetto Berries
- Chaste Tree Berry
- Hawthorn Berries
- Bugleweed
- Dandelion Leaf
- Parsley Leaf
- False Unicorn Root

HERBAL FORMULAS—DETOXIFIERS

- Lymphatic System
- Prostate
- Liver/Gallbladder
- Circulation Formulas
- Blood

HERBAL FORMULAS—STRENGTHENERS

- Endocrine Glands
- Adrenal Glands
- Thyroid Gland
- Pancreas
- Male Reproductive
- Prostate
- Liver/Gallbladder
- Circulation Formula
- Blood

LYMPHATIC SYSTEM

STRUCTURES — Spleen, thymus, appendix, tonsils, lymph nodes, lymph vessels, and lymph fluid.

DIET — A living, raw food diet consisting mainly of fruits which are full of antioxidants and astringents. They clean, enhance, rebuild and restore the health of your cells. The "kings" of these fruits are grapes and lemons.

SINGLE HERBS—DETOXIFIERS

- Poke Root
- Blood Root
- Fenugreek

- Mild Cayenne Pepper
- Cascara Sagrada
- White Oak Bark
- Cleavers
- Red Clover
- Blue Flag
- Plantain
- Red Root
- Yellow Dock

SINGLE HERBS—STRENGTHENERS

- Yellow Dock
- Poke Root
- Blue Flag
- White Oak Bark
- Reishi Mushroom
- Maitake Mushroom
- Shiitake Mushroom

HERBAL FORMULAS—DETOXIFIERS

- Lymphatic System
- Kidneys and Bladder
- Stomach and Bowel
- Liver/Gallbladder

- Blood Formula

HERBAL FORMULAS—STRENGTHENERS

- Kidneys and Bladder
- Stomach and Bowel
- Liver/Gallbladder
- Immune System
- Blood Formula

NOTE — The organs of your eliminative system are tied to your lymphatic system. Work with both systems. Your lymph and blood send their wastes into your eliminative channels (this includes your kidneys and colon) to be excreted.

IMMUNE SYSTEM

STRUCTURES — Lymphatic system, which includes the thymus and spleen, bone marrow, immune cells (lymphocytes, monocytes, basophils, macrophages, T-lymphocytes, B-cells, helper T and B cells, etc.), liver and beneficial parasites.

DIET — A living, raw food diet alkalizes and helps remove acids, foreign proteins and substances from the tissues that cause inflammatory immune responses. This enhances and eases the function of your immune system.

SINGLE HERBS—DETOXIFIERS

- Poke Root

- Blood Root
- Blue Flag
- Bugleweed
- Red Clover Flower
- Fenugreek Seed
- Plantain Leaf
- Oregon Grape Root

SINGLE HERBS—STRENGTHENERS

- Reishi Mushroom
- Shiitake Mushroom
- Astragalus Root
- Kelp/Bladderwrack
- Antler (Elk or Deer)
- Panax Ginseng
- Echinacea (all types: Purpurea, Angustifolia and Pallida)
- Siberian Ginseng
- Maitake Mushroom
- Schizandra Berries

HERBAL FORMULAS—DETOXIFIERS

- Lymphatic System formula
- Lymph Nodesformula

HERBAL FORMULAS—STRENGTHENERS

- Immune Formula #1, for general use
- Immune Formula #2, (Super-Immune) for general use, bone marrow strengthening and improved B-cell production.
- Adrenal Glands
- Thyroid Gland
- Spleen
- Liver/Gallbladder

INTEGUMENTARY SYSTEM

STRUCTURES — Skin, nails, hair, oil and sweat glands.

DIET — A living, raw food diet is highly cleansing and strengthening to the liver and skin. Raw fruits and vegetables alkalize and dissolve fatty deposits in the skin and liver (stones). These foods also enhance the function of your thyroid gland and increase body heat and elimination through your skin.

SINGLE HERBS—DETOXIFIERS

- Dock Family (Yellow Dock and Oregon Grape Root)
- Milk Thistle
- Poke Root
- Chaparral
- White Oak Bark

SINGLE HERBS—STRENGTHENERS

- Dock Family (Yellow Dock and Oregon Grape Root)
- Milk Thistle
- Horsetail
- Comfrey Root and Leaf

HERBAL FORMULAS—DETOXIFIERS

- Lymphatic System
- Liver/Gallbladder
- Stomach and Bowel Blood
- Circulation Formulas

HERBAL FORMULAS—STRENGTHENERS

- Liver/Gallbladder
- Stomach and Bowel
- Blood
- Circulation Formulas

OTHER — A Liver/Gallbladder Flush (Chapter 9) and skin brushing (Chapter 9) are also recommended.

INTESTINAL SYSTEM

STRUCTURES — Colon, lymphatic system, urinary system, immune system and the skin.

DIET — A living, raw food diet is rich in "electrical" fiber and nutrition for optimal elimination.

SINGLE HERBS—DETOXIFIERS

- Cascara Sagrada
- Psyllium Seed
- Flax Seed
- Dock Family
- Marshmallow
- Slippery Elm
- White Oak Bark

SINGLE HERBS—STRENGTHENERS

- Cascara Sagrada
- Mullein
- Chickweed
- Dock Family
- Marshmallow
- Slippery Elm
- Gentian

HERBAL FORMULAS—DETOXIFIERS

- Stomach and Bowel
- Liver/Gallbladder
- Lymphatic

- Kidneys and Bladder
- Parasite—for microorganisms
- Parasite—a general formula Strengtheners
- Stomach and Bowel
- Liver/Gallbladder
- Kidneys and Bladder
- Parasite—for microorganisms

OTHER — A Liver/Gallbladder Flush is also recommended.

MUSCULAR SYSTEM

STRUCTURES — Muscles, tendons, and connective tissue.

DIET — A fresh, raw food diet consisting of lots of green leafy vegetables and vegetable juices helps to rebuild strong muscle tissue. These foods are high in superior amino acids and minerals, especially usable calcium.

SINGLE HERBS—DETOXIFIERS

- Poke Root
- Plantain
- Blood Root
- Fenugreek Seed
- Chaparral
- White Oak Bark

- Blue Flag
- Red Clover
- Burdock Root
- Dandelion Root

SINGLE HERBS—STRENGTHENERS

- Alfalfa
- Kelp
- Panax
- Ginseng
- Comfrey Root and Leaf
- Horsetail

HERBAL FORMULAS—DETOXIFIERS

- Lymphatic System
- Circulation Formulas
- Lymph Nodes

HERBAL FORMULAS—STRENGTHENERS

- Bones
- Thyroid Gland
- Adrenal Glands

NERVOUS SYSTEM

STRUCTURES — The brain, spinal cord (Central Nervous System), the Autonomic Nervous System, sensory organs (eyes, ears, nose, olfactory nerves, etc.).

DIET — A living, raw food diet consisting primarily of fruits. These foods hold the highest electromagnetic energy of all foods (alkalizing) and promote nerve and brain regeneration.

SINGLE HERBS—STRENGTHENERS

- Gotu Kola
- Ginkgo Biloba
- Skullcap
- Kelp
- Saw Palmetto Berries
- Chaste Tree Berries
- Panax Ginseng
- Siberian Ginseng
- Parsley Root and Leaf
- Hawthorn Berries
- Astragalus Root
- Licorice Root

SINGLE HERBS—ANTISPASMODICS

- Lobelia

- St. John's Wort
- California Poppy
- Passion Flower
- Skullcap

SINGLE HERBS—RELAXANTS

- Valerian
- St. John's Wort
- Passion Flower
- California Poppy

HERBAL FORMULAS—DETOXIFIERS

- Lymphatic System
- Lymph Nodes
- Stomach and Bowel Formulas

HERBAL FORMULAS—STRENGTHENERS

- Brain and Nervous System
- Adrenal Glands
- Thyroid Gland
- Kidneys and Bladder
- Neuromuscular Spasms

NOTE — Many of the herbs listed strengthen the adrenal glands, which in turn increases low neurotransmitter production. By increasing low neurotransmitter production (adrenal insufficiency), you will strengthen your nervous system.

REPRODUCTIVE SYSTEM

STRUCTURES — Testes, ovaries, sperm, ova, mammary glands and prostate gland. The reproductive system works hand-in-hand with your glandular system.

DIET — A living, raw food diet energizes the gonads and the glandular system. A raw food diet is also an anti-inflammatory to these tissues (prostate, uterus, etc.).

SINGLE HERBS—DETOXIFIERS

- Saw Palmetto Berries
- White Pond Lily
- Poke Root
- White Oak Bark

SINGLE HERBS—STRENGTHENERS

- Kelp
- Chaste Tree Berries
- False Unicorn
- Saw Palmetto Berries
- Panax Ginseng Root
- Siberian Ginseng Root

- Damiana Leaf
- Astragalus Root
- Licorice Root
- Black Cohosh
- Red Raspberry Leaf
- Pumpkin Seed
- Black Haw Root

HERBAL FORMULAS—DETOXIFIERS

- Lymphatic System
- Prostate
- Female Reproductive

HERBAL FORMULAS—STRENGTHENERS

- Adrenal Glands
- Thyroid Gland
- Male Reproductive
- Female Reproductive
- Prostate

NOTE — It is not advisable to use Panax-type Ginseng in the presence of inflammation or cancer. Panax-type Ginseng may promote estrogen and testosterone, which can stimulate or feed these processes.

RESPIRATORY SYSTEM

STRUCTURES — Lungs, trachea, bronchi, bronchial tubes and alveoli.

DIET — A diet of raw foods is not mucus-forming or congesting. The effects of these foods is the opposite; they help clean the lungs, throat, bronchi, etc. Fruits are especially good!

SINGLE HERBS—DETOXIFIERS

- Mullein
- Fenugreek
- Pleurisy Root
- Lobelia
- Elecampane
- Comfrey Leaf
- Horehound

SINGLE HERBS—STRENGTHENERS

- Mullein
- Lobelia
- Elecampane
- Comfrey Leaf
- Horehound

HERBAL FORMULAS—DETOXIFIERS

- Lungs
- Lymphatic System
- Strengtheners Lungs
- Neuromuscular Spasms
- Adrenal Glands

SKELETAL SYSTEM

STRUCTURE — Bones, cartilage and connective tissue.

DIET — A living, raw food diet, which includes dark-green leafy vegetables, alkalizes and nourishes the whole system, especially the skeletal/ muscular system. These vegetables have a high content of electrolytes (alkaline minerals: calcium, magnesium, sodium and potassium). Raw vegetables are high in calcium and magnesium with the proper balance of phosphorus. This is vital for bone regeneration.

SINGLE HERBS—DETOXIFIERS

- Black Walnut Hull
- White Oak Bark

SINGLE HERBS—STRENGTHENERS

- Oat Straw
- Horsetail
- Kelp

- Comfrey Root and Leaf
- Black Walnut Hull
- Alfalfa
- White Oak Bark
- Chickweed

HERBAL FORMULAS—DETOXIFIERS

- Lymphatic System
- Lymph Nodes
- Blood

HERBAL FORMULAS—STRENGTHENERS

- Bones
- Adrenal Glands
- Blood
- Kidney and Bladder
- Pancreas
- Thyroid Gland

URINARY SYSTEM

STRUCTURES — Kidneys, bladder, ureter and urethra.

DIET — A raw food diet is essential because of its high alkalizing effect upon the urinary system. Acidosis, especially from high protein diets, deteriorates this system rapidly.

SINGLE HERBS—DETOXIFIERS

- Corn Silk
- Juniper Berries
- Saw Palmetto Berries
- Pipsissewa
- Uva Ursi
- Couch Grass Root
- Parsley
- Dandelion Leaf

SINGLE HERBS—STRENGTHENERS

- Juniper Berries
- Saw Palmetto Berries
- Pipsissewa
- Uva Ursi
- Lespedeza
- Couch Grass Root
- Parsley
- Dandelion Leaf

HERBAL FORMULAS—DETOXIFIERS

- Kidneys and Bladder
- Lymphatic System
- Prostate
- Blood

HERBAL FORMULAS—STRENGTHENERS

- Kidneys and Bladder
- Adrenal Glands
- Blood
- Prostate

ALL SYSTEMS

SINGLE HERBS—TONICS

- Panax Ginseng
- Astragalus
- Gotu Kola
- Siberian Ginseng
- Antler
- Alfalfa
- Fo Ti
- Pau d'Arco

- Chaste Tree Berries

SINGLE HERBS—PARASITE ELIMINATION

- Black Walnut Hull
- Pau d'Arco
- Wormwood
- Male Fern
- Cloves
- Garlic
- Grapefruit Seed extract

HERBAL FORMULAS—TONICS

- Immune #2 (or Super-Immune)
- Male Reproductive
- Female Reproductive
- Endocrine Glands
- Thyroid Gland
- Adrenal Glands

HERBAL FORMULAS—PARASITE ELIMINATION

- Parasite—a general formula
- Parasite—for microorganisms
- Lymphatic System
-

MODULE 8. 5

Pharmaceutical Antibiotics vs. Nature's Anti-Parasitics

In this book, I've discussed parasites, which encompass bacteria, fungi, and worms, and their role in the natural world. As we delve into the comparison between chemical medications and herbs, it's crucial to grasp two fundamental concepts.

Firstly, the notion of "diseases" is misleading—what truly exists are varying levels of acidosis and toxicity within the body.

Secondly, attempting to counteract acidosis and toxicity with more of the same (such as chemical medications) is counterproductive, toxic, harmful to cells, and often more lethal. In my perspective, among the various forms of chemical treatments, antibiotics particularly stand out for the adverse effects they generate in the body.

The allopathic medical philosophy revolves around the "germ theory," championed by Louis Pasteur, who believed that microorganisms present in many disease processes were the definitive "cause" of these diseases. He overlooked the possibility that these microorganisms might merely be a secondary consequence of the actual cause. In contrast, the naturopathic standpoint has consistently regarded parasites as secondary to the true origins of disease—namely, toxicity and acidosis. (Much of this was covered in Chapter 5, where we explored parasites and the underlying causes of disease.)

Over the last few generations, human organs and glands have experienced considerable weakening. Our cellular structures and functions have been compromised by our lifestyle and dietary choices, and these vulnerabilities have been transmitted to subsequent generations. With each iteration, cells have grown progressively weaker, while the body's inflammatory responses to toxicity have intensified, and the lymphatic pathway (lymph system) has become obstructed to a significant extent. This has substantially impacted the immune system's effectiveness. Our capacity to digest and absorb nutrients has markedly declined. When all these factors are combined, it becomes evident why cells become susceptible to parasites.

It's important to bear in mind that parasites serve as a natural mechanism for keeping the body clean. They consume waste products from metabolism and digestion, along with other toxins, and they also eliminate weakened or dying cells. As this process can be life-threatening in individuals who are toxic, weakened, and congested, modern medical science has endeavored to retaliate. Hence, the emergence of antibiotics came into being.

The Bad News

At least 2 1/2 million people enter the hospital each year from adverse reactions to chemical medications. At least 180,000 people die each year from chemical medications. (Some have estimated this to be over 500,000). —*Washington Post*

Around 100,000 people die each year from iatrogenic diseases (caused by allopathic physicians).
100,000 people die each year from hospital errors. You have a 1 in 200 chance of dying in a hospital from hospital errors. — *Discovery News*

Humans themselves have created a great many strains of microorganisms, especially bacteria. These include M.R.S.A. (methicillin-resistant staphylococcus aureus), Sinorhizobium meliloti bacterium and the Rhizobia (RMBPC) bacterium, just to name a few. From these and many others we see conditions like "hoof and mouth" disease, M.R.S.A. infections, and "Mad Cow Disease." Many of these conditions lead to death.

Viruses are a whole different subject. Many deadly and debilitating viruses have been created due to contamination; in the search for weapons of biological warfare; and even as forms of simple population control. For a frightening look into the subject of viruses and their use by the scientific community, refer to Emerging Viruses by Leonard G. Horowitz.

Now let's look at antibiotics, both the pharmaceutically manufactured and the natural.

PHARMACEUTICAL ANTIBIOTICS

Pharmaceutical antibiotics are often referred to as sulfa drugs. Many of them primarily contain sulfur derivatives along with other highly toxic chemical compounds. This particular form of sulfur is inorganic in nature and tends to accumulate within the body over time. Excessive consumption of sulfa drugs can lead to the development of allergies or immunity towards them.

Sulfur possesses inhibitory properties that target intestinal and lymphatic tissues, causing decreased activity in these areas. When an individual experiences symptoms such as a cold or flu-like condition, usually due to congesting foods like sugars or dairy products, a specific sequence unfolds: A triggering factor—such as an overload of bacteria, fungi, harsh weather conditions, or increased weakness—prompts the body into a healing or cleansing response. However, the conventional medical approach perceives this as a disease demanding treatment.

As the congestion or mucus contains microorganisms, it is characterized as an "infection." Antibiotics are then prescribed to suppress and ostensibly eliminate these symptoms.

Yet, these sulfa drugs actually impede the lymphatic system, halting the body's natural efforts to eliminate the congestion.

The congestion and toxicity should be eliminated, not merely suppressed. Otherwise, the body ends up storing these toxins. The added sulfur and other chemicals from the medication can accumulate in various tissues like the intestines, lymph nodes, etc. Killing the microorganisms within the toxic congestion is insufficient; the toxic congestion itself must be eliminated.

Continuously suppressing the body's inherent cleansing mechanisms contributes to a gradual decline in cellular health or the formation of tumors. This approach also triggers a perpetual inflammatory response by the immune system. Given the modern context, the eventual outcome of this scenario is often some form of cancer.

Let's examine the example of CIPRO, a commonly used antibiotic that gained attention during the anthrax scare until its detrimental side effects became apparent to the public. These side effects encompass a range of impacts on various bodily systems, including:

GI — Nausea, vomiting, diarrhea, oral candidiasis, dysphagia, intestinal perforation, dyspepsia, heartburn, anorexia, pseudo-membranous colitis, flatulence, abdominal discomfort, GI bleeding, oral mucosal pain, dry mouth, bad taste.

CNS — Headache, restlessness, insomnia, nightmares, hallucinations, tremor, lightheadedness, confusion, seizures, ataxia, mania, weakness, drowsiness, dizziness, psychotic reactions, malaise, depression, depersonalization, paresthesia.

GU — Nephritis, crystalluria, hematuria, cylindruria, renal failure, urinary retention, polyuria, vaginitis, urethral bleeding, acidosis, renal calculi, interstitial nephritis, vaginal candidiasis, glucosuria, pyuria, albuminuria, proteinuria. SKIN — Rashes, urticaria, photosensitivity, flushing pruritus, erythema nodosum, cutaneous candidiasis, hyperpigmentation, edema (of lips, neck, face, conjunctivae, hands), angioedema, toxic epidermal necrolysis, exfoliative dermatitis, Stevens-Johnson syndrome.

OPHTHALMIC — Blurred or disturbed vision, double vision, eye pain.

CV — Hypertension, syncope, angina pectoris, palpitations, atrial flutter, myocardial infarction (heart attacks), cerebral thrombosis, ventricular ectopy, cardiopulmonary arrest, postural hypotension.

RESPIRATORY — Dyspnea, bronchospasm, pulmonary embolism, edema of larynx or lungs, hemoptysis, hiccoughs, epistaxis.

HEMATOLOGIC — Eosinophilia, pancytopenia, leukopenia, neutropenia, anemia, leukocytosis, agranulocytosis, bleeding diathesis.

MISCELLANEOUS — Super-infections; fever; chills; tinnitus; joint pain or stiffness; back, neck or chest pain; flare-up of gout; flushing; hyperpigmentation; worsening of myasthenia gravis; hepatic necrosis; cholestatic jaundice; hearing loss. After ophthalmic use: Irritation, burning, itching, angioneurotic edema, urticaria, maculopapular and vesicular dermatitis, crusting of lid margins, conjunctival hyperemia, bad taste in mouth, corneal staining, keratitis keratopathy, allergic reactions, photophobia, decreased vision, tearing, lid edema. Also, a white, crystalline precipitate in the superficial part of corneal defect (onset within 1-7 days after initiating therapy; lasts about 2 weeks and does not affect continued use of the medication). Contraindications include: never use in children and lactating mothers.

This information is taken from the*RN's NDR-93 (Nurse's Drug Reference)* by George R. Spratto and Adrienne L. Woods.

As you can see, the side effects of CIPRO are shocking, and the FDA allows this! It makes you question the FDA and who really controls it. (The FDA is supposed to be a consumer protection agency.) I learned of CIPRO's devastating side effects from one of my clients who developed a urinary tract infection and went to his medical doctor, instead of asking me first. His wife called me from the Emergency Room when he developed three blood clots and had a heart attack as a probable result of consuming CIPRO, which he had just started taking three days earlier.

Each antibiotic, depending upon its chemical composition, has its own set of side effects. Not only do they kill your overgrowth bacteria, they also kill your beneficial digestive bacteria, and at the same time increase the growth of fungi and yeasts. They also inhibit your immune system and lymphatic system, making it very difficult for your body to clean and properly protect itself. As previously stated, this eventually leads to cellular death and the degeneration of your body.

NATURE'S ANTIBIOTICS

Now, let's delve into the natural remedies that counteract the effects of toxic human lifestyles. Nature's creations are inherently multifaceted, designed with various purposes and responses. A prime illustration of this complexity is found in the botanical kingdom. Herbs are distinct from hybrid vegetables due to their active principles, which confer unique actions within the body. Consider Black Walnut Hull as an example. It serves as a potent antibiotic, anti-fungal, antiworm, anti-protozoa, and anti-fluke agent, while also acting as a cellular strengthener. Moreover, it enhances the immune system, supports cleansing through astringent properties, and boosts the lymphatic system. Rich in calcium, it contributes to bone and connective tissue strength. This is just a glimpse into the capabilities of this single herb.

What's even more remarkable is that Black Walnut Hull does not indiscriminately eliminate beneficial bacteria as chemical antibiotics do, and it carries no harmful side effects. The wonders of nature's design never cease to astonish!

This same principle holds true for the effects of nearly all herbs. While a few toxic herbs exist, they are not utilized in this context. Non-toxic herbs are also sources of nourishment. In other words, they abound in vitamins, minerals, and a wide array of nutritive components.

Let me illustrate with a case, one among the countless individuals I've assisted. A female client of mine contracted E. coli infection. The source of the infection remained uncertain —it could have been from a restaurant, improperly cleaned vegetables, or even the fish she consumed on the day she fell ill.

Her condition rapidly deteriorated, prompting her to seek medical attention at the Emergency Room. Subsequently, she was admitted to the hospital and put on potent antibiotics. Having followed a healthy regimen for about a year, her body had grown highly sensitive to toxins. The antibiotics exacerbated her condition, subjecting her to a host of side effects that were unfortunately disregarded by the medical staff.

Her husband became deeply concerned and eventually removed her from the hospital after a protracted dispute with her medical doctor. This physician ominously predicted that she would not survive more than two days if she left the hospital. Astonishingly, within three days under my guidance, she was up and about, feeling considerably better. This recovery was achieved through dietary adjustments and herbal formulas, all of which left her free of side effects and without tissue damage.

As you acquaint yourself with the genuine origins of disease and the nature of parasites, this newfound understanding will liberate you. Embracing the principles of nature will spare you from unnecessary suffering and provide a path to healing.

And God said, "Behold, I have given you every herb-bearing seed which is upon the face of all the earth."

— Genesis 1:20

CHAPTER NINE

Tools for Healthy Living

This chapter will introduce you to or reintroduce you to alternative health approaches beyond dietary considerations, which can significantly aid you on your wellness journey. As you delve into the pages ahead, you will step through a doorway of golden opportunities into an expansive and incredible realm. This realm is replete with truths, enlightening information, novel hobbies, and methods to amplify your ultimate potential for growth.

Within the initial section, you will become acquainted with Nine Healthy Habits that can be seamlessly integrated into your daily routine to elevate your health. Some of these practices, such as exercise and deep breathing, may already be part of your regimen. Others, like dry skin brushing and foot reflexology, might be entirely new experiences for you.

In Module 9.2, you will find comprehensive guidance on several supplementary tools that we have suggested throughout this book, including the Liver and Gallbladder Flush.

Embrace a sense of joy and contentment as you embark on this journey. Always remember that this is your life, your physical vessel, and your decision-making power. The boundless wonders of nature await your exploration. Revel in the myriad tools that the divine has crafted for your benefit.

MODULE 9.1

Nine Healthy Habits

HABIT #1
BE GOOD TO YOURSELF

It's often said that we come into this world alone, we live our lives within our own selves, and eventually, we depart alone. Embrace the company of the person you are with – yourself! Treasure every fleeting moment. Many individuals haven't truly delved into understanding themselves, and a significant number may even find it challenging to genuinely appreciate who they are. During a moment of meditation, I heard a voice saying, "You are my creation." That was the instant I comprehended that all existence is an expression of the divine. We are all inherently divine, regardless of our appearance, intelligence, or perceived virtues and flaws. We are merely utilizing our physical forms. Our essence as souls far surpasses the vessels we inhabit.

Embrace self-love, but do so without fostering ego. Emulate the sun that radiates its light and warmth upon all living things, without discrimination or division. Love all things, for all entities are manifestations of the divine. You possess divinity within you; it's your responsibility to yourself and to all life to nurture your well-being and find happiness. Extend kindness to yourself and to all existence around you.

HABIT #2

MEDITATION: RELAX! RELAX! RELAX!

Stress has a constricting effect on various aspects of our body, including circulation, bowel function, organ operation, and glandular activity. This constriction can lead to discomfort and weaken tissues, resulting in conditions such as constipation, lower back pain, adrenal gland and kidney issues, anxiety, heart problems, and compromised digestion, among others.

Meditation stands out as an exceptional tool for achieving relaxation. It offers the ability to unwind every muscle and cell within you. As the body finds its relaxation, this tranquility extends to the mind and emotions, which are often the root causes of stress. Meditation is a simple and enjoyable practice that, with persistence, can be performed anywhere, at any time.

Commence your meditation routine by locating a peaceful environment where you won't be disturbed. Dedicate about thirty minutes. If possible, establish a regular practice, beginning at the same time each day. Find a comfortable position, sitting or lying down, in which you won't be disrupted.

Shut your eyes and take roughly ten deep breaths, making use of abdominal breathing if you can. Gradually ease into a state of relaxation, granting your mind a respite from constant thinking. Your intention is to observe while you completely relax. You might start from your toes and gradually work your way upward, relaxing each part of your body. Unwind your legs, arms, torso, and facial muscles. Allow yourself to attain a sensation of weightlessness, akin to a drifting feather, devoid of any inclination or yearning. Observe and listen, all the while maintaining profound relaxation, as if you're an audience member watching a movie. If you consciously shift your attention elsewhere, do so purposefully.

Meditation is your personal time to be with yourself, detached from external influences and the ceaseless chatter of the mind and emotions. Through meditation, previously sealed doors can open, ushering in genuine healing. Your connection and understanding of the divine will expand significantly. By opening yourself up as described above, you allow spirit to course through you unimpeded. This flow can bring about profound healing, and if you're receptive, you might encounter unexpected experiences. It's much more rewarding to listen to the divine than to direct your own words towards it.

Remember, just *be*.

HABIT #3

EXERCISE

In earlier eras, we might have lived as nomads and foragers, covering great distances to gather food for survival. During those times, movement would have been an integral part of our daily existence. The role of movement in our overall health cannot be overstated. A significant portion of our blood and lymphatic circulation, especially in the lower parts of our body, relies on muscle activity. It's noticeable that after prolonged periods of inactivity, whether sitting or lying down, we often experience stiffness until we start moving again. The degree of stiffness tends to be less pronounced in individuals with lower levels of toxicity.

There is an array of effective exercise options to choose from. Walking, swimming, rebounding (using a mini-trampoline), tai chi, stretching, and yoga are some of the excellent choices. These activities can be adapted to suit almost any physical condition, allowing individuals to engage in them either partially or fully.

Maintaining an active lifestyle is important. If you're starting from a weakened state, it's advisable to gradually build up your activity level. However, aim to increase your daily activity as much as your circumstances allow. Exercise plays an essential role in the journey toward achieving good health.

HABIT #4

DEEP BREATHING

The air we inhale serves as the life force for our physical bodies, essential for our survival. This process has a natural cycle where we take in oxygen, carbon, hydrogen, and nitrogen from plants through breathing, and then exhale carbon dioxide —a crucial breath that sustains plant life. Among these elements, oxygen holds immense significance as it acts as an energizer, alkalizer, and oxidizer. The air we breathe, created by plants and trees, is alkaline, while the carbon dioxide we exhale is acidic. Given that we are primarily alkaline beings, it's crucial that we learn proper breathing techniques and engage in deep breathing. This deep breathing process introduces negative ions into the system, establishing a cationic condition within the body. In contrast, shallow breathing contributes to over-acidity, creating an anionic state in the body. Just as carbon dioxide is a primary fuel for plants, oxygen and simple sugars are the main sources of energy for our cells.

Unfortunately, many of us have not been taught proper breathing techniques and have become "shallow breathers." When our breath becomes shallow, our vitality is similarly diminished. Human beings are intricately connected to nature, and it's only when we allow our egos to separate us from nature that diseases can take root.

Deep breathing holds the power to invigorate the system, enhancing circulation and lymphatic flow. Beyond its physical benefits, deep breathing also has a calming effect on the mind and emotions, fostering a sense of peace and alignment with ourselves and the natural world.

Across various spiritual traditions, the breath is referred to as prana, chi, ki, life force, spirit, mana, the ECK, and other names. Some individuals claim to subsist primarily on air, such as a Catholic nun reportedly living solely on snow in the Himalayas. In the past, I experimented with attempting to sustain myself solely on air, living as a hermit in Florida's national forests and state parks. For six months, I consumed only oranges with the hope of eventually eliminating even those. However, my energy levels became so intense that I experienced out-of-body sensations and felt disconnected from this world. It was difficult for me to interact with others, given the limited understanding of true reality and our ability to conncct with all forms of life on Earth. Eventually, I found balance by incorporating raw fruits and vegetables back into my diet.

To enhance the oxygen levels in your body, try the following deep-breathing exercise. Lie on your back on a couch, floor, or bed. Focus on relaxation and place your right hand on your abdomen, slightly above your navel. Inhale through your nose without moving your shoulders, watching your hand rise and fall with each breath. This technique involves breathing into the lower parts of your lungs. As you inhale, allow your abdomen to expand, causing your hand to rise, and then exhale through your mouth. As you exhale, your abdomen will naturally contract, lowering your hand.

After several breaths, attempt to increase your oxygen intake by first breathing into your abdomen, causing it to expand. Then proceed to fill the upper portions of your lungs by inhaling more air into the upper thoracic region, raising your shoulders. Exhale gently.

Another approach involves filling the lower portions of your lungs by expanding your abdomen with your inhalation. Continue to inhale, filling the upper lungs and elevating your chest and shoulder areas for complete inhalation. Once fully filled, exhale gently.

Practice deep breathing in any position until it becomes a habit to take deeper, fuller breaths. This practice assists in alkalizing the body, enhancing cellular respiration, and facilitating the elimination of acidic gases. It's an excellent exercise to perform before meditation or as a technique to induce calmness. By immersing yourself in nature and embracing its elements, you can experience enhanced vitality, a sense of youthfulness, and a profound connection to the world around you.

HABIT #5

DRY SKIN BRUSHING

In previous sections, we thoroughly discussed the skin and its various disorders (refer to Chapter 5, Module 5.9 for instance). It's crucial to remember that your skin serves as an avenue for eliminating approximately two pounds of metabolic waste and toxins every day. As your largest elimination organ, it plays a vital role in maintaining your overall health. Accumulation of acids and toxins within the skin layers can lead to conditions such as rashes, pimples, and boils. Therefore, prioritizing proper skin care is essential.

Daily cleansing of the skin through baths or, ideally, showers is important. Installing a water softener or a reverse osmosis (R/O) system in your home is a valuable consideration, as inorganic minerals present in hard water can clog and block skin pores. Using pure, soft water, in contrast, can make a noticeable difference in the health of your skin and the texture of your hair.

Another effective method for promoting skin health is dry skin brushing. This practice aids in the removal of dead skin cells, enhances circulation, and stimulates lymphatic flow. It allows the skin to breathe more effectively. All you need is a long-handled vegetable-fiber brush, typically found at health food stores. It's important not to use a nylon-bristle brush for this purpose. Start by brushing your feet, legs, and hands. The direction of brushing doesn't matter significantly, though brushing towards the center of your body can be beneficial. Since your hands and feet house numerous nerve endings, you'll experience a tingling sensation as your nervous system gets stimulated. This method of skin cleansing contributes significantly to achieving vibrant and healthy skin. Over his lifetime, Dr. Jensen, who conducted seminars on health, provided attendees with an understanding of what healthy skin should look like. Even until his passing at the age of ninety-three, his skin remained as soft and healthy as that of a baby's.

Make an effort to spend time outdoors in the fresh air while wearing as few clothes as possible. Allow your skin the opportunity to breathe and rejuvenate. This connection with nature can offer immense benefits to the health of your skin and your overall well-being.

HABIT #6

SAUNAS AND STEAM BATHS

Sweating holds a critical role in your daily detoxification process. Often referred to as the third kidney, your skin eliminates a substantial amount of waste, including by-products and toxins—equivalent to the excretion performed by your lungs, kidneys, and bowels. This makes your skin your body's largest organ for elimination. However, when thyroid function is diminished or if you lead a sedentary lifestyle, your body's ability to sweat effectively is compromised. This can lead to the accumulation of toxicity in the subcutaneous layers of the skin, resulting in issues such as dry skin, rashes, pimples, rosacea, dandruff, and dermatitis. Sweating holds a crucial place in your journey towards improved health.

Saunas and steam baths offer significant benefits, particularly when complemented by various essential oils. When using public facilities, it's wise to be cautious about their cleanliness standards, both in terms of physical hygiene and the environment's psychic energy. Private saunas can be built or purchased, providing you with a controlled environment for this purpose. If saunas aren't accessible, you can create a steam bath using your own bathtub. You can enhance the cleansing effects by incorporating herbs like mustard or cayenne pepper into the water. (For additional treatments, refer to the instructions on cold sheet treatments in Module 9.2.)

HABIT #7

SLANT BOARDING

A slant board is a simple apparatus consisting of a board or table fixed at an angle of approximately 45 degrees. By lying down on this board with your head positioned lower than your feet, you can facilitate improved circulation to the brain and enhance lymphatic flow in your lower extremities. Over years of living in an upright position, the effects of gravity can take a toll on the body. This can lead to reduced cerebral circulation and the accumulation of fluid (edema) in the legs and feet. As a consequence, skin and organs may start to sag and prolapse, interfering with their optimal functionality. Engaging with a slant board offers a method to restore healthier blood flow to the brain, thus benefiting internal organs by alleviating some of the pressure imposed by gravity.

HABIT #8

COLOR THERAPY (SUNLIGHT)

All forms of life, in various ways, draw energy and healing properties from the sun. Sunlight encompasses a spectrum of colors, each contributing to a distinctive form of healing energy for the body. Each individual color ray carries a unique impact on tissues, bestowing a specialized form of healing. Collectively, these color rays unite to create a potent healing energy that permeates every cell within the body, providing nourishment, healing, and comfort to each one.

However, it's important to maintain a sense of equilibrium when engaging with the sun. The sun possesses acidic qualities, and excessive exposure can be just as detrimental as insufficient exposure. Many individuals already carry an excess of acidity within them. This is a contributing factor to why some people may find the sun uncomfortable or experience sunburn easily. As your body becomes more alkaline, your ability to appreciate the sun's healing attributes increases. Embrace the energies of nature and divinity, allowing them to bathe you in their regenerative powers.

A wealth of literature on color healing is available (references can be found in the Bibliography for some recommendations).

Further exploration of this subject will occur later in this chapter, where you will delve into the distinctive properties of various colors and their capacity to heal. Delving into color theory is an enjoyable pursuit, and as you incorporate a heightened awareness of colors into your daily life, you may find your dreams also imbued with vibrant hues. The universe encompasses an array of colors beyond our imagination. Open yourself to the elevated energies of the divine; it promises an exhilarating journey.

HABIT #9

FOOT AND HAND REFLEXOLOGY

Accumulations of acid crystals, including uric, phosphoric, carbonic, and lactic acids, as well as cellular waste products, tend to build up beneath the nerve endings in your feet. Given that these nerve endings correspond to various parts of your body through reflexes, the presence of these acids and toxins can exert a detrimental influence on related areas. For instance, nerves that terminate in the heart also conclude in the hands and feet. If acid crystals or toxins impede the function of these nerve endings, it may result in symptoms such as heart palpitations, elevated blood pressure (particularly while standing or walking), chest discomfort, and more. This phenomenon extends to all organs and glands, as the nerves supplying them also conclude in the hands and feet.

A daily practice of massaging the soles of your feet and the palms of your hands can help disintegrate these acid crystals and toxic accumulations, thereby alleviating associated symptoms. Reflexology, which operates on these principles, is a remarkable field of study. I've personally used reflexology techniques to revive three individuals who were experiencing cardiac arrest. This simple yet powerful practice has the potential to alleviate considerable suffering. I encourage you to delve into the knowledge of reflexology, as it is a valuable system for enhancing your well-being.

MODULE 9.2

Four Healthy Tools to Assist Your Detoxification ... and Your Life

TOOL #1

LIVER AND GALLBLADDER FLUSH

This process helps to remove liver stones and gallbladder stones.

Items Needed

8-ounces of pure, cold-pressed, extra virgin organic olive oil.
6 to 8-ounces of freshly squeezed (if possible) pink grapefruit juice or the juice of 2 lemons.
Freshly squeezed apple juice (enzymes assist with reducing nausea).
Optional: a preparation to aid in the softening of possible stones, such as Phosfood Liquid®, produced by Standard Process Laboratories.
Optional: Intestinal cleansing formula.

Suggested Preparation

Three days of eating mainly raw fruits and vegetables (organic preferred).
One 8-ounce glass of freshly juiced apple juice in the morning and one in the evening, for three days.

Three days of bowel detoxification. Use an intestinal cleansing formula, with formula strength depending upon your bowel regularity. Use a gentle formula if bowels move at least one time daily; a moderate-strength formula if bowels move at least once in a two-day period; and a strong formula for bowels that resist regular movement.

In lieu of herbal detoxification, an individual may choose to take an enema one-day prior to the flush. It is important that your bowels are moving well.

Optional: You can add 45 drops of Phosfood Liquid to your apple juice, two times a day (A.M. + P.M.). This will help loosen and soften any stones you might have.

NOTE: No solid foods should be consumed after noontime on the day of the flush (fresh fruit juices or distilled water are acceptable).

Directions

Stop all fluid intake at 6:30 P.M., or thirty minutes before the flush is started.

Begin the flush between 7:00 P.M. and 9:00 P.M., or as you wish.

Mix or blend 8-ounces of olive oil with 6 to 8 ounces of pink grapefruit juice or the juice of two lemons.

Consume at a rate that best suits you. You may wish to consume it all at one time, or you may consume 1/4 cup every 15 minutes, or you may drink it even more slowly. After the olive oil is consumed you should retire for the evening, lying on your right side.

Considerations

If nausea and/or vomiting sensations are experienced, the olive oil/citrus juice mixture can be chased with small amounts of freshly made apple juice. Resume consumption of the mixture as soon as possible. If the feeling of nausea continues, consume only as much of the mixture as you possibly can, then go right to bed, lying on your right side.

Watch stools for stones. Stones are usually green, but may be yellow, red or black. Stones range from a pea-size to that of a quarter, or larger. Most liver or gallbladder stones are soft in nature, as they are lipid/bile stones. With degenerative problems, the liver and gallbladder flush should be supervised by a health care professional.

TOOL #2

DISTILLED WATER

Natural water from various sources like springs, wells, rivers, and lakes, as well as tap water, contains mineral elements acquired from contact with soil and rocks. Unfortunately, many water sources also contain impurities including chemicals from various sources such as pollution, sewage, and pesticides.

The minerals found in these water sources are classified as inorganic. It is important to understand that there is a significant distinction between the minerals found in the Earth and those found within the human body. Earth minerals are considered inorganic and lack the same electrical frequency as the minerals found in the human body and within plant life.

These elemental (earth) minerals are relatively inert and possess low electromagnetic charges.

Rainwater, or distilled water, is charged with the energies of soil and minerals as it falls and gets absorbed into plant roots. This water, combined with the energy of the sun, transforms inorganic minerals into tissue salts within the plants. These tissue salts are essential for building and sustaining the plant's structure.

During the growth of plants, through enzymatic processes, the constituents evolve into compounds. The minerals in plants are referred to as "cell salts," as many of them form synergistic compounds. These compounds are interdependent, requiring each other and other substances for proper absorption and utilization within animal and human cells. Animals, particularly humans, require a higher-frequency nutritional source than elemental minerals.

Inorganic minerals, if they manage to permeate the intestinal wall, function merely as stimulants. Due to their low electrical charge, they cannot cross cell membrane barriers. For instance, inorganic iodine is used in medical settings for imaging purposes, but it only stimulates the thyroid and can potentially lead to inflammation and thyroid issues.

Distilled water is considered a powerful solvent. It's the only form of water that can be consumed by the body without causing damage to tissues. It aids in dissolving nutrients for absorption into cells and eliminates cellular waste and toxins. Moreover, distilled water can dissolve inorganic mineral substances lodged within the body's tissues, facilitating detoxification. It's crucial to note that distilled water doesn't leach out essential body minerals. Blood tests conducted during distilled water fasts have shown improved electrolyte balances. Distilled water effectively removes minerals that have been rejected by cells and are obstructing normal bodily functions.

Hydration is essential, and consuming water-rich foods like raw fruits and vegetables is beneficial. In their raw state, these foods consist of 60 to 95 percent water. Alongside this, drinking at least two 8-ounce glasses of distilled or R/O (reverse osmosis) water daily is recommended.

When brewing herbal teas, it is advisable to use distilled water. Distilled water's lack of minerals helps extract compounds from the herbs more efficiently, resulting in a stronger tea. If distilled water isn't accessible, R/O water is a suitable alternative. Installing an R/O filter under the sink can provide convenient access to this type of water. However, it's important to avoid over-hydration and follow one's natural instincts.

NOTE: Never drink with your meals. This dilutes your digestive enzymes and affects proper food digestion.

TOOL #3

CASTOR OIL PACKS

Castor oil, also referred to as Palma Christi (Palm of Christ), has a longstanding history of therapeutic use spanning centuries. Notably, the renowned medical intuitive Edgar Cayce frequently recommended castor oil packs for various health issues. Initial studies conducted at the George Washington School of Medicine suggest that these packs can enhance immune system functioning, aid in dilation, and soften tissues and muscles.

Castor oil packs, when applied to the abdomen, contribute to detoxification of the body. They can also offer relief for conditions such as pain syndromes, slipped discs, tumors, tinnitus, inflammation, as well as for organs that are hardened or swollen, including the liver, spleen, kidneys, lymph nodes, and bowels. Topical application may even aid in loosening or dissolving cancerous masses. These packs prove particularly beneficial for respiratory problems like asthma.

Detoxifying the lungs is a challenge, especially for clients who rely on inhalers. Inhalers can trap toxins within lung tissues instead of facilitating their elimination. This congestion can persist at an interstitial level, affecting the nervous system and causing spasms. For comprehensive relief from conditions like asthma, lung detoxification is essential.

Castor oil packs play a vital role during spasmodic episodes when clients require enhanced airflow. Additionally, an alternative to inhalers involves ingesting 1 teaspoon of Lobelia tincture every ten minutes to counter spasms. This herbal remedy substitutes the inhaler. It's important to note that some individuals may be accustomed to using inhalers and could need minimal inhaler use during the detoxification process. The focus should be on elimination rather than suppression.

Furthermore, castor oil packs are valuable for addressing female health concerns. These include alleviating abdominal discomfort and bloating, managing ovarian and uterine fibroids and cysts, addressing endometriosis, and easing menstrual discomfort.

Castor oil packs are easy to use.

Items Needed

Soft, flannel cloth (cotton or wool).
Cut flannel to the appropriate size (example 10 inches to 12 inches for abdomen).
Cold-pressed castor oil (available at most health food stores).
Wax paper or plastic wrap.
Heat source (a non-electric source is preferable such as a hot water bottle. However, you can use an electric blanket or heating pad, if necessary).

Directions

Fold the cloth into a two-to-four-inch thickness.
Saturate the cloth with the cold-pressed castor oil.
Apply the cloth directly to the skin in the area that needs the treatment. Place a piece of wax paper or plastic wrap over the soaked flannel cloth. Apply heat over the wax paper or plastic wrap (if the temperature of the heat source is too hot, wrap in a towel).
Maintain in place for at least an hour.
Leave on overnight, if necessary.
The recommended frequency for use of castor oil pack is three to seven times per week.
The flannel pack does not need to be discarded after one application. It may be kept in a glass container in the refrigerator for future use.

During this treatment, be aware of the thoughts and feelings that may arise. It is common during a detoxification process to experience toxic thoughts and feelings from the past. Don't worry, these are being released along with the physical toxins.

TOOL #4

COLD SHEET TREATMENT

The cold sheet treatment is a potent hydrotherapy technique that was advanced and brought into public awareness by the late Dr. John Christopher and popularized by Dr. Richard Schulze. It can serve as a valuable tool in aiding the process of detoxification. This procedure holds significant strength, actively encouraging the expulsion of bodily toxins through the skin.

Given its robust nature and potential to cause exhaustion, I advise against employing the cold sheet treatment in cases of extreme debilitation, such as advanced stages of cancer. While the treatment's benefits in such situations are evident, the risk of exacerbating the lack of energy in individuals already experiencing significant depletion is considerable and should be avoided.

NOTE: If you or your patient is way too weak, I would prefer to build the energy in these clients before I purge them with this cold sheet method. You *can* detoxify too fast. When you go on a 100% raw food diet and take high quality herbal formulas, this can be a very powerful process by itself.

The following is a basic cold sheet treatment that anyone can do at home with the assistance of a mate or friend.

Step 1

I recommend initiating a raw food diet for several days prior to embarking on the cold sheet treatment. This dietary adjustment will effectively cleanse the bowels of decaying animal matter. As you initiate the treatment, it might be beneficial to administer an enema on the evening you begin. Dr. Richard Schulze advocates for a garlic implant following this enema, which can be performed using a rectal syringe. Dr. Schulze proposes blending eight to ten sizable garlic cloves with a mixture comprising 50 percent apple cider vinegar and 50% distilled water. It's noteworthy that this concoction can be quite potent for individuals who primarily consume raw foods, yet it remains an option for individuals with higher levels of toxicity. It's worth acknowledging that heightened health often corresponds with increased sensitivity to pungent foods.

Step 2

Begin by preparing an exceedingly hot bath, making sure the water is as hot as your tolerance allows without causing any discomfort or burns to the skin. Take 1 ounce of Dry Mustard herb and enclose it in a small cotton bag or pouch. Similarly, place another cotton bag containing 1 ounce of finely ground Ginger Root. If you desire a more potent effect, you can add another cotton bag with Cayenne Pepper, although I recommend initially attempting the cold sheet treatment without it.

Submerge these herb-filled cotton pouches into the hot bathwater, allowing them to diffuse their contents throughout the water. To protect sensitive areas of your body such as genitals and nipples, apply petroleum jelly (e.g., Vaseline®). Stay immersed in the hot water for approximately 10 to 15 minutes, as you aim to induce sweating by generating a fever-like state through the application of heat.

For enhancing the heat-generating process and ensuring sufficient hydration, consider consuming a hot herbal tea made from Yarrow or Ginger Root. This combination of heat and the diaphoretic qualities of the herbs, particularly Yarrow, will prompt perspiration. This, in turn, stimulates the blood and lymphatic systems, promoting increased circulation and toxin elimination via the skin.

While undergoing the treatment, it's advisable to drink as much of the herbal tea as you can manage. If you experience dizziness or faintness, you might place a cool washcloth on your forehead or the back of your neck with the assistance of someone else. It's wise to have a tincture of lobelia on hand in case of muscle spasms, although it's preferable to prevent the situation from reaching that point.

Before commencing the treatment, place a white, double-bed-sized cotton sheet in your refrigerator's freezer or immerse it in a container of ice water. This chilled sheet will be needed immediately after you exit the hot bath.

Step 3

Step into the bathtub and immerse your entire body, excluding your head, in the water. This immersion has a stimulating and expanding effect, particularly if Cayenne Pepper has been included in the mix. Stay in the water for as long as you can comfortably endure, and even try to push yourself a bit further.

Upon exiting the bath, have your assistant wrap the previously chilled cotton sheet, which you had stored in the freezer or ice water, around your body. Surprisingly, you won't perceive the cold sensation due to your elevated body temperature. Instead, you'll find this contrast of your heated body and the cold sheet to be quite enjoyable. The combination of your elevated body temperature and the cold sheet creates an additional drawing effect on the skin, facilitating the extraction of further toxins.

Step 4

After the cold sheet treatment, proceed directly to bed while wrapped in the cold sheet. To avoid wetting your bed, place a plastic or waterproof covering underneath your bedding. Lay a cotton sheet over the covering. Then, have your assistant layer another cotton sheet over you, followed by a cotton or wool blanket, effectively cocooning you for the night. For added stimulation, immune response, and potential anti-parasitic effects, a "garlic paste" can be applied to the soles of your feet.

Throughout the night, rest and allow yourself to sleep. In the morning, take a look at the sheet that was wrapped around you. You'll likely notice some evidence of the toxins that were drawn out from within your body. Following this, take a shower to cleanse your skin thoroughly, and consider incorporating dry skin brushing into your routine. It's important to continue your raw food diet, focusing on fresh fruits, juices, and distilled or R/O water. Ensure that your bowel movements are regular.

Remember, there are various natural therapies at your disposal to aid in the detoxification process. Patience is key, as your body has its own pace of response. The foundation of it all lies in your dietary choices. Enjoy your journey towards vibrant health and embrace it as your personal endeavor. Trust your own body's wisdom, be intuitive, and avoid pushing yourself excessively. With persistence, you'll be astonished at how swiftly and deeply you can attain good health. From there, vitality will be well within your reach. Take it one day at a time until healthy living becomes your natural way of life.

The natural force within each of us is the greatest healer of disease.

— Hippocrates

MODULE 9.3

The Bottom Line

Break free of the chains that bind you to this world. "Become like little children," free to enjoy the present moment. The present moment is eternal, and pure awareness (which is what you are) only lives in the present moment. Remember, it is thought that is based in time. Past and future are only concepts of the mind, as memory and desire weave your future.

Use the natural laws of God to create a vibrant state of health. Look to the power and expansion of the infinite, not the limitation and confinement of the finite. Realize that you are God's expression and that what you experience, God experiences. Why else would God create?

See every moment as a spiritual experience. Feel and see the divine in all things. The future is unimportant; it doesn't matter what changes the earth will make to cleanse itself. What is important is you and your survival. One day it will be time for you to leave your body, so spend time alone with yourself and get to know who you truly are.

Years ago, a very old master told me "that alone exists." Everything is born alone, lives separate from everything else, and passes (dies) alone. Get to know who you are in this alone state. Most people cannot live without a TV or radio. They fear this aloneness. At the physical and emotional levels, souls have become code-pendent because of this fear and this longing for God. Use prayer, meditation or contemplation; not to petition God, but to listen to and experience God. God is omnipresent;

there is no place God is not. If you are constantly talking, thinking or desiring, how will you experience or be able to recognize this eternal presence of God?

When It's Your Time to Move On

In extreme cases, and in some advanced cancer cases, failure to get well may indicate that it is a person's turn to leave this planet. Our physical, emotional, and mental bodies are only our vehicles while we're on a journey in this creation. They can't and won't last forever.

One should never fear God or the journey that one takes. "You" can never die—only your bodies die. You, as soul, live forever. This physical world is one of the hardest of God's worlds to function and live in. If it is your time, it can be experienced as a blessing and a great joy to move on to the next world. When I have journeyed out of my physical body I have found nothing but joy, awareness, ecstasy and pure love.

Always fill yourself full of love and God. If everyone did this at all times, this world would be a much different place. Live in every moment for the moment and forget the past. Live in the "Now" and the future never comes. Learn to enjoy every moment, regardless of what medical condition you have or how chronic and hopeless it seems. Make your life what you want it to be. If you want your body to be healthy, then so be it – make it healthy. It is up to you, and you alone, to make it healthy. You choose.

Open the doors of exploration and allow yourself to grow and expand. This will remove the stress out of all your bodies and will allow healing to take place. True healing is integrated; treatment is specific, separate. Healing is expansive; treatment is constricted or limited. See everything and everyone as God's expression and give divine love to all. When you experience the beauty of total love and God, then true vitality will be yours. Keep your heart opened at all times.

Learn to step back from thought and emotions and observe. "Be" your true self. This is what true prayer and meditation is all about—separating yourself from your bodies so you can have true communion with God. Clean and strengthen yourself in every way.

All the Herbs mentioned in this book can be purchased from www.drmorses.com. Discount Coupon - GAUTAM

Appendixes

APPENDIX A

Basal Temperature Study for Thyroid Function

The basal temperature test is quite accurate when the temperature is tested in the axilla (armpit) each morning for a period of 4 days. If the temperature is consistently low, then there is a hypo or under-functioning of the thyroid gland in spite of what any other laboratory analyses indicate.

How to Take Your Own Basal Temperatures

At night, before retiring, shake down a thermometer and lay it beside your bed, on your night table, or chair. BE SURE IT IS SHAKEN DOWN.

Next morning, on awakening, don't get up or move around. Place the thermometer under your armpit pressing your arm against your bare body. Relax and LEAVE THE THERMOMETER THERE FOR 10 MINUTES BY THE CLOCK. Take it out, read it, and write down your results.

This record of your early morning basal temperature is a great aid in determining hypothyroidism. The most important issues of hypothyroidism are metabolism and calcium utilization.

Normal reading is between 97.8° to 98.2°

When your basal temperature is below 97.8, this shows varying degrees of hypothyroidism. When your temperature is above 98.2, this may indicate hyperthyroidism.

Basal temperatures between 97.0 and 97.8 are much easier to cure than temperatures in the 96s or 95s. These temperatures are chronically low, requiring much more aggressive detoxification and herbal therapy. Raw thyroid glandulars and organic iodine may be needed with low basal temperatures. Most under-active thyroid conditions are congestive in nature, coming from mucus, acids, and foreign proteins that literally clog the tissues of the thyroid. Hyperthyroidism, especially, is also a congested condition. Detoxification is the main key to eliminating these thyroid conditions.

Today, many people have genetically weak thyroids. The answer is always the same: detoxify and strengthen these tissues and the body. Give it time. It could take you a year or more to change these chronic levels.

Date_____Temperature_____

Date_____Temperature_____

Date_____Temperature_____

Date_____Temperature_____

For menstruating females, also do temperatures on the second and third days of your period.

Date_____Temperature_____
Date_____Temperature_____
Date_____Temperature_____
Date_____Temperature_____

ADDITIONAL READINGS

Date_____Temperature_____

Date_____Temperature_____

Date_____Temperature_____

Date_____Temperature_____

APPENDIX B

The Family of the Natural Sciences

Nature provides a diverse array of natural healing methods, some of which remain undiscovered. What's remarkable about these natural therapies is the way they affect your well-being. Some may initially cause discomfort as they penetrate deep into your tissues to release toxins, while others offer a gentle, soothing experience that enhances your energy flow and raises your awareness. These natural therapies have a profound impact not only on your physical health but also on your mental and emotional well-being.

Distinguishing between addressing the root cause and merely alleviating symptoms is crucial. Nature's healing methods can broadly be categorized into two groups: treatment systems and detoxification systems. Interestingly, certain treatment systems, such as massage, actually facilitate detoxification. Both treatment and detoxification systems are essential in today's world due to the depth of tissue weakness and toxicity we often encounter. However, from my personal perspective, I lean toward detoxification modalities because they offer lasting results. Your ultimate objectives should revolve around revitalizing and restoring weakened or degenerative tissues to a state of vibrancy. Embrace the use of nature's therapies as you embark on a journey to cleanse and reshape both your physical and spiritual selves, and enjoy the process.

ACUPUNCTURE & ACUPRESSURE

Acupuncture and Acupressure are therapeutic systems that employ either fine needles or applied pressure to alleviate stagnant energy, particularly in regions of the body experiencing weakness or congestion.

The body naturally directs its energy towards areas where irritation or congestion is present, often leading to pain and discomfort. By mobilizing stagnant energy, we enhance the circulation of both blood and lymph through these affected areas. This, in turn, boosts the immune system, promotes better nutrient delivery, increases antioxidant and electrolyte responses, and aids in the elimination of inflammation and toxins that have accumulated in these stagnant regions.

Acupuncture and Acupressure have significantly improved the quality of life for countless individuals. When combined with detoxification methods, these two techniques form an incredibly effective duo, offering a comprehensive approach to enhancing well-being.

BIO-ELECTROMAGNETICS

From the ongoing spiritual resurgence, a new field known as Bio-electromagnetics or Energy Medicine has emerged. This scientific discipline closely aligns with the principles of quantum physics and encompasses the study of electricity and electromagnetic energies, along with their impact on cellular, tissue, organ, and glandular functions. It emphasizes that the study of electrical currents ultimately leads to an understanding of the divine and the divine's creations because everything is fundamentally energy.

All matter, in its essence, is condensed energy. The absence of energy implies non-existence, including consciousness itself. Consciousness represents pure energy, simultaneously static and dynamic—a paradoxical concept. In this view, the Creator, God, is pure, boundless energy, while creation embodies this pure energy in a condensed and structured form. As pure energy extends into creation, it generates electrical currents, and the energy emitted by these electrical currents is referred to as electromagnetic energy.

Each individual atom emits electromagnetic energy through its movement. When atoms cluster together to form compounds and structures, these energies combine, producing a diverse spectrum of colors—a testament to the boundless beauty of creation. This energy flows from the core of one's consciousness or soul, passing through the mental realms of the mind, entering the emotional realms (the astral level), and finally manifesting in the physical world. The colors and frequencies of this electromagnetic energy vary depending on the type of structure the soul assumes—whether human, animal, plant, or mineral. An individual's awareness and lifestyle shape the experience of this energy, as all life in creation is defined by energy. Blockages in the flow of this energy result in dis-ease.

Creation itself is a continuous flow of energy. To maintain harmony, one must consume and align with energies that resonate with their level of awareness. These energies are found in various forms, including foods, thoughts, emotions, and external influences. One's level of awareness can evolve as spiritual growth occurs. Discord in these energies can lead to the onset of dis-ease.

Energy is categorized as either "endogenous," internal to the body, or "exogenous," external to the body. Energy exists in a vast spectrum of bands and frequencies, ranging from low-frequency direct currents (DC) to mid-level radio waves, microwaves, radar, and infrared currents, and finally, high-level X-rays and gamma rays.

Ionization, the breakdown of structures into other forms, is essential for life, as it reflects the ever-changing nature of existence. Creation is perpetually in flux, growing and expanding.

The term "electro-pollution" describes the detrimental effects of electrical currents and their associated electromagnetic energies on tissues. High-ionization sources like X-rays and gamma rays can harm biological tissue, while even lower-ionization sources like ultraviolet and some visible light bands can have negative effects. Non-ionizing bands, such as those used in radio, microwaves, radar, and infrared, though considered non-ionizing, may still potentially harm brain and nerve tissue with prolonged exposure. These non-ionizing bands are further categorized as thermal (heat-producing) and non-thermal (non-heat-producing), with the former being more destructive to biological tissue.

In the medical field, non-thermal, non-ionizing energy bands are utilized for observing and diagnosing tissue weaknesses, exemplified by instruments like the EKG and EEG.

Human understanding of the life force and its mechanisms is progressing. The pursuit of truth and an open-minded approach to exploring the realms of divinity, both within and beyond, remain essential.

Note: When you are acidic, this condition changes the electromagnetic energy of the body, which causes increased thermal energy and ionization. This damages the tissues throughout your body.

AROMATHERAPY— USING ESSENTIAL OILS

I've always held the belief that when you breathe in a substance, you essentially consume it. Aromatherapy relies on harnessing the potent properties of essential oils derived from plants to enhance, heal, stimulate, and revitalize bodily tissues. These essential oils can be administered through inhalation, ingestion, or absorption into the skin. It's worth noting that while the FDA doesn't recommend ingesting essential oils, many people worldwide do consume them, especially considering that when applied to the skin, they are indirectly ingested.

Essential oils are incredibly concentrated and are often considered among the most powerful compounds within a plant. They have profound and far-reaching effects on bodily tissues, and when used thoughtfully and with care, they can yield highly valuable results. Consider incorporating essential oils as a complementary approach to improving your health. Different oils, much like various herbs, can have specific effects on different organs or processes within the body. For furthcr information in this field, you can consult the bibliography for additional resources.

Essential Oils and Their Benefits

BASIL OIL — Anti-spasmodic. Use for migraines, mental clarity, nervous system support (due to anxieties, etc.), thyroid support (due to depression), adrenal gland support.

BERGAMOT OIL — For skin conditions, congestive conditions of the respiratory tract, sinuses, lymphatic system, inflammation, urinary tract system, parasites, endocrine glands. This oil is said to affect the hypothalamus of the brain.

BIRCH OIL — For arthritis, pain, detoxifying, lymphatic congestion and skin conditions.

CHAMOMILE OIL — A smooth muscle relaxant; use for allergies, bladder, anxieties, and digestion.

CINNAMON OIL — For digestion, parasites (cinnamon has anti-bacterial properties), cardiac issues, increasing circulation, support for the kidneys, toothaches.

CLARY SAGE OIL — This hormone balancer provides glandular support to the lymphatic system. Also use to support the nervous system, as a tonic, and for headaches.

CLOVE OIL — For respiratory congestion, rheumatism, allergies (clove provides lymphatic support), stress, toothaches, and tuberculosis. Strong anti-parasitic.

CORIANDER OIL — For the pancreas (helps digestion), for cardiac support, for circulation, and for pain.

CYPRESS OIL — Lymphatic. Use for arthritis, hot flashes, pancreatic support, and circulation.

EUCALYPTUS OIL — For any lung congestion or condition, diabetes, headaches, sinus congestion, lymph congestion, or kidney inflammation.

FENNEL OIL — Respiratory conditions, especially asthma; constipation; digestion; liver support.

FRANKINCENSE OIL — Immune system support, lymphatic system support, for enhancing red blood cells, for tumors, inflammation, and urinary tract support.

GALBAUN UMOIL — Said to enhance spirituality. An anti-parasitic due to its anti-bacterial properties. Use for lymphatic support, for stress, and for circulation.

GERANIUM OIL — For the pancreas (particularly in cases of diabetes, or for digestion), for liver/gallbladder; a detoxifier; urinary system support; for skin; for the lymphatic system.

GINGER OIL — A digestant. Use for the pancreas, for circulation, arthritis, cramps, tooth-aches, as a laxative, and for hangovers.

GRAPEFRUIT OIL — Lymphatic support. Use for skin, liver, glandular support. An anti-parasitic.

HYSSOP OIL — Anti-parasitic (anti-bacterial, viral, anti-fungal). An expectorant for the respiratory system. Also supports the lymphatic, urinary and digestive systems. This is a strong oil. Use with caution!

JASMINE OIL — For inflammation (itis's), for adrenal support (in cases of anxiety), liver conditions, respiratory issues, nervous system support, and for muscles.

JUNIPER OIL — Urinary tract, especially kidneys; for diabetes (because this oil supports the pancreas); for endocrine glands; "ego" issues; adrenal glands; gout; lymphatic system support. (Strong oil—use with caution!)

LAVENDER OIL — Great for kidneys and bladder, headaches, earaches, and as a relaxant for the nervous system. This oil slowly feeds the nerves. Use as a liver and gallbladder detoxifier. Also works well for all skin conditions, including burns.

LEMON OIL — For the pancreas (in cases of diabetes, and for digestion, among other uses). Provides lymphatic support; helps the urinary tract (kidneys and bladder); heals scar tissues; helpful in cases of bleeding.

LEMON GRASS OIL — For conditions involving connective tissue; also used as a digestant (helps the pancreas, liver, etc.); great for the lymphatic system, urinary tract, respiratory system, nervous system; and help for the muscles.

MARJORAM OIL — Supports the adrenal glands (for anxiety, nervous system issues, stress). Great for the thyroid (for depression, headaches, or in cases of bruising). An anti-fungal. Supports the respiratory tract and the muscles. Helps in removal of ticks. Relieves inflammation.

MOUNTAIN SAVORY OIL — Anti-microbial, including bacterial, fungal, and viral properties. Said to be somewhat of a tonic.

MYRRH OIL — Helps inflammation, respiration congestion, and hyperthyroidism. Use for its anti-fungal, anti-bacterial, and sedative properties.

NUTMEG OIL — A digestant (helps the pancreas), and a laxative. Helps relieve vomiting. Support for the heart.

ORANGE OIL — Helps the spleen, adrenal glands (anxiety, stress, shock, etc.), heart, liver and blood. Also used for anti-fungal properties and as a laxative.

OREGANO OIL — An anti-parasitic (due to its anti-fungal, bacterial, viral components); good for immune system support.

PATCHOULY OIL — Helps the nervous system, the lymphatic system, and the glandular system especially the adrenals in conditions of anxiety and stress, and the thyroid in cases of depression, headaches, fever. Good for the skin; use as a diuretic; use for mental clarity, and for allergies where lymphatic support is needed.

PEPPERMINT OIL — Ideal for respiratory congestion; for use as an anti-spasmodic; a great digestant (helps the pancreas, liver, etc.). Use for skin conditions; for inflammation; for urinary tract support; and mental clarity. Helps relieve morning sickness, shock, nausea, dizziness and fatigue. Use for gallstones, and for toothache.

ROSE OIL — Supports the endocrine glands; good for issues involving the emotions; useful for lung congestion, TB, impotency, ulcers, skin conditions, depression (due to its thyroid supporting properties.) Contains hemostatic properties (useful in stopping both internal and external bleeding).

ROSEMARY OIL — Use for inflammation, liver conditions, skin conditions, endocrine glandular support, pancreas support (for diabetes), epilepsy, gout, cardiovascular conditions (heart and circulation), mental confusion and conditions, respiratory and sinus congestion, stress. Also useful in childbirth.

ROSEWOOD OIL — Anti-parasitic properties (bacterial, fungal, etc.).

Useful to the skin, liver, nervous system, adrenals (to ease stress, anxiety, worry).

SAGE OIL — Another great detoxifier, which aids in lung, lymphatic, sinus, liver, skin, and circulatory congestion and obstructions. Sage is also a good diuretic and aids digestion. Useful for inducing sweating, which encourages skin elimination. Also said to be anti-bacterial, anti-fungal, and anti-viral.

SANDALWOOD OIL — Believed to have positive effects on the DNA and RNA. Useful as a digestant by supporting the pancreas and liver. Good for the bladder, thyroid support (especially with depression, calcium issues), skin conditions, stress, and vomiting. Contains anti-fungal properties.

SPEARMINT OIL — Similar to Peppermint, Spearmint supports the liver, urinary tract, and lymphatic system. Good for respiratory conditions, and as a relaxant to the nervous system. Contains anti-fungal properties.

SPRUCE OIL — Use for inflammation (various itis's), urinary tract support, anti-fungal properties, and hypothyroidism in conditions relative to the bones, skin, sweating.

TARRAGON OIL — A digestant (which supports the pancreas, liver). Use for inflammation (various itis's), as a laxative, and as an anti-parasitic. Valuable in cases of anorexia, and for support of the nervous system.

TEA TREE OIL (MELALENCA) — A great oil for support of the immune and lymphatic systems. Useful for shingles, as an anti-fungal, or antiviral. Good for burns, shock, and eliminating warts.

THYME OIL — Anti-parasitic for all types of parasites: fungal, bacterial, viral, or worms. Use in cases of lung congestion, stress, anxiety and tension (when adrenal glands need support), skin disorders, thyroid-related problems (like depression or skin conditions), lymphatic/congestive conditions, tumors, nausea, gout, cardiac problems, circulation, and throat congestion.

WILD TANSY OIL — Provides support for the immune system, lymphatic system, adrenal glands (especially emotional issues).

WHITE LOTUS OIL — Useful as tonic. Uplifting, said to bring euphoria. Spiritual properties. Immune system enhancing. Anti-cancer properties.

In my sister's herb shop we have a sauna in which we use essential oils. This offers a great benefit to the body, especially in assisting elimination through the skin, lungs, kidneys and even the bowels. Using oils in this way can literally pull the toxins from your skin. I recommend using Eucalyptus, Birch, Sage or Lavender oil (see their properties and uses above).

Essential oils can also be burned in oil lamps or special essential-oil burners. They can be used in the bag of your vacuum cleaner, which allows the essential oils to neutralize many toxic particles that escape from your sweeper. This method also spreads the oil throughout the area that you are vacuuming.

Let the aroma of the oils invigorate you and enhance your life in endless ways.

CHIROPRACTIC AND KINESIOLOGY

Chiropractic is a therapeutic approach centered on the relationship between the spine and the nervous system. A trained chiropractor employs various methods to manipulate the spinal column, making precise adjustments to specific vertebrae. These adjustments aim to open up energy pathways and alleviate blockages in the flow of energy to various parts of the body.

Kinesiology is a diagnostic feedback system that involves assessing the strength of specific muscles. The underlying theory is that muscles weaken when any part of the body is compromised or in a weakened state. By essentially "asking" the body targeted questions and then testing the strength of the muscles, a skilled kinesiologist can pinpoint which system requires attention and determine the most effective approach for strengthening it.

When used in conjunction, chiropractic and kinesiology have provided relief and healing to many individuals enduring suffering. This combination is particularly significant because spinal vertebrae often become misaligned due to weak and toxic muscles. Muscles play a crucial role in supporting the skeletal system, and the body often stores toxins in muscles as a protective measure to safeguard vital organs. The consumption of dairy products, refined sugars, and starches can contribute to lymphatic congestion, ultimately leading to muscle and tissue weakness. Consequently, certain muscles may become weaker than others, causing stronger muscles to pull bones out of their proper alignment.

Injuries can also disrupt the skeletal system's alignment. When the skeletal system is out of place, it can result in severe pain and discomfort, and in some cases, even convulsions. Incorporating detoxification alongside chiropractic care can offer a comprehensive approach to healing the muscular and skeletal systems.

COLON THERAPY

See section 6.9 on "Healthy Bowel Management" in Chapter 6.

COLOR THERAPY

Without color, life would not exist. The energies that make up the millions of colors create, support and sustain the untold dimensions that exist beyond our sight. The power of colors to enhance tissue is phenomenal. I developed a color therapy machine years ago and had great fun experimenting with colors and their effects upon the body. The sun is the ultimate provider of color therapy. Full-spectrum rays surround and flow through us, healing and embracing our cells. All life looks to the "light," one way or another.

As we have discussed, energy creates, supports, sustains and changes the universe. This energy manifests from consciousness, and extends out into creation. As it moves, it gives off colors (light) and music (sounds). These energies, their colors and music, are both dramatic and subtle. Duality dictates that colors or energies move between hot (acid) and cold (alkaline), or light (acid) and dark (alkaline).

Everything that exists has a main energy or energies that support or sustain it, whether this is a human, animal, plant, planet or universe. An example of this would be a planet, like Mother Earth, where gemstones play a major role in channeling these energies that sustain her. There are also lay lines or electromagnetic energy lines that crisscross the earth. Where they meet is said to be a place of very high energy—a place where more spiritually-minded people tend to congregate and live. Sedona, Arizona is an example of such a place.

Another example of energy centers is found within the bodies of animals and humans. There are basically seven main energy centers within each of us. These main energy centers correspond to different aspects or different bodies that we use. Most people cannot see these types of energies. Those who can we call psychic; however, anyone can train himself or herself to see these. Your ability to achieve anything depends upon the degree of your desire for it. These centers of energy are "seen" as follows:

First Center

Dimension: physical (survival)
Location: base of spine (fourth sacral)
Color: red

Second Center

Dimension: physical (social, healing)
Location: 2 inches below the naval
Color: orange

Third Center

Dimension: emotional (astral, survival)
Location: solar plexus
Color: yellow/pink

Fourth Center

Dimension: emotional (healing, astral)
Location: center of chest (heart) first, second, third thoracic
Color: green

Fifth Center

Dimension: mind (survival)
Location: throat first through third cervical
Color: sky blue

Sixth Center

Dimension: mind (healing)
Location: third eye, pineal gland
Color: indigo

Seventh Center

Dimension: ego (crown)
Location: crown of head, pituitary gland
Color: purple/violet

Eighth Center

Dimension: soul itself
Color: yellow/white

The above main centers are expressed through your physical body and are called chakras.

When one has physical, emotional or mental disease, these centers will begin to shut down respectively. These energies emanate from and through your physical body. Your aura, or the electromagnetic energies emanating from you, can be read and analyzed to determine weaknesses or strengths.

In the aura, white or yellow are the colors of Consciousness. The main creative and sustaining energies of Earth, divided into five basic influences or elements, are seen in the aura in the following colors:

Air element = violet
Fire element = red
Ether element = blue
Water element = orange
Ground element = green

The following are examples of colors and the specific tissues that they affect.

Color Energies and Tissues They Affect

RED	ORANGE	YELLOW	GREEN	BLUE	VIOLET
Prostate gland	Respiratory stimulant	Overall vitality	Pituitary	Liver	Individuality
Colon	Stomach	Spinal cord	Cell activation	Pelvic area	Sexual organs (females)
Muscles	Solar plexus	Growth	Cleansing	Cerebral (brain tissue)	Lymphatic system
Red blood cells	Parathyroid/ Thyroid	Immune system	Healing	Blood	Stomach
Excretory		Heart	Muscle builder	Small intestines	Menstruation
Organs (general)		Lymphatic activator	Tissue builder	Oxygenation of tissues	Digestive system (pancreas)
Liver (energizer)		Cerebral stimulant		Adrenal glands	Pregnancy
Adrenal glands		Bones			Lower extremities
		Nervous system			Parathyroid
		Brain			Spleen Immune
					Blood

By using different colors, or electromagnetic frequencies, therapeutically, we can affect tissue in a positive way. It will respond or function in a greater capacity. Today, we need all the healing power we can get because of the severe hypo-conditions that most of us have in our cells, tissues, organs and glands as a result of our diets and genetics.

Nature offers us an abundance of tools to assist us in the quality of our expression while we live on this planet. Take control. Use all of these tools available to you, to obtain your goals.

Below is a list of foods and their specific colors. Eat more of the foods that fit the area of your body you wish to work on.

Foods and Their Specific Colors

RED	ORANGE	YELLOW	GREEN	BLUE	VIOLET
cherry	carrot	carrot	romaine	blueberry	pear
watermelon	orange	cantaloupe	lettuce	blackberry	asparagus
strawberry	tangerine	corn	spinach	plum	celery
tomato	pumpkin	lemon	celery	grape	parsnip
yams	rutabaga	grapefruit	parsley	all blue-skinned fruits & vegetables	potato
watercress	melon, some	mango			
radish	yam	onion			
cabbage	garlic	papaya			
onion	nuts, some	persimmon			
garlic	all orange-skinned fruits & vegetables	squash			
peppers		orange			
ginger		tangerine			
eggplant		turnip			
beet		peach			
parsley					

In creation there is always duality or opposites. Without opposites there would be only one thing – God! Opposites give us matter, energy, time and space. There are always two processes or forces at work in nature: anabolism and catabolism. Anabolism is the process of growth, repair, building, enhancement and dynamic energy. The essential opposite to this is catabolism, which is the destructive or the "tearing down" side. This side affects change; balances out over-growth; maintains the shape and size of forms; and destroys the weak, to make room for the strong. Catabolism creates the wastes from metabolism, while anabolism moves these out through the lymphatic system. Life in these material worlds requires duality for its existence. We need to understand both sides of life's essential processes.

Colors add beauty and elevate the consciousness in one's life. Surround yourself in color, harmonious music, and the energy of God. You will then know what true vitality really is.

FLOWER ESSENCES

Nature is so beautiful and powerful. One of its most beautiful creations is the flower. I love to go to flower gardens and embrace the loving energies of these most precious gifts. Without these "balancing" gifts of royal beauty, life on this planet would truly be dull.

Have you noticed the multitude of aromas found in the flower kingdom? Each aroma affects your physical, emotional, mental and soul bodies in an uplifting and healing way. Each flower is designed, like each herb, to enhance and expand the consciousness of your cells, your emotions, and your thoughts. Edward Bach was the modern day founder of a healing modality that uses flowers to enhance each facet of your life. Kathren Woodlyn Bateman has created a fantastic selection of flower essences (Flower Essences of Running Fox FarmsTM in Worthington, Massachusetts). I have used these formulas to balance the emotional trauma that people have experienced in hospital Emergency Rooms, in the Oklahoma City bombing, and in mental health clinics. I have seen these subtle energies work with amazingly positive results.

In physics you learn that all things exist as energy fluctuating between two poles. These energies can be disruptive to the emotional and mental parts of ourselves, or they can be harmonious, yielding balance and upliftment. This is important to know because what you think and what you feel affects your health as much as what you eat.

Many flower essence formulas have been created. They are similar to herbal formulas in that the quality of the formula depends upon the quality of the flower and the ability of the practitioner who made it. Of all the formulas created, "Emergency Relief" by Bach Flower Essences is the most famous. Many companies have copied this one to some extent. "Emergency Relief" can be used in almost any traumatic experience, especially when shock is involved. "Moonshine Yarrow" (by Fox Mountain) is another great formula for shock, anxiety attacks, and especially for depression.

Most men typically do not think or dream in color. One night I was meditating on this subject and had a vivid out-of-body experience in a heaven that was crystalline, where all the trees and plants flashed an endless variety of colors and hues. This experience changed the way I looked at, and dreamt about, life. Flower therapy is very much a part of color therapy and aromatherapy. We just need more of it.

Flowers can also be eaten for their nutritional and energetic values. Nasturtiums, daisies, and dandelion flowers are just some of these edible beauties. Enjoy the "Power of the Flower." You will be surprised as God's rainbow foods enhance, calm, expand and revitalize you. Add plenty of flowers and flower essences into your life and it will help you open your heart and bring forth the music of God.

GEM STONE THERAPY

Gemstone therapy is an ancient practice that has spanned thousands of years. In this tradition, various gemstones, including rubies, were ground into fine powders and ingested as a remedy for sickness and disease. The vibrational and stimulating properties of these inorganic compounds were believed to have a beneficial effect on biological tissues. Additionally, certain gemstones were worn as jewelry, typically around the neck or on the arms, and sometimes placed directly over the affected area. Crystal therapy, which is a form of gemstone therapy, is still widely utilized today for purposes like absorbing disease and directing healing energy toward weakened parts of the body. This is achieved by positioning a crystal over the afflicted area and allowing the crystal's energy to work its healing magic.

Gemstones are believed to possess significant power, often beyond what humans currently comprehend. Exploring this field is a captivating endeavor, as it encompasses an exciting and mysterious science.

To learn more about this subject I recommend *Love is in the Earth* by Melody (Earth-Love Publishing House, 1995); *Crystal Enlightenment* by Katrina Raphaell (Aurora Press, 1985); and *Cunningham's Encyclopedia of Crystal, Gem and Metal Magic* by Scott Cunningham, (Llewellyn Publications, 1987).

HERBOLOGY

Whether you refer to it as phytotherapy, botanical medicine, or herbology, the non-hybrid plants created by nature possess the remarkable power to heal, cleanse, and rejuvenate tissues. In the realm of science, there's a tendency to extract, isolate, and administer specific constituents from plants in mega-doses to address bodily symptoms. However, it's essential to recognize that this approach may not align with the original intent of plants. The holistic power of the whole plant is often potent enough when harnessed correctly. I've been using herbal formulas for over twenty-five years, long before they became trendy. My primary goal has always been to empower individuals to heal themselves rather than merely treating their symptoms. I've administered substantial quantities of herbs to individual patients, as herbs can be incredibly potent and robust. There are only a few herbs that I do not recommend due to their toxic nature, but these are typically exotic and not commonly used in mainstream herbology.

Beyond their various medicinal properties, which encompass anti-inflammatory, astringent, bitter, stimulant, antispasmodic, and more, herbs also offer substantial nutritional value. They are rich sources of vitamins, minerals, tissue salts, flavins, amino acids, sugars, and even possess unique electromagnetic energies. I encourage the study and experimentation with botanicals. Without the benefits they provide, humans may struggle to mitigate the numerous damaging effects they have had on the planet.

HOMEOPATHY

Homeopathy is a therapeutic system that relies on remedies derived from animal parts, plants, and minerals. These remedies are prepared in very mild strengths and dosages. The fundamental principle of homeopathy is "like treats like." In other words, if a person has symptoms similar to those caused by a particular substance, they would be administered minute amounts of that substance as a treatment. For example, in the case of poison ivy exposure, the homeopathic remedy would involve consuming poison ivy in highly diluted amounts.

Homeopathy primarily operates by stimulating the body's immune response rather than directly promoting tissue healing. Homeopathic remedies are formulated based on the essence of their constituents, focusing on their electromagnetic energy rather than their potency. It's important to note that homeopathy is not a deep detoxification and regenerative approach but is often effective in relieving symptoms and improving well-being.

HYDROTHERAPY (KNEIPP THERAPY, AND OTHER FORMS)

Hydrotherapy, also known as water therapy, has been utilized for thousands of years. In modern times, credit is given to the late Sebastian Kneipp, a Catholic priest in Bavaria, for refining and popularizing hydrotherapy on a global scale.

Water can serve as a powerful tool for stimulating both blood and lymphatic circulation. It acts as a transporter of elements and toxins, facilitating their movement to and from cells through the gastrointestinal tract or the skin. The benefits of heat are well-known, as it dilates blood vessels and enhances circulation. The body employs internal methods like diaphoresis (sweating and fevers) and histamine responses to increase blood and lymphatic flow. By enhancing circulation to the body's tissues, hydrotherapy contributes to improved delivery of nutrition, oxygen, immune responses, and electrolyte balance (alkalization) – all crucial factors in tissue circulation. Conversely, cold has a constricting effect and can impede energy circulation to tissues. Combining these aspects of stimulation, hydrotherapy involving alternating hot and cold applications can produce remarkable responses in disease situations.

One can even view the act of drinking water as a form of hydrotherapy. Many individuals do not consume an adequate amount of water, either as a beverage or through cooked foods.

Water plays a vital role in the oxidation and ionization processes of the body. It is indispensable for promoting proper bowel movement, hydration, and the functioning of the renal system (kidneys and bladder).

Mineral baths, another facet of hydrotherapy, can be highly effective in stimulating tissue. However, excessive exposure to water rich in heavy minerals may have adverse effects, potentially leading to dry and crusty skin, coarsening of hair texture, and hindrance of hair growth by blocking hair follicles. It's crucial to note that excessive stimulation isn't the key to vitality; what matters more is maintaining dynamic energy balance.

IRIDOLOGY

Iridology is a science and field of study that focuses on the examination of the iris of the eye and its correlation with the various tissues in the body. It provides an incredibly detailed roadmap, offering insights into the functioning and dysfunctions of individual cells.

Dr. Bernard Jensen, a respected figure in the field, referred to Iridology as the "Master Science." Through the iris of the eye, Iridology provides an intricate depiction of a person's genetics, tissue strengths and weaknesses, as well as the presence of congestion or toxicity within the body. It reveals obstructions, prolapsed conditions, and accumulations of chemicals. Furthermore, it not only identifies tissue weaknesses and congestion but also quantifies the extent of these issues. A neuro-optic analysis, which delves into the study of the eyes, is a valuable tool for gaining a profound understanding of one's physical body.

For practitioners, Iridology not only offers insights into individual cells but also provides information about the structures and systems of the body. This is crucial for identifying reflex conditions, particularly the interconnectedness between the gastrointestinal (GI) tract and the various cells throughout the body. In the conventional medical world, there are often cases where symptoms lack a known origin or association with reflex areas of toxicity or weakness. Iridology bridges this gap by offering comprehensive information.

Iridology essentially serves as a form of soft tissue analysis, offering valuable insights that are much needed in today's world of diagnosis and analysis. The eyes, often referred to as the windows of the soul, also provide a window into the physical body. Iridology is a science that is accessible for individuals to learn and is highly recommended, as it can unravel the mysteries of one's genetics and unveil weaknesses within the body.

MASSAGE (ALL TYPES) AND REFLEXOLOGY

The golden hands of a good massage therapist are truly magical as they reshape and restore the tissues of your body. There are so many forms of massage—from light stimulation and relaxing massage, to deep tissue and sacral cranial massage. Massage work is an important field in many ways, from assisting the body to heal itself from injuries, to promoting lymphatic drainage and detoxification. The body stores toxins in muscles, sparing as long as possible the major organs. But, in storing these toxins the body becomes stiff and sore, driving us to exercise to stimulate lymph flow. When we have the inability to exercise or we become too toxic, massage is extremely vital.

Foot Reflexology, noted in Chapter 9, is a special form of massage and a most valuable tool. I have saved several people from cardiac arrest with my thumb and their left foot. The power of stimulating the nervous system and lymphatic system by pressure to points on the hands and feet cannot be underestimated. Toxicity and acid crystals build up under the nerve endings in the hands and feet. This toxicity can cause a multitude of symptoms from high blood pressure to gallbladder weakness.

NAPRAPATHY AND POLARITY THERAPY

Naprapathy encompasses Dr. Randolph Stone's Polarity Therapy combined with manipulation. "Polarity" refers to a type of energy balancing. Naprapathy is a combination of chiropractics (structural realigning), kinesiology, polarity therapy and nutrition. Its goal is to remove energy obstructions by manipulating the muscles and skeletal system. My old friend Dr. Rudy Splavic was taught by Dr. Stone, and was a naprapath for fifty years. When he was age eighty-six I saw him work miracles on people, completely changing their posture and structure after thirty years of deformity. He could tell you the year of your injury or when the disease began; and could feel a hair under seven sheets of paper. However, some modern naprapaths swing toward conventional medicine.

Always seek to know your practitioner. It is important to keep your body, and its injuries, in balance. It is equally important to learn why they get out of balance.

NATUROPATHY

The term "naturopathy" was coined by Benedict Lust, but its roots can be traced back to the practices of Hippocrates and even earlier. Naturopathy is a science that revolves around a 100% natural and organic approach to detoxification and nutrition, ultimately leading to tissue regeneration. This foundation paves the way for genuine vitality and long-lasting health.

Naturopathic practitioners exclusively rely on natural remedies and nature's resources to achieve these objectives. It is considered one of the most comprehensive sciences globally, encompassing a wide array of disciplines such as chemistry, physics, hydrotherapy, vibrational therapy, color therapy, phytotherapy (herbal medicine), massage therapy, thermotherapy, electrotherapy, bio-electromagnetic therapy, emotional therapy, reflexology, raw food therapy, fasting therapy, proper food combining, and many more. At the heart of naturopathy lies the principles of detoxification and alkalization.

The fundamental premise of naturopathy is that disease is a natural process. When the body becomes acidic and accumulates substances like mucus, pus, parasites, chemicals, preservatives, antibiotics, pesticides, and carbon by-products, it cannot maintain good health.

Naturopathy is truly holistic, addressing not only the physical body but also emotions, mind, and soul. Recognizing that human beings are highly interconnected entities, naturopathy acknowledges that diseases can manifest on multiple levels, often unbeknownst to the patient. Naturopathy opens the doors to explore and address these various levels, allowing individuals to reconnect with life on a spiritual plane. Many consider naturopathy to be the most advanced and comprehensive healing modality available, as it delves into the root causes of health issues rather than merely addressing their effects.

Naturopathic Medicine

Naturopathic medicine is a system or modality similar to naturopathy. However, it is more treatment-minded than naturopathy. Naturopathic physicians use orthomolecular science (vitamins and minerals), tissue salts, glandular supplements and other separated constituents to treat symptoms in an effort to correct the cause of the problem. Naturopathic medicine uses some detoxification principles and stresses diets consisting mainly of fresh fruit, vegetables and grains.

VIBRATIONAL THERAPIES (ENERGY HEALING)

This is a large category and could include Therapeutic TouchTM, magnet therapy, crystal therapy (gem stone therapy), radionics, qi gong (Chinese energy healing), spiritual healing, psychic healing, fengshui, biofeedback, and the like. Even though each of the above modalities is uniquely different, they all use "spirit" in one way or another to affect tissues, increasing circulation and elimination. These therapies change the vibrational energy of cells, thus improving cellular respiration and vitality. Our magnetic energies become out of balance by toxicity, acidic foods, negative thoughts, negative derogatory emotions and unhappiness.

Vibrational therapies move stagnant or restricted energies and allow this energy to circulate through cells and tissues better. This reduces or eliminates pain, increases overall circulation, and stimulates elimination. This increases tissue function and repair.

We are only at the first stage of new discoveries in this area. Vibrational therapies will dominate the future, in one form or another.

ALLOPATHIC MEDICINE

Allopathic medicine, in my opinion, should be limited to emergency medicine, diagnostic procedures and surgeries. Emergency medicine has saved hundreds of thousands of lives, and many surgeries are essential to life, as humans have literally destroyed their health and the tissues in their bodies.

I spent many years involved in emergency medicine, and especially enjoyed anything that dealt with the heart. However, there are a lot of hospital Emergency Rooms that could learn about nature and how to apply more non-invasive techniques that could save even more lives and increase the quality of life for many, many more. There are far too many tissue-damaging techniques used in Emergency Rooms today, including chest compressions, which crack or break the sternum.

Many surgeries are unnecessary, however. They often cause the patient great distress, and in many cases, a dismal future. Open-heart surgery, for example, can mostly be avoided. Nature can clean out the vascular system in short order if the patient is willing to change his/her lifestyle. In fact, eighty to ninety percent of all dis-eases can be cured without chemical medicine or invasive procedures. Naturopaths are non-invasive and seek a cure for the cause of the problem.

Conclusion

Avoid a future of immobility, despair, sexual impotence and massive diseases. Don't wait until it is too late. Become healthy now. Health, vitality and fun can give you a new life of freedom, tranquility, vibrancy and longevity.

It is beyond the scope of this book to cover all the natural therapies that currently exist, for which I send out my deepest apologies. I have tried to give you an overview of the most well-known and important ones. Each one deserves much more recognition. Each natural modality is a science within itself, offering you a magnificent journey to restoration of the self. Read, study, and learn all you can about each one and enjoy what they have to offer you. The Bibliography at the end of this book will suggest many fine books that will help you in your study.

It is time that each individual takes responsibility for his/her own health issues. Empower yourself. You will enjoy how your body feels as it becomes more vital and dynamic. If you seek anything, seek to be vibrantly healthy: physically, emotionally, mentally and spiritually.

NOTE: The sciences described above are the greatest tools that nature offers you in restoring your vitality. However, they are only as good as the practitioner who uses them. A director of the American Medical Association was once interviewed on the news program 60 Minutes and asked about how people could protect themselves from poor M.D.s. His response was to quote the old adage, "Let the buyer beware [*Caveat Emptor*]."

I challenge you to make your life a masterpiece. I challenge you to join the ranks of those people who live what they teach, who walk their talk. Live with passion!

— Anthony Robbins

APPENDIX C

All About Blood Analysis

This Appendix will teach you a lot about blood chemistry and help you to interpret the results of any blood-work that your healthcare practitioner may suggest for you. This Appendix consists of four parts:

1. An overview of the most common types of blood analysis.

2. A sample Laboratory Report to familiarize you with how results are
tabulated.

3. A detailed description of each blood test, explaining why it is used and what diseases or conditions its results may indicate.

4. The shortcomings of blood analysis.

PART I
OVERVIEW OF BLOOD ANALYSIS
Most Common Blood Analysis Ordered

The "Complete Blood Count and Differential Count," abbreviated as "CBC and diff." This analysis includes:

RBC

• Red Blood Cell Count

- Hemoglobin (HGB)
- Hematocrit (HCT)
- MCV (Mean Corpuscular Volume)
- MCH (Mean Corpuscular Hemoglobin)
- MCHC (Mean Corpuscular Hemoglobin Concentration)
- **WBC**
- White Blood Cell Count and Differential Count
- Neutrophils
- Lymphocytes
- Monocytes
- Eosinophils
- Basophils
- Platelet count

CANCER

(CARCINOEMBRYONIC ANTIGEN) — A protein that normally appears in fetal gut tissue. However, it is also found in the bloodstream of adults with colorectal tumor and other carcinomas including breast, pancreatic, liver and gastric (stomach). It is also found in non-cancerous (benign) conditions including ulcerative colitis, diverticulitis and cirrhosis.

CA 19-9 — Useful tumor marker (antigen) for liver and pancreatic cancers. It is primarily used in the diagnosing of pancreatic carcinoma (70 percent). CA 19-9 markers can also indicate gastric cancers, colorectal cancer, pancreatitis, gallstones, cirrhosis and cystic fibrosis.

CA 15-3 — A tumor marker best used for meta-static breast cancer. It can also be elevated in ovarian disease, non-malignant breast masses and non- breast malignancies.

CA 125 — An epithelial cell tumor marker for ovarian cancer.

AFP (ALPHA-FETOPROTEIN) AND HCG (HUMAN CHORIONIC

GONADOTROPHIN) — Germ cell tumor markers for the ovaries.

PSA (PROSTATE-SPECIFIC ANTIGEN) — Aglyco-protein found in the cytoplasm of prostate epithelial cells. Elevated PSAs can indicate inflammation and/or cancer of the prostate. The higher the PSA levels, especially above 5, the more likely that this inflammation has become cancer.

Blood Typing

Human blood is categorized according to the presence or absence of blood antigens. These antigens are called **ABO** and **Rh** Antigens. The two major antigens that comprise ABO blood typing are the **A** and **B** antigen, which serve as the basis for the ABO system.

Type A blood contains type A antigens. Type B blood contains type B antigens. Type AB blood contains type AB antigens. Type O blood does not

TUMOR MARKERS (ANTIGENS) CEA

Contain type A or B antigens.

The presence or absence of Rh antigens (factors) determines whether your blood is Rh-positive or Rh-negative.

Blood typing is important for transferring blood from one person to another. Antigens are the immunity of the individual and reflect one's ability to fight pathogenic invasions.

Other Common Terms and Tests Used

Electrolyte Panels: Show glucose and blood serum electrolytes.

Thyroid Panels: Show T4s (Thyroxin), T3s (Systemic converted Thyroxin), and TSHs (Thyroid stimulating hormone, from pituitary).

Lipid Profile Panels: Show cholesterol (LDLs and HDLs) and blood triglyceride levels.

PART II

HOW TO INTERPRET YOUR BLOOD TESTS

General Chemistry

GLUCOSE — In general, basic serum glucose levels may be an indicator of many conditions within the body. Elevated levels may indicate diabetes mellitus, hyperparathyroidism,

Cushing's disease, stress, pancreatitis, corticosteroid and diuretic therapy, pheochromocytoma, and cellular acidosis. Decreased levels may indicate hypoglycemia, hypothyroidism, liver disease and Addison's disease.

MINERALS — The minerals sodium, potassium, chloride and calcium are the main electrically-charged cations and anions, which constitute the body's electrolytes.

SODIUM — Sodium is the most abundant cation (positively charged) mineral in extracellular fluids. Therefore, it is the major salt in determining extracellular osmolality (transportation) of nutrients and constituents. Blood sodium is a direct result of the balance between dietary intake and kidney (renal) excretion and reabsorption.

Many hormones affect this balance of sodium by controlling the excretion through the kidneys (e.g., aldosterone, ADH, NH, etc.)

Low sodium levels create hyponatremia (low sodium), which can create weakness, confusion, coma and death. Too much sodium (hypernatremia) creates thirst, dry mucus membranes, convulsions, restlessness, etc. Many drugs can create both hypo- and hypernatremia, including antibiotics, steroids, laxatives, diuretics, sulfides, heart medications, etc.

Cancer will also decrease sodium levels. The body will use any alkaline component in it to fight acidosis. Sodium has a strong affinity for oxygen and is a vital inorganic metal in maintaining electrolyte balance.

POTASSIUM — Potassium is one of the major cations within the cell. There is almost forty times more potassium in a cell as opposed to the fluid that surrounds a cell. Potassium is affected by sodium reabsorption by the kidneys. Aldosterone lowers potassium by increasing kidney excretion. Your body always seeks to maintain the acid-based balance within it. Acidosis pulls potassium out of a cell, causing electromagnetic changes which affect cell wall permeability of nutrients and the electro-potentiality of a cell. Symptoms of elevated blood potassium (hyperkalemia) include nausea, vomiting, irritability, diarrhea, depressed electrical depolarization of the heart, muscle contractility, (S.O.B., chest pain, etc.) and acidosis. Low serum levels (hypokalemia) include a decrease in the contractility of smooth, skeletal and cardiac muscles, which can cause a host of symptoms including pain, paralysis, general weakness, and cardiac arrhythmias.

Sample Blood Tests

	RESULT	OUT OF RANGE	REFERENCE RANGE	REFERENCE UNITS
GENERAL CHEMISTRY				
Glucose	103		mg/dL	70-115
Sodium	142		meq/L	133-145
Potassium	4.3		meq/L	3.3-5.3
Chloride	104		meq/L	96-110
Carbon dioxide	33		meq/L	21-24
Bun	10		mg/dL	6-27
Creatinine	0.8		mg/L	0.5-1.5
Calcium	9.7		mg/dL	8.4-10.6
Total Protein	7.5		g/dL	5.9-8.4
Albumin	3.6		g/dL	3.4-4.8
Bilirubin Total	0.3		mg/dL	0.0-1.2
Alkaline Phosphatase	98		u/L	51-131
SGOT (AST)	19		u/L	0-50

SGPT (ALT)	23		u/L	0-50
THYROID TESTING				
T3 uptake	32.0		Percent	25.0-40.0
T4	10.7		ug/dL	4.9-11.7
T7	3.42		Calc.	1.25-4.55
TSH (ultra sensitive)		L < 0.010	uiu/m/L	0.350-4.950
MISCELLANEOUS CHEMISTRY				
CEA	1.9		ng/mL	0.0-5.0
CBC, PLATELET CT, AND DIFF				
White Blood Cell (WBC) Count	505		4.0-10.5	X 10-3/uL
Red Blood Cell (RBC) Count	4.42		4.10-5.60	X 10-6/uL
Hemoglobin		12.2 L	12.5-17.0	G/dL
Hematocrit	36.7		36.0-50.0	%
MCV	83		80-98	fL
MCH	27.6		27.0-34.0	pg
MCHC	33.2		32.0-36.0	G/dL
Platelets	183		140-415	X 10-3/uL
Polys	44		40-74	%
Lymphs	43		14-46	%
Monocytes	10		4-13	%
Eos	3		0-7	%
Basos	0		0-3	%
Polys (Absolute)	2.4		1.8-7.8	X 10-3/uL
Lymphs (Absolute)	2.4		0.7-4.5	X 10-3/uL
Monocytes (Absolute)	0.6		0.1-1.0	X 10-3/uL
Eos (Absolute Value)	0.2		0.0-0.4	X 10-3/uL
Baso (Absolute)			0.0-0.2	X 10-3/uL
Lipid Panel w/LDL/HDL Ration				
LDL/HDL Ratio	2.5		0.0-3.6	Ratio units

CHLORIDE — Chloride is an extracellular anion. It's considered one of the body's main electrolytes and serves to maintain electrical neutrality. Being a companion with sodium, its fluctuation mostly matches sodium, especially in fluid retention. However, chloride is not always affected by cancer like sodium is. In many cancers, the body will use its sodium to help alkalize this highly acidic condition. Chloride also helps maintain acid/alkaline balance. Chloride replaces intracellular bicarbonate in the neutralization of carbon dioxide, thus maintaining the alkaline balance of the cell and its fluids. Hypochloremia is low chloride levels and hypercloremia is elevated chloride levels.

Hypochloremia

Hyperactivity of nerve and muscle tissue
Hypotension
Difficult and shallow breathing
Acidosis
CHF
Over-hydration
Vomiting
Chronic respiratory

Hyperchloremia

Weakness
Fatigue
Dehydration
Cushing's Syndrome
Multiple myeloma
Kidney dysfunction
Anemia

CALCIUM — Serum Calcium is used as an indicator of parathyroid function and calcium metabolism. This test is very inaccurate in determining calcium utilization. Blood calcium levels can rise or fall from cancer, chemical medication, detoxification, excessive milk drinking, high protein diets, vitamin-D supplementation, hyper-/hypo- or parathyroidism, renal failure, inflammation of the bones, malabsorption, pancreatitis, and other conditions.

CALCIUM-IONIZED — Ionized calcium does not bind with albumin, so is unaffected by albumin imbalances. Therefore it is seen as a more accurate picture for hyperparathyroidism.

CARBON DIOXIDE — Carbon dioxide levels are used to determine acidosis or alkalosis. It can also be an indicator of poor oxygenation, electrolyte imbalance (cellular), neutrality of extra and intracellular fluids, poor elimination (from kidneys and lungs), renal failure, salicylate toxicity, diabetic ketoacidiosis, starvation, shock, emphysema, and other conditions.

BUN (BLOOD UREA NITROGEN) — This test measures the amount of urea nitrogen in the blood. Urea is a substance formed in the liver as the end result of protein metabolism. As amino acids are catabolized (broken down or changed), ammonia is formed and then converted mostly to urea.

Urea is also formed in the lymphatic system. These ureas are transported to the kidneys for elimination. One can determine toxic levels of protein consumption, liver metabolism (of proteins) and kidney excretory functions by urea levels in the blood. Most kidney conditions create low levels of urea.

High levels can reflect over-consumption of proteins, GI bleeding, liver inflammation, and deterioration. Extracellular protein toxicity can also be a factor.

BUN and creatinine combo tests are used as renal function indicators. Dehydration or over-hydration can affect blood ureas, as well as many drugs, including aspirin and diuretics.

Prostatitis and hypertrophy of the prostate gland can also cause abnormal urea levels. Malnutrition and lack of proper protein digestion and synthesis is also a big factor.

CREATININE — Creatinine is a product of catabolized creatine. Creatine is used for skeletal muscle contraction and strength. Creatinine is excreted entirely by the kidneys and can be an indicator of kidney or muscle breakdown (decreased levels). Increased levels can be an indicator of inflammation of the kidneys, urinary obstructions, dehydration, CHF, diabetes, shock or trauma.

TOTAL PROTEIN — Proteins are formed from building materials called amino acids. They are used in all structural and most functional aspects of the body. They are constituents of muscle, cell membrane walls, hormones, enzymes, neurotransmitters, and hemoglobin, and used as transport vehicles. Proteins significantly contribute to the osmotic pressure within the vascular system. This is significant to nutrient transport and metabolism.

ALBUMIN — Albumin is a protein formed within the liver. It constitutes almost 60 percent of the total protein of the body. Albumin has many responsibilities including maintenance of cellular osmotic pressure, and transportation of enzymes, hormones, etc. Albumin levels can give an insight into liver conditions, hepatitis, cirrhosis, cancer, malnutrition, wasting conditions including those of the vascular and intestinal (Crohn's) systems.

BILIRUBIN TOTAL — Bilirubin is one of the best indicators of liver function. It can become elevated during detoxification as the urine eliminates water-soluble toxins. There is indirect (unconjugated) or direct (conjugated) bilirubin depending upon the organ involved, (spleen or liver, respectively). Provides insight as to the proper functioning of these organs and the inflammation or damage therein. Obstructions of these organs, as well as the bile duct, such as with tumors or stones, will increase bilirubin levels. Other conditions that increase these levels include pernicious anemia, sickle cell anemia, hemolyte anemia, and damage from drug consumption.

ALP (ALKALINE PHOSPHATASE) — Alkaline phosphatase is a phosphatase enzyme that works in the presence of an alkaline environment. ALP is found mostly in the Kupffer's cells of the liver, bile tract epithelium (surface cells), and in the bones. When acidosis is present in these tissues, depending upon the degree (tumors, inflammation, cancer, etc.), the ALP will increase. The elevation of ALP can also be a result of healing fractures and normal bone growth, among other things. Many drugs and chemicals can play a major role in affecting ALP levels. These include antibiotics, heart medications, fluorides, oral contraceptives, oxalates, sulfates, and cyanides. Low levels can indicate hypothyroidism, pernicious anemia, excess vitamin-B ingestion. Some doctors give mega B-vitamin injections to drive ALP down when they are high. As previously stated, increased levels may indicate cancer (liver, gallbladder, bone, etc.), however, normal growth factors can also affect ALP levels.

AST (ASPARTATE AMINOTRANSFERASE) — Formerly SGOT (serum glutamic-oxaloacetic transaminase), AST is an enzyme found in liver cells, heart muscle cells, skeletal muscle cells, and to a smaller degree in kidney and pancreatic cells. The elevation of AST may suggest liver inflammation, as in hepatitis, cirrhosis and cancer, as well as myocardial infarction (heart attack), muscle conditions like myositis and myopathy, and renal disease and pancreatitis.

ALT (ALANINE AMINOTRANSFERASE) — Formerly SGPT (serum glutamic-pyrovic transaminase) . ALT is an enzyme formed predominately in liver cells. However, it is found in heart muscle cells, skeletal muscular cells, and kidney cells, like AST. ALT enzyme is considered a specific in liver conditions such as hepatitis, cirrhosis, cancer, and necrosis.

Drugs and chemicals will affect both AST and ACT enzymes. These include antibiotics, aspirin-type drugs, heart medications, and many others. The list is a long one.

Immune Panel

WBC (WHITE BLOOD CELLS) — Basically, white blood cells (leukocytes) are the body's armed forces, which protect it from foreign bodies—substances including proteins, chemicals and weakened or dying cells. When WBCs are elevated we know the body is fighting something. That something could be inflammation from foreign substances, tissue necrosis, or weakness and toxicity This all leads to what is called infection. Trauma and stress also may affect WBCs.

When WBC count is low, ask yourself "Why are they low now?" "Why is my body under-producing them?" Or, "Why are they not getting into my bloodstream?" These questions may lead you to consider the presence of bone marrow weaknesses or disease, chemical and radiation therapies (which suppress and kill bone marrow cells), and/or a highly congested lymphatic system. All of these situations and more will affect the body's WBCs. Low WBC count is called **Leukopenia** ("penia" meaning "deficiency"). Elevated WBCs are called leukocytosis. An increase in total WBCs may indicate inflammation (acidosis), infection (acidosis), trauma, stress, and tissue neurosis. A decrease of WBCs may indicate drug toxicity, dietary deficiency, bone marrow failure or disease.

There are many types of white blood cells (leukocytes). They include:

Cell Types	% In Body
Neutrophils	55% – 70%
Lymphocytes	20% – 40%
Eosinophils	01% – 04%
Basophils	0.5% – 01%
Monocytes	02% – 08%

Most immune panels provide what is called a differential count. Each type of immune cell has its own function. When the percentage of any particular type of WBC changes, it will give insight into what condition the body is fighting. For example, neutrophils indicate inflammation, lymphocytes indicate anything from infection to cancer, monocytes indicate conditions from parasites to ulcerative issues (types of tissue destruction).

The following are some of the causes related to the increase or decrease of individual WBCs.

Neutrophils

Cause of increase: (Neutrophilia) Acute infection, inflammatory conditions, e.g., arthritis (rheumatoid and others), rheumatic fever. Any "itis," including gout, trauma, leukemia and stress.

Cause of decrease: (Neutropenia) Overgrowth of bacteria, anemia, viral involvements (like hepatitis or measles) radiation therapy, chemical or drug toxicity.

Lymphocytes

Cause of increase: (Lymphocytosis) Viral or bacteria involvements, multiple myeloma, lymphatic cancers, infectious hepatitis, radiation exposure.

Cause of decrease: (Lymphocytopenia) Sepsis, lupus, leukemia, drug or chemical toxicity, steroid use, and radiation exposure.

Eosinophils

Cause of increase: (Eosinophila) Parasites, allergies, skin conditions, e.g., eczema. Also, leukemia.

Cause of decrease: (Eosinopenia) Allergic reactions, stress, hyperthyroidism.

Basophils

Cause of increase: (Basophilia) Leukemia, fibrocystic conditions. Cause of decrease: (Basopenia) Allergic reactions, stress, hyperthyroidism.

Monocytes

Cause of increase: (Monocytosis) Inflammatory processes, viral involvements, tuberculosis, parasites, ulcerative conditions.

Cause of decrease: (Monocytopenia) Drug and chemical toxicity, steroid use.

Immune cells should be working *for* us. These cells live within the ocean of the lymphatic system. When the lymphatic system becomes congested and impacted this will highly compromise the function of immune cells in many ways.

Parasites, including bacteria and protozoas, are secondary to the cause. In other words, toxicity and/or acidosis are the cause of immune system weakness. Parasites and immune response are secondary. The answer to these conditions is always detoxification. Detoxification always cures the cause.

RBC (RED BLOOD CELLS) — Red blood cells, or erythrocytes, carry oxygen to the cells. These are measured by the total number of RBCs in $1mm^3$ of venous blood. Within each red blood cell are numerous molecules of hemoglobin. These molecules are full of iron that binds oxygen and carries it forth. Many things affect red blood cells. They can become weakened, become out of shape, and begin sticking together, etc. However, this is mainly due to acidosis and low enzyme function within the vascular system.

Weakness and the other factors mentioned will affect the RBC's ability to carry and transport oxygen, remove carbon dioxide, and other functions. This can create a multitude of problems from low oxidation reactions to acidosis and anemia. One can experience any number of symptoms ranging from chronic fatigue, fatigue of the thyroid and adrenals, to debility. As stated, inflammatory conditions from acidosis are major factors affecting RBCs.

Dehydration will lead to increased RBCs and overhydration will lead to decreased RBCs. Diet, organ failure, cancer, anemia, hemorrhages, and drug and chemical therapy will decrease RBCs.

Again, detoxification is the only true answer to restoring red blood cells to their true, individual potentiality. Alkalization separates them while increasing hemoglobin content and capacity. Detoxification cleans the liver and spleen, and removes the chemicals and any metals that affect RBCs, or any cell for that matter.

Detoxification will restore total blood work to within normal ranges again, without compromising homeostasis.

HEMOGLOBIN — The red blood cells contain molecules called hemoglobin. Hemoglobin is a conjugated protein that consists of *hemo*, which bonds with iron, and *globin*, a simple protein (amino acid). There are hundreds of different types of hemoglobin. However, basically they bond to oxygen and glucose and transport these elements to the cells for energy and oxidation purposes. The clinical implications of this test are closely related to the RBC count.

Increased levels may suggest COPD, CHF, dehydration, or other conditions. A decrease in hemoglobin may suggest anemia, cancer, lupus, kidney disease, splenetic conditions, and nutritional deficiency. Normal hemoglobin levels are called normochromic, high levels are hyperchromic, and low levels are called hypochromic.

Old RBCs are broken down (phagocytized) by macrophages in the spleen, liver or red bone marrow. When this happens, the iron from the hemoglobin is reused immediately to produce new RBCs, or is stored in the liver. The globin portion is converted back to amino acids. The heme that is left is converted to bilirubin, which is then excreted by the bile.

HCT (HEMATOCRIT) — Hematocrit is the percentage of RBCs (erythrocytes) in any given volume of blood. Your hematocrit should closely relate to your RBC count and hemoglobin count. Increased levels may indicate dehydration, severe diarrhea, trauma or shock, burns, or other conditions. A decrease in hematocrit levels may indicate anemia, cirrhosis of the liver, cancer, hyperthyroidism, hemorrhage, bone marrow failure, rheumatoid arthritis, malnutrition, or normal pregnancy.

MCV (MEAN CORPUSCULAR VOLUME) — The MCV test is a measurement of the volume or size of a single red blood cell. This is beneficial in classifying anemias. The greater the MCV volume, the larger (or macrocytic) the cells are; and the lower the MCV volume the smaller (or microcytic) a red blood cell is. MCV volumes are calculated by dividing the hematocrit by the total RBC count. MCVs may indicate liver conditions, alcoholism, pernicious anemia, or other problems. A lower MCV finding may suggest iron deficiency anemia.

MCH (MEAN CORPUSCULAR HEMOGLOBIN) — MCH signifies the average amount (weight) of hemoglobin within an individual red blood cell.

MCHC (MEAN CORPUSCULAR HEMOGLOBIN CONCENTRATION) — The MCHC is a measurement of the average percentage or concentration of hemoglobin within an individual cell. This factor is obtained by dividing the total hemoglobin concentration by the hematocrit.

RDW (RED BLOOD CELL DISTRIBUTION WIDTH) — This is a measurement of the width of the red blood cells. This is helpful in classifying the type of anemia that one might have.

PLATELETS (THROMBOCYTES) — Platelets are essential to the ability of the blood to clot. They are the bridges and spider webs for perforations of tissue. They bind so the body can repair. Low platelet levels are indicative of bone marrow and/or spleen weakness or disease. Infections, drugs and hemorrhages are also related to low platelet counts. Below *50,000* is critical.

MPV (MEAN PLATELET VOLUME) — MVP deals with platelet size reflecting bone marrow weakness or function.

I.P.D. Profiling Panels

CHOLESTEROL (LDL AND HDL) — Cholesterol is essential for the formation of steroids (anti-inflammatory: anabolic type), bile acids and cellular wall membranes.

Cholesterol can only be used by the body in its free form. It is synthesized by the liver or metabolized from dietary cholesterol (meats mainly). This free cholesterol is then bound or connected to transporters (lipoproteins) for transport through the blood to the cells. Note: In cooked meats, lipids become bonded and are no longer free.

There are two types of lipoproteins: LDL's Low-density proteins, and HDL's High-density proteins. Seventy-five percent of the body's free cholesterol binds to the low-density proteins and 25 percent to the high- density proteins. LDLs bring the most abundant type of cholesterol. It leads some to think that the elevation of this type of bound cholesterol is an indicator of arteriosclerotic disease. This thinking is unreasonable to me. When you examine why cholesterol is produced and how it is used by the body, you realize that cholesterol production is linked to steroid use, in particular, to inflammatory responses, and to the rebuilding of cells when cell destruction has taken place.

Because the liver synthesizes and metabolizes cholesterol, low cholesterol levels can be associated with liver diseases (like inflammation, hypo-function, narcosis, and cancer), as well as malabsorption, hyperthyroidism, some anemias, sepsis and stress.

Increased levels of cholesterol may create or indicate low adrenal function, inflammatory conditions, nephrosis, biliary cirrhosis, dietary habits (over-consumption of meats), pregnancy, hypothyroidism, high blood pressure, or other conditions.

What elevated or decreased cholesterol levels indicate is quite different than what they cause. For example, low blood pressure is indicative of adrenal medulla weakness and sodium imbalances, which can reflect adrenal cortex weakness. When the cortex of the adrenal glands is weak, the body's response to inflammation from acidosis (mostly dietary and hormonal) will be low. Therefore, the production of cholesterol by the liver will increase, thus increasing blood serum levels. Cholesterol is an anti-inflammatory lipid used by the body in response to inflammation and cellular destruction.

In time, without correcting the above, blood pressure will swing from low to high (arteriosclerotic syndrome). One can also experience diabetes, hyperthyroidism, hypercholesterolemia, hyperlipidemia, high blood pressure, heart attack, strokes, arteriosclerosis, nephrosis, and other conditions.

The answer to the above of course will always lead you back to the same thing—detoxification. Alkalize and energize, and your body will clean and rebuild itself.

TRIGLYCERIDES (TG) — Triglycerides are similar to cholesterol in that they are lipids. Triglycerides act as a source of stored energy and for healing inflammatory conditions. Triglycerides (like cholesterol) also bind with lipoproteins for transportation throughout the body. These lipoproteins include: **VLDs**—Very low-density lipoproteins and

LDLs—Low-density lipoproteins.

Triglycerides are synthesized by the liver from glycerol and other fatty acids. Being similar to cholesterol, triglycerides have the same biological and pathogenic response. Anything that causes acidosis (from alcohol consumption to meat eating) will elevate lipids.

Thyroid Profile Panels

T3 (TRIIODOTHYRONINE) — The T3 or triiodothyronine study shows the amount of T3 in the blood. This is used to determine if there is overactive or under-active thyroid involvement.

T4 (THYROXINE) — This study shows the amount of T4 (thyroxine) present in the blood. Elevated levels have been associated with hyperthyroidism and Wilson's Syndrome—the inability of the body to convert T4s into T3s. Low levels of T4 have been associated with hyperthyroidism. T4, as with most hormones, needs protein transporters. TBG or thyroid-binding globulin (a protein) is one of the transporters of T4 or thyroxine. Elevated serum proteins from acidosis or protein toxicity may increase T4 or T3 levels.

T3 uptake reflects the thyroid-binding globulin (TBG) and thyroid-binding prealbumin (TBPA) in the blood. This test is done to weed out elevated or decreased T3 or T4 levels by other factors, such as, oral contraceptives, pregnancy, or kidney disease.

TSH (THYROID-STIMULATING HORMONE) AND TRH (THYROTROPIN-RELEASING HORMONE) —
TSH is a thyroid-stimulating hormone produced in the anterior portion of the pituitary gland. This hormone (TSH) activates or stimulates the thyroid gland to produce and release thyroxine (T4s). When the thyroid is weak (hypothyroidism) or the pituitary is hyperactive, TSH levels will be elevated. This is in response to the need for more thyroid hormone, thyroxine, which is vital to metabolism and heart function. Low levels of triiodothyronine (T3) and thyroxine (T4) stimulate TRH and TSH release.

TSH study is also used to determine primary hypothyroidism (from the thyroid itself), or secondary hypothyroidism (hypothalamic caused).

Remember that all things work together in creation to form one God. This is true also of your body and its glands. Specific glandular function can be a result of the gland itself being toxic and weak, or due to other related glands that are affecting it.

Because all things are interwoven and interlocked, conventional "treatment" never works.

NOTE: In thirty years of clinical observation, it is my opinion that blood T3, T4 and TSH levels are the least accurate of thyroid tests. This is why the Basal Temperature Test was created. (See Appendix A.) I have seen a tremendous number (80 percent) of hypothyroid cases missed by the medical profession because they treated the blood test, not their patient.

PART III

SHORTCOMINGS OF BLOOD ANALYSIS

Using blood analysis to determine body conditions and diagnose tissue weaknesses is one of the least accurate of the diagnostic tools available today. However, when combined with tissue analysis, Iridology, physical symptomatology, reflexology, and kinesiology, it can provide as close a total picture as you can get of the internal condition of your body.

With blood analysis alone one can only hypothesize what *might* be going on in the body, and this of course *greatly* depends upon the interpreter. A blood type analysis does not accurately reflect electrolyte imbalances, hormone levels, glucose fructose utilization, and the true nature of the immune response. Each of these factors can affect, and thus skew, the results.

Electrolyte Imbalances

Your blood can show normal levels of calcium, for example, but at the cellular level you could be highly deficient. Blood level minerals do not show utilization or storage factors. Serum levels of minerals can change due to emotional issues, blood-drawing techniques, and homeostatic (balance) needs. Also, excess mineral and toxic metal accumulation is hard to detect from blood analysis because of the removal by the spleen, liver or other tissues for storage or protection. Your body must keep the blood and serum as clean and balanced as possible or death can result.

Hormone Levels

Your blood is the most inaccurate medium in showing hypoactive hormone production. Thyroid (T4 and T3) hormone activity is much better indicated by the Basal Temperature Test, which was created for this purpose. (See Appendix A.) Adrenal steroid and neurotransmitter production are also not measured properly by blood tests.

Glucose/Fructose Utilization

Your blood can show serum glucose levels, but test results can't indicate the degree of transport.

True Immune Response

Your blood can show high or low levels of immune cells (basophils, for example), but can't indicate why the immune system is responding as it is. Most immune responses are interpreted wrongly, especially without the understanding of detoxification.

Your blood carries many cellular metabolites, parasites, liver wastes and the like. These are filtered out through your spleen, kidneys, intestines and lungs. Because of this your blood's environment is always changing, giving rise to the ever-changing chemistry of the body.

Your blood analysis can be a great tool to help you to put the "pieces" of the puzzle together. It can help you determine excessive carbon buildup, excessive tissue breakdown, and electrolyte disturbances through low serum levels. It can alert you to liver, heart, kidney and muscle tissue breakdown. It can also give you clues to systemic acidosis and immune response creating inflammatory issues, and much more.

APPENDIX D

Tissue Mineral Analysis (TMA)

Your hair is quite unique among the body's tissues, as it requires nearly the same elements for growth and repair as other tissues. Being the second most metabolically active tissue in your body, it can serve as a sort of "archive" of your metabolic activity. The initial inch or so of your hair provides insights into the past two months or so of your body's metabolic processes. As it continues to grow, it essentially preserves a record of both intra- and extracellular metabolic activities.

Hair analysis surpasses blood analysis in reliability when it comes to indicating the utilization, storage, and elimination of substances at the cellular level. Hair is regarded as an excretory tissue, capable of revealing levels of minerals, heavy metals, and toxic elements within the body. This precision is highlighted by the FBI's use of hair analysis in forensic labs to detect the ingestion of hazardous substances like arsenic, enabling them to determine not only the approximate time of ingestion but also level fluctuations. Additionally, hair analysis can offer more definitive insights than blood and urine tests when it comes to identifying the body's storage of toxic elements, as recognized by the Environmental Protection Agency (EPA), which favors hair as the preferred tissue for assessing toxic metal exposure.

Numerous factors can influence the accuracy of hair analysis, including the presence of hair treatment products like dyes, bleaches, and shampoos.

Understanding cellular-level activity is crucial, and hair provides valuable indicators in this regard, as it is where these processes largely occur. As Dr. Emanuel Cheraskin noted in his book "Diet and Disease," minerals have intricate connections with all other nutrients, and without optimal mineral levels in the body, the utilization of other nutrients is compromised. Minerals also play essential roles in hormone production and activity, sometimes acting as "electric" transporters and stimulators, while also influencing enzyme activity.

Tissue mineral analysis is a key tool for comprehending certain symptoms in your body. Many naturopaths and healthcare practitioners incorporate hair (tissue) analysis into their practice, offering dietary recommendations that may not always align with natural health principles.

Conclusion

Analyzing blood, hair, saliva, and urine should be complemented by iris analysis and clinical observations, in addition to considering the body's symptoms. Relying solely on the examination of body fluids as diagnostic tools can lead to misinterpretation of systemic conditions.

It's important to recognize that detoxification processes can significantly alter the results of blood, hair, saliva, and urine analyses. This can potentially mislead inexperienced physicians or healthcare practitioners into believing the body is facing health issues when, in fact, it is merely undergoing a cleansing process. For instance, blood cholesterol levels and cancer markers (antigens) may substantially increase during the early stages of detoxification but are likely to return to normal ranges once the body has completed its cleansing.

In summary, a comprehensive approach that includes multiple diagnostic methods, such as iris analysis, clinical observation, and symptom assessment, is essential for a more accurate understanding of a person's health status, especially when interpreting results from blood, hair, saliva, and urine analyses. It's crucial to avoid jumping to conclusions based solely on these analyses, as they can be influenced by detoxification processes.

There is only one true healing modality... detoxification. It will bring the body's chemistry back into equilibrium (balance), and will remove the toxic metals and substances that do not belong there.

Always Follow Your Highest Excitement

Bibliography

Aihara, Herman. *Acid & Alkaline*. *CA:* George Ohsawa, Macrobiotic Foundation, 1986.

Alexander, Joe. *Blatant Raw Foodist Propaganda!* CA: Blue Dolphin Publishing, 1990.

Amber, Reuben. *Color Therapy*. NM: Aurora Press, 1983.

Anderson, Mary. *Colour Healing*. NY: Harper & Row Publishers, 1975.

Andrews, Ted. *How to Heal with Color*. MN: Llewellyn Publications, 1992.

Arlin, Dini, Wolf. *Nature's First Law: The Raw Food Diet*. *CA:* Maul Brothers Publishing, 2nd edition, 1997.

Arlin, Stephen. *Raw Power! Building Strength and Muscle Naturally*. *CA:* Maul Brothers Publishing; 2nd edition, 2000.

Balz, Rodolphe. *The Healing Power of Essential Oils*. WI: Lotus Light Press, 1st edition, 1996.

Bensky, Dan & Barolet, Randall. *Chinese Herbal Medicine: Formulas and Strategies*. WA: Eastland Press, Inc., 1990.

Bethel, May. *Healing Power of Herbs*. *CA:* Melvin Powers, Wilshire Book Co., 1968.

Blunt, Wilfrid and Sandra Raphae. *The Illustrated Herbal*. NY: W.W. Norton & Company, 1979.

Boxer, Arabella and Philippa Back. *The Herb Book. A Complete Guide to Culinary Herbs*. NJ: Thunder Bay Press, 1994.

Bragg, Paul and Patricia. *The Miracle of Fasting*. Health Science, 3rd edition, 1999.

Brennan, Barbara Ann. *Hands of Light*. NY: Bantam Books, 1987.

Brown, Deni. New *Encyclopedia of Herbs and Their Uses*. NY: Dorling Kindersley Publishing, 1995.

Brown, Donald. *Herbal Prescriptions for Better Health. CA:* Prima Publishing, 1996.

Carrington, Hereward. *The Natural Food of Man. CA:* Health Research, *1963*.

Christopher, John.*School of Natural Healing*. UT: Christopher Publications, 1996.

Cohn, Robert. *Milk—The Deadly Poison*. NJ: Argus Publishing, Inc., 1998.

Copen, Bruce. *A Rainbow of Health*. England: Academic Publications, 1974.

Culpepper, Nicholas. *Culpepper's Color Herbal*. MA: Storey Books, 1997.

Culpepper, Nicholas. *Culpepper's Complete Herbal and English Physician*. UK: FoulSham & Co., Ltd., 1995.

Deoul, Kathleen. *Cancer Cover-Up (Genocide)*. MD: Cassandra Books, 2001.

Dodt, Colleen. *The Essential Oils Book: Creating Personal Blends for Mind and Body*. VT: Storey Communications, Inc., 1996.

Douglass, William Campbell.*Milk of Human Kindness Is Not Pasteurized*. GA: Last Laugh Publishers, 1985.

Dubelle, Lee. *Proper Food Combining Works— Living Testimony*. CO: Nutri Books, Corp., 1987.

Dubin, Dale. *Rapid Interpretation of EKG's* . FL: Cover Publishing Co., 6th edition, 2000.

Dykeman, Thomas, Elias, and Peter. *Edible Wild Plants*. Benedict Lust Publications, Inc., 1990.

Ehret, Arnold.*Mucusless Diet Healing System*. Benedict Lust Publications, Inc., 2001.

Ehret, Arnold. *Rational Fasting*. Benedict Lust Publications, Inc., 2001.

Ehret, Arnold. *The Definite Cure of Chronic Constipation*. Benedict Lust Publications, Inc., 2002.

Fathman, George and Doris. Live *Foods: Nature's Perfect System of* Human Nutrition. NY: Cancer Care Inc., 1986.

Feeney, Mary. The Cardiac Rhythms: A Systematic Approach to *Interpretation*. PA: W.B. Saunders Co., 3rd edition, 1997.

Foster, Steven. *Herbal Renaissance*. UT: Gibb Smith Publisher, Revised edition, 1993.

Foster, Steven, and Yue Chongxi. *Herbal Emissaries: Bringing Chinese Herbs to the West*. VT: Healing Art Press, 1992.

Fratkin, Jake. *Chinese Herbal Patent Formulas —A Practical Guide*. CO: Shya Publications, 1985.

Gaeddert, Andrew. *Chinese Herbs in the Western Clinic*. CA: Get Well Foundation, 1998.

Gladstar, Rosemary. *Herbal Healing for Women*. NY: Fireside Simon and Schuster Inc., 1993.

Glasby, John. *Dictionary of Plants Containing Secondary Metabolites*. PA: Taylor and Francis Inc., 1991.

Grauer, Ken. *A Practical Guide to ECG Interpretation*. Year Book Medical Pub., 2nd edition, 1998.

Griffin, LaDean. *Please Doctor, I'd Rather Do It Myself... With Herbs!* UT: Hawkes Publishing, Inc., 1979.

Gurudas. *Flower Essences and Vibrational Healing*. CA: Cassandra Press, 2nd edition, 1989.

Harborn, Jeffrey, and Herbert Baxter, editors. *Phytochemical Dictionary: A Handbook of Bioactive Compounds from Plants*. PA: Taylor and Francis, 2nd edition, 1999.

Heinerman, John. *Medical Doctor's Guide to Herbs*. UT: Woodland Publishing, 1987.

Hey, Barbara. *The Illustrated Guide to Herbs*. NJ: New Horizon Press.

Hobbs, Christopher. *Ginkgo: Elixir of Youth*. CA: Botanica Press, 1990.

Hobbs, Christopher. *Handbook for Herbal Healing*. Culinary Arts Ltd., 1994.

Hobbs, Christopher. *Milk Thistle—The Liver Herb*. CA: Botanica Press, 2nd edition, 1993.

Hoffmann, David. *The New Holistic Herbal*. MA: Element Book Ltd., 3rd edition, 1991.

Holmes, Peter. *Jade Remedies: A Chinese Herbal Reference for the West (Volume 1)*. CO: Snow Lotus Press, Inc., 1997.

Horowitz, Leonard G. *Emerging Viruses, AIDS & Ebola, Nature, Accident or Intentional? MA: Tetrahedron, Inc., 1998.*

Hotema, Hilton. Long Life in Florida. Health Research, Reprint edition, 1962.

Hunt, Ronald. *The Seven Keys to Color Healing*. NY: HarperCollins, 1989.

Jensen, Bernard. *Beyond Basic Health. CA:* Bernard Jensen, 1988.

Jensen, Bernard. *Developing a New Heart Through Nutrition and a New Lifestyle. CA: Bernard Jensen, 1995.*

Jensen, Bernard. *Doctor-Patient Handbook*. CA: Bernard Jensen Enterprises, 1978.

Jensen, Bernard. *Goat Milk Magic*. *CA:* Bernard Jensen, 1994.

Jensen, Bernard. *Herbs: Wonder Healers*. *CA:* Bernard Jensen, 1992.

Jensen, Bernard. *Iridology: The Science and Practice in the Healing Arts (Volume* II). CA: Bernard Jensen Enterprises, 1982.

Jensen, Bernard. *Iridology Simplified*. *CA:* Bernard Jensen, 1980.

Jensen, Bernard. *What is Iridology?* Illustrated. CA: Bernard Jensen, 1984.

Katz, Michael and Ginny.*Gifts of the Gemstone Masters*. OR: Gemisphere, 1989.

Keville, Kathi. *Herbs for Health and Healing*. PA: Rodale Press, Inc., 1996.

Kloss, Jethro. *Back to Eden*. Benedict Lust Publications, Inc., 1981.

Kroeger, Hanna. *Parasites—The Enemy Within*. CO: Hanna Kroger, 1991.

Kulvinskas, Viktoras. *Life in the 21st Century*. IA: 21st Century Publications, 1981.

Kulvinskas, Viktoras. *Love Your Body or How To Be A Live Food Love* . IA: 21st Century Publications, 1972.

Kulvinskas, Victoras. *Survival Into the 21st Century Publications*, 1975.

L'Orange, Darlena. *Herbal Healing Secrets of the Orient*. NJ: Prentice *Hall, 1998.*

Liberman, Jacob.Light—Medicine of the Future. NM: Bear and Company, 1992.

Lopez, D.A., R.M. Williams and M. Miehike. Enzymes—The Fountain of Life. Germany: The Neville Press, Inc., 1994.

Lu, Henry. Chinese System of Food Cures— Prevention and Remedies. NY: Sterling Publishing Co., Inc., 1986.

Mauseth, James. *Botany: An Introduction to Plant Biology*. MA: Jones & Barlett Pub., 3rd edition, 2003.

McBean, Eleanor. *The Poisoned Needle*. Health Research, Reprint edition, 1993.

McDaniel, T.C. *Disease Reprieve*. PA: Xlibris Corporation, 1st edition, 1999.

Meyer, Clarence. *The Herbalist*. IL: Meyer-books, 1986.

Miller, Neil Z. *Vaccines: Are They Really Safe and Effective? (A Parents Guide to Childhood Shots)*. NM: New Atlantean Press, Revised and updated edition, 2002.

Monte, Tom. *World Medicine—The East /West Guide to Healing Your Body*. NY: G.P. Putnam's Sons, 1993.

Murray, Michael. *Natural Alternatives for Weight Loss*. NY: William Morrow and Company, Inc., 1996.

Meyer, Joseph. *The Old Herb Doctor*. IL: Meyer-books, 2nd edition, 1984.

Naturopathic Handbook of Herbal Formulas: A Practical and Concise Herb User's Guide. CO: Kivaki Press, 3rd edition, 1994.

Olsen, Cynthia. *Australian Tea Tree Oil Guide* . WI: Lotus Press, 3rd edition, 1998.

Parachin, Victor. *365 Good Reasons To Be A Vegetarian* . NY: Avery Penguin Putnam, 1997.

PDR for Herbal Medicines. NJ: Medical Economics Co., 2nd edition, 2000.

Pedersen, Mark. *Nutritional Herbology: A Reference Guide to Herbs*. IN: Wendell W. Whitman Co., 3rd edition, 1998.

Pizzorno, Joseph. *Total Wellness*. *CA:* Prima Publishing, 1996.

Rector, Linda.*Renewing Female Balance*. CA: Healthy Healing Publications, Inc., 4th edition. 1997.

Rector, Linda. *Renewing Male Health and Energy*. CA: Healthy Healing Publications, Inc., 2nd edition, 1997.

Royal, Penny. *Herbally Yours*. UT: Sound Nutrition, 3rd edition, 1982.

Sandman, Amanda. *A-Z of Natural Remedies*. NY: Longmeadow Press, 1995.

Sanecki, Kay. *The Book of Herbs*. NJ: Quantum Books Ltd., 1996.

Santillo, Humbart. *Food Enzymes: The Missing Link to Radiant Health*. AZ: Hohm Press; 2nd edition, 1993.

Santillo, Humbart. *Natural Healing with Herbs*. AZ: Hohm Press, 1991.

Scalzo, Richard. *Naturpathic Handbook of Herbal Formulas— A Practical and Concise Herb User's Guide*. CO: Kivaki Press, 3rd edition, 1994.

Schauenberg, Paul. and Paris, Ferdinand. *Guide to Medicinal Plants*. CT: Keats Publishing, Inc., Reprint edition, 1990.

Shelton, Herbert.*Food Combining Made Easy*. Ontario: Willow Publishing, 1982.

Swahn, J.O. *The Lore of Spices*. MN: Stoeger Publishing Company, 2002.

Tenny, Louise. *Today's Herbal Health* . UT: Woodland Publishing, 5th edition, 2000.

Thie, John. *Touch for Health*. *CA:* Devorss and Co., Publishers, 1979.

Thomas, Lalitha. *10 Essential Herbs*. AZ: Hohm Press, 2nd edition, 1995.

Tierra, Michael. *Planetary Herbology*. WI: Lotus Press, 1987.

Tierra, Michael. *The Way of Herbs*. NY: Pocket Books; Revised edition, 1998.

Tilden, John. *Toxemia: The Basic Cause of Disease*. FL: Nat'l Health Assoc, 1974.

Tompkins, Peter and Christopher Bird. *The Secret Life of Plants*. NY: HarperCollins, 1989.

Twitchell, Paul. *Herbs the Magic Healer*. CA: Eckankar, 1971.

Walker, Norman. *Colon Health: The Key to a Vibrant Life*. TN: Associated Publishers Group, 2nd edition, 1997.

Walker, Norman. *Water Can Undermine Your Health* . AZ: Norwalk Press, 1996.

Walker, N.W. *Become Younger*. AZ: Norwalk Press, 2nd edition, 1995.

Walker, N.W. *The Vegetarian Guide to Diet and Salad*. Longman Trade/Caroline House, Revised edition, 1995.

Walker, N.W. Fresh Vegetable and Fruit Juices: What's Missing in Your Body? Longman Trade/Caroline House, 1995.

Walker, N.W. Pure and Simple: Natural Weight Control . AZ: Norwalk Press, 1981.

Walker, N.W. The Natural Way to Vibrant Health . Longman Trade/Caroline House, 1995.

Weiss, Rudolf Fritz. Herbal Medicine. NY: Thieme Medical Pub., 2nd edition, 2001.

Werbach, Melvyn and Michael Murray. Botanical Influences on Illness—A Sourcebook of Clinical Research. CA: Third Line Press, 2nd edition, 2000.

Wigmore, Ann. The Hippocrates Diet and Health Program. NJ: Avery Penguin Putnam, 1984.

Wigmore, Ann. The Wheatgrass Book. NJ: Avery Penguin Putnam, 1984.

Wolfe, David. The Sunfood Diet Success System. CA: Maul Brother's Publishing, 3rd edition, 2000.

Made in the USA
Coppell, TX
27 May 2025

49968621R00350